The Development and Management of Visitor Attractions

This book is dedicated to Susan Horner and John Michael Richard Swarbrooke for all their love and support.

It is also dedicated to my parents, Maureen June Swarbrooke and John Wilfred Samuel Swarbrooke, who did everything they could to give me the best possible start in life.

Finally, I dedicate this book to my grandparents, Flora Swarbrooke, John Henry Swarbrooke, Lilian Walker and Frank Walker, who helped me understand who I am.

The Development and Management of Visitor Attractions

Second edition

John Swarbrooke

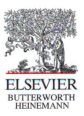

ELSEVIER
BUTTERWORTH
HEINEMANN

AMSTERDAM · BOSTON · HEIDELBERG · LONDON · NEW YORK · OXFORD
PARIS · SAN DIEGO · SAN FRANCISCO · SINGAPORE · SYDNEY · TOKYO

Elsevier Butterworth-Heinemann
Linacre House, Jordan Hill, Oxford OX2 8DP
30 Corporate Drive, Burlington, MA 01803

First published 1995
Reprinted 1995, 1996, 1997, 1998
Reissued with new cover 1999
Reprinted 2000
Second edition 2002
Reprinted 2003, 2005

Permissions may be sought directly from Elsevier's Science and Technology
Rights Department in Oxford, UK: phone: (+44) (0) 1865 843830; fax: (+44) (0) 1865
853333; e-mail: permissions@elsevier.co.uk. You may also complete your request
on-line via the Elsevier homepage (http://www.elsevier.com), by
selecting 'Customer Support' and then 'Obtaining Permissions'

British Library Cataloguing in Publication Data
Swarbrooke, John
    The development and management of visitor attractions. –
    2nd ed.
    1. Tourist trade – Management   2. Tourism – Management
    I. Title
    338.4'7'91

Library of Congress Cataloguing in Publication Data
Swarbrooke, John.
    The development and management of visitor attractions/John Swarbrooke. –
    2nd ed.
    p. cm.
    Includes bibliographical references (p.).
    1. Tourism. 2. Leisure industry.   I. Title.
    G155.A1 S885 2001
    338.4'7910–dc21   2001043888

ISBN 0 7506 5169 5

For information on all Butterworth-Heinemann publications visit our
website at www.bh.com

Working together to grow
libraries in developing countries

www.elsevier.com | www.bookaid.org | www.sabre.org

ELSEVIER   BOOK AID
            International   Sabre Foundation

Composition by Genesis Typesetting, Rochester, Kent
Printed and bound in Great Britain

Contents

Contents

Preface to the first edition

This book is designed to be a comprehensive text on the complex subject of visitor attractions, particularly human-made attractions. The book examines the process of developing visitor attractions and discusses the main issues involved in their management.

Given the vital importance of attractions in the tourism industry as the main motivators of travel, it is surprising that there is at present no other text in the UK or other countries which covers this subject in such depth and with the same breadth. It is hoped that the book will appeal to both students and practitioners. For tourism students it will help them understand the role of attractions in tourism, while for hospitality students it will give them an insight into a specific type of tourism facility management. Business studies students will find in it an interesting application of management principles to a sector of a major service industry. The book should also be of interest to students of other subjects such as planning, leisure and recreation, museums, environmental management and finance. However, the book is also designed to be a useful handbook for practitioners working in the industry, in the public, private and voluntary sectors. It is written in a straightforward way and contains many practical ideas relating to the development and management of visitor attractions.

The book is split into three main parts:

- Part One sets the context by defining what we mean by attractions, looking at their role in tourism as a whole, examining the attraction product and market, and outlining the business environment of attractions.
- Part Two explores the issues involved in the development of new attractions, including feasibility studies, financing, design and project management.
- Part Three considers the challenges involved in managing attractions such as marketing, financial management, operations management and human resource management.

In Part Four are then a number of case studies designed to illustrate different points about the development and management of attractions. The final part looks at the future of the attraction sector.

I hope the fact that I spent ten years as a manager in the tourism industry before moving into the academic world will help to guarantee that the book is a good blend of challenging ideas and practical advice. As far as possible I have tried to ensure that a number of key themes, which I feel to be vitally important for an understanding of visitor attractions, run through the whole book. These are:

- All attractions exist within a rapidly changing business environment which requires them to be constantly vigilant so that they can anticipate and respond to these changes.
- Attractions live within a competitive market even if it is not always easy to identify the competitors.
- While the principles of attraction development and management are similar for all attractions, it is important to recognize that there are differences between attractions in the public, private and voluntary sectors, reflecting their different motivations and objectives.
- In terms of attraction management it needs to be appreciated that while for clarity and ease of reading the management issues are split into chapters, such as marketing and operations, in reality they are all interlinked and interdependent.
- Marketing, in the widest sense of the word, is at the core of successful human-made attractions.

As far as is possible in a single volume of limited length, the book takes an international perspective on attractions, using examples from a number of countries. However, in the space available it is impossible to give a full picture of the attractions sector in more than one country. This is a pity as it would have been interesting to look at the situation in the USA, or France or the rapidly changing countries of Eastern Europe. Readers in other countries should interpret my comments in the context of their own national situation.

A further result of the restriction on the length of the book has been the decision largely to exclude special events and natural attractions. This is not a serious problem as readers will find a significant quantity of material on the management of natural attractions while event management is now covered in several good texts by authoritative authors like Getz and Hall.

The limitations of space have also imposed another constraint, namely the need to generalize about a subject which is incredibly varied. This inevitably leads to oversimplification in places, although I have been at pains to point this out to the reader wherever I felt it was particularly significant.

I would like to conclude by acknowledging all the help I have received in writing this book. First I must thank all those attractions whose management and staff unselfishly offered their time to supply me with information. They are too numerous to mention at this stage, but readers will see them clearly identified in the text, while those who have made particularly valuable contributions are listed in the acknowledgements. Second, I would like to express my gratitude to all the people I worked with during my ten years in the tourism industry who taught me so much; and to my customers during those years who helped teach me what marketing is really all about. I must also thank all my students, who have helped me refine my ideas and have given me a lot of job satisfaction.

As far as the production of the book is concerned, I gladly acknowledge the debt I owe to several people: Kathryn Grant of Butterworth-Heinemann who made the task easier by being very understanding; Joan Butt who produced all the diagrams; and Judy Mitchell who deciphered my awful writing and typed the text perfectly and quickly.

I must also thank my parents for bringing me up in a way that allowed me to develop my critical faculties and my ability to analyse and debate issues. Furthermore, I owe them both an enormous debt for the sacrifices they made, so that I could have more opportunities than they ever had. Sadly, it is a debt I can never repay.

Last, but not least, I have to thank two special people. First, my partner, Sue Horner, for putting up with all the disruption to our lives which I caused when writing this book. I could not have finished it without her help. And I must thank our little (or not so little now) son, John, for always making me smile and showing me that there is much more to life than work.

All that remains is for me to wish you happy reading. If you find the book useful then all my efforts will have been worthwhile.

John Swarbrooke
1995

Preface to the second edition

Much has changed since this book was first published six years ago.

New attractions have opened all over the world, from the Guggenheim Museum in Bilbao to Sony Wonder in New York. Attractions such as aquariums have boomed worldwide. At the same time, many traditional attractions have undergone facelifts and relaunches.

The growth of the supply of attractions has been stimulated by public funding, such as the National Lottery in the UK, with questions being raised about their long-term viability.

There have also been developments in the ownership of attractions. United States based Universal has taken a share of Port Aventura in Spain, while fellow American corporation, Six Flags, has moved into Holland. It is clear from these examples that globalization is at work in the attraction sector, as elsewhere. In the UK, Vardon has sold its interest in the Sea Life Centres and the Pearson corporation has sold the Tussauds Group.

Overall, visitor numbers have been a little less impressive than many commentators predicted in the mid-1990s. The growth in the supply of attractions has created real concerns about the long-term ability of the market to keep pace with this growth.

Technological developments such as the growth of the Internet, and virtual reality have started to have a greater impact on attraction marketing and product development in the few years since this book was first published.

More courses about the development and management of visitor attractions have been developed in universities and colleges around the world. Much progress has been made by academics in studying aspects of attraction management, particularly in the museums sector. And yet, sadly, there are still hardly any textbooks that focus on the management and development of all types of visitor attractions as a whole.

This fact, together with the changes that have taken place in the intervening six years, have convinced the author that now is the right time to produce a new edition of this book.

The new edition of the book has two main purposes:

1 To update the contents of the book to ensure they reflect the state of the attractions sector at the beginning of the new millennium.
2 To offer an international perspective of the subject in contrast to the more UK-based emphasis of the original edition.

Since the publication of the first edition of this text, the author has been fortunate enough to travel and visit attractions all over the world, including in Austria, Brazil, Finland, France, Greece, Hong Kong, Italy, Ireland, Indonesia, Malaysia, Malta, Norway, Palestine, Portugal, Russia, Singapore, Spain and the USA. The author hopes that he will be able to use these experiences to offer a truly international perspective of the subject.

Feedback from readers has suggested that the structure of the book is popular, and therefore the new edition will use the same structure.

The main change with the new book is the inclusion of new data, examples and case studies. There are also new sections on issues which are topical in the attractions sector today.

The author has also added exercises and discussion points for this edition, to help the reader develop their understanding of the subject.

In spite of all these improvements, much of the core text remains as it was in 1995, because the principles which underpin good practice in attraction development and management have not changed fundamentally since 1995.

I hope that you will find this second edition useful and that it will stimulate you to take a greater interest in this vitally important sector in the future.

John Swarbrooke
2001

Acknowledgements

The author would like to thank the following people who have helped him in some way while he was working on this book:

M. Frédéric Bonnichon, Directeur, Vulcania™, France
Mrs Betty Fromer, Editora Aleph, Sâo Paulo, Brazil
Mr Sergei Kurilov, Government of the Autonomous Republic of Sakha-Yakutia, Russian Federation
Mr Adriano Piazzi, Editora Aleph, Sâo Paulo, Brazil
Dr Dimitrios Skalkos, Ioannina, Greece
Ms Marina Sukueva, Government of the Autonomous Republic of Sakha-Yakutia, Russian Federation
Mr Graeme Thomas, formerly of the British Embassy, Athens, Greece,

staff and students at the following institutions:

Dublin Institute of Technology, Ireland
Institut Management de Hôtelier International, Cergy-Pontoise, France
Sheffield Hallam University
UNIP, Sâo Paulo, Brazil
University of the Aegean, Greece
University of Bethlehem, Palestine

and all the airlines, airports, hotels, trains and education institutions that have provided the time and space for me to write this book.

Figures

Tables

Part One

The Context

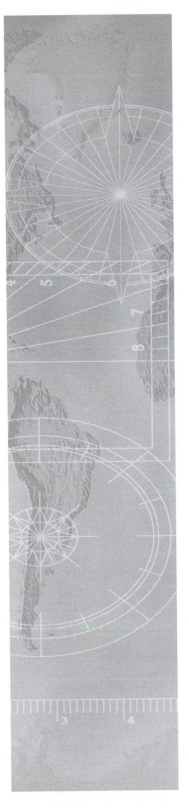

Introduction

Attractions are arguably the most important component in the tourism system. They are the main motivators for tourist trips and are the core of the tourism product. Without attractions there would be no need for other tourism services. Indeed tourism as such would not exist if it were not for attractions.

Definitions

Attractions are a very complex sector of the tourism industry and are not well understood. There are few books specifically about attractions and there is no generally accepted definition that is relevant to all visitor attractions, although there are several which are worthy of repetition here, including the following:

> The attraction must be a permanently established excursion destination, a primary purpose of which is to allow public access for entertainment, interest, and education, rather than being primarily a retail outlet, or a venue for sports, film, or theatrical performances. It must be open to the public without prior booking, and should be capable of attracting day visitors or tourists'. (British Tourist Authority, quoted in *Travel and Tourism Analyst*, 2000)

Writing in *Travel and Tourism Analyst*, Stevens criticized this definition, saying: 'It reveals a myopic, restricted and outdated view of the attractions sector. It ignores the rapidly changing nature of consumer demand that has fuelled recent developments'. Furthermore, the British Tourist Authority definition would exclude 'temporary' attractions such as the Millennium Dome in London, expositions and all other events and festivals.

Likewise, the definition would exclude those sporting venues which have developed related visitor attractions such as football club museums, and the Euro 2000 attraction at PSV Eindhoven in the Netherlands. Many more similarly ambitious projects are planned in places as diverse as Cardiff, UK, and Toronto, Canada.

There are some alternative definitions of attractions which are broader and seem more in tune with recent developments in the sector. One of these is:

> A visitor attraction is a feature in an area that is a place, venue or focus of activities and does the following things.
>
> 1 Sets out to attract visitors/day visitors from resident or tourist populations, and is managed accordingly.
> 2 Provides a fun and pleasurable experience and an enjoyable way for customers to spend their leisure time.
> 3 Is developed to realize this potential.
> 4 Is managed as an attraction, providing satisfaction to its customers.
> 5 Provides an appropriate level of facilities and services to meet and cater to the demands, needs, and interests of its visitors.
> 6 May or may not charge an admission for entry. (Walsh-Heron and Stevens, 1990)

One reason it is difficult to come up with a definition that encompasses all attractions is that it is a diverse and complex sector.

The sector is fragmented geographically, with different interpretations and approaches being taken in the USA and Europe for example. Furthermore, it is split into several very different subsectors such as heritage and theme parks. These are two reasons why there is no single industry voice which operates for attractions.

This also explains why it is so difficult, often, to gain data on the attraction sector in different countries. As Stevens has noted: 'Overall data about this sector is first difficult to access in many countries, second, incompletely collected and third, prone to the idiosyncratic influences of individual [attraction] owners. As such it is difficult to find comparative information and relevant time-series data' (Stevens, in *Travel and Tourism Analyst*, 2000).

In general terms, attractions tend to be single units, individual sites or clearly defined small-scale geographical areas that are accessible and motivate large numbers of people to travel some distance from their home, usually in their leisure time, to visit them for a short, limited period. This definition clearly excludes uncontrollable and unmanageable phenomena that are sometimes described as attractions, such as climate. Therefore, this definition implies that attractions are entities that are capable of being delimited and managed.

A typology of attractions

While no clear definition exists, attractions can be split into four main types:

1 Features within the *natural environment*.
2 *Human-made buildings, structures and sites that were designed for a purpose other than attracting visitors,* such as religious worship, but which now attract substantial numbers of visitors who use them as leisure amenities.
3 Human-made buildings, structures and sites that are *designed to attract visitors and are purpose-built to accommodate their needs, such as theme parks.*
4 *Special events.*

Please note that the word 'visitor' is used here to cover all visitors from local residents to foreign tourists and includes both excursionists/day-trippers and the staying visitor. We will return to this issue later in the chapter.

There are two important differences between these types of attractions. The most obvious is that the first three are generally permanent while the last category covers attractions which are temporary and usually have a limited lifespan which is known in advance. The second major difference is between the first two types of attraction, where tourism is often seen as a problem and a threat, and the last two types, where tourism is generally perceived to be beneficial and an opportunity.

With natural attractions and human-made attractions that were not purpose-built to attract tourists the emphasis is on visitor management to cope with the problems caused by the visitors. The main concerns are the environmental impacts of tourism, such as pollution and erosion, together with the effect of tourism on the original purpose of the site or building whether it be farming on a hillside or religious worship in a cathedral.

On the other hand, the aim of attractions which are purpose-built to attract tourists is often to increase visitor numbers and maximize the economic impact of tourism. Most special events also fit into this category, although for some traditional events too many visitors can be a threat as they change the original purpose and content of the event, for example deeply significant religious festivals that evolve into superficial entertainment for visitors.

This typology, which puts attractions into one of four main groups (Table 1.1), is a useful tool to help us understand this complex subject but it is important to recognize that the boundaries between these categories are not always clear-cut and can overlap.

Natural	Human-made but not originally designed primarily to attract visitors	Human-made and purpose-built to attract tourists	Special events
Beaches	Cathedrals and churches	Amusement parks	Sporting events:
Caves	Stately homes and	Theme parks	watching and
Rock faces	historic houses	Open air museums	participating
Rivers and	Archaeological sites and	Heritage centres	Arts festivals
lakes	ancient monuments	Country parks	Markets and fairs
Forests	Historic gardens	Marinas	Traditional customs
Wildlife:	Industrial archaeology	Exhibition centres	and folklore events
flora and	sites	Garden centres	Historical anniversaries
fauna	Steam railways	Craft centres	Religious events
	Reservoirs	Factory tours and shops	
		Working farms open to	
		the public	
		Safari parks	
		Entertainment complexes	
		Casinos	
		Health spas	
		Leisure centres	
		Picnic sites	
		Museums and galleries	
		Leisure retail complexes	
		Waterfront developments	

Table 1.1 The four categories of attractions

Touring circuit attractions	Longer-stay attractions
Roadside scenic areas	Resorts
Outstanding natural areas	Camping areas
Camping areas	Hunting and water sports areas
Water touring areas	Organization camp areas
Homes of friends or relatives	Vacation home complexes
Unusual institutions	Festival and event places
Shrines and cultural places	Convention and meeting places
Food and entertainment places	Gaming centres
Historic buildings and sites	Sports arenas and complexes
Ethnic areas	Trade centres
Shopping areas	Science and technology centres
Crafts and lore places	Theme parks

Source: Gunn (1988).

Table 1.2
Attractions classified by length of stay

Kinds of attractions	Dependency upon natural resources	Dependency upon other than natural and cultural resources	Dependency upon cultural resources
Touring circuit:			
Roadside scenic areas	✪	○	○
Outstanding natural areas	✪	○	○
Camping areas	○	✪	○
Water touring areas	✪	☆	☆
Homes: friends/relatives	☆	✪	☆
Unusual institutions	○	✪	○
Shrines, cultural places	☆	✱	✪
Food, entertainment	☆	✪	○
Historic buildings/sites	☆	○	✪
Ethnic areas	☆	✱	✱
Shopping areas	☆	✪	☆
Crafts, lore places	☆	✱	✪
Longer stay:			
Resorts	✪	✱	☆
Camping areas	✪	✱	○
Hunting, water sports	✪	☆	○
Organization camps	✪	☆	○
Vacation home complexes	✪	○	○
Festival, event places	○	✪	✪
Convention, meeting places	☆	✪	☆
Gaming centres	☆	✪	○
Sports arenas, complexes	○	✪	○
Trade centres	○	✪	✱
Service, technical centres	○	✪	○
Theme parks	☆	✪	○

Note: ✪ Highly dependent; ✱ Dependent; ☆ Somewhat dependent; ○ Low or no dependency.
Source: Gunn (1997).

Table 1.3 Resource dependency of attractions

American academics such as Gunn have also sought to produce typologies of attractions that reflect the situation in the USA. Table 1.2 is an attempt to distinguish between short-visit and longer-visit attractions, while Table 1.3 focuses upon the level of dependency on natural and cultural factors.

The scope of attractions

The brief and selective list in Table 1.1 clearly shows that there are a variety of different types of attractions within our four categories. Even this table which is far from comprehensive, shows how difficult it is to draw clear lines between these four categories and treat them as mutually exclusive. A few examples will illustrate this point.

While many cathedrals were not designed to be tourist attractions, some were built on pilgrimage routes or the site of religious shrines. If one believes that pilgrimages were one of the earliest forms of tourism then such cathedrals are early examples of purpose-built tourist attractions. Their problem today is not that they were not purpose-built for tourism but that they were designed for another type of tourism and find it difficult to accommodate the needs of the modern leisure tourist.

Country parks rely on the natural environment to attract visitors but their operators manage them with the express aim of attracting and accommodating visitors.

Railways are a functional method of transport but when steam was replaced by diesel and electricity the old locomotives and railway stock were saved by enthusiasts and used to create picturesque steam railways that attract hundreds of thousands of visitors every year.

Open-air museums such as Ironbridge in Shropshire and developments such as the Albert Dock in Liverpool use old buildings that were designed as places to live and work to create popular attractions.

As mentioned earlier in the chapter, some special events were not originally developed to attract visitors and have become tourist attractions over time, while some have been created specifically to attract tourists.

In spite of these 'grey areas', the typology is helpful in gaining an understanding of this complex and potentially confusing subject. However, it is important to acknowledge that other commentators have produced different ways of categorizing attractions. Gunn divided attractions into short-stay touring-circuit attractions and longer-stay focused attractions. As Gunn has commented, these are based on two types of tourism, namely attractions 'that satisfy touring markets for travellers on tours involving many separate locational stops and those at or near longer-stay destinations' (Gunn, 1988).

Inskeep favours a three-category typology, namely:

- natural attractions that are based on features of the natural environment
- cultural attractions that are based on humans' activities
- special types of attractions that are artificially created (Inskeep, 1991).

Finally, Lew in 1987, in a review of studies of attractions, suggested that such studies took one or more of three perspectives towards attractions, namely:

- an ideographic listing of attractions
- an organizational perspective which takes account of factors such as capacity, spatial and temporal scale
- a cognitive perspective incorporating tourists' perceptions and experiences of attractions (Lew, 1987).

There are a number of other issues that need to be discussed to help to clarify our understanding of attractions.

Visitor attractions and tourist attractions

The term 'tourist attraction' is actually a misnomer since most visitors to attractions are not tourists in the accepted sense of the word, except in a few exceptional cases, such as Disney World in Florida or Legoland in Denmark. In other words, they are usually day-visitors rather than staying visitors and often they come from the region in which the attraction is located. It is therefore more accurate to talk about visitor attractions rather than tourist attractions.

Attractions and destinations

Attractions are generally single units, individual sites or very small, easily delimited geographical areas based on a single key feature. Destinations are larger areas that include a number of individual attractions together with the support services required by tourists. There is a strong link between the two and it is usually the existence of a major attraction that tends to stimulate the development of destinations, whether the attraction is a beach, a religious shrine or a theme park. Once the destination is growing other secondary attractions often spring up to exploit the market.

Attractions, support services and facilities

The idea that attractions are distinctly different from support services and tourism facilities like hotels, restaurants and the transport system is clearly an oversimplification for two main reasons. First, many attractions are increasingly developing services such as catering and accommodation on site to increase their income. Second, some support services and tourism facilities are attractions in their own right. Many famous restaurants attract people to travel hundreds of miles to visit them, for example that of Paul Bocuse near Lyon in France. There are numerous hotels that function as attractions such as Gleneagles in Scotland which is a Mecca for golfers, while some modes of transport such as Concorde and the Orient Express also meet our definition of an attraction.

The growth of resort complexes such as Disneyland Paris, Center Parcs and Club Med centres is blurring the distinction between attractions and support services, just as they are also making it difficult to separate attractions from destinations.

Attractions and activities

As far as activities are concerned, attractions are a resource that provides the raw material on which the activity depends. For example, sunbathing makes use of beaches, sailors use marinas and music fans visit folk festivals.

Some attractions are a resource for a number of different activities, some of which may be conflicting, in which case they will need to be managed to reconcile the needs of the users with the conservation of

Sector	Main types of attractions owned	Main motivations for ownership and operation
Public, i.e. government, local authorities, nationalized industries	Museums and galleries, ancient monuments, archaeological sites, historic buildings, country parks, forests	*Main priority*: Conservation *Other priorities*: Education, public access and increased leisure opportunities for the community, income, visitor management, catalyst for tourism development
Private, i.e. commercial organizations	Theme parks, zoos, marinas, entertainment complexes, leisure shopping	*Main priority*: Profit *Other priorities*: Entertainment, maximize visitor numbers and market share, exploit growth markets
Voluntary, i.e. trusts and charities including the National Trust in the UK and many Ecomusées in France which operate under the 1901 Law on Associations	Historic buildings (especially stately homes), heritage centres, open-air museums, steam railways	*Main priority*: Conservation via income from visitors *Other priorities*: Education, visitor management

Table 1.4 The ownership of attractions

the resource. There are many examples of this, including the use of rivers and reservoirs by anglers and powerboat enthusiasts. Table 1.4 illustrates the conflicts that can exist between the use of attractions for leisure and their use for other purposes such as water supply and conservation.

The classification of visitor attractions

There are a number of ways of classifying attractions based on variables such as ownership, scale, catchment area, location and visitor numbers, to mention just a few.

Ownership

The ownership of attractions in terms of the public, private and voluntary sectors is very important. The three sectors tend to own different types of attractions and their motivation for owning and operating these attractions tends to be different. This is illustrated in Table 1.4. One feature of attraction ownership is the number of organizations in the public, voluntary and private sectors that each own a number of attractions. In the UK there are several organizations that own and operate a number of attractions, of which probably the three most important are those below.

English Heritage

This is a government agency that operates some of the most important historic buildings and monuments in England. Their main aim is to conserve these properties. In recent years they have started to improve visitor facilities and have struggled to reconcile the needs of conservation and the desires of visitors at places like Stonehenge. Parallel organizations exist in respect of Scotland, Wales and Northern Ireland.

The National Trust

The National Trust is a voluntary body covering England, Wales and Northern Ireland which was established in the Victorian age. It owns historic houses and land. The former are open to the public to raise money so that the Trust can further its main activity, which is conservation. It even rents out some of its properties as holiday homes to raise income. The Trust runs a membership scheme and it is Britain's largest membership organization in the field of conservation, green issues and the environment. An equivalent organization exists in Scotland.

The Tussauds Group

In the UK, perhaps the major private sector attraction operation is the Tussauds Group which owns Alton Towers, Chessington World of Adventure, Madame Tussauds and Thorpe Park. All of these attractions are large scale and well established. The Tussauds Group was sold by its former parent company, Pearson, to Charterhouse Development Corporation for £352 million in 1999. However, in the global attraction market, particularly in the theme park sector, such larger corporations play a key role.

Premier Parks/Six Flags

This US based corporation now owns thirty-five parks worldwide which received 47.5 million visitors in 1999 (*Travel and Tourism Analyst*, 2000). Most of their parks are in the USA, but in 1999 they announced that they were investing in the Walibi Flevo Park in the Netherlands which would be rebranded as Six Flags Holland.

Walt Disney Attractions

In 1999 Walt Disney Attractions operated nine parks in the USA, Japan and Europe with a combined attendance of 89.2 million visitors (*Travel and Tourism Analyst*, 2000). Many people see Disney as a benchmark for the theme park business, in particular.

Primary and secondary attractions

Primary attractions are those which are the main reason for taking a leisuretrip. They tend to be those attractions where visitors will spend most of their time either because the site is a vital resource for a preferred activity or it is necessary to spend several hours at least on the site to enjoy all its elements and to obtain value for money. In the latter case the attractions are often those with relatively high entrance charges. Based on these two explanations of primary attractions, it is clear that two good examples are beaches and theme parks respectively.

In contrast, *secondary attractions* are those places visited on the way to and from the primary attractions. Their role is usually to break a long journey, to provide an opportunity for eating and drinking, or to give the trip some variety. Visits to secondary attractions may be as short as a few minutes. They can be used as a compromise solution to please members of the family or party who may have not wanted to visit the primary attraction but were overruled in the decision-making process. Examples of common secondary attractions include craft centres, picnic sites and markets.

It should be noted, however, that these are generalizations and that what is a primary or secondary attraction is different for each visitor, depending on their preferences, attitudes and interests. For some leisure shopping is a way to pass a few minutes on the way home at the end of a day out, while for others it would be the primary attraction of a day trip.

In order to maximize their income from visitors many primary attractions are trying to develop their sites so that visitors will not feel the need to visit secondary attractions. They are increasingly adding retail and catering outlets, which are themed and specialized, and are attractions in their own right. Many attractions also run events programmes so as to attract new customers who might not otherwise visit the attraction.

Catchment area

There are enormous varieties in the size of the catchment areas from which attractions draw their visitors. Many attractions are local with most of their visitors coming from within a few miles. These attractions are seen as local leisure facilities rather than as part of a tourism product. Examples of such attractions include small-scale local authority museums and country parks.

Other attractions have regional catchment areas, drawing most of their visitors from the region in which they are situated. The size of this region may vary from country to country but it will often be measured in tens of miles. In the UK most theme parks have a regional catchment area, for example Camelot in North West England and the American Adventure in the East Midlands. Evidence shows that theme parks need populous regional catchment areas to ensure their viability. However, these regional catchment areas are not mutually exclusive and may well overlap, with people in some areas falling within the catchment area of two theme parks. For example, people in London are part of the catchment area for both Chessington World of Adventures and Thorpe Park.

Relatively few attractions have primarily national catchment areas. Such attractions are generally the market leaders in their field, like Alton Towers in the UK, or are located in major tourist destinations which have a national catchment area. This latter factor accounts for the national and international catchment area of many attractions in London and Paris.

Only a handful of attractions enjoy an international catchment area. These tend to be the unique attractions which are, literally, world famous. Examples of such attractions include Disney World, the Pyramids at Giza, the Grand Canyon and the Olympic Games, wherever they are held.

Determining the size of a catchment area is difficult for two reasons. First, it is not just the distance that people travel but how long it takes them to travel to the attraction that matters. The catchment area map will therefore not show an attraction surrounded by a neat circle but rather an irregular shape determined by road patterns and public transport systems. Second, the chief criterion for determining the catchment area has to be the overwhelming majority of visitors coming from within the area rather than all visitors. Otherwise small local museums could be said to have an international catchment area if just a few overseas tourists visited them.

Visitor numbers

Attractions can be classified according to how many visitors they receive. The variety is enormous such as the 12.5 million visitors a year at Disneyland Paris, and 12 million people who annually visit Notre Dame in Paris. The highest number of visitors is often found at theme parks, and internationally renowned ancient monuments and historic buildings. Conversely, the smallest number of visitors is usually seen at small specialist private museums and local authority museums.

There is clearly a close link between visitor numbers and the population of the catchment area.

Location

Different types of attraction are found in different types of location, namely rural, coastal and urban. Most natural attractions, except beaches, are found in rural areas, in relatively isolated areas, as are many historic houses. Theme parks, too, are often found in rural areas but they are often deliberately located next to major roads for easy accessibility to help maximize visitor numbers. Coastal resorts are the traditional home of amusement parks, entertainment complexes and large marinas.

In terms of attractions there are two main types of urban areas. There are the historic towns and cities which are usually rich in cathedrals, heritage centres, health spas and arts festivals. On the other hand, there are the industrial cities with strong traditions of manufacturing industry which are usually venues for major sporting events, industrial heritage, conference and exhibition centres, and factory visits, where tourism may be being used as part of an urban regeneration campaign.

Size

Attractions can be classified according to the size of their site. Their size varies from a few hundred square metres for some craft centres and small museums to hundreds of hectares for major theme parks. Size of site and the capacity of the attraction are clearly interrelated.

Target markets

It would be possible to classify attractions according to their target market or markets. The market could be looked at or subdivided in a number of ways based on any of a number of variables, including the following:

- age
- sex
- stage in the family life cycle: children, young single adults, young couples, young couples with babies, growing family, 'empty-nesters' and old age
- social class: A, B, C1, C2, D, E
- place of residence
- day-visitors versus staying visitors
- individuals or groups
- type of transport used to travel to the attractions
- when they visit the attraction – season, month, day of the week, and time of day
- the personality of visitors and their lifestyles.

Benefits sought

The other customer-orientated way to classify attractions would be to look at them in terms of the benefits visitors expect from visiting them. There are many such benefits but the following brief list will provide a general idea of the range:

- status
- nostalgia
- learning something new
- economy and value for money
- good service
- a variety of on-site attractions to satisfy a family with different tastes and preferences
- easy accessibility

Classification	Emphasis
Natural (Scottish Highlands, Yosemite)	Purpose-built (Universal Studios, Six Flags parks)
Outdoor (San Diego Zoo)	Indoor (Smithsonian Museums)
Heritage-based, not purpose-built for tourism (English cathedrals)	Purpose-built for tourism (Stockman's Hall of Fame, Australia; Jorvik Viking Centre, UK)
Special global events (Olympics)	Local festivals/events (Local parades, exhibitions)
Drawing power (high) (Great Barrier Reef, Australia)	Drawing power (low) (local recreation, sites)
Ownership (Star City Casino)	Stewardship (Banff World Heritage Area, Canada)
Content themes: historical (Sovereign Hill, Australia); cultural (Amish communities); music (Branson, Nashville, USA); sporting (events, museums, Hall of Fame); military (Gallipoli, Culloden); art (the Prado/Louvre); marine (aquaria); animals (zoos, sanctuaries)	

Source : Pearce, Benchendorff and Johnstone (2000).

Table 1.5
Some classifications of tourist attractions

- good catering
- clean environment
- exercise
- obtaining a sun tan
- buying a souvenir
- excitement
- light-hearted entertainment.

Pearce, Benchendorff and Johnstone have produced a multicriteria attraction classification which is illustrated in Table 1.5.

Conclusion

This chapter has looked at what we mean by visitor attractions, how they relate to destinations, tourism facilities and activities, and how they can be classified. However, it must be stressed that, because of the complexity of the subject and the great number of types of attractions that exist, it is very difficult to generalize about attractions and, yet, this very diversity means we must generalize if we are to try to make sense of the subject.

Discussion points and essay questions

1 Critically evaluate the definition of attractions given in this chapter and then devise and justify your own new definition.
2 Discuss the factors which influence the size of the catchment area of an attraction.
3 Compare and contrast the benefits visitors may expect from a visit to:
   (a) a gallery of modern art
   (b) a theme park
   (c) a farm-based attraction.

Exercise

Select ten attractions of various kinds from your region. Analyse each attraction in terms of:

- the type of attraction
- who owns the attraction and what are the objectives of the attraction managers
- the location of the attraction
- history of the attraction.

What does this exercise teach you about the scope and nature of the attractions sector?

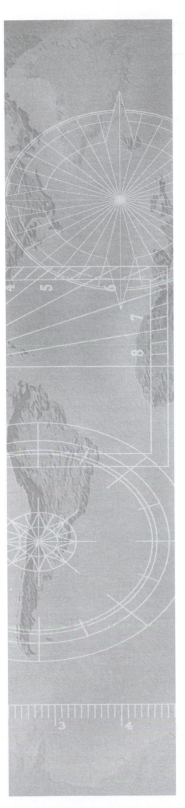

The role of visitor attractions in tourism

There are three main aspects to the role of visitor attractions in tourism which this chapter will explore:

1 The historical development of attractions from their earliest beginnings to the present day, and their relationship with the growth of tourism.
2 The link between attractions and other sectors of tourism, notably destinations, transport and tour operation.
3 Their economic, social and environmental impacts and the use of attractions in urban regeneration, economic development, regional policy and national economic development.

Historical development

Tracing the historical development of attractions is more difficult than it might at first appear, for two main reasons. First, it is difficult to decide how many people have to visit a site before it justifies the term 'attraction'? Were the pyramids of Egypt an attraction in Roman times when they received perhaps a few dozen Roman visitors a year? Or did they only really become a true attraction when they were made accessible to thousands of tourists every year through the rise of tour operators and improved transport services? Likewise, the Grand Canyon has existed for millions of years. Did it become an attraction when it was first discovered by the Native Americans, or was it not until it was made accessible by transport developments and started to be exploited by the fledgling mass tourism industry that it truly became a tourist attraction?

Second, there is the issue of the reason for visiting a place. Are sites only attractions when people visit them primarily for pleasure and entertainment in the widest sense of the word, rather than out of a sense of duty or obligation. For example, are shrines and cathedrals only attractions when the majority of visitors use them for pleasure and enjoyment rather than visiting them as an expression of religious devotion? The same discussion could also take place in relation to many traditional events and festivals. In England, for example, when did well-dressing in Derbyshire cease to be a religious activity that was designed to guarantee the future well-being of the local community and become a visitor attraction?

Natural attractions and the human-made attractions that were not designed primarily to attract tourists are clearly the oldest type of attraction. They have become attractions slowly over a period of time because of a variety of factors, including changes in society and technological developments. Conversely, most attractions that were designed specifically to attract tourists are of a more modern era and have been true attractions from their first day of existence. Events and festivals can be of either type depending on whether they are traditional events that have been adopted by tourists, such as the Trooping of the Colour in London, or those which have been created specifically to attract tourists, like many of the numerous arts festivals that have sprung up recently in Europe.

What is clear is that the number of attractions worldwide and the number of people visiting them have grown dramatically in recent decades. This reflects the enormous growth in international tourism since 1950 and the rise of domestic excursion-taking in the developed countries over the same period. There are a number of reasons for this growth, including:

- increased disposable income
- more leisure time in terms of paid holidays, a two-day weekend for most people, and the ability to build up extra holiday through 'flexitime' systems
- developments in technology, leading to sophisticated reservation systems and better aircraft
- the growth of personal mobility through mass car ownership
- education
- the media which provide images and information about destinations and attractions
- increased marketing of destinations and attractions as governments and private companies recognize the economic benefits of tourism
- the rise of the package holiday, which helped make travel affordable for most people and took the fear out of travelling to other countries.

These factors are clearly common to both tourism generally and attractions specifically, thus proving the point that the growing popularity of attractions is inextricably linked to the rise of the tourism industry.

Earliest beginnings

No one really knows which were the first attractions in the world. However, it is known that the Greeks and Romans sometimes travelled substantial distances to visit sites for pleasure. Most of these sites were of artistic or architectural interest. The pyramids of Egypt were also an attraction for Roman travellers. While such sites stimulated the imagination of Romans and pleased them aesthetically, they also made use of waterfront villas for recreational activities such as fishing and bathing. The Romans took this love of water-based attractions to all the areas they colonized; hence, for example, the creation of the baths at Bath. There is little, if any, evidence of any attraction-visiting elsewhere in the world on a significant scale during the same period or indeed for a further thousand years. This is not to say that such evidence may not be found in future years through the efforts of archaeologists.

The medieval period

The medieval period in Europe saw the rise of tourism based on religion. This was arguably the first example of mass tourism, which saw the growth of services geared to the needs of the religious traveller such as hostels and guidebooks. The attractions in this case were the religious shrines that were the objective for pilgrimages. Travellers ventured great distances to visit these sites and, so, well-established routes developed, linking numerous shrines such as on the route of St Jacques de Compostella. As well as being a religious devotion, visiting these shrines was also an opportunity for socializing and seeing new sights. It should be remembered that while Christian shrines in Europe were attracting large numbers of pilgrims the shrines of other religions, such as Mecca in Saudi Arabia, were also being visited by substantial numbers of visitors.

The Renaissance

In contrast to the tourism of the medieval period, which was relatively large scale, the non-religious tourism of the Renaissance era was an elitist activity enjoyed by few people. It involved visiting a variety of attractions including many where the main appeal was aesthetic, as well as religious. The nature and culture of exotic lands were also a major attraction for Renaissance travellers.

The seventeenth and eighteenth centuries

The next stimulus for the growth of tourism based on specific attractions was a concern with health in the latter part of the seventeenth century and during the whole of the eighteenth century. This concern led to two major types of attraction developing. The first were spas based on mineral waters, such as Bath and Royal Tunbridge Wells. Here socializing was as much a part of the attraction as the health-giving properties of the water. The second type of attraction was sea-bathing based on the view that sea water had medicinal properties. One therefore bathed in it for health reasons rather than for pleasure. The origins of the seaside resorts of Scarborough and Margate, for example, date back to this era and these beliefs. This development clearly also took place in other countries at the same time, notably Germany, Belgium, France and the former Czechoslovakia.

These years also saw a particular type of attraction-based tourism, namely the 'Grand Tour'. This was an established itinerary that focused on historic and cultural sites, mainly in France and Italy. It was often undertaken by the younger members of the aristocracy and was seen as part of their education.

The nineteenth century

Industrialization and the development of railways in a number of European countries stimulated the growth of attraction-visiting in the nineteenth century among the less well-to-do sections of society. Until then tourism had mostly been the preserve of the social, economic and political elites. It was in this century that bathing began to be seen as a pleasurable activity in its own right, and resorts grew up based on good beaches and accessibility from urban areas. These towns and cities themselves gained new attractions in this century in the shape of great museums, galleries and parks, which were generally created by paternalistic industrialists. Many of the museums and galleries displayed items collected by eighteenth-century travellers who had undertaken the 'Grand Tour'. Many of the artefacts brought back by these travellers were also to be found in Britain's stately homes, which were occasionally opened to select members of the public in the nineteenth century.

The elite discovered two new types of attraction during this century. The first was the climate of Southern Europe in winter, particularly the French Riviera and Biarritz, where their desire for leisure activities was met by the development of casinos for example. The second attraction was the mountains of the Alps with the opportunities they offered for mountaineering and skiing. Here activity rather than relaxation and sightseeing were the attractions.

Into the twentieth century

The late nineteenth and early twentieth centuries was a popular period for event-based attractions such as the numerous 'Great Exhibitions' and the revival of the Olympic Games.

Recent decades

Since the end of the Second World War the number and range of attractions available has multiplied dramatically. The package tour and developments in air travel have made attractions in distant lands accessible to far more people than ever before. The rise of car ownership has allowed people to visit more isolated attractions within their own country, which were previously inaccessible by public transport. Furthermore, the growth in tourism since 1950 and the recognition of its economic benefits has led to the growth of purpose-built attractions, designed specifically to attract tourists, and to encourage them to spend their money. This accounts for the rise of theme parks, for example, whose mission is to entertain and amuse. Unlike other forms of human-made attractions that were not designed specifically for tourism, such as cathedrals and stately homes, they would not exist without tourism.

In many ways, the 1980s were a watershed in the development of attractions. Changes in lifestyles, increases in leisure time and disposable income, technological developments and new consumer tastes combined to bring to prominence novel types of attractions in Europe. These include leisure shopping complexes, waterfront developments, IMAX cinemas and visits to working factories. Rightly or wrongly, many of these were identified with the concept of 'postmodernism'.

At the same time, there was a worldwide growth in heritage attractions, particularly those concerned with social history and more recent periods of history such as the late nineteenth and twentieth centuries. However, the growth of such attractions stimulated an intense debate about their legitimacy. Many heritage attractions were criticized for allegedly being nostalgic and distorting history to attract tourists, by authors like Robert Hewison in his 1987 book, *The Heritage Industry*. This was also the era when dusty old-fashioned museums in Europe began to be remodelled to incorporate more visitor-friendly and interactive displays.

The 1980s and early 1990s was also the period in which governments around the developed world began, deliberately, to use attractions as tools of government urban regeneration and regional development policies. For example, this was the era of the 'garden festivals' in the economically depressed cities of the UK.

By the end of the 1980s it could be said that in the USA, Northern Europe and Japan, for example, attractions had 'come of age' and matured.

However, in other parts of the world the sector was at a much earlier stage of development. In the 1980s there were no major theme parks in South East Asia (excluding Japan), the Middle East, South America or Africa. And in most of these regions the museums remained largely traditional, uninspiring and relatively undervisited.

However, it is in this era that we saw the first stirrings of the massive latent attraction sector in South East Asia, with proposed major projects in countries such as South Korea and Malaysia. In South America, Africa and the Middle East, the 1980s saw very little evidence of the emergence of a modern attractions sector. This was due to a variety of reasons, in different places, including:

- a lack of recognition of the potential role of inbound cultural tourism and a lack of commitment to heritage management
- relatively low levels of economic development and unequal distribution of wealth which often limited the potential domestic market for attractions

- inadequate infrastructure to support the development of attractions
- political and/or economic instability which discouraged the sub-stantial investment required for the development of attractions
- an emphasis in tourism policy and tourism marketing on 'traditional' natural attractions such as beaches and wildlife.

Attractions and other sectors of tourism

We have now established that there is a close correlation between attractions and tourism, as both an activity and an industry. It is appropriate therefore that we should now explore this relationship in more detail, looking at tourism sector by sector.

Destinations

As we saw in the previous chapter, popular attractions tend to grow into destinations and services such as hotels, restaurants and shops gather around the attraction to meet the needs of visitors. It could be said that attractions are the original grain of sand around which the destination 'pearl' grows.

Most of the world's largest and most successful destinations developed from one major attraction. Thus Luxor's fame is based on its pyramids, Canterbury on its cathedral, Orlando on Disney World, and Ober-ammergau on its passion plays. The marketing of these destinations tends to focus on these attractions so that they are often the symbol of the destination in the minds of tourists.

While some destinations remain based on a single attraction, such as Lourdes with its shrine, most develop new attractions to satisfy visitor demand and lengthen their stay. This latter pattern is perhaps best illustrated through Figure 2.1, although it must be observed that not all destinations pass through all these stages. This is obviously an idealized model that presupposes a greenfield site with no existing development. In reality, most attractions are located within villages, towns or cities, with established services and infrastructure geared to the needs of residents. Clearly, the model relates to physical attractions rather than events and festivals.

In due course, and in line with product life cycle theory, it may be that destinations may reach a fifth stage where some of the original attractions go into decline and the pattern of support services changes accordingly. Perhaps this phenomenon is already being seen in some British seaside resorts where entertainment facilities and other traditional attractions are closing and hotels are being converted into nursing homes.

Until recently, there was in most destinations a clear distinction between attractions and support services including accommodation, catering and retailing. Most of the attractions and services were in the hands of separate owners in both the public and private sectors. Furthermore, it was generally quite easy in the past to distinguish between attractions and destinations. However, there are now a number of examples in Europe, and even more outside Europe, of attractions in

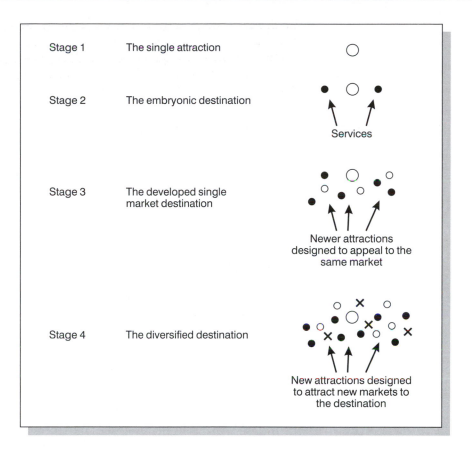

Figure 2.1
Attractions and the
development of
destinations

the ownership of a single organization which are, in effect, destinations. They combine entertainment and support services on one site, albeit a very large site covering many hectares. A prime example of this is Disneyland Paris; such attractions are arguably destinations in their own right. Tourists feel no need to leave the site at all during their stay as it is capable of accommodating all their needs. There are now many such 'attractions' around the world, particularly in the USA and the countries of the Pacific Rim.

Transport

Attractions enjoy a close relationship with transport systems in a number of ways:

1 Transport networks make attractions physically accessible to potential visitors and are thus an important factor in determining the number of visitors an attraction is likely to attract. As most people travel to attractions by car or bus, road links are by far the most important element of the transport network for attractions.

2 The existence of major attractions leads to the development of new public transport services to meet the demand of visitors. For example,

Billund Airport in Denmark has developed to make it easier for visitors to reach Legoland, while a new airport has been opened in Knock in Ireland for the convenience of pilgrims visiting the shrine there. Likewise the French government has extended the TGV rail network to include Disneyland Paris.

3 Transport is also important within destinations to make travel between attractions, and between attractions and services, as easy as possible to encourage visitors to use as many of the destination's facilities as possible.

4 Modes of transport can often be an attraction in themselves, with passengers being encouraged to see using them as a type of special event. For example, there is the 'once-in-a-lifetime' trip on Concorde or the Orient Express, while at another level there are the ferry journeys which, because of the excellent facilities on board, are described as 'mini-cruises'.

5 Novel methods of on-site transport are used to move visitors around the attraction in ways that will add to the enjoyment of their visit. Such methods include the monorail at Alton Towers, canal boats at Wigan Pier, 'time-cars' at the Jorvik Centre in York, and trains at Beamish Open Air Museum.

Tour operation

Attractions are vitally important to the tour operators who put together package holidays. Their relationship takes a number of forms, including the following:

1 Operators prefer to base their holidays in destinations that combine a variety of attractions and services that will appeal to their customers.

2 Excursions taken away from the base destination are a valuable source of income for operators and they therefore like destinations which have a range of attractions within a short distance that can be visited on day, half-day and evening excursions. Often it is better if these attractions are very different from those at the destination itself so that visitors will feel they will enjoy a new experience by visiting them. That is why in many beach resorts based on sunbathing and watersports the excursion programmes featured by tour operators are to historic buildings, old villages or 'traditional events'.

3 The growth of holidays in the off-peak season is dependent upon the availability of sufficient attractions to keep the visitors occupied. In many places the range of attractions available to visitors outside the peak holiday season is severely restricted.

4 Specialist attractions are vital to the provision of special interest holidays by tour operators, such as vineyards for wine tours and good shows for theatre weekends.

5 The quality of attractions is important as some visitors may take the same holiday again in the future because of enjoyable experiences at attractions on the first holiday.

We have clearly demonstrated that the development of attractions over the centuries has been instrumental in the growth of tourism and that there are strong links between attractions and other sectors of tourism. It is not surprising, therefore, that attractions also share many of the impacts of tourism generally.

The impact of attractions

Attractions can have three main types of impact, namely, economic, environmental and sociocultural, and these are usually interrelated.

Economic impact

To examine the economic impact of attractions it is best to divide the effects into those which are positive and those which are negative.

Attractions can benefit an economy in several ways:

1 The major attractions such as the Trooping of the Colour, the Wimbledon Tennis Championships and the heritage attractions of London encourage thousands of overseas visitors to visit Britain. This brings valuable foreign currency and contributes to improving the balance of payments situation of the country as a whole. This is undoubtedly one of the reasons why the French government was keen to see the Disneyland Paris resort develop in France rather than in another country.

2 Attractions in general provide central government with an income through the taxes paid by employees and the sales taxes paid on items bought by visitors, for example. However, the government may also own many of the leading attractions, as is the case with the Tower of London, and thus receive a direct income from entrance charges paid by visitors. This income can then be used to help conserve the country's heritage. An interesting example of the use of attraction income, though not a government-owned attraction, is the opening of Buckingham Palace to visitors with the express intention of raising money to fund the renovation of Windsor Castle, which is a government property, following the fire of 1992.

3 Attractions provide jobs, directly and indirectly. The British Tourist Authority has estimated that in 1992 there were nearly 5552 attractions in the UK which employed some 84 000 people (British Tourist Authority/English Tourist Board, 2000). However, because of the seasonal and part-time nature of many attraction jobs the real figure is some 47 000 full-time job equivalents. Small attractions provide very few jobs while even the largest rarely employ more than 100 full-time job equivalents. Different types of attractions tend to generate different amounts of employment. For example, the British Tourist Authority found that, in 1992, gardens employed nine staff on average compared with an average of twenty-five employees at wildlife attractions.

4 Visitor expenditure has a multiplier effect within the local and regional economy, and helps support a number of jobs indirectly in fields such

as food production, catering, crafts and souvenir production. There is also a multiplier effect from the employees at the attractions spending their salaries.

5 Many attractions in the UK are owned by local authorities and voluntary bodies, such as the National Trust. The income from these attractions can help to subsidize other activities of the organization, such as the provision of leisure facilities and the conservation of buildings.

On the negative side, however, the conservation and management of attractions is very costly and much of the burden falls on central government. There are hundreds of such attractions in the UK, owned by the government. The cost of opening them to the public rarely covers their running costs. They are, in purely financial terms therefore, arguably liabilities rather than assets. Other negative economic impacts of attractions include:

1 Jobs are often poorly paid and, in the case of those in museums and capital-intensive leisure projects, cost more money to create than to produce jobs in some other sectors of the economy.
2 Many local-authority owned attractions, particularly sports facilities and museums, lose money and are therefore a net drain on the local authority budget.
3 Where local authorities do fund attraction projects from their own limited resources there is often an opportunity cost in relation to how else the money might have been spent.

This is just a brief outline of some of the key economic impacts of attractions. There are, however, several excellent detailed case studies on this subject which readers with a particular interest in this field may find valuable. First, there is the work of Peter Johnson and Barry Thomas (1992a) on the North of England Open Air Museum at Beamish, in County Durham, which was published in their book, *Tourism, Museums and the Local Economy*. A survey of their main conclusions follows, together with data on the economic impact of Center Parcs in Nottinghamshire.

North of England Open Air Museum, Beamish, County Durham • • •

In its first year, the attraction opened over twenty weekends and received around 50 000 visitors. By the late 1980s the attraction was welcoming some 500 000 visitors per annum, over half the visitors coming from outside the region. However, the growth has not been constant; numbers fell from just over 300 000 to around 200 000 between 1979 and 1985.

Beamish is funded by local authorities and grants from other bodies and there is also a trust fund that helps finance the continuing development of the attraction. The museum is now being very successful in generating income so that less than a third of its total income comes from the local authorities.

The late 1980s were a particularly good time for Beamish. In 1986 a new visitor centre opened and the museum was named Museum of the Year. Then in 1987 Beamish went on to be awarded the accolade of European Museum of the Year. By 1988–9 the museum was employing 137 full-time equivalent staff and was receiving £1.1 million in income. Its capital expenditure in the same year was some £302 000.

In 1990 Johnson and Thomas made an interesting study of the labour force at Beamish in the late 1980s. Among their conclusions were the following points:

- Employee costs including national insurance and pensions represent about 60 per cent of the attraction's annual expenditure. This compares to other costs such as supplies and services (24 per cent) and the maintenance of premises (11 per cent).
- Half of all employees were female.
- Some 80 per cent of staff were described as being 'manual' labour.
- About 65 per cent of staff were paid weekly, while 35 per cent were paid monthly.
- Peak period employment was 70 per cent higher than off-peak employment.
- Half of all staff lived within a 3-mile radius of the attraction.
- The labour force in 1989 was three times the size of that in 1978.
- Staff numbers had grown more rapidly than the number of visitors but less rapidly than admission income.
- As well as the people employed on site it was estimated that a further 100 jobs were supported outside the site by the attraction.
- The cost of job creation in terms of public revenue expenditure at Beamish was £1855 at 1988 prices. This was more than the cost of creating jobs in museums and galleries in Ipswich and Glasgow but far less than the cost of job creation in Merseyside in museums and galleries (£2658).

Johnson and Thomas carried out a comparative study of Beamish and other European open air museums at the end of the 1980s, the main conclusions of which were:

- Beamish received a lower percentage of public sector subsidy per visitor than most other open-air museums.
- UK open-air museums, including Beamish, are much younger than those in Scandinavia and the Netherlands.
- Beamish was the largest open-air museum of the ten that were studied; it was nearly twice the size of the second largest museum, the Ulster Folk and Transport Museum.
- Beamish was the most visited of all the UK open-air museums and out of the ten studied was second only to the Skansen Museum, in Stockholm, Sweden, which received 1.7 million visitors.
- On the other hand, Beamish came only fifth in terms of the number of staff employed.
- In terms of income, Beamish was second only to the Skansen museum.

- Only two other museums (Ironbridge and the Black Country Museum) of the ten studied received less public sector revenue subsidies.
- Between 1980 and 1989, while most open-air museums in the UK experienced a growth in visitors, most of those in the Netherlands and Scandinavia received fewer visitors.

Center Parcs UK, Sherwood Forest, Nottinghamshire[1] • • •

Between 1986 and 1993 total investment on the construction of the complex exceeded £150 million. Of this, some £14 million was paid directly to purchase local labour or supplies from local businesses around the site. The construction of the site created over 600 job-year's worth of work and generated some £7 million of wages and salaries, and income for the self-employed, in the area.

The Sherwood Forest site employs more than 700 people, in a variety of jobs. Nearly 300 of these jobs are in domestic services where 95 per cent of jobs are part-time, of less than 20 hours per week. On the other hand, over half of the other 400 jobs on site are full-time or, at least, involve more than 30 hours per week. More than 90 per cent of all staff live within a 10-mile radius of the complex, and 17 per cent of them were unemployed before they obtained a job at the site.

Center Parcs in Sherwood Forest, according to the Rural Development Commission Report in 1991, bought 27 per cent of the goods and services it required from local depots. Each week around a ton of meat and poultry were being purchased from one butcher in a local town which represented a quarter of the butcher's entire turnover. Several subcontractor services, the report said, had had to expand their workforce substantially to meet the needs of Center Parcs. There are still opportunities for local suppliers, of food and souvenirs for example, to sell to Center Parcs if they can offer new product lines or undercut the prices of non-local suppliers. It has been estimated that the money spent by Center Parcs with local suppliers supported some eighty-six full-time equivalent jobs in 1990.

In addition to the economic benefits occurring from expenditure by Center Parcs, there are also the benefits that come from the money spent by the attraction's visitors. Some 58 per cent of visitor expenditure took place on the site while the other 42 per cent occurred in the area on the journey to or from the complex, in 1990. Surveys have estimated that the off-site expenditure by Center Parcs visitors amounted to around £1 million per annum, mostly on shopping and petrol, in 1990. In 1990 it was estimated that each party of visitors using the self-catering villas spent about £240 (at 1990 prices) on purchases such as food and drink, shopping and an average of two visits to local attractions in the area.

The Rural Development Commission's report of 1991 found that the multiplier effect in the local area of Center Parcs was between 1.3 and 1.4.

While the Center Parcs development did bring economic benefits for the local community, it did not stimulate the local economy dramatically. That may be because complexes such as Center Parcs encourage the majority of visitor spending to take place on site, which limits the potential spin-off benefits for the local area.

The UK government has attempted to evaluate the economic impact of attractions it has helped fund. The results of these surveys were published in two volumes in 1990 by the Department of the Environment. One looks at the first three garden festivals that took place in 1984, 1986 and 1988 in Liverpool, Stoke-on-Trent and Glasgow respectively (Department of the Environment/PA Cambridge Economic Consultants, 1990a). The other looks at a sample of twenty projects in areas in need of urban regeneration (Department of the Environment/PA Cambridge Economic Consultants, 1990b).

Although at both national and local levels attractions have positive and negative economic impacts, the conventional wisdom appears to be that, on balance, attractions are generally an economic benefit. However there are great varieties in the benefits and costs of attractions, depending on factors such as the type of attraction, its size and where it is located.

Environmental impact

In contrast to the case of the economic impact of attractions, the general view seems to be that attractions have an overall negative impact on the environment. The nature of the impact tends to vary depending on the nature of the attraction and it is possible to identify two very different types of environmental impact that relate to the four-part typology of attractions outlined in the previous chapter. In the case of natural attractions and human-made attractions that were not designed for tourism, the problem is one of the impact of visitors on the attraction itself. Conversely, in the case of the other two types of attraction, namely attractions which are purpose-built for tourism and special events, it is the effects of the attraction on the environment which is the cause for concern.

Almost by definition visitors have a negative impact on the natural environment. Vegetation is eroded by walkers and valuable flowers are taken home as souvenirs. Wildlife is killed by accident or by design and habitats are damaged. Geological features suffer from graffiti and erosion, while air and water quality suffer from pollution. Tourism income can help with the conservation of the natural environment but tourism is usually more of a threat than an opportunity for the natural environment.

In the case of attractions that were not originally created with tourism in mind, such as cathedrals and stately homes, the problem is generally one of trying to accommodate large numbers of people in buildings and spaces that were not designed for the purpose. The negative effects therefore tend to be wear and tear, erosion, accidental damage and litter. For example, unique memorial stones set in the floors of cathedrals can be worn away. In fairness it should be remembered that the income from visitors can be used to fund conservation work and thus benefit the environment.

For both these types of attraction the main aim of managers must be to try to manage the attraction and the visitors in a way which tries to minimize the negative impact of visitors on the attraction itself.

On the other hand, the attractions that were designed specifically to attract tourists tend to have different problems, as they have been designed especially to accommodate the modern visitor. The environmental impact of these attractions can include inappropriate and unattractive buildings and structures, and large unsightly car parks. Their construction may also involve the destruction of parts of the natural environment. Depending on their size and nature, they may also be sources of pollution in terms of noise and air and water quality. Many operators are now very sensitive to these problems and are attempting to develop in more environmentally friendly ways. One example of this is the Center Parcs' development at Sherwood Forest in Nottinghamshire. Yet again, however, there is another side to the story. In some areas, particularly old industrial towns and cities, the creation of new purpose-built attractions has brought environmental improvements through the refurbishment of derelict buildings and the reinstatement of derelict land. Good examples of this are the Albert Dock complex in Liverpool, and the waterfront developments in Boston and Baltimore, in the USA.

Even this short discussion suggests that, in many instances, on balance, the environmental impact of attractions is a negative one. The problem is often exacerbated by the fact that many attractions are in 'honeypot' areas which attract large number of visitors on certain days at specific times of the year, namely on Sundays in the summer and on public holidays. Therefore it is often not the number of visitors per annum that is the main problem but, rather, their concentration in time and space.

Sociocultural impact

It is becoming increasingly recognized that attractions also have a sociocultural impact, and this, too, tends to depend on the type of attraction. For the natural attractions and those human-made attractions and traditional events that were not designed for tourism, the impact is often a negative one, which again revolves around how the visitors affect the attraction and its traditional, existing uses and users. Crowds at natural attractions can ruin the atmosphere and sense of space, but using rural attractions for recreation can improve the health of people. The ability to visit beautiful, relatively unspoilt places can often serve as a way of relaxing and 'recharging the batteries' of people from less attractive areas who may have monotonous or stressful jobs. As far as the human-made attractions that were not built to attract tourists, such as cathedrals, are concerned, the presence of visitors who see the building as a tourist sight rather than a place of worship can have a detrimental effect on the quality of experience for the worshipper. Likewise, the presence of too many tourists at old-established religious festivals who see the event as a source of entertainment rather than a serious part of community life, can change the nature of the event and destroy the experience for the local residents.

With regard to the attractions that are purpose-built to attract visitors and the events that have been created to encourage tourism, the concern is the impact of the attraction and its users on the local community or even on the national culture. The key point here is often the extent to which these attractions reflect the needs and desires of the local people and how accessible they are to local people. In the case of mixed-use waterfront developments and heritage centres, which are freely accessible to local people and are usually attractive to them, the new attractions will often be seen as a positive development that increases the range of leisure opportunities for local people. Alternatively, where new attractions are seen to be out of keeping with the local area and locals are prevented from using them, as happens in many parts of the world, a sense of resentment towards the visitors is the most likely result.

Often, whether or not a created attraction is seen to have a positive or negative sociocultural impact on an area is judged by the degree to which the real or perceived benefit of the attraction, jobs and visitor expenditure for example, are enjoyed by local people rather than outsiders.

Occasionally new attractions that introduce alien features and values to a country for the first time can be seen as a threat to national culture. For example, a French intellectual is reported to have described Disneyland Paris as a 'cultural Chernobyl'! Whether attractions can actually pose a threat to national cultures or whether their location in a country reflects that country's acceptance of the culture represented by the attraction, or whether the attractions themselves are modified by the indigenous culture, is as yet a debate without a conclusion.

Attractions and urban regeneration, regional policy and national economic development

In recent years, governments and local authorities all over the world have recognized the potential of tourism as an economic development tool. Sadly, while they have focused on the potential economic benefits of tourism they have not always appreciated the economic, environmental and sociocultural problems that tourism can cause. They have therefore sought to use tourism generally, and attractions specifically, as a way of achieving urban regeneration, regional development and national economic development, not always successfully.

Urban regeneration in the UK

The industrial towns and cities of the UK suffered heavily in the early 1980s from a recession which decimated many traditional manufacturing industries on which these places relied. Central government felt the need to try to regenerate these areas to improve the economic situation and to alleviate the serious social problems that had developed in many such towns and cities.

Tourism was chosen as one of the key ways of achieving this goal, with government often working through non-elected development corporations to achieve the aim rather than working with local authorities with whom they were often embroiled in political conflict. Many attractions were funded by central government to try to achieve urban regeneration, including the following examples.

Garden festivals ● ● ●

Tens of millions of pounds were invested in five garden festivals in Liverpool (1984), Stoke-on-Trent (1986), Glasgow (1988), Gateshead (1990) and Ebbw Vale (1992). It was hoped that the festivals would create new uses for derelict land and would put depressed industrial areas on the tourism map. However, it has proved difficult to maintain the momentum after the festivals ended, and it has been decided that there will be no more garden festivals.

Waterfront developments ● ● ●

Drawing on the experience of the Eastern Seaboard in the USA, considerable sums of public money have been invested in waterfront developments that tend to be mixed-use developments featuring retail units, leisure facilities, offices and homes. Some of these have been very successful in attracting visitors, such as the Albert Dock in Liverpool which attracts several million visitors annually, but the benefits have not always reached the most deprived and disadvantaged sections of the community.

Decentralized national museums ● ● ●

Several internationally renowned London-based museums have set up subsidiary attractions in provincial cities to help stimulate regeneration. For example, a Tate Gallery was established in Liverpool and the National Museum of Photography, Film and Television – a branch of the Science Museum – was established in Bradford.

However, these development have not always been successful. For example, part of the Tower of London weaponry collection was transferred to Leeds to form the Royal Armouries attraction, which has failed to reach its visitor number targets since it opened.

National Lottery and Millennium Projects ● ● ●

Since the mid-1990s, the National Lottery has provided huge sums of money to attraction projects, many of them with the specific aim of acting as a catalyst for urban regeneration. For example, between 1997 and 2002 it has been estimated that thirteen National Lottery/Millennium Commission funded projects would open in the UK, with an average capital cost of £58 million (*Travel and Tourism Analyst*, 2000).

However, it has been argued that as soon as these projects – such as London's Millennium Dome and National Centre for Popular Music in Sheffield – are seen as being unsuccessful, they have harmed the cause of urban regeneration in these places. They have also raised questions about whether any project which requires such heavy public or voluntary sector 'subsidies', is actually a viable project, at all.

As well as these central government initiatives that have met with mixed success, many local authorities have also undertaken attraction projects to try to achieve urban regeneration. Examples of this in the UK include heritage attractions such as Wigan Pier and sport facilities such as the Don Valley Stadium, Ponds Forge and the Arena in Sheffield.

Regional development in France

In France, the main aims of government policy on spatial development are regional development and rural development rather than urban regeneration. Both central and local government, as well as the voluntary sector, have used attractions to try to achieve these objectives. This is illustrated by the following three examples.

Nausicaa, Boulogne-sur-Mer • • •

This modern, aquarium-based attraction was developed in the resort of Boulogne to attract tourists to the Nord-Pas-de-Calais. It is designed to exploit the inbound tourism opportunities offered by the Channel Tunnel and counter the threat of the tunnel by encouraging French people to visit Boulogne rather than South East England.

Across Europe and the USA, aquariums have been used to help regenerate urban areas. Elsewhere in France, the Oceanapolis complex was developed to help rejuvenate the remote city of Brest.

La Cinéscénie du Puy-du-Fou, Vendée • • •

La Cinéscénie du Puy-du-Fou is a live interpretation of scenes from the history of the local area. It is enacted by local volunteers in the grounds of a ruined chateau, and is managed and controlled by local people. A few facts and figures will serve to illustrate the scale of the event.

- The action takes place on a site covering 15 hectares.
- There are 700 actors including fifty on horseback.
- Some 4000 people from the local community dress up in costume to enhance the visitor experience.
- There are lasers and fireworks and the *son et lumière* which is part of the show features some 1500 projectors.
- About 300 artillery pieces are used every evening, all of which are controlled by computer.
- One hundred and fifty seats are equipped with equipment which translates the show into four languages.

Visitor numbers for the Cinéscénie have grown steadily over the years:

1978	82 000
1983	200 000
1991	317 000
1999	400 000.

Research conducted in the mid-1990s showed that 42 per cent of visitors were in organized groups that visit on tours arranged by coach operators or travel agents, while about 38 per cent of visitors came as individuals or families. The rest of the visitors were made up of diverse groups (18 per cent) and educational groups (2 per cent).

Although the event was set up to help the area attract more visitors, about 30 per cent of visitors are from the local area, and well over half the total number of visitors are from the region. Interestingly, just over 3 per cent come from the Paris region, which is surprising given how important the Paris region is in the French domestic tourism market.

The association which runs the event is voluntary, and is also responsible for running the local Ecomusée. Its aim overall is to protect the area's heritage and develop its cultural life. In recent years the profits made by the association from the event have been used to help cultural projects in the surrounding fifteen communes that make up the 'Pays du Puy-du-Fou', including:

- an archaeology club
- a research centre in relation to local traditions
- a school of popular dance
- a riding school
- a steam train that travels 22 kilometres through local woodland.

The surplus generated also funded the creation of a reconstructed eighteenth-century Vendée village, complete with craftsmen and musicians in the early 1990s. Later in the decade a medieval village was added along with a jousting area and a Viking invasion reconstruction.

The Cinéscénie specifically, and the Ecomusée in general, represent possibly Europe's most impressive example of voluntary action creating a major attraction and then using the profits to help develop the local community and culture.

Futuroscope near Poitiers • • •

Futuroscope is, quite simply, a unique attraction. It is a mixture of a high-technology, 'hands-on' theme park, educational institutions and a state-of-the-art industrial complex, based on the latest technological developments. It is also very unusual in that the stimulus for the project came from the local authority, the Conseil Général de la Vienne. Indeed, the local authority is still the dominant player in the mixed economy body that runs the site. The underlying concept behind the project is the idea of using high technology in a number of forms to act as a catalyst to economic development in what was otherwise a rather underdeveloped part of Western France.

Futuroscope has three main elements. The first is 'le Parc Europeen de l'Image', a theme park devoted to moving images. It features the latest in Kinemax and Omnimax technologies. There is even a circular cinema where images are projected through the full range of 360°. This park is open eleven months a year and there are hotels, restaurants and gift shops on site, together with gardens and water areas on which boat trips are offered.

The second element is an education complex which has a number of separate institutions, including:

- a research centre looking at the future of mankind
- a school for secondary school level students
- a number of departments of the University of Poitiers
- a college that trains engineers and researchers
- the National Centre for Distance Learning
- an international centre for the diffusion of legal knowledge across national boundaries
- an institute that studies social change across Europe.

Again, high technology is the core of most of the education centres.

Third, there is an industrial complex that is unique in France. There is a teleport which links the businesses that are based on site with other companies all over the world through the very latest in telecommunication technology. There is also a congress centre with a capacity of 1000 delegates and an exhibition centre of 1500 square metres. The industrial complex covers some 1200 hectares.

The whole site is covered in ultra-modern buildings, resembling something from a science fiction film. It has been developed in phases, with something new coming on stream most years. The decision to develop Futuroscope was taken in 1983 and the theme park element opened to the public in 1987. In its first year the theme park attracted some 225 000 visitors. The numbers then developed as follows:

1987	225 000
1990	900 000
1993	1.9 million
1999	3 million.

According to Davidson (1994), 88 per cent of visitors expressed a desire to return to Futuroscope. At that time 6 per cent of visitors were foreigners but this figure is now significantly higher. Futuroscope is modestly priced and a ticket costs about half as much as a ticket for Disneyland Paris.

There are a number of reasons for the success of Futuroscope including:

- the fact that the on-site technology, which is the main attraction, remains at the leading edge of technological developments
- the development of the regional transport network including the TGV and the A10 motorway which links the area to Paris, and the development of direct seasonal air services from the UK to Poitiers
- joint promotions with organizations such as Kodak and Philips.

In terms of its wider aims, the park has been an important catalyst for economic development. Davidson states that by the early 1990s the park had created 2000 jobs directly and a further 13 000 indirectly. Indirect job creation is now even higher.

The park has also fuelled the growth of tourism in the region, with visitors regularly filling hotel beds up to 30 kilometres from the park. Between 1987 and 1993 Davidson (1994) writes the park largely accounted for an 82 per cent increase in the number of two-star hotel rooms alone. The 2001 brochure promoted twenty-nine hotels ranging from no frills motels to four-star luxury properties. These hotels offer more than 1000 rooms and, two-thirds of them were less than ten years old.

Futuroscope appears to be proving wrong those people who state that the French do not like theme parks, or perhaps Futuroscope is not a traditional theme park.

National economic development in Spain

Because of the importance of tourism in the Spanish economy and the problems caused by tourism in some coastal areas of Spain, together with the need to change its image as a tourist destination and attract new markets, the Spanish government used special events in 1992 to try to strengthen the national tourism industry. The main events were the Summer Olympics in Barcelona, the Exposition (Expo) in Seville, and the celebration of Madrid as the 'European City of Culture'. The only problem with using events like this is the need to find a way of maintaining the momentum created by the events after they are over. The events in Barcelona and Seville are described in more detail in the following sections.

The 1992 Olympics, Barcelona, Spain[2] • • •

The lead-in time to the XXV Olympiad in Barcelona was six years, from Barcelona being granted the Olympics in 1986, to the Games taking place in 1992. The total cost of the project has been estimated at something over 700 000 million pesetas (approximately £3500 million at January 1995 exchange rates), of which nearly 30 per cent was spent on road improvements. The Olympic Village was a wholly private development comprising two tower-blocks (a hotel and an office block), together with a shopping centre and a conference facility.

There were also some 2000 apartments on the site together with an associated marina and beach. The main Olympic stadium, created in 1929, was enlarged to a capacity of 60 000 in the mid-1980s. There was also a Sports Palace with a capacity of 17 000, the Vall d'Hebron area of 82 hectares of parks, sports facilities, housing and hotels, together with a sports centre developed from an old railway station.

Clearly, all of these facilities are available to the citizens of Barcelona now that the Olympic Games are over. Furthermore, the Games created 5500 new good quality bedspaces that have become part of the city's tourist infrastructure. The Games also led to the expansion of Barcelona airport so it is now able to handle some 12 million passengers per annum.

As well as the legacy of the Games, the event itself provided excellent public relations for Barcelona as a city, and Spain as a country. It has been estimated that some 3500 million people around the world watched the Olympic Games on television; in all there were some 2400 hours of live transmission of the Games. Furthermore, many people in the region became actively involved in the Games. For example, some 100 000 people, mostly from the region, volunteered to help with the Games.

The aim of the organizers was to ensure that the city and the region would enjoy these benefits at no extra cost to the taxpayer. They planned to achieve this through encouraging the private sector to develop the facilities, and through generating as much income as possible.

The main sources of income were:

- the sale of television rights, which contributed a third of all income. For example, it is estimated that NBC from the USA paid around 400 million US dollars for the rights to televise the Olympics
- lotteries and the sale of commemorative stamps, which raised some 20 per cent of all the income of the Games
- the marketing of corporate symbols which contributed a further 20 per cent of all income.

However, the Olympic Games were not just a beneficial event for Barcelona, they were also a good opportunity for major companies to raise their profile worldwide through their sponsorship of the Games. Major sponsors included Coca-Cola, Kodak, Philips, National Panasonic, 3M and Mars. The last named company dedicated over £15 million to promotional activity relating to the Olympic Games in the UK alone.

The Olympic Games are now a major international media event, a global marketing opportunity for world-famous brands, and an opportunity for sponsors to raise their worldwide profiles. Furthermore, the Olympic Games now often make an operating profit, in contrast to most other major sports events which often lose money. It is not surprising therefore that Atlanta and Sydney spent millions of pounds attracting the 1996 and 2000 Games respectively, and Manchester may yet make a third bid to host the Olympic Games.

Since it hosted them in 1992, Barcelona has built on the success of the Olympic Games and has developed as a leading European city break destination. For example:

- the city has exploited its links with artists such as Miró
- the redevelopment of the waterfront and the opening of new leisure attractions in the former docklands has widened the market appeal of the city
- the promotion of sport tourism, particularly visiting the stadium of FC Barcelona with its excellent museum.

However, the success of Barcelona has created its own problems such as rising prices and crime, although tourism has undoubtedly played a major part in helping restructure the city economy.

Expo '92, Seville, Spain • • •

Expo '92 took place between April and October 1992 in the southern Spanish city of Seville. The total cost of the Expo has been estimated at nearly 184 000 million pesetas and the organizers hoped to attract 36 million visitors and visitor expenditure of some 66 000 million pesetas (approximately £330 million at January 1995 exchange rates). Their plan was for the rest of the costs to be met by sponsorship and the liquidation of infrastructure, for example. In the event, however, visitor numbers did not live up to these expectations.

Mary Januarius, writing in *Leisure Management* in 1992, described the Expo as, 'an international fiesta, an architectural showcase, a spectacular tourist attraction, and an obligatory stop-off for government officials and Heads of State from all around the world'. The Expo was a huge exhibition with each exhibitor contributing a pavilion or building which contained their exhibits. There were 111 participating countries, together with every Spanish region and a limited number of major corporations. The theme of the Expo was the 'Age of Discoveries' to coincide with the five-hundredth anniversary of Columbus's discovery of the Americas. This in itself was a subject of heated controversy.

As well as the pavilions which contained many unique, high-technology exhibits, many visitors were also attracted to the Expo by the daily and varied entertainment programme. Evening entertainment proved particularly popular with visitors to the site.

The 215-hectare site was designed to be capable of coping with up to 200 000 visitors a day. An additional 12 000 hotel beds and 25 000 campsite places were made available while a further 30 000 bedspaces were made available under the special Seville Open City Programme. Accommodation prices rose dramatically during the Expo.

There were some operational difficulties, however, such as queues of up to two and a half hours to enter some pavilions and problems when pavilions were closed so that VIPs could pay them a visit. Nevertheless, while in the early days after the project was announced it was heavily criticized by local people, in the event there was also considerable local pride.

The challenge since 1992 has been to find a use for the site after the event has ended. It is planned that the site will be converted into a technological research and development centre, with about 40 per cent of buildings remaining. However, this scheme still looks ambitious in the light of Spain's current economic difficulties. In the long run, there is little doubt that Expo '92 has left a valuable legacy for the Seville of the future in terms of transport improvements, better telecommunication links and more hotel beds. In financial terms, however, the event has left the public sector with major debts. It is a matter of opinion to what extent the event was cost-effective in the short and longer terms.

Purpose-built attractions, designed specifically to attract tourists, are commonly used to help achieve development goals and they can be located where they are most needed. Specially created events and festivals are often used for the same reason. However they also have the advantage of not being fixed in space and type, so that the latter can be arranged at the time and place where they are most needed. They can also be easily moved to a new location if required, and specialist events have the power to attract new markets to visit areas they would not otherwise want to visit. These factors make events and festivals probably the most effective type of attraction in terms of achieving economic development objectives.

Conclusion

This chapter has attempted to look at the role of attractions in the field of tourism as a whole. It has explored their historical development and the role of attractions in the growth of tourism, and has looked at the relationship between attractions and other sectors of the tourism industry. Finally, the chapter has briefly examined the impact of attractions and has looked at their use as a tool for economic and social development.

Discussion points and essay questions

1 Discuss the likely impacts of the opening of a new theme park.
2 Discuss the factors that led to the growth of heritage attractions in the 1980s and 1990s.
3 Critically evaluate the extent to which attraction projects can stimulate regional development and urban regeneration.
4 Discuss the way in which single attractions can act as a catalyst for the development of new destinations.

Exercise

Select a new or recently developed attraction in your region or country. For your chosen attraction, evaluate its positive and negative environmental, economic and social impacts. Then decide whether these impacts, overall, are positive or negative. Justify your decision and indicate any difficulties you experience in carrying out this exercise.

Notes

1 The information in this section is based on a report produced by PA Economic Consultants for the Rural Development Commission (1991) and a paper presented by Clive Gordon at the 'Tourism in Europe: The 1992 Conference', which was held in Durham, UK, in July 1992.
2 This information largely comes from an article by Professor Terry Stevens (1991). Further details of this article are contained in the Bibliography.

The visitor attraction product

What is a product?

The commonly used word 'product' is in reality a complex concept that needs careful definition. A number of possible definitions already exist, including the following: 'A product is anything that can be offered to a market for attention, acquisition, use, or consumption that might satisfy a want or need. It includes physical objects, services, persons, places, organisations, and ideas' (Kotler, 1994b).

Many well-established definitions are mainly concerned with products that are manufactured goods. However, the rise of service industries, including tourism, in recent years has led to the development of other definitions designed to modify the idea of a product to reflect the complexity of industries where the product is a service rather than a manufactured good. There is now a general recognition that in many service industries the product is actually a combination of tangible goods and intangible services. This idea has come to be known as the 'product/service mix', and is summed up by the following definition: 'The product/service mix is the combination of products and services, aimed at satisfying the needs of the target market' (Renaghan, 1981).

What is the attraction product?

It is the author's view that most attractions are a classic example of this idea that the product is in fact a product/service mix. Although primarily intended to cover the hospitality industry product, the following definition is equally applicable to the majority of attractions:

> A product is an offering of a business entity as it is perceived by both present and potential customers. It is a bundle of benefits designed to satisfy the needs and wants, and to solve the problems of, specified target markets. A product is composed of both tangible and intangible elements: it may be as concrete as a chair or dinner plate or as abstract as 'a feeling'. The utility of a product derives from what it does for the customer. (Lewis and Chambers, 1989)

If this definition is applied to most types of attractions we can see that it works. A theme park such as Alton Towers, for example, consists of tangible elements such as the rides, and intangible elements associated with the rides such as excitement or fear. Museums have physical artefacts but they also offer visitors the opportunity to indulge in feelings of nostalgia. The pleasure of visiting cathedrals is derived both from the physical features of the building such as stained-glass windows and stone sculptures, and the intangible elements such as the atmosphere and the spiritual value of the place. Likewise natural attractions are a combination of the physical element such as beaches, together with intangibles, for example, the romantic feelings associated with being on a beach with a partner at one's side. Even many events can be a product/service mix. If one is attending a concert the aesthetic and intangible pleasure which comes from the music is a vital element of the product, but the comfort of one's seat and its location in the theatre are also important.

The visitor attraction as a service product

There are thought to be a number of special characteristics of services that distinguish them from manufactured products. Most of these relate to the idea that 'services are consumed in the process of their production' (Sasser, Olsen and Wyckoff, 1978).

First, *the staff involved in producing and delivering the product are part of the product itself*. Their attitudes, behaviour and appearance are crucial to the way the product is perceived by the customer. Customers are directly exposed to the strengths and weaknesses of the staff in services, whereas they never see the people who produce manufactured products generally. This is clearly true for attractions such as events, and for purpose-built attractions, hence the emphasis placed on staff recruitment, training and performance by Disney at its theme parks. The same phenomenon exists for most natural attractions but it may be harder to see as customers may not come into contact with the service deliverers, for example, the people who maintain footpaths and those who clean the beaches.

Second, *the customers themselves are involved in the production process*. Their use of the product will reflect their own attitudes, expectations and experiences; in other words, they will customize the product to some degree. Therefore, for an elderly person a heritage centre which looks at the period when they were a child will be a very different product than it will be for a child growing up today for whom the heritage centre tells stories about things which are totally outside their own experience, and about which they have no strong feelings. The product is therefore different for every customer and to some extent they shape the product in their own image. This is true for all types of attractions from cathedrals to forests to theme parks.

Third, because of the factors outlined in the first two points it is clear that *service products are not standardized*. The production process is a continuous one with the customer directly involved and the product changing all the time to reflect the changing relationship between the service, the deliverer, the customer and the resources on which the product is based. This is very important when it comes to the development of quality management systems and is in direct contrast to manufactured goods where the production process generally guarantees standardization, except in the case of malfunctions. In this respect attractions are clearly services and their product is never standardized. For example, the product of a theme park is constantly changing, depending on factors such as the attitude of the staff, and the weather.

Furthermore, the product is perishable and cannot be stored. It is produced and consumed at one and the same time. For example, the airline seat ceases to exist as a product to be sold when the aircraft takes off, or the restaurant meal that one could buy at 10 p.m. is no longer available at 11 p.m., after the restaurant has closed. For service products that are generally pre-booked, such as airline seats, this leads to discounting to encourage last minute purchases. Even if the price paid is lower than the normal price, it at least contributes towards covering the fixed costs of the flight. Likewise, hotel room prices may well be discounted for people enquiring about accommodation late in the day, when it is clear that the hotel will not be full, for once the morning comes the hotel room will have ceased to exist as a saleable product.

This result of perishability is also seen in attractions where pre-booking is normal, such as theatres where standby tickets may be offered, but not where pre-booking is not usual such as theme parks. The fact that the product cannot be stored makes it difficult to manage the balance between supply and demand. This is crucially important for attractions where demand tends to be highly seasonal. Capacity planning and utilization are therefore vital management tasks given the lack of ability to store the product.

Fifth, there is no tangible product to carry home, which has a number of implications. If a manufactured product does not work it can be taken back and exchanged. However, as services provide no tangible product and are produced and consumed at the same time it is virtually impossible to sort out problems in the same way. Shattered dreams cannot be replaced. This means it is important that service providers get it right the first time. The intangibility of the product also means that, unlike in the case of manufactured goods, consumers cannot inspect the product before purchasing. In this situation the sources of information on which purchasing decisions are made assume a great importance for marketers. They will often be based on word-of-mouth recommendation, past experience, the media and literature produced by the organization offering the service. This is true for all attractions and this explains why good customer service, effective public relations and quality literature are integral elements of attraction marketing.

Sixth, the surroundings of the service delivery process are a feature of the service. A factory producing goods is designed to be functional and its appearance does not matter, because it will usually never be seen by customers. In service industries, on the other hand, the environment in which the service is delivered must be both functional and attractive to the customer. Museum layouts therefore have to facilitate the free flow of visitors and appeal aesthetically to visitors at the same time.

Visitor attractions and tourism products

As well as service products generally, some commentators have said there are also characteristics of service products that are rather more specifically related to tourism.

The first contention is that tourism products are unusual because they offer shared use rights only to the purchaser. Whereas the purchaser of a car can choose whom to share it with, the charter flight seat purchaser has no choice over who they share the aircraft with and the holiday-maker on the beach has to share the sand with anyone else who chooses to be there at the same time. Likewise, the theme park visitor has to share the whole park and all the rides with other visitors. If the different users have conflicting expectations and attitudes this can result in problems. For example, noisy youngsters and elderly people in a museum are not really compatible, and the same is true of naturists and non-naturists on a beach. What is more, the need to share an attraction may in itself reduce the quality of the experience even if the other users do not have conflicting aims. For example, a beach at sunset will be far less romantic if the couple have to share it with a thousand other couples!

While it is occasionally possible to buy exclusive use rights to tourism products, the sharing of tourism products generally, and attraction products specifically, is a key factor in the debate about the impact of tourism and the need for visitor management. The impacts and the role of visitor management will depend on who is sharing with whom and how complementary or not they are to each other.

Second, it is assumed that consumers buy only temporary use rights to tourism products. This is clearly true. Holiday-makers only have the use of their accommodation for one or two weeks, for example. Most attractions are the same. One buys a ticket to use a theme park for a day or to see one performance at the theatre. There are, however, usually no such time limits on the use of natural attractions.

Third, is the idea that in tourism, customers travel to the product rather than vice versa. In general terms this is true for both tourism generally and attractions specifically. Almost all attractions are fixed in space so that to enjoy them visitors must travel to them. Even events tend to take place in specific locations. Indeed, the mode of transport used to visit an attraction may be an integral part of the overall visit experience.

The visitor attraction product as an experience

Because of the characteristics discussed above it is now usual to see the visitor attraction product as an experience, which begins with the anticipation of visiting the attraction and the planning of the trip. There is then the visit itself, including the journey to and from the attraction, and the time spent at the attraction. Finally there are the memories once the visit is over.

There are a number of elements that affect the experience:

1 The tangible elements of the product. At a theme park these could include the rides, shops and restaurants, and the cleanliness of the site.
2 The service delivery element, including the appearance, attitudes, behaviour and competence of the staff.
3 The customers themselves in terms of their expectations, behaviour and attitudes.
4 A range of factors which are largely outside the control of either the attraction operator or individual customers such as the mixture of people using the attraction at any one time, traffic congestion on the roads leading to the area in which the attraction is located, and the weather.

This complex interrelationship of factors ensures that the experience is different for every customer.

While visitor attractions are an excellent example of the idea of products as experiences, they are not the only ones. The same is true of a number of other services such as meals in restaurants.

The three levels of products

Kotler (1994b) says the product planner needs to think about the product at three levels, as illustrated in Figure 3.1.

The *core product* is what the customer is really buying. It consists of the main benefit or benefits the purchaser identifies as a personal need that will be met by the product. These are often intangible and highly subjective attributes such as atmosphere, experience, relaxation or convenience. The customers look for a product that will be a solution for their problems or needs. In general they therefore buy a product for the benefit it brings them rather than because of the specific attributes of the product.

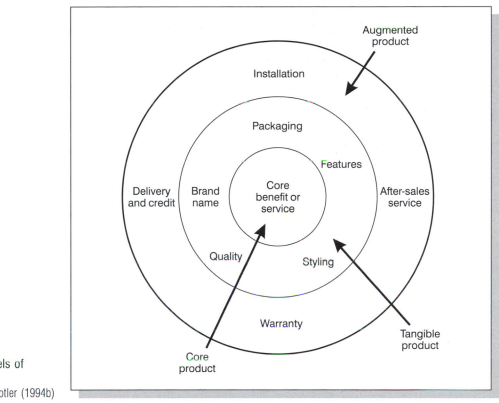

Figure 3.1
The three levels of product
Source: after Kotler (1994b)

Marketers then need to turn the core product into a tangible product, an entity which customers can purchase to satisfy their needs. This tangible product can have up to five characteristics including features, brand name, quality, styling and packaging.

Finally there is the augmented product which includes all the additional services and benefits the customer receives, both tangible and intangible. The augmented product is the 'total product bundle that should solve all the customers' problems, and even some they haven't thought of yet' (Lewis and Chambers, 1989).

This model, put forward by Kotler, was clearly developed with manufactured products in mind. However, it does apply, with modifications, to services such as attractions, as illustrated in Figure 3.2 with the example of a theme park.

Whereas Kotler envisages all the elements of the augmented product being under the control of the producer, for service products such as attractions some, such as the weather, are outside the control of the service deliverer. The weather is a good example of the fact that the augmented product has potential negatives as well as benefits. The management skill in this situation lies in trying to turn these negatives into benefits such as providing wet-weather facilities at outdoor attractions.

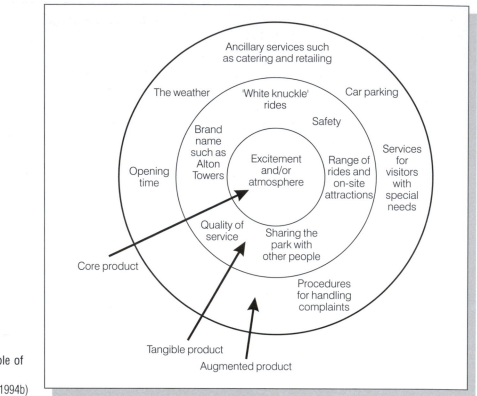

Figure 3.2
The three levels of
product: the example of
a theme park
Source: after Kotler (1994b)

Interestingly, Lewis and Chambers (1989), writing about the hospitality industry product, have a different view of the three levels of the product. They talk about formal, core and augmented products. They define the formal product as what the customer thinks they are buying; it is in fact what the customer can easily articulate. In truth, however, it may not be the real underlying reason why the customer is buying the product. They may be covering up the real needs which are making them purchase the product or they may not be aware of the more deep-seated needs. This is often seen in the case of attractions where people say they visit for fun and enjoyment while the real core product may be a much more complex set of motives and needs.

Benefits sought from the product

People visit attractions in the hope of receiving benefits. There are a wide variety of potential benefits and the particular benefit a customer looks for and expects to enjoy on a specific visit depends on two major factors. The first is the *nature of the visitors* themselves in terms of their age, lifestyle, stage in the family life cycle, past experiences and personality, for example. These criteria will determine the main benefits a particular customer looks for and will also dictate whether or not visitors see

Customer characteristics	Main benefits sought
Elderly people	Economy Passive activities Nostalgia Easy access
Families with young children	Entertainment for the children Special children's meals in catering outlets Economy
Adventurous personalities	Excitement Challenges New experiences
Health-conscious	Exercise Healthy food Clean and safe environment
Fashion-conscious	Status Being seen at a fashionable attraction or taking part in a fashionable activity
Car driver	Easy access by road Good and free or inexpensive car parking Lack of traffic congestion
Urban dweller	Peace and quiet Contrast with home environment Aesthetically pleasing environment

Table 3.1
Customer characteristics and benefits sought

particular attributes of the attraction product as a benefit or a weakness. They will affect the way visitors perceive the attraction. This is important for managers because if customers do not perceive something as a benefit then it is not a benefit in reality, even if the manager feels it should be seen as a benefit by the customer. Some of the ways in which these criteria and others could influence the customer's view of benefits are illustrated in Table 3.1.

Clearly this categorization is based on stereotyping, for example, the idea that all elderly people have little money and limited mobility. In reality, customers are far more complex and heterogeneous, and the benefits they seek reflect this diversity. Furthermore, society is changing dramatically so that characteristics that would traditionally have been used to predict visitor preferences, such as social class, are becoming arguably less useful. At the same time there are phenomena which are becoming more important determinants of the types of benefit that will be sought, such as the growing concern with green issues.

In reality, using just a single characteristic is inadequate and the benefits sought will reflect the interrelationship of the numerous characteristics of a particular customer. For example, someone is not just

Types of attraction	Main benefits sought
Theme park	Excitement Variety of on-site attractions Atmosphere The company of other users Value for money Light-hearted fun
Beach	Sun tan Sea bathing Economy Company of others or solitude
Cathedral	History Aesthetic pleasure derived from architecture Atmosphere, sense of peace and spirituality
Museum	Learning something new Nostalgia Purchasing souvenirs
Theatre	Entertainment Atmosphere Status
Leisure centre	Exercise Physical challenges and competing against others Status

Table 3.2
Types of attraction
and benefits sought

an elderly person. They could be either sixty years old and very healthy or eighty and confined to a wheelchair. They could be wealthy or poverty-stricken. Perhaps they are adventurous or they could be timid and shy. They might like to be alone or be gregarious.

The characteristics of the customer are only half the story. The second factor which influences the benefits sought is the *type of attraction* itself. Certain types of attractions are commonly associated with particular types of benefits. Table 3.2 shows just a few examples of this relationship.

Again, this is a gross simplification, one that assumes that all attractions within a certain type are the same and offer similar benefits. But this is not true. Some theme parks specialize in 'white-knuckle' rides that offer excitement while others concentrate on traditional, gentle rides that appeal to a wider range of people. Some museums are very formal with everything in glass cases and with an atmosphere that makes people talk in whispers as if they were in a church. Others encourage people to touch the exhibits and are lively, noisy places.

The key to success in the development of attractions depends on the ability to match the product being offered with the benefits which are sought from the product by the customer.

Branding

Kotler (1994b) defines a brand as 'a name, term, sign, symbol, or design or combination of them intended to identify the goods or services of one seller or group of sellers and to differentiate them from those of competitors'. Brand names and logos or trademarks encourage people to buy the particular product because for customers they represent familiarity and safety. For example, the Disney brand attracts visitors who feel they know what sort of product to expect when it carries the Disney name. There are other well-known brand names in the attraction world such as the National Trust. However, branding is weaker in the visitor attraction sector than it is in many other parts of tourism or industry as a whole, for two main reasons. First the development of brand images requires large amounts of expensive advertising and most attraction operators cannot afford such promotional activities. Second, some attraction operators, particularly in the public and voluntary sectors, do not believe that they have competitors as such. They therefore do not see the need to develop strong brand identities to differentiate them from competitors.

At the same time, we are also seeing the concept of 'brand extension' in the attractions sector, where well known brands use attractions to raise the profiles of their brands. As Jones (2001) says, these brands, 'create a visitor experience which embodies the values of the brand, stimulates the further interest of consumers and provides a profitable additional revenue stream'. Jones quotes a range of examples of this phenomenon such as Legoland and the Wimbledon Lawn Tennis Museum. It is clear that this phenomenon is at the heart of the rise of industrial or factory tourism, which is referred to elsewhere in this book.

Packaging

Packaging is easy to understand in the case of manufactured goods but what does it mean in the context of the visitor attraction product? The answer depends on our definition of packaging. For goods it is the external wrapping that is designed to make the product attractive to potential purchasers. Packaging is also used to make it easier for customers to pick up, transport and use goods. Using the same two definitions of packaging, it could include the following elements in relation to the attraction product.

- providing information and signposting to help visitors find the attraction
- attractive entrances to attract passing trade
- combining the attraction with other facilities and services to make it more attractive or accessible, for example inclusive rail travel and admission charges
- selling the product by making it part of the package offered by another organization with its own client base such as a tour operator or coach company.

Price

Fixing the price of the attraction product is difficult for a number of reasons, including the following:

1 Many of the organizations that operate attractions in the public sector are subsidized and do not look for an economic rate of return on their investment. Market pricing is therefore inappropriate and their pricing will be more dependent on social or political factors.
2 The 'price' of buying the attraction product usually has three components:
   (a) the direct cost of using the attraction, for example, the entrance charge at museums
   (b) the cost of extra discretionary purchases made by visitors, such as meals and souvenirs
   (c) the cost of travelling to and from the attractions which can often be far greater than the direct cost of using the attraction.

The many possible permutations of these three costs make the pricing issue a very complex one.

- Some attractions operate an all-inclusive price covering all on-site activities, facilities and services while others charge on an item-by-item-basis.
- A number of attractions have no entrance or usage charge at all. For example most natural attractions, some human-made attractions like churches and country parks, and many events are to all intents and purposes free, except for the cost of travelling to and from them.
- The lack of perceived competition in some sectors of the attraction's business and confusion over what exactly constitutes competition in other sectors makes it difficult to operate pricing based on what competitors are charging.
- The prices charged for direct use of the product tend to vary depending on who the customer is, with discounts being offered to groups and concessions being offered for families, the elderly, students and those who are unemployed.

Attractions and the product life cycle

There is a view that products pass through several stages during their lifetime. This is the basic premise behind the concept of the product life cycle, a model which was originally based on manufactured products. At each stage of its life it is thought that the product and its market have different characteristics that require different strategic marketing responses.

Figure 3.3 shows the traditional product life cycle while Table 3.3 illustrates the characteristics and strategic responses at each stage.

There are a number of points that need to be made in relation to the standard product life cycle model.

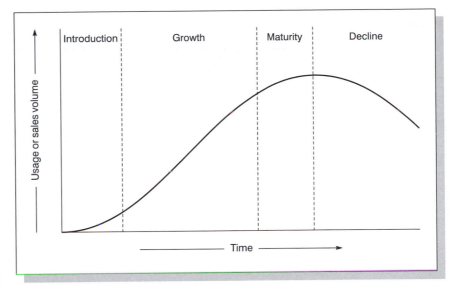

Figure 3.3
The product life cycle
Source: after Kotler (1994b)

1 The shape of the life cycle is not always the almost '5'-shaped curve; it may be bi-modal, namely with two peaks, or skewed, perhaps with growth not occurring until the last quarter of the timescale.
2 Product life cycles can vary dramatically in their time span. Staple products in traditional markets may have a life cycle measured in decades while products in fashion-conscious markets may last only a few weeks.
3 Many products never enter the growth stage. They are tested and fail and are therefore abandoned even though substantial investment may have been made in research and development.
4 Decline is not inevitable. Many products will be relaunched before they enter the decline stage. There is no guarantee that relaunches will be successful, although some products can have a number of relaunches so that their life-cycle curve looks like a succession of waves.
5 Relatively few attractions fail at the introduction stage, although many attractions never get beyond the feasibility study stage.

Product life cycle is generally accepted as being a relevant if simplistic model for manufactured goods and service products. But to what extent can the model be usefully applied to the attraction product?

Product life cycle is perhaps most relevant to attractions which are human-made and created specifically to attract visitors, so for the time being we will concentrate on this category of attraction. While the principles apply in general to these attractions there are a number of interesting points that can be made about the application of product life cycle to this type of attraction.

1 The shape of the curve is often skewed in the way shown in Figure 3.4, particularly in the case of the bigger attractions. Such attractions

	Introduction	Growth stage	Maturity stage	Decline stage
Characteristics:				
Sales	Low	Rapidly rising	Peak	Declining
Costs	High per customer	Average per customer	Low per customer	Low per customer
Profits	Negative	Rising	High	Declining
Customers	Innovative	Early adopters	Middle majority	
Competitors	Few	Growing number	Stable number, beginning to decline	Declining
Marketing objectives	Create product awareness and trial	Maximize market share	Maximize profit while defending market share	Reduce expenditure and 'milk' the brand
Strategies:				
Product	Offer a basic product	Offer product extensions, service, warranty	Diversify brands and models	Phase out weak items
Price	Use cost-plus	Price to penetrate market	Price to match or better competitors	Cut price
Distribution	Build selective distribution	Build intensive distribution	Build more intensive distribution	Become selective: phase out unprofitable outlets
Advertising	Build product awareness among early adopters and leaders	Build awareness and interest in the mass market	Stress brand differences and benefits	Reduced to level needed to retain hard core of loyal customers
Sales promotion	Use heavy sales promotion to entice trial	Produce to take advantage of heavy consumer demand	Increase to encourage brand switching	Reduce to minimal level

Sources: Kotler (1994b); Middleton (1994).

Table 3.3 The characteristics and strategic responses at each stage of the product life cycle

reach their maximum numbers of visitors relatively quickly in their lifespan. This may be because the major ones attract considerable media coverage in their early days which encourages the mass market to visit them earlier than would be the case for products that do not achieve such media attention. Furthermore, large attractions need to achieve high visitor numbers early in their life because they often have to pay back their capital costs over a relatively short period for two main reasons. First, it is difficult to borrow money for attraction products over a long period of time because they are seen as high-risk investments. Second, the life cycle is relatively short, so it is important that most of the original capital cost is paid back before expensive relaunches are required. Should constant relaunching not take place the attraction sooner or later goes into a steady decline.

2 Some attractions have a bi-modal profile because they achieve a spectacularly successful if temporary relaunch based on a change of core attraction or massive new product development. This model is shown in Figure 3.5.

3 As competition increases and customers become more sophisticated and demanding the life cycle of purpose-built attractions is getting shorter. The period between introduction and the need for relaunch can be as little as a year or two.

4 Some attractions, on the other hand, are never allowed to die even if the decline stage has become terminal. The traditional model is based on the private market where products will ultimately be 'killed off' when they are no longer producing satisfactory financial returns on the investment. However, some attractions such as local authority museums and heritage centres may simply become fossilized because to close them would be politically and socially unacceptable. Likewise small privately owned museums will often never close, even if they receive only a few dozen visitors a year, because they are run as hobbies rather than for profit.

5 Relatively few attractions fail at the introduction stage. The last major example in the UK was the Britannia Theme Park in Derbyshire, in the mid-1980s. However, many attractions never get beyond the feasibility study stage.

6 Most attractions undergo one or more relaunches during their life. These relaunches can take a number of forms including:
   (a) new rides or themes at theme parks
   (b) the introduction of new methods of interpretation at museums
   (c) improved support services such as retailing and catering at all kinds of attractions.
   A good recent example of a re-launch is the Jorvik Centre in York, UK, which was given an £8 million refurbishment in 2000–1. The cost of relaunching the product can be very expensive in terms of investment in product development and spending on promotion to make the market aware of the product development.

7 The price charged for the product does not tend to change over the life cycle in the way envisaged in the classic models, although at all stages pricing is related to what competitors are charging, where competitors can be identified.

8 Unless the new attraction is very innovative it is likely to have a large number of competitors from the beginning, whereas the traditional life-cycle model says competitors will be few in number at the beginning.

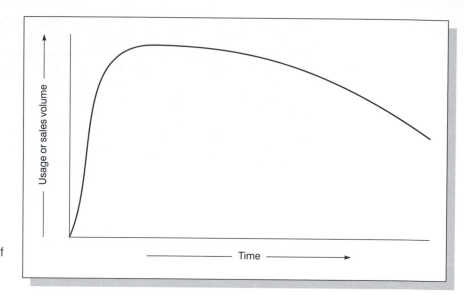

Figure 3.4
The product life cycle of some purpose-built attractions

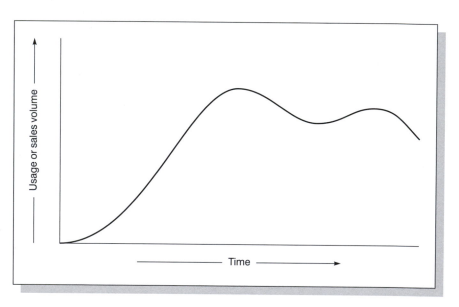
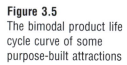

Figure 3.5
The bimodal product life cycle curve of some purpose-built attractions

When does the introduction stage begin? In the case of natural attractions, is it when the forest is first planted, or when the first local residents start to use it for recreation or when it starts to attract people from further afield? Characteristics such as sales and profits are hardly applicable and no charge is usually made for using the forest. It is also rare for forests to be marketed in the way manufactured products are, so the strategic responses and marketing objectives appear to be of little relevance to this type of attraction.

If we move on to look at those attractions that were not designed to attract tourists but have become visitor attractions over time, the model again appears of relatively little relevance for similar reasons. Taking a cathedral as an example, does it enter the introduction stage when it is built, when it first welcomes local worshippers or when it becomes an attraction for tourists from outside the area who are visiting it for enjoyment rather than because of religious devotion? Unlike the goods on which the model is based the aim of such attractions is not to maximize sales and profits but perhaps to use the income from visitors to help support their other activities such as conservation and education. For attractions like these phrases such as strategic responses and marketing objectives have little meaning for, to use management theory terminology, the attraction business is not their core business.

It is also difficult to think in terms of competition for attractions such as Notre Dame, the Egyptian pyramids and, now, Buckingham Palace, which are all unique. The model envisages that the number of competitors will rise over the lifetime of the attraction but these attractions are all specifically products of the time when they were first built so that no true competitors, offering exactly the same product or experience, will ever exist. Finally, the decline phase is seen as a problem in the classic model but for this type of attraction, which probably has more visitors than it can accommodate, it could be seen as good news, rather than as a problem.

This leads on to the idea that for natural attractions and those human-made attractions that were not designed to attract tourists, the maturity stage may not be a function of market saturation and competition. Instead it may reflect the fact that, during peak times at least, the attraction has reached its physical capacity.

It is also probably true that, for all four types of attractions we have considered so far, the life cycle of the individual attraction is related to another life cycle. That is, the life cycle of the area as a tourist destination and the stage it has reached in its life cycle as a destination. Attractions may stimulate the onset of the growth stage in the development of the destination but they can also help cause, as well as suffer from, the decline stage of a destination's life-cycle.

Trends in the attraction product

The 1980s

In the 1980s new types of attractions appeared and some well-established attractions were relaunched and given a new lease of life. These developments resulted from a number of factors including:

- changes in consumer tastes and preferences
- the introduction of new technologies
- the use of attractions by the public sector as a tool of economic development and urban regeneration.

Many of the trends in the attraction product took place in a number of countries rather than in just one but it has to be said that many of them originated in the USA. In some fields, however, the UK was also a major innovator. We will start by looking at the newer types of attraction and then go on to look at the well-established ones that have been relaunched.

While not a new product as such, *theme parks* grew dramatically in the early 1980s. The market leaders in this business, the Disney Corporation, expanded their operations to Japan and France. In the UK the majority of theme parks were first opened in the 1980s. France, too, saw an explosion of theme parks, such as that based on the traditional children' book character Asterix or the Futuroscope science and technology park near Poitiers.

The 1980s also saw the advancement of the concept of *waterfront developments*, mixed-use developments that were based on docks, riverbanks or canal sides. They tended to include uses such as offices, housing and retailing as well as leisure. They were first used in the USA as part of the regeneration of run-down port cities such as Baltimore. The government in the UK tried to use the idea to regenerate the dockland areas of cities like London and Liverpool.

Large amounts of public money were poured into these projects and some of them, like the Albert Dock in Liverpool, attract several million visitors annually. The perceived success of such attractions led to other waterfront developments in smaller ports like Hull and on canals in cities like Leeds and towns like Burnley and Wigan.

The 1980s, in particular, also saw the rise of new types of *museums* reflecting changing ideas of what constitutes history and a certain spirit of nostalgia for the recent past born out of the rapid social and economic change experienced in recent years. First there has been a growth in *open-air museums* that celebrated local and regional lifestyles, usually over the last century or two, through the use of authentic exhibits. This idea originally developed in the USA and Scandinavia, but some of the best examples were in France and the UK. The Ecomuseés of France used authentic artefacts in their original location to tell themed stories about a small geographical area.

They were usually based on a local economic activity, and could be found in both urban areas and rural areas. The original, and perhaps still the best known, is Le Creusot but there are now dozens of others. In the UK, similarly, museums were based in industrial areas where the old industries were in decline or had disappeared. They included Beamish in County Durham, the Black Country Museum at Dudley and, most famously of all, Ironbridge in Shropshire. In the 1980s there was also a growth in so-called heritage centres, which interpreted local history in an imaginative way, for example, Wigan Pier in Greater Manchester.

A number of other types of attractions developed rapidly, in the 1980s including the following:

- *Leisure shopping complexes* designed to exploit the growth in disposable income and changing lifestyles in the 1980s. In these centres shopping is almost a form of entertainment with themed food outlets and performing entertainers. Examples in the UK include the Metro Centre at Gateshead and Meadowhall near Sheffield, although the most famous example in the world is at West Edmonton in Canada.

- *Factory tourism*, in other words, visits to working factories to see industry in action, mainly manufacturing industry. Perhaps the interest in this form of tourism grew at this time in response to the decline of many traditional manufacturing industries in the so-called developed countries.
- Many towns and cities started *arts festivals* in the 1970s and 1980s to attract the economic benefits that can come from tourism and to improve the image of their town or city.
- *Wildlife and science-based attractions* that combine entertainment and education, such as the chain of Sea Life Centres in the UK, and La Villette in France.

These developments were largely concentrated in the USA and Europe, and to a lesser extent in Asia. It is in these countries that the volume of domestic demand and incoming international tourism in the 1970s and 1980s stimulated the development of these new products. However, there were some types of attractions that were developing in other countries at the same time. For example, resort complexes that combined attractions and support services on the one site have been developing, largely to meet the demand of inbound international tourists in places such as Southern Africa, Mexico and Australia. Similar complexes developed in the 1980s in the USA and Europe to meet largely domestic demand, such as the Center Parcs complexes in the Netherlands, France and the UK.

As well as these relatively new types of attractions, some well-established types of attractions underwent radical change in the 1980s in response to changing market trends and funding arrangements. Some old-established museums installed new 'hands-on' exhibits based on new technology, began to offer sophisticated catering and opened large retail outlets. They started to emphasize customer care and market themselves professionally. Increasingly the emphasis was on entertainment as well as education, and in this respect the line between them and theme parks became more blurred in some instances. Some museums began to appear more like theme parks based on historical themes rather than traditional museums.

Another type of attraction which changed in the 1980s was the zoo. The rising public interest in conservation and animal welfare led to a change of emphasis of many zoos, from entertainment to promoting themselves as agents of conservation.

The early 1990s

The attractions world in the early 1990s was dominated by the opening of Euro-Disney [now Disneyland Paris] east of Paris, the largest attraction project ever seen in Europe. Arguments raged about how the opening of this mega-attraction would affect visitor numbers at other attractions in Europe.

Table 3.4
The nature of the attraction product in the early 1990s: theme parks, farm attractions and industrial tourism

Characteristics	Theme parks	Farm attractions	Industrial tourism attractions
Main attraction for visitors	Rides Atmosphere Entertainment	Animals Outdoor activities Countryside location Children's entertainment	Chance to see industry in action Opportunity to buy products direct
Main motivation of operators	Profit Market share	Profit or supplementary income Education Diversifying farm business	Boosts corporate image and sales Staff morale improvement Additional income
Size	12 to 800 acres (average: 30 to 40 acres)	10 to 200 acres but farm size does not matter, visitors generally will use small part of it	From workshops to massive factories, but visitors are usually allowed access to small areas
Main services and facilities	Rides Live entertainment Animals Gardens and lakes Special events Education centres Corporate hospitality Function facilities Retailing Catering Parking	Animals Countryside access Interpretation and exhibitions Crafts and arts Small-scale retailing and catering	Factory tour Retail outlet Interpretation Usually limited catering and visitor services
Visitor numbers	From 300 000 to 2 million (average: 830 000)	Generally in range of 40 000 to 50 000	6000 to 120 000
Charges	Average £7 to £10 for adults	Adult – £2 average	Adult – £1.50 average
Opening times	Usually seasonal 100–220 days per annum	Seasonal, usually about half of the year	All year round but usually only Monday to Friday
Length of stay	6–7 hours	Relatively short (1–3 hours)	Relatively short (1–2 hours average)
Staff numbers	Between 75 and 200 permanent and up to 400 seasonal	2–4 full-time permanent and 3–5 permanent part-time plus casual or voluntary labour	Few, mainly part-time or part of duties of full-time factory employees

Characteristics	Theme parks	Farm attractions	Industrial tourism attractions
Staff training	Well-developed, usually in-house	Very limited	Limited in-house training
Turnover	Up to £18–£20 million	£10 000–£220 000	£20 000–£1.5 million; 75% comes from retail
Profit/turnover ratio	20–25% of turnover	10–40% of turnover	0–10% depending on the cost centre structure
Marketing budget	Range of £24 000 to £1 million, 3–14% of turnover	Average 50% of turnover, £5000–£10 000	Average 4–6% of turnover average with range of £2000–£14 000
Development costs	Less than £5 million to over £30 million	Average £50 000	£15 000–£1 million
Other points	Significant local benefits especially through the provision of jobs No major theme park is more than 15 years old	Limited local economic benefits but is useful education resource Virtually all are less than 15 years old	Local benefits include protecting existing jobs through the extra income generated and strengthening the local tourism product Most have been developed in last 15 years

Sources: Paynter (1991); Product Development Department, English Tourist Board (1992); Wooder (1992).

However, the supply of attractions continued to grow in Europe. In the UK, for example, it is estimated that over 700 new attractions opened between 1988 and 1992, most of them in the last two years of this period. Many of these were relatively new forms of attraction such as craft centres, farm-based attractions, factory-based attractions, hand-on science centres, heritage centres and theme parks, the latter reaching a peak of fashionability during this period.

Table 3.4 shows the nature of three types of attractions which were particularly popular in the UK, in the early 1990s.

During this period the aquariums 'boom' hit the UK with the opening of Sea Life Centres all over the UK, developed by Vardon, which has since sold these attractions. In the same period, in the UK, the Lego Corporation announced that it was to develop a Legoland attraction on the site of the Windsor Safari Park which had closed.

But in the UK, an economic recession began in 1991 which depressed the market and contributed towards the postponement of projects such as the proposed Battersea Power Station Theme Park.

The difficult, highly competitive market also led to an increase in improvements to existing attractions to make them more appealing.

In the rest of Europe new leisure and theme parks opened such as Port Aventura at Salou in Spain, while museums such as the Louvre in Paris were remodelled.

Commentators at first thought that the new political and economic situation in Eastern Europe would increase the attraction market in these countries and lead to the development of new attractions. However, the severe economic problems in these countries ensured that this did not happen.

In Asia, on the other hand, the so-called 'tiger economies' developed an ever greater taste for attractions, primarily theme parks and leisure shopping complexes. This was the era when projects such as Lotte and Everland in South Korea developed strongly.

The rapidly developing if rather unstable, economies in South America also stimulated the growth of leisure attractions, of the same types as those popular in Asia, albeit on a smaller scale.

However, in Africa and the Middle East we saw relatively few significant developments in the attractions field in the early 1990s.

The USA continued to dominate the global attractions business in terms of both volume of demand and innovations. In 1993, for example, 275 million people were estimated to have visited amusement/leisure parks in the USA.

Recent developments in the attraction product

Let us now bring the story up to date. We will conclude this chapter by looking at recent developments in the attraction product.

Overall, the past few years have seen rapid growth in the supply of attractions, which has put pressure on many long-established attractions, for the new ones offer state-of-the-art experiences, meeting the needs of today's customers. Many commentators believe that the future of traditional attractions is now threatened by the growth of new types of attractions.

Key trends in the attractions sector in recent years include:

1 Increasing concentration of ownership in the hands of major corporations with the financial capability to continue to innovate and rejuvenate their attractions.
2 The development of attractions which are designed to be complete destinations that combine leisure attractions, catering, retailing, and often accommodation.
3 The growth of new types of attractions such as sporting venue-based attractions, a trend which has been well covered by Stevens.
4 Public funding has stimulated the growth of some types of attractions such as those in the UK, which have National Lottery funding.
5 The opening of many new modern art galleries and non-traditional museums.

In recent years, we have also seen the continued growth and evolution of modern forms of attractions such as industrial tourism.

We will now look at developments which have taken place in recent years in different types of attractions.

Several major *theme parks* have opened since the early 1990s around the world, including:

- Islands of Adventure Park, Florida
- Terra Mitica, a £260-million park in Benidorm, Spain
- New Universal Studios Theme Park in Osaka, Japan
- Disney California Adventure in Anaheim, USA.

Otherwise, in general, there have been few new major theme park projects, in Europe and the USA. Instead, great attention has been paid to updating existing parks and introducing new high-technology, and 'white knuckle' rides.

Stevens (2000) suggests that 'the focus of investment . . . has shifted from the theme park per se to the inclusive all-weather mixed retail entertainment and leisure developments in out of town locations'. He calls these places *urban family entertainment centres*, and cites the 'Heron City' concept as a leading example of the phenomena. Each centre costs around £50 million and the first opened in Madrid in 1999, with others following in Stockholm, Lille and Barcelona. Stevens (2000) also quotes other examples, in his report on the future of attractions, including:

- the £700 million Trafford Centre in Manchester, UK
- the COEX Plaza complex, a 95 000 square metre site in Seoul, South Korea.

In the first edition of this book we noted the rise of *industrial tourism* where tourists visited workplaces. This market will also be discussed in the next chapter. However, at this stage we should note that three developments have taken place in this sector:

1 The opening of new attractions located at the workplaces themselves, such as the Opel Live attraction at Russelheim in Germany and the new Wedgwood Visitor Centre in 'The Potteries', UK – a case study featuring the latter is to be found in Part Four of this book.
2 The creation of state-of-the-art attractions, away from the actual workplace, but still in the local area of production. This category includes the World of Coca-Cola in Atlanta, USA.
3 The development of attractions in major cities which are designed to promote leading brands, but which are located nowhere near the actual place of production. This trend is well illustrated by Sony Wonder in New York.

In recent years we have seen the opening of a new generation of *modern art museums* such as the new Tate Modern in London and the

Guggenheim Museum in Bilbao, Spain. Such projects have often been located in cities trying to establish themselves as tourist destinations or, as in the case of London, in less fashionable areas of established city destinations.

Sports stadia have begun to be developed more as visitor attractions rather than just as venues for sporting events. Stevens has studied this phenomenon and suggested that this is a result of a process of evolution, illustrated in Table 3.5.

In many stadia the first element of the 'attractionization' process has been the opening of a museum about the team[s] for whom the stadium is home. Good examples of this are Old Trafford, Manchester, UK, and Neu Camp, Barcelona. Other attractions, based on the main national

Phase	Title	Description
One	The classical	The civic focus for community assembly and celebration in an amphitheatre setting exemplified by the Coliseum in Rome and the sixty other such amphitheatres of the period, many of which are now heritage visitor attractions
Two	The ballpark	Neighbourhood facilities dedicated to a single sport, basic and with a limited range of facilities for spectators
Three	Modernist super stadium	Often built in greenfield locations on fringes of urban areas with a dramatic visual presentation, designed for a range of sports but a tendency to be soulless and unattractive on non-event days
Four	Neoclassical ballpark	Postmodernist recognition of the strengths of the early ballparks but adding quality amenities and services thus building on the architectural appeal to create an attractive venue with a strong sense of place
Five	Regenerated stadium	Upgrading of existing phase three stadia adding amenities and facilities to enhance their ability to host multievents and sports and to operate on a year-round basis. Often located with limited resources for expansion
Six	Millennium	Multipurpose venues designed with a high specification for amenities, facilities and services, often including a sports attraction and making a strategic contribution to the development of a region's tourism profile
Seven	Post-millennium	A complex designed primarily as a destination attraction but with the potential to host major sports events
Eight	The sports village	A multifaceted, comprehensive destination incorporating stadia, attractions, themed bars and retailing, with hotels

Source: Stevens and Associates (2000).

Table 3.5 The phases of evolution of the stadium

Venue	Cost (£ million)	Opening date	Comment
Theatres/cinemas:			
Sadler's Wells Theatre	30.0	1999	Rebuilt 1600 seats
Royal Opera House	3.0	End 1999	Extended, renovated
Round House, Camden	n/a	2000	Redevelopment
British Film Institute	20.0	April 1999	Largest cinema screen in Europe (IMAX Cinema, South Bank)
Royal National Theatre	2.0	2003	Modernization, phase 1
Royal Albert Hall	0	End 2003	Upgrade front and back stage
Museums/galleries:			
New National Maritime Museum, Greenwich	19.6	Spring 1999	Renovation: eleven new galleries
Shakespeare's Globe Exhibition	n/a	September 1999	Shakespeare's world sixteemth century to the present day
Gilbert Collection Somerset House	5.0	Early 2000	New decorative art gallery
Tate Gallery of Modern Art, South Bank	130.0	May 2000	New: in old Bankside power station
National Portrait Gallery	14.0	Spring 2000	New wing, café etc.
Docklands Museum	6.0	Early 2001	New
Wallace Collection	10.5	Summer 2000	Four new galleries
Science Museum	45.0	Summer 2000	New Wellcome Wing of medicine and technology
British Museum Great Court	97.0	September 2000	Total redevelopment of inner court
Royal Artillery Museum	25.0	May 2001	New: at Royal Arsenal site
Tate Gallery of British Art	8.8	2001	Relaunch of current Millbank gallery
Miscellaneous:			
London Zoo 'Web of Life'	4.4	n/a	New building with biodiversity theme
Millennium Experience	758.0	December 1999	Dome exhibition, live shows
Vinopolis	18.0	July 1999	'City of Wine', audiovisual history, tastings, restaurants, etc.
FA Premier League Hall of Fame, County Hall	8.5	April 1999	Football museum
British Airways London Eye, South Bank (for five years)	n/a	December 1999	135-metre high ferris-wheel
Excel, Royal Victoria Dock	n/a	Autumn 2000	Phase one of new conference and exhibition venue
New National Stadium, Wembley	120.0	2003	Redevelopment core of England's bid for World Cup

Sources: Respective attractions/venues; London Tourist Board, quoted in *Travel and Tourism Intelligence*, City Report, No. 2 (1999).

Table 3.6 Selected major new attractions and renovations being planned for development in London 1999–2003

stadium have been developed as museums of the various sports played there. A good example of this is the Gaelic Athletics Association Museum and Visitor Centre at Croke Park, Dublin, Ireland. On other occasions the stadium or sports venue has become the site of a major general leisure attraction, such as the ICON (Baileys Centre) at Leopardstown Race-course, Ireland.

In addition to all these major attractions, it is important to recognize that many smaller attractions have opened and existing attractions have been refurbished. However, the evidence appears to be that the smaller attractions are finding it difficult to compete with the larger attractions.

Today, all over the world, major attraction projects are being completed and are adding to the global supply of attractions. This point is illustrated in Tables 3.6 and 3.7 which list projects due to be undertaken in London and Auckland between 1999 and 2003.

Several of these projects subsequently ran into difficulties, most notably the Millennium Experience and the new National Stadium, Wembley. However, they clearly illustrate the trends in the attraction product towards sports stadia, leisure retail and multipurpose enter-tainment complexes, and show how much investment is taking place around the world in the attraction sector.

Project	Cost (NZ$ million)	Work
Under construction:		
Viaduct Basin	n/a	America's Cup project to accommodate syndicate bases, shops, apartments, hotels
Civic Entertainment Centre	75	Force Corporation project for multiplex food outlets and tourist information
Auckland Museum	40	Ongoing refurbishment of museum
Proposed/planned:		
Sky City Entertainment Centre	100	Interactive entertainment complex and possible hotel development
Quay Park	750	Magellan Corporation recreation and entertainment centre
Britomart project	n/a	Retail mall and hotel development by Pacific Capital Assets, for completion in 2000
Eden Park expansion	100	Construction of 13 000-seat stand by Eden Park Trust Board
Mount Smart Indoor Stadium	35	15 000-seat indoor stadium project
Ellerslie Racecourse	7	Facility upgrade due in 1999–2000

Sources: JLW; media reports; *Travel and Tourism Intelligence*. City Report, No. 2. (1999).

Table 3.7 Major attraction projects in Auckland

The geography of attraction development is also changing. While the USA remains dominant in the sector, the attractions business is now taking off in regions such as the Middle East, particularly in the Gulf States. American-influenced forms of attractions are also growing in Asia and South America.

Trends in both the types of attractions and the geography of attractions can be clearly seen if we look at eight planned projects identified by Stevens in his *Travel and Tourism Analyst* report of 2000:

- the Metropolitan Ecological, Entertainment and Culture Complex in Santiago, Chile
- the Harbour FEST Leisure and Entertainment project in New York
- the new Guinness Hop Store Visitor Centre in Dublin, Ireland
- the new media theme park at Mainz, Germany
- the Parc del Barca sport, culture, leisure, and entertainment complex project at the Neu Camp Stadium, Barcelona, Spain
- the World of Rugby Visitor Experience project at the new Millennium Stadium in Cardiff, UK
- the 'all-weather' themed resort and attraction concept, Legend Court, in Wales
- The active searching for potential theme park sites in Hungary, Slovakia, and the Czech Republic, by theme park operators

Conclusion

This chapter has shown that the visitor attraction product is a complex concept and that in reality there are a large number of different attraction products. It has looked at the attraction as a service product, a tourism product and an experience. It has examined the product from both ends, namely the product that is offered to the customer and the benefits the customer seeks from the product. The chapter has explored the ways in which the attraction product has developed and has considered the application of product life cycle theory to the attraction product.

The chapter concluded by discussing trends in the attraction product since the 1980s and the development of new attractions up to the present day.

Discussion points and essay questions

1 Compare and contrast the attraction product with the tourism product and the product in other service industries.
2 Account for the rise of aquariums, urban family entertainment centres and sports stadia as visitor attractions.
3 Discuss the implications of the growth in the supply of attractions in London, identified in Table 3.6.

Using visitor numbers over a period of years for a selection of attractions:

- produce a life-cycle graph for each attraction
- suggest which stage each attraction is going through in the life cycle, justifying your suggestions
- account for the shape of the life-cycle curve of each attraction.

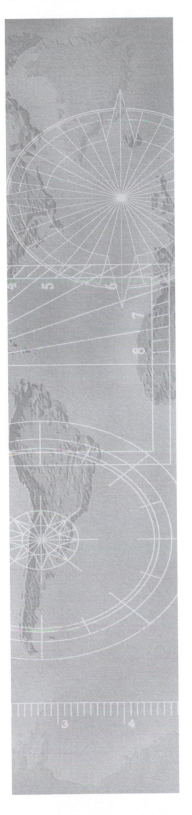

The visitor attraction market

Introduction

The factor that determines whether or not an attraction is successful is how the market responds to the product it offers. It is therefore vital that attraction developers and managers understand the market for visitor attractions. Unfortunately, this is not as easy as it sounds for in reality there does not appear to be a single attraction market that can be easily defined, identified and measured. Instead there is a hierarchy of attraction markets, as Figure 4.1 shows.

Even this model is clearly an oversimplification of the situation. When we talk about the whole population being the potential market, what population are we talking about? That of the local area perhaps, or the region, the country, in which the attraction is situated, or indeed the whole world. We know that for some attractions at least visitors from other countries are a very important part of their market while other attractions hardly ever see a foreign visitor.

The same is true when we go on to the next level in the hierarchy, namely, the actual population that visits attractions, the so-called 'effective market'. This, too, is difficult to define as we have to use a qualifying time period. We might say that the effective market is those people who have visited an attraction in the previous twelve months. But this disguises the important distinction between occasional attraction users and those who visit attractions frequently.

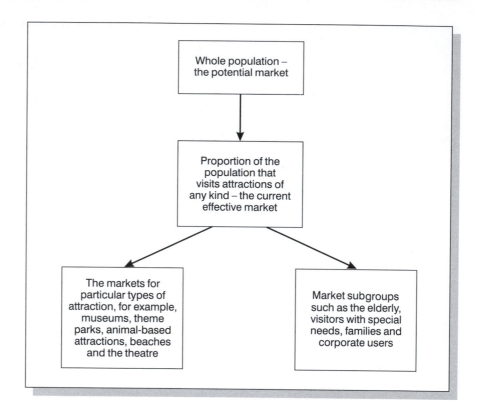

Figure 4.1
The hierarchy of attraction markets

Finally, in terms of the model, there are the markets for the different types of attractions and there are different subgroups within the market as a whole. However, the markets for different types of attractions are not mutually exclusive. Many of them are strongly interrelated, such as the market for museums, theatres and historic buildings. Furthermore, the subgroups are not homogeneous. For example, elderly people vary dramatically in terms of their health, wealth and interests.

Given these complexities it is not surprising that market research in the attractions field is generally weak, in three main ways. First, as much of the attraction sector lies in the private sector many key facts and figures (visitor numbers and spending for example) are commercially sensitive and are not published. Second, we know relatively little about why people visit attractions in general and why they choose to visit particular attractions specifically. There are notable exceptions to this generalization, however, such as the work done on the heritage attraction market in the Isle of Man by Prentice. Third, at many attractions where no entrance charge is made there tends to be no monitoring of visitors in any way so that even visitor numbers are not accurately recorded.

The nature of demand

As with most products the demand for attractions can be split into four main types, as illustrated in Figure 4.2. *Effective demand* means people

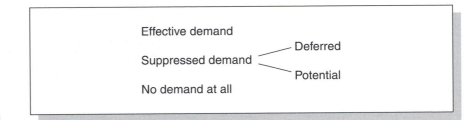

Figure 4.2
The nature of demand

who want to visit attractions and do visit attractions; in other words, the existing effective market. *Suppressed demand* consists of those people who are not currently visiting attractions but would like to visit attractions. These people fall into one of two categories. In the case of *deferred demand* they are not visiting attractions because of a problem on the supply side. Perhaps the theatre is fully booked for the show they want to see. *Potential demand*, on the other hand, is where people want to visit attractions but there is a problem on the demand side. They may be ill or have no money, or may feel they have no spare time. The people within the suppressed demand category are crucial to attraction operators as they represent potential new customers if the obstacles to them visiting attractions can be removed. The theatre, for example, could probably put on more performances of the show if demand substantially exceeded supply. Where there is no *demand at all*, in other words, no desire to visit attractions, it is very difficult for attraction operators to try to convert these people into users and it may be that the cost of trying is simply not cost-effective.

Motivators and determinants

Whereas the preceding section focused on what people do, the concept of motivators and determinants looks at why they do what they do. Motivators are those factors which make people want to visit attractions. Determinants are those factors which determine, first, whether somebody will be able to visit an attraction at all and, second, if they can visit, what type of attraction they will visit and what kind of visit it will be.

Motivators

Clearly the motivators will vary from person to person and will be different for different types of attraction. A brief list of some of the main ones will suffice to give an idea of the breadth of motivators that exist. Table 4.1 illustrates some of the main motivators for four different types of attraction. While some of the motivators appear to be the same, for different attractions, they are not. For example, the atmosphere that attracts people to theme parks is not the same as that which attracts people to health farms. In addition, there are, as can be seen from Table 4.1, significant differences in motivators between different types of attractions.

Theme park with 'white knuckle' rides	Prestigious opera	Free local museum	Health farm
Excitement	Status	Education	Health
Atmosphere created by the interlinking of all users	Aesthetic pleasure of enjoying the music	Nostalgia	Relaxation
Light-hearted fun	The extraordinary nature of the event	Economy	Status
New experiences and sensations	Sharing the event with other like-minded people who one believes will abide by the conventional code of behaviour at such events	Easily accessible	Escape from routine and to be pampered for a limited time
The opportunity to buy particular types of food and souvenirs		Previous experience and familiarity	Atmosphere

Table 4.1 Main motivating factors by type of attraction

However, it is all too easy to exaggerate the differences between motivators for visiting different types of attractions. Ultimately all people visit attractions for enjoyment; it is the individual's own definition of what constitutes enjoyment for them personally that creates the range of motivators. Furthermore most people find it difficult to articulate what their motivations are for visiting attractions because they are not used to analysing their behaviour in such detail.

Determinants

As we said earlier, determinants are of two types, namely those that dictate whether people can visit an attraction or not, and those that determine the types of trip that will be made and the type of attraction that will be visited. Some of the major determinants are outlined in Table 4.2.

It is possible to further divide determinants into:

- personal determinants such as personal circumstances, personal experiences, the prejudices and perceptions of the individual and the knowledge about attraction operations that the person possesses
- external determinants such as the views of friends and relatives, the media and the marketing activities of the attraction industry.

Determinants are very personal and can sometimes be removed or alleviated. What stops one person travelling to attractions will not stop another and one factor such as disposable income can help overcome another determinant. For example, an affluent person could perhaps pay for someone to relieve them of their responsibilities as a carer for the day so they could visit an attraction. Furthermore determinants can also be influenced by external agencies; in other words, the local

Determinants of whether or not *any* visit to an attraction can be or will be made	Determinants of the type of attraction that will be visited and the type of trip that will be taken
State of health	State of health
Disposable income	Disposable income
Real or perceived leisure time	Real or perceived leisure time
Commitments to family or friends as a carer	Commitments to family or friends as a carer
Fear of travel	Fear of particular modes of travel
	Interests and hobbies
	Who else will be visiting the attraction as part of the party
	Information available to the potential visitor
	Past experience
	Word of mouth recommendation
	Weather
	Mobility
	The existence of special events
	Fashions
	Entrance charges and whether or not they are all-inclusive or there are extras such as car parking

Table 4.2 Determinants and visitor attractions

authority might provide a professional carer for the day so that the person who cares for someone day in, day out, can visit an attraction by way of a break.

Individual decision-making

Until now we have focused on the market as a whole, although we have acknowledged that the market, in reality, consists of a number of subgroups. However at the root of all markets is the individual consumer and so it is appropriate now to take a brief look at how the individual makes a decision about visiting attractions. Figure 4.3 gives a stylized picture of the decision-making process.

While this is a useful model, it is generalized and is based on the idea that people always behave in a wholly rational manner. In fact, as we know, people do not behave totally rationally; their behaviour is tempered by their perceptions and prejudices, and influenced by the level and type of information they have. The model is also based on the idea that at the start of the process the potential visitor is a 'blank sheet'. However, the visitor usually has previous experiences that influence their present and future behaviour and once they have been actual visitors at an attraction it becomes part of their experience that will influence their future behaviour. In other words, the model needs a feedback loop from the actual visitor position to the potential visitor position.

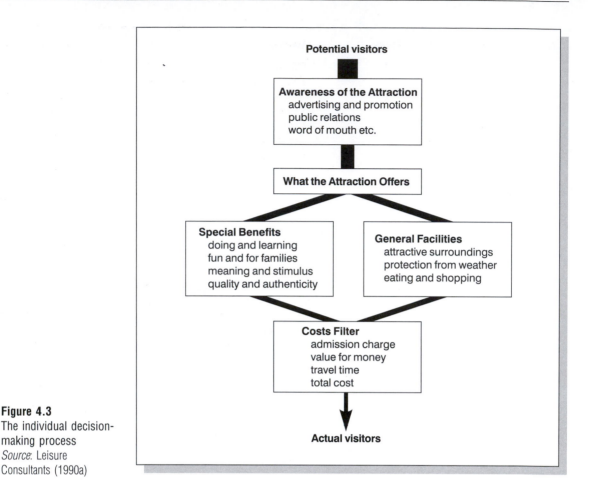

Figure 4.3
The individual decision-making process
Source: Leisure Consultants (1990a)

Decision-making and theme parks

In general, we know relatively little about how people make decisions about whether or not to visit attractions. However, McClung has done some interesting research on this subject in relation specifically to theme parks. McClung's research, published in 2000, identified the factors which potential theme park visitors took into account when deciding whether to visit theme parks in general, or particular theme parks specifically.

Tables 4.3, 4.4 and 4.5 show the preferences of the sample of potential visitors in relation to overall park characteristics, on-site attractions and themselves. McClung concluded that the four most important factors influencing decisions as to whether or not to visit a theme park were:

- climate
- preference for particular types of theme parks
- their children's desire to visit
- cost.

Rank	Variable	Index[1]
1	Climate	1.20
2	Preference for this type of park	1.09
3	Children	1.07
4	Cost	0.99
5	Crowds	0.97
6	Distance	0.94
7	Lodging	0.79

Note: 1 Mean/grand mean.

Source: McClung (2000)

Table 4.3
Influencing factors:
park visitors

Rank	Variable	Label	Index[1]
1	Attraction 8	Exhibits/attraction promoting learning	1.191
2	Attraction 5	Variety/quality of restaurants	1.177
3	Attraction 10	Animals in their natural habitat	1.140
4	Attraction 6	General shows and entertainment	1.106
5	Attraction 11	Animal shows	1.035
6	Attraction 2	Water rides	1.026
7	Attraction 3	Thrill rides	0.970
8	Attraction 4	Big-name entertainment	0.965
9	Attraction 9	Rides for small children	0.947
10	Attraction 1	Roller coaster	0.929
11	Attraction 13	Cartoon characters	0.919
12	Attraction 7	Movie-based rides entertainment	0.818
13	Attraction 12	Gifts of souvenir shops	0.776

Note: 1 Mean/grand mean.

Source: McClung (2000)

Table 4.4
Attractions in rank
order

This research was conducted in the USA and it would be interesting to see if different results could be obtained in Europe, for example. If climate were a major factor in Europe, then Disneyland Paris would presumably not be receiving 12.5 million visits a year, and Blackpool Pleasure Beach 6.9 million! Nevertheless this research represents a good example of academics trying to understand the role of motivators and determinants in relation to theme park visiting.

Decision-making and museums

Research was published in 2001, by MORI and the Council for Museums, Galleries and Libraries which looked at attitudes of people in the UK towards museum visits. It noted that only 28 per cent of those surveyed in November/December had visited a museum or gallery in the past

Rank	Variable	Label	Index
1	Theme 11	Educational exhibits	1.170
2	Theme 9	Exotic animals	1.090
3	Theme 2	Technology	1.058
4	Theme 5	Botanical gardens	1.043
5	Theme 8	Wilderness	1.028
6	Theme 3	History	1.025
7	Theme 7	River trips	1.018
8	Theme 4	Foreign cultures	0.984
9	Theme 10	Live entertainment	0.969
10	Theme 13	Water rides	0.963
11	Theme 12	Animal shows	0.952
12	Theme 6	Flower displays	0.949
13	Theme 1	Fantasy	0.937
14	Theme 14	Nightclub	0.814

Source: McClung (2000)

Table 4.5
Themes in rank
order

twelve months. It went on to look at the reasons why people chose *not* to
visit museums and galleries. These factors are identified in Figure 4.4. It
is interesting that some of these reasons are outside the control of
museums – notably the health problems of the respondent – but the main
reason relates to a failure to offer an attractive product.

Even more interesting were the results of the survey of children. Many
museums encourage children who visit on school trips to revisit with

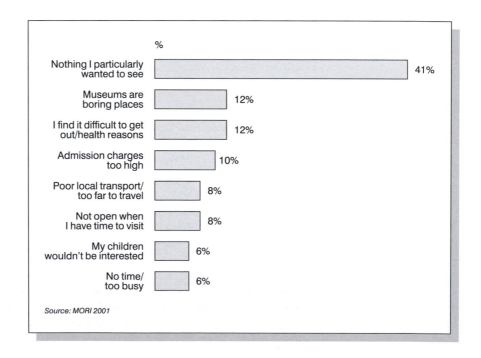

Figure 4.4
Reasons for not
visiting museums
or galleries
Source: MORI (2001)

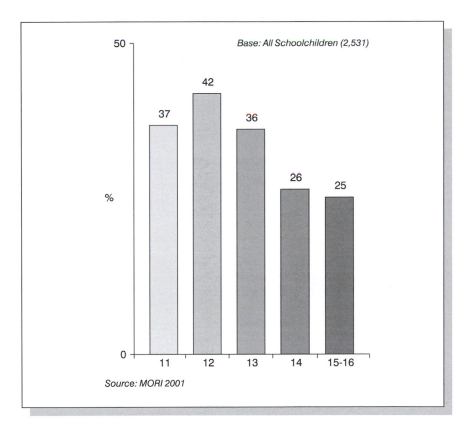

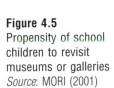

Figure 4.5
Propensity of school
children to revisit
museums or galleries
Source: MORI (2001)

their families or friends. Figure 4.5 shows that only a minority of young people do this and the percentage falls significantly the older the young person becomes.

The research went on to identify the things that would make young people visit museums more and gain greater enjoyment from their visit. These factors are illustrated in Table 4.6 and give clear indications to museum managers of the young market expectations and desires.

Market segmentation and the visitor attraction market

One way of trying to deal with the complexity of the attraction market and to look at the market in a way which is helpful for marketing purposes is the technique of market segmentation. Segmentation means splitting a population into subgroups or segments whose members show similar characteristics, needs and buying behaviour.

There are four classic ways in which markets are segmented:

1 Geographical, in other words, categorizing people on the basis of their geographical characteristics, for example, where they live.
2 Demographics, which means dividing the population into groups on the basis of their demographic characteristics such as age, sex and race.

	All responses (%)	Which ONE would you most like (%)
Interactive *computer games* about the objects on display	61	11
Internet access	58	9
Handle the objects on display	58	11
Working models which young people can use	54	6
A *shop* selling the sorts of things young people want to buy	53	3
More *places to sit and talk*	51	3
Staff available to answer questions etc.	51	6
Actors in the museum	44	6
Art and craft materials for use during your visit	43	4
Display objects in the setting they would have been found	40	1
Dance and drama programmes for young visitors	40	8
Other *young people* to guide you around the museum	36	3
The opportunity to be involved in *organizing displays/ producing labels/writing about the objects* on display	31	2
Other	3	
Don't know/not stated	16	

Note: Base: all (2.531).
Source: MORI (2001)

Table 4.6 Things that would make visits to museums and galleries more enjoyable

3 Psychographic, which differentiates people on the basis of their attitudes and opinions, for example.
4 Behaviouristic. This puts people into groups in terms of their relationship with particular types of products, for example whether or not they are first time users, or the benefits they seek from using a particular product.

Geographical segmentation

Traditionally the main geographical criterion on which attraction markets have been segmented is where the people within the market live. This is because the market for attractions tends to be related to a geographically defined catchment area such as the region or the particular city in which the attraction is located. The size of this area varies from one type of attraction to another. For example, most theme parks have a regional or national catchment area while local authority museums tend to draw most of their visitors from the local area. Identifying the catchment area is crucial because its population size determines likely visitor numbers and because it helps marketers to decide where to place advertisements for the attraction.

However, if one just considers the place of permanent residence of visitors a false picture of the market may emerge, because for people on holiday their place of residence is not the place from which they started their day trip to the attraction. Their day trip will have begun either from a commercial accommodation establishment or from the home of a friend or relative with whom they are staying. This means that marketers must often target these people not where they live but in the place where they are staying. In many areas the normal catchment area of an attraction is swelled by visiting holiday-makers from further afield, who may make the difference between the attraction being viable and not being viable. This is particularly the case in regions with a relatively small resident population but large influxes of tourists, such as Cornwall in the UK, Malta and the Canary Islands.

The concept of geographical segmentation can also be applied to attractions in other ways. People from urban areas may seek out rural attractions because this represents a change of environment, while others may look for attractions in a area with a better climate than that of their home area.

Demographic segmentation

Demographic segmentation is well established in the tourism industry generally and the attractions field specifically. Indeed, many of the well-known tourism marketing stereotypes are built on demographic segmentation. For example, museums are seen as being for older people while theme parks are for the young. Shopping is seen as a favourite activity with women, men are thought to prefer golf courses, and other attractions are described as being for families.

This latter aspect of demographics has always been particularly important and there has been a view that you can determine people's desires and needs in relation to their position in the so-called 'family life cycle', which is illustrated in Figure 4.6.

Figure 4.6 is clearly a gross oversimplification and is in many ways outdated. Yet, the planning and marketing of many attractions often appears to be based on this model. However, just a few points will illustrate how it is no longer a true reflection of society, if it ever was:

1 Children are maturing more quickly now and are becoming more independent of their parents at an early age.
2 Many people never become part of a couple and many couples now do not have children.

Stage in family life-cycle	Likely preferences and needs at attractions
Child	New experiences. Other children to play with. Paternal guidance and support
Teenager	New experiences. Excitement. Status. More independence from parents. Other teenagers. Active participation
Young adult	New experiences. Freedom of action. Other young adults. Active participation
Young couple	New experiences. Romance. Solitude
Young couple with baby	Facilities for babies. Convenience for people with babies
Growing family	Economy – family ticket for example. Something for all the family
Empty nesters	Chance to learn something. More passive participation
Elderly	Watching rather than doing. Economy. Company of other people. Easy accessibility for people with mobility problems

Figure 4.6
The family life cycle and visitor attractions

3 A large proportion of families are single-parent families with different needs from the traditional two-parent family.

4 The model is based on the nuclear family which is no longer representative of society as a whole and certainly not of the traditions of some ethnic minorities where the extended family is far more important.

5 It is wrongly assumed that elderly people are poor and have health problems. While this is true for some elderly people it is patently not true for all elderly people.

However, there is another way in which this model is particularly unsuitable for attractions and that is that much attraction-visiting is not based on the family group. Particularly among younger people, there is a tendency to visit in groups whose members are often not related and who visit attractions either as friends or as members of educational parties. There are also many older people who visit attractions as part of coach parties, rather than in family groups.

While much attention has focused on demographic variables such as age, sex and family situation, relatively little attention has been focused on other important variables such as race, religion, language and nationality. These are clearly important issues which merit further investigation in a multicultural society such as Britain.

Social class • • •

In some countries, social class is seen as an important determinant of tourist behaviour. In the UK for example, people are grouped in traditional social classes (A, B, Cl, C2, D, E or Upper, Middle and Working Class) on the grounds that attraction-visiting behaviour is related to class. In other words, As and Bs visit museums while theme parks are more popular with people in the Cl, C2 and D classes. There are clearly problems with this approach. First, defining class has always been a problem and the criteria on which such definitions are based in Britain would not be accepted in other countries. Indeed, in many other countries it is difficult to define classes as such. Second, British society has undergone dramatic changes in recent years and it is arguable that the basis on which class has been defined in Britain is at least partly outdated.

These first two segmentation methods are, as we have seen, rather crude and tend to be based on assumptions that all people living in an area or all people who share a demographic characteristic will behave in a particular way. The next two methods take a different approach. They focus on the individual in terms of their attitudes and opinions on the one hand and their behaviour on the other.

Psychographic segmentation

This method is based on the idea that it is the attitudes or opinions of individuals which dictate their behaviour as consumers and it therefore tries to group people on the basis of shared attitudes and opinions. This method works on the basis that these attitudes and opinions come from two main sources.

Lifestyle • • •

In this case, people are grouped according to their lifestyle. This approach gained ground in the 1980s with the recognition of 'designer lifestyles'. Lifestyle is a matter of how individuals live, how they see themselves and how they want others to see them. Lifestyles result from the combination of many factors including education, occupation, income and social contacts. What is particularly interesting is that people's lifestyles influence all their decisions as consumers as they try to develop a lifestyle which reflects their idea of how they want to be seen and which reinforces the way they see themselves. Their decisions on which attractions to visit are just as much a part of this as the clothes they buy, the car they drive and the newspapers they read. Some of the lifestyle types that are particularly relevant to attraction operators are the 'health-conscious' (important for health clubs and sports centres), and the 'environmentally aware' (may hold strong views on zoos).

The conventional wisdom in marketing currently is that there has been a major shift in the nature of the lifestyles of many people, particularly those in the younger age groups. The materialistic lifestyles of the 1980s are supposed to have given way to the more caring lifestyles of the 1990s. If true, this has important implications for attraction operators – particularly in terms of concerns over green issues, animal welfare and business ethics.

Anyone looking at advertisements for consumer products generally on television and in the press will quickly see that 'lifestyle marketing', namely, marketing based on segmentation on the basis of lifestyles, is now very fashionable. However, this has not yet extended through much of the tourism industry generally and most attractions specifically. But perhaps it should, for this is arguably a more realistic method of segmentation in the complex societies of developed countries in the 1990s.

Personality • • •

Individuals can be segmented on the basis of shared personality traits which influence their decisions as consumers in relation to attractions. For example, it is more likely that one will find adventurous people bungee-jumping or riding on 'white-knuckle' rides and that a higher proportion of people at theme parks will be gregarious extroverts than you might find in an archaelogical museum. Nevertheless, this is not only a gross stereotype but it also implies that all people choose for themselves which attraction they visit, which is often not true. Many go as part of a group where a decision to visit a particular attraction is often a majority decision where some may have to go along with a decision that does not reflect their own preferences.

Behaviouristic segmentation

This method of segmentation groups people according to their relationship with a particular product such as a specific attraction or type of attraction. This covers a number of variations, some of which are listed below:

- *Purchase occasions*: whether or not the people buy the product regularly or occasionally or never. For example, for some, a trip on Concorde may be a once-in-a-lifetime experience while for others it is a regular activity.
- *Benefits sought*: in other words, what are people hoping to gain from visiting an attraction. It could be knowledge from a museum, excitement from a theme park, or economy from a country park where no charge is made for admission.
- *User status*: this means are people non-users, ex-users, potential users, regular users or first-time users.

- *Readiness stage*: namely, are people unaware of the product, aware and interested, desirous of visiting the attraction, or actually intent on visiting it and planning the visit right now?
- *Attitude to the product*: this means identifying people who are enthusiastic or positive about the attraction or merely indifferent, and those who are negative or downright hostile to it.
- *Loyalty to the product*: whether people feel a loyalty towards the attraction or would happily go somewhere else instead, if it was cheaper or looked more exciting for example.

Other methods of segmentation

So far we have applied classic segmentation techniques to the attraction market. However, a number of commentators have argued that there are other ways of segmenting the tourism market generally that may be applicable to the attraction market. Some of these are briefly outlined below:

- *Visit party composition*: this approach argues that behaviour is often related to the composition of the visit party and that, therefore, the market should be segmented on the basis of whether people visit as individuals, families, or groups for example.
- *Visit type and purpose*: here the market is split into groups of a particular type, such as school parties and corporate hospitality clients for example, who have specific reasons for visiting the attraction.
- *Method of travel*: this divides the market in relation to how people travel to the attraction (private car, coach, bike, walk or train).

In the end, the fact is that no one method is satisfactory on its own for segmenting the complexities of the attraction market or any other market for that matter. In isolation they are all one-dimensional and it is only when two, three, or more are combined and blended in an appropriate way that an accurate picture of the market can be compiled. Furthermore, it is important to recognize that segmentation is usually carried out to help improve the effectiveness of marketing activity so that the method chosen will be that which also meets the attraction's marketing objectives.

Segmentation and the theme park market

As yet, little empirical research has been done on the segmentation of the theme park market, except for some rather crude demographic segmentation.

One exception to this standard is the work of Fodness and Milner (2000), which used a perceptual mapping approach to segmenting the theme park market, based on parks in Florida. They were concerned to see how this segmentation could be used by marketers to predict visitor behaviour.

Trip planning variables	Cluster 1, n = 71	Cluster 2, n = 71	Cluster 3, n = 32
Planning time ($x^2 = 14.4$)[1]:			
< 2 weeks	9.9	9.9	3.1
2 weeks – 1 month	9.9	4.2	3.1
1–3 months	23.9	38.0	38.0
3–6 months	23.9	12.7	31.3
6 months–1 year	26.8	33.8	21.9
> 1 year	5.6	1.4	3.1
Information sources used:			
Automobile clubs[2,3]	28.2	53.5	54.8
Brochures[2]	31.0	28.2	25.8
Guide books[2]	23.9	19.7	9.7
Friends or relatives[2]	49.3	42.3	61.3
Welcome centres[2]	46.5	57.7	54.8
Local tourist offices[2]	12.7	18.3	19.4
Magazines[2]	19.7	21.1	25.8
Newspapers[2]	16.9	7.0	12.9
Past experience[2,4]	23.9	7.0	12.9
State travel guide[2,3]	12.7	22.5	6.5
Travel agency[2]	11.3	11.3	6.4
Mean number of sources used[5]	3.0	3.0	3.1

Notes: 1 Significant at alpha = 0.05.
2 x^2 test of dependency.
3 Significant at alpha = 0.001.
4 Significant at alpha = 0.01.
5 ANOVA F test of differences.

Source: Fodness and Milner (2000)

Table 4.7 Comparison of trip planning characteristics across multiple attraction visitor segments (percentage except where indicated)

The researchers established three separate 'clusters' of theme park visitors with their own fully homogeneous characteristics.

It is clear from the results illustrated in Tables 4.7 and 4.8 that different segments or 'clusters' do have different patterns of behaviour in terms of theme park visiting that could be exploited by marketers.

The leisure paradox

Attraction visiting involves time and money, so the concept of the 'leisure paradox', as illustrated in Figure 4.7, is highly relevant to the attractions market. This largely realistic generalization implies that the ability to pay, and the amount of time people have available to visit attractions varies greatly with stages in the family life cycle.

Figure 4.8 shows that available time also varies between men and women and between retired, employed and unemployed people.

Trip behaviour variables	Cluster 1, n = 71	Cluster 2, n = 71	Cluster 3, n = 32
Mobility (F = 0.9):			
Number of destinations visited	2.8	2.6	2.9
Attraction visitation (F = 1.7):			
Number of attractions visited	3.5	3.2	3.6
Lodging type (percentage):			
Hotel/motel[1]	45.7	52.4	36.0
Friends or relatives[1]	16.5	15.7	26.9
Campgrounds/RV park[1]	20.6	15.5	18.1
Timeshare unit[1]	4.6	7.2	7.3
Condominium, apartment, home[1]	10.6	9.2	8.5
Other[1]	1.9	–	3.1
Number of lodging types[1,2]	1.5	1.4	1.7

Notes: 1 ANOVA F test of differenes.
2 Significant at alpha = 0.01.
Source: Fodness and Milner (2000)

Table 4.8
Comparison of trip behaviour characteristics across multiple attraction visitor segments

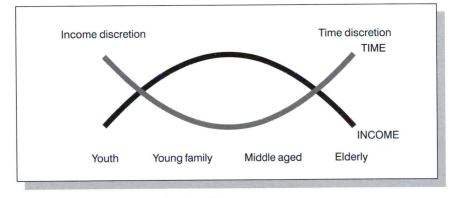

Figure 4.7
The 'leisure paradox'
Source: The Henley Centre

Participation levels in the attractions market

It is important to remember that not everyone visits attractions; some people, particularly the elderly, may not visit a formal visitor attraction in a year. Families and young single adults are perhaps the groups with the greatest participation levels in the market, and even then many such people may not visit an attraction in a single year.

MORI poll research published in March 2001 indicated that in the twelve months from November/December 1998 to November/December 1999, 20 per cent of people visited no attractions of any kind including cinemas, museums, theme parks, the theatre, sporting events, wildlife parks, cathedrals or concerts.

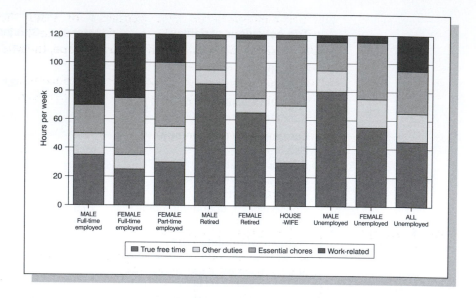

Figure 4.8
Free time availability
(average hours per
week)
Source: Henley Centre
(1989)

Of those who did visit attractions, the cinema was most popular but even then only 52 per cent had visited a cinema in the past twelve months. The most popular forms of visitor attractions, with the percentage of respondents having visited them in the past twelve months were as follows:

Museums	8 per cent
Stately home or castle	28 per cent
Theme park	25 per cent
Wildlife park	23 per cent.

Frequency of attraction-visiting

Most adults in developing countries take leisure day trips. Data published in *Insights* in May 2001 showed that 85 per cent of adults in the UK said they had taken such a trip within the previous two weeks. It was estimated that 5.9 billion such day trips were taken in the UK in the same year. However, it is vital to recognize that these trips are largely *not* to visitor attractions as they are understood in this book. Most represent trips to restaurants, visiting friends, going shopping, going walking, swimming or visits to cinemas. The vast majority of such visits take place to urban areas and the average round trip is less than 16 miles.

However, in the UK, as elsewhere, for most people, visits to actual visitor attractions as discussed in this book, are an 'out of the ordinary' activity, and such visits will rarely take place more than once a month. While some people do visit particular types of attractions – such as craft centres and museums, reasonably frequently – generally attraction-visiting is not a very frequent activity for most people. For many types of attraction, such as theme parks, one visit a year is the norm for most people.

Participation levels and frequency of visits, however, does vary between countries and cultures with Japan and the USA being above the UK average, and countries in Eastern Europe, the Middle East and Africa below the UK average.

For example, as far as theme parks are concerned, Page (2000) suggests that visits per capita to theme parks vary between regions of the world, as follows:

USA	0.6
Japan	0.6
Australia	0.5
Europe	0.2.

The international attractions market

The author cannot currently present a comprehensive view of the worldwide attractions market because:

- different countries still define attractions in different ways to each other which makes the presentation of comparable data impossible
- some countries do not appear to collect data systematically concerning attraction-visiting
- when data are published they are often already two or three years out of date.

Nevertheless, in this section an attempt will be made to produce some meaningful comments on the current situation in Europe, North America, Japan and Australia.

The attractions market in European cities

Most European cities have well-established attractions, although they vary greatly depending on the nature of the city and its history. They differ, too, in terms of visitor numbers, due to the size of the resident population and the popularity of the city as a tourist destination. Table 4.9 identifies the top attractions in six European cities, to illustrate these points.

The attractions market in North American cities

North America is often seen, understandably, as the home of the attractions business, the place from which most new ideas originate. Most North American cities certainly have a wide variety of attractions as we can see from Table 4.10.

The attractions market in Japan

Japanese people love visiting attractions and the country has the world's most visited attraction – Tokyo Disneyland – which received 17 500 000 visitors in 1999 (*Amusement Business*, 2000).

Barcelona[1]	Copenhagen[2]	Glasgow[3]	London[4]	Paris[5]	Rome[6]
1 L'Aquarium 1 600 000	1 Tivoli 3 400 000	1 Kelvingrove Art Gallery and Museum 1 100 000	1 British Museum 5 600 000	1 Notre Dame 12 000 000	1 Vatican 3 100 000
2 Poble Espanyol de Montjuic 1 400 000	2 Zoo 1 200 000	2 The Time Capsule 700 000	2 National Gallery 4 800 000	2 Montmartre 6 000 000	2 Colosseum 2 300 000
3 IMAX 1 100 000	3 National Museum 400 000	3 Museum of Transport 400 000	3 Westminster Abbey 3 000 000	3 La Tour Eiffel 5 720 000	3 Villa 'Este 600 000
4 Sagrada Familia 1 100 000	4 Louisiana, Museum of Modern Art 400 000	4 Gallery of Modern Art 400 000	4 Madame Tussauds 2 800 000	4 Musée de Louvre 5 180 000	4 Borghese Gallery 500 000
5 Museu Picasso 1 000 000	5 Experimentarium 400 000	5 New Lanark Village 400 000	5 Tower of London 2 600 000	5 Centre Pompidou 4 420 000	5 Palatine Hill 500 000
6 Museu F.C. Barcelona 900 000	6 Carlsberg Glyptotek 400 000	6 Botanical Gardens 400 000	6 Tate Gallery 2 200 000	6 La Villette 3 460 000	6 Castel Sant'Angelo 500 000
7 Espai Gaudi 600 000	7 Rundetarn 400 000	7 Burrell Collection 300 000	7 St Paul's Cathedral 2 000 000	7 Versailles 2 650 000	7 Hadrian's Villa 300 000
8 Fundació Miró 400 000	8 State Museum of Art 400 000	8 Aquatec 200 000	8 National History Museum 1 900 000	8 Musée d'Orsay 2 280 000	8 Ostia Antica 300 000
9 Parc d'Attractions Tibidabo 400 000	9 Arken, Museum of Modern Art 200 000	9 St Mungo Museum 100 000	9 Science Museum 1 600 000	9 L'Arc de Triomphe 1 170 000	
10 Museu Nacional d'Art Catalunya 400 000		10 Cathedral 100 000	10 Chessington World of Adventure 1 600 000	10 Natural History Museum 1 120 000	

Notes: 1 Figures for 1998.
2 Figures for 1998 – monuments, museums and sites only.
3 Figures for 1997.
4 Figures for 1998.
5 Figures for 1997 – monuments and museums only.
6 Figures for 1998 – monuments and museums only.

Source: Travel and Tourism Intelligence (1999–2001)

Table 4.9 The top attractions in six European cities

Chicago	Montreal	New York
Navy Pier (8183)	Casino (5756)	Times Square area (20 000)
Lincoln Park Zoo (3000)	Vieux Port (4250)	Central Park (15 000)
Shedd Aquarium/Oceanarium (1981)	Centre Molson (guided visits, special events, Canadian hockey) (1998)	South Street Seaport (10 000)
Museum of Science and Industry (1750)	La Ronde (1200)	Ellis Island and Statue of Liberty (5000)
Art Institute of Chicago (1537)	Hippodrome (1169)	Metropolitan Museum of Art (5000)
Field Museum of Natural History (1451)	Botanical Gardens and Insectarium (1014)	American Museum of Natural History (3500)
Sears Tower Skydeck (1302)	Biodôme (871)	Empire State Building (3500)
Chicago Cultural Center (623)	Musée des Beaux-Arts (400)	World Trade Center Observation Deck (1800)
Museum of Broadcast Communications (500)	Granby Zoo (335)	Museum of Modern Art (1700)
Chicago Children's Museum (472)	Olympic Park (305)	Guggenheim Museum (900)
Adler Planetarium (460)		Brooklyn Museum of Art (600)
Chicago Symphony Orchestra (273)		National Museum of the American Indian (400)
DuSable Museum (171)		Museum of the City of New York (400)
Chicago Historical Society (143)		United Nations (400)
		Whitney Museum of American Art (300)
		Frick Collection (300)
		New York Historical Society (100)

Source: Travel and Tourism Intelligence, City Reports, No. 3 (1997); No. 2 (1999); No. I (2000)

Table 4.10 Leading attractions in three North American cities, 1998 (attendances in 000s in brackets)

Table 4.11 shows the number of visitors to attractions in the Tokyo area alone. As we can see from this table, it is estimated that more than 100 million visits were made to some 340 attractions in the Tokyo area in 1999. This figure is particularly impressive when one considers that it excludes shopping centres in a country renowned for its love of leisure shopping.

The attractions market in Australia

The attractions sector varies greatly between the major cities as can be seen from Table 4.12.

Because of their different bases it is difficult to compare these figures, but we can see variations between the cities with gambling and shopping being key attractions in Melbourne, nature topping the list in Perth, and shopping and a single building being the most popular attractions in Sydney.

	No. of facilities	Total yearly entrance (facilities replying)	No. of facilities replying to survey	Average no. of visitors per attraction	Total estimated visitors
Art gallery	50	9 064 706	(43)	210 807	10 540 350
Museum	151	11 288 805	(138)	81 803	12 352 253
Zoo	7	5 184 630	(6)	864 105	6 048 735
Aquarium	5	3 098 625	(4)	774 656	3 873 280
Botanical garden	20	2 564 787	(17)	150 870	3 017 400
Historical attraction	8	1 660 461	(8)	207 558	1 660 464
Leisure/theme park	14	10 551 670	(12)	879 306	12 310 284
Park/garden	24	2 894 737	(10)	289 474	6 947 376
Sports centre	23	4 514 379	(3)	1 504 793	34 610 239
Hot springs	5	248 000	(2)	124 000	620 000
Children's play-park	3	1 748 835	(3)	582 945	1 748 835
Viewpoint/tower	3	4 954 396	(3)	1 651 465	4 954 396
Exhibition venue	7	23 643 000	(3)	7 881 000	55 167 000
Theatre	9	1 941 613	(9)	215 734	1 941 613
Show-room	11	5 470 000	(9)	607 778	6 685 555
Total	340	88 828 644	(289)	307 366	104 504 287

Source: *Travel and Tourism Intelligence* (2000)

Table 4.11 Number of visitors to tourist attractions in Tokyo by type of attraction, 1999

Melbourne[1] (1995)	**Perth[2] (1997)**	**Sydney[3] (1996)**
Crown Casino 450 000	Botanical/public gardens 314 000	Shopping 1 900 000
Queen Victoria Market 340 500	National/state parks 296 000	Sydney Opera House 1 700 000
Melbourne Central 240 000	Zoos, animals, marine parks 243 000	Sydney Harbour 1 600 000
Royal Botanic Gardens 220 000	Historic and heritage sites 198 000	The Rocks 1 300 000
Melbourne Zoo 135 000	Wineries 185 000	Beaches 1 100 000

Notes: 1 Estimated number of international visitors at individual attractions.
2 Number of international visitors at particular types of visitor attractions.
3 Number of international visitors to individual attractions and types of attraction.

Source: *Travel and Tourism Intelligence*, City Reports, No. 1 (1999), No. 4 (1999), No. 3 (2000)

Table 4.12 The top five attractions in terms of international visitors in Melbourne, Perth and Sydney

	Percentage of visitors who are domestic	Percentage of visitors who are international
Melbourne Central	96	4
Crown Casino	95	5
Melbourne Zoo	86	14
Rialto Observation Deck	79	21

Source: *Travel and Tourism Intelligence*, City Reports No. 1 (1999)

Table 4.13
Domestic and international visitors to selected attractions in Melbourne, 1995

However, there are also differences in preferences in Australia between domestic and international tourists, as we can see from Table 4.13.

This phenomenon is seen all over the world, sometimes in even more extreme proportions.

The UK attractions market

In 1999, there were an estimated 404 million visits to attractions in the UK, with total spending of around £1400 million. The visitor figures for this year represented an increase of 1.2 per cent compared with 1998. However, as we can see from Figure 4.9, this overall average figure masked significant variations between different types of attraction.

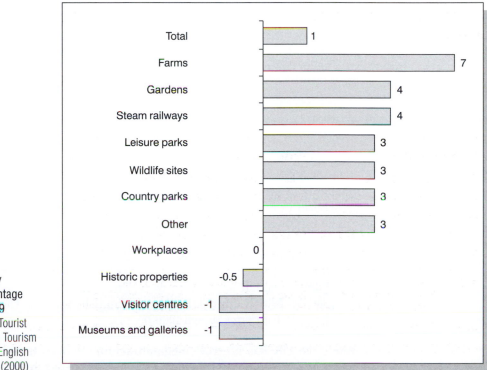

Figure 4.9
Visits trends by category percentage change, 1998–9
Sources: British Tourist Authority/English Tourism Council (1999), English Tourism Council (2000)

In the ten years from 1989 to 1999, attraction visiting rose by a modest 11 per cent in the UK as a whole. Again this masked differences with attraction visits growing by 27 per cent in Northern Ireland but by only 1 per cent in Wales.

Over the same decade, the change in attendance at different types of attractions ranged from a fall of 6 per cent for wildlife attractions to a rise of 11 per cent for museums and galleries, and of 76 per cent for farm attractions.

Within the UK, the geographical distribution of attraction visits in 1999 is illustrated in Table 4.14.

Region/country	Number of visits (000s)	(%)	Average number of visits per site	Per 1000 square kilometres	Per head of population
Cumbria	7 438	2	52 400	1 090 000	15.1
Northumbria	14 447	4	57 800	1 681 000	5.6
North West	34 616	9	108 500	4 715 000	5.4
Yorkshire	27 167	7	65 500	1 763 000	5.4
Heart of England	60 936	15	70 900	2 402 000	6.5
East of England	36 653	9	48 400	1 396 000	6.2
London	52 860	13	191 500	33 498 000	7.4
West Country	37 205	9	57 200	1 894 000	10.2
Southern	25 312	6	62 200	2 214 000	5.6
South East	31 150	8	61 900	3 388 000	7.6
ENGLAND	327 783	82		2 513 000	6.7
Northern Ireland	9 111	2	42 200	676 000	5.4
Scotland	49 627	12	46 600	644 000	9.5
Wales	17 846	4	50 400	859 000	6.1
UK	404 367	100		1 673 000	6.9

Source: British Tourist Authority/English Tourism Council (1999); English Tourism Council (2000)

Table 4.14 Visits to tourist attractions by region/country in 1999

From Table 4.14 it is clear that attraction visiting is spread very unevenly around the UK with London clearly dominating the market, whichever criteria we use.

The top three UK destinations for attraction visits in 1999 were:

Westminster, London, UK   22 279 499
Blackpool, UK   9 619 308
Edinburgh, UK   7 619 012
Source: British Tourist Authority/English Tourism Council (1999); English Tourism Council (2000).

While the UK has no true 'mega-attraction', it does have a number of major attractions, the top twenty of which are listed in Table 4.15.

Alton Towers	2 650 000	Westminster Abbey, London	1 268 215
Madame Tussauds, London	2 640 000	Edinburgh Castle	1 219 720
Tower of London	2 422 181	Flamingo Land, Yorkshire	1 197 000
Natural History Museum, London	1 739 591	Drayton Manor Park, Staffs	1 174 448
Legoland, Windsor	1 620 000	Windermere Lake Cruises	1 140 207
Chessington World of Adventures	1 550 000	St Paul's Cathedral, London	1 076 222
Science Museum, London	1 480 000	London Zoo	1 067 917
Royal Academy, London	1 390 000	Chester Zoo	965 721
Canterbury Cathedral	1 350 000	Victoria and Albert Museum	945 677
Windsor Castle	1 280 000	Thorpe Park, Surrey	926 000

Sources: British Tourist Authority/English Tourism Council (1999); English Tourism Council (2000)

Table 4.15 Top twenty attractions charging admission in 1999

In the UK as a whole, 16 per cent of attraction visitors are overseas tourists, but in London they represent 44 per cent of visits. By contrast, in North West England only 4 per cent of visits are made by international tourists. Overseas visitors have preferences for particular types of attractions in the UK. For example, they represent 33 per cent of all visitors to historic properties but only 5 per cent of wildlife attraction visitors.

Around 31 per cent of all visitors to UK attractions in 1999 were undertaken by children, both with their families and on school trips. Children visit some attractions more than others, with 46 per cent of all visits to farm attractions being made by children but only 17 per cent of garden visits.

An interesting finding of the *Sightseeing in the UK* (British Tourist Authority/English Tourism Council, 1999) survey was that 47 per cent of all UK attractions have opened since 1980 but that these attractions only received 29 per cent of all visits in 1999. Hence, it can be seen that recent attractions are attracting fewer visitors, on average, than those developed before 1980.

The same survey contained some other interesting facts about the UK attraction market, namely:

- 13 per cent of all UK attractions reported reaching their maximum capacity on an average of twenty-eight days in the year
- 49 per cent of attraction income came from admission charges or donations
- 41 per cent from retailing and 10 per cent from catering.

Finally, there are clearly great differences in the market for different types of attraction in the UK. Some of the differences for six types of attraction in 1999 are outlined in Table 4.16.

	Country parks	Farms	Leisure parks	Steam railways	Visitor centres	Workplaces
Number of properties	290	247	85	106	489	382
Number of visits	70 755 430	9 791 978	41 466 026	5 274 728	19 821 685	10 049 346
% opened since 1990	7	45	24	14	52	35
% opened since 1980	34	84	55	49	80	60
Trend in visits 1998–9 (%)	+2.8	+7.2	+2.8	+4.2	−1.2	+0.3
Overseas visitors (%)	4	5	6	6	17	16
Children (%)	34	46	43	32	29	22
Average days open	351	259	235	164	255	293
Maximum capacity reached (% of days open)	28	31	30	37	32	31
Days maximum reached	15	11	7	5	16	15
% charging admission	10	78	73	96	45	29
Average adult charge	£3.17	£3.29	£7.69	£4.70	£2.69	£2.81
Average child charge	£2.14	£2.10	£6.22	£2.57	£1.66	£1.54
Change in revenue (%)	+11	+11	+11	+10	+3	+4
Government ownership (%)	10	0	0	0	6	0
Local authority ownership (%)	73	7	2	3	34	2
Private ownership (%)	16	93	98	97	60	98

Sources: British Tourist Authority/English Tourism Council (1999); English Tourism Council (2000)

Table 4.16 Analysis of country parks, farms, leisure parks, steam railways, visitor centres and workplaces

The market for different types of attractions

As we saw from the UK, different types of attractions have very different markets. Let us now look at this point in relation to theme parks and industrial tourism.

Theme parks

Table 4.17 lists the top twenty amusement/theme parks in the world.

The dominance of the USA in this field is clear by the fact that twelve of these top twenty attractions are in the USA. However, the recent growing interest in theme parks in Asia is shown by the fact that six of them are in Asia, including the market leader. Interestingly, while Europe dominates the international tourism market it has only two attractions in the top twenty.

Every American visits an amusement/theme park at least once a year, on average, as can be seen from the figures in Table 4.18.

McClung, in 2000 published interesting research outlining the demographic profile of theme parks visitors in the USA with non-visitors. While limited in scope, the research included some interesting results:

- frequency to visit theme parks was high in the 24–44 age group but low in the 45+ segment

Rank	Park	Country	Attendance (million)
1	Tokyo Disneyland	Japan	17.45
2	Magic Kingdom	USA	15.20
3	Disneyland	USA	13.45
4	Disneyland Paris	France	12.50
5	Epcot	USA	10.10
6	Disney – MGM Studio	USA	8.70
7	Everland	South Korea	8.64
8	Disney Animal Kingdom	USA	8.60
9	Universal Studios (Orlando)	USA	8.10
10	Blackpool Pleasure Beach	UK	6.90
11	Lotte World	South Korea	6.10
12	Yokohama Sea Paradise	Japan	5.67
13	Universal Studios (Hollywood)	USA	5.10
14	SeaWorld Florida	USA	4.70
15	Huisten Boch	Japan	4.03
16	Nagashima Spa Land	Japan	4.00
17	Busch Gardens Tampa	USA	3.90
18	Six Flags Adventure	USA	3.80
19	SeaWorld California	USA	3.60
20	Knotts Berry Farm	USA	3.60

Source: Amusement Business (December 1999)

Table 4.17
Top twenty amusement/theme parks worldwide, 1999

Year	Attendance (million)	Revenue (US$ billion)
1990	253	5.7
1991	260	6.1
1992	267	6.5
1993	275	6.8
1994	267	7.0
1995	280	7.4
1996	290	7.9
1997	300	8.4
1998	300	8.7

Source: Amusement Business, Harrison Price Company Service Annual Survey; US Census Bureau; IAAPA (1999)

Table 4.18
Estimates of attendance and revenues at US amusement/theme parks, 1990–8

Theme	Percentage	Rank
Nature	66.7	1
Fantasy	46.7	2
Adventure	44.8	3
Futurism	44.7	4
History and culture	37.1	5
International	32.4	6
Movie	27.7	7

Source: Wong and Cheung (1999)

Table 4.19
Theme preferences of respondents by frequency of higher ranking

- families with children are much more likely to visit theme parks than those without children
- theme park visitors, in general, were rather higher earners than the non-visitors (McClung, 2000).

In 1999 Wong and Cheung published a fascinating study of the amusement/theme park market in Asia, looking at the types of theme Asian visitors prefer. Their research focused on Hong Kong, and covered visits by Hong Kong people to both Asian and American theme parks. Their preferences for different types of theme are shown in Table 4.19.

Industrial tourism

Stevens in 2000 looked at industrial tourism, in other words, tourism based on existing current industries rather than past industries. This field covers a variety of types of attraction, but the sector as a whole has seen fresh growth in recent years. For example, it has been estimated that in France some 5500 industrial sites are open to visitors, with around 10 million visitors per annum (Stevens, 2000). Table 4.20 lists a number of the world's most popular industrial tourism attractions.

However, most industrial tourism attractions are on a smaller scale than those shown in Table 4.20. It is clear from the industry attractions we have today that tourists are attracted to particular types of workplaces and industrial sites which have one or more of the following characteristics:

- famous brands
- products which are made in a traditional and/or 'picturesque' way
- places where the visitor can buy the product, preferably at a better price than in the high street
- exclusive, luxury high-status products such as champagne and perfume
- products where the production process involves high levels of skill
- controversial industry sites such as nuclear power stations

Name of company	Country	Industry	Visitors per annum
Hershey	USA	Chocolate	2 000 000
Coca-Cola	USA	Drinks	1 000 000
Kellogg's	USA	Food	1 000 000
Swarovski	Austria	Crystal	650 000
Cadbury	England	Chocolate	500 000
Waterford Crystal	Ireland	Glass	400 000
Guinness	Ireland	Beer	400 000
Parfumerie Fragonard	France	Perfumes	300 000
BNF Sellafield	England	Nuclear energy	200 000
Glenfiddich	Scotland	Whisky	180 000
Heineken	Netherlands	Brewing	90 000

Source: Stevens and Associates (2000)

Table 4.20
Examples of leading 'industry' visitor attractions (000s)

- very large-scale production such as steel plants
- sites with a high public profile such as airports and television studios.

Cross-cultural differences in attraction-visiting

As the tourism market becomes ever more internationalized, the issue of cross-cultural differences in tourist behaviour assumes ever greater significance. However, little empirical research has been conducted on these differences in relation to attractions-visiting.

It would, for instance, be interesting to see how the preferences for different themes at theme parks identified by Wong and Cheung compare to those of European or American tourists. However, the author would like to look at three examples of cross-cultural differences in attitudes to attractions that have been researched.

Kau, in 2000, published an excellent piece of research on cultural differences in attitudes towards the Tang Dynasty Village in Singapore, although the field research data are now rather old. The research involved 639 Asian tourists and 379 Caucasian tourists. Before looking at the Tang Dynasty Village, respondents were asked to identify which Singapore attractions they had most enjoyed. The results of this question, shown in Table 4.21, indicate significant differences in the satisfaction with different attitudes between the Asian and Caucasian tourists.

Tables 4.22 and 4.23 indicate relatively small differences between the two ethnic groups in terms of awareness, intention to visit, disruption, and willingness to pay.

However there were differences in terms of their levels of interest in different planned attractions as can be seen from Table 4.24, and their motivators were also significantly different in some ways, as can be seen from Table 4.25. As Table 4.26 illustrates, there were also major differences

Place of interest	Caucasian (%)	Asian (%)
Sentosa Island	41.9	63.6
Orchard Road	34.8	30.1
Chinatown	24.2	9.2
Zoological Garden	22.1	14.2
Botanical Garden	13.9	10.7
Jurong Bird Park	9.7	19.9
Haw Par Villa (Dragon World)	7.4	14.7
Elizabeth Walk/Merlion Statue	3.2	8.3
Chinese Garden	2.9	6.8
Science Centre	2.4	3.7

Source: Kau (2000)

Table 4.21
Place of interest
enjoyed most

	Caucasian	Asian
Awareness[1]		
Yes	13.2	25.3
No	86.8	74.7
Intention of visit[2]		
Yes	94.7	95.3
No	5.3	4.7
Best description[3]		
An attraction for entertainment shopping and food	29.6	26.6
Universal Studio of the East	7.7	14.7
Largest historical and cultural theme park	62.7	58.7
Total (all categories)	100.0	100.0

Notes: 1 Chi-square value = 21.08; level of sign. = 0.000.
2 Chi-square value = 0.1666; level of sign. = 0.6832.
3 Chi-square value = 10.66; level of sign = 0.0048

Source: Kau (2000)

Table 4.22
Awareness,
intention of visit
and description of
theme park (in
percentage
distribution)

Category	Caucasian (S$)	Asian (S$)	p=value[1]
1 Admission only	18.14	17.92	0.866
2 Admission plus transport, guided tour and lunch	36.36	40.37	0.055

Notes: 1 Level of significance for t-test.
Source: Kau (2000)

Table 4.23
Admission fee
respondents willing
to pay

Attraction/activity	Mean value[1]	Asian	p-value[2]
Tang delicacy tasting	4.150	4.046	0.125
Chinese cultural show	4.058	3.551	0.000
Terracotta soldiers display	3.651	3.698	0.578
Calligraphy demonstration	3.444	3.209	0.006
Motion-picture making	3.356	3.845	0.000
Kung fu demonstration	3.103	3.401	0.001
Photograph-taking in Tang costume	2.916	3.376	0.000
Horse/camel riding	2.825	3.390	0.000
Fortune telling	2.652	2.820	0.075

Notes: 1 Measured on a five-point scale ranging from 1 (not at all interested) to 5 (most interested).
2 Level of significance for t-test.

Source: Kau (2000)

Table 4.24
Interest in the planned attractions and activities

Statement[1]	Mean value Caucasian	Mean value Asian	p-value[2]
1 When I travel I like to know more about a country's culture and history	4.512	4.274	0.000
2 I enjoy local cuisine when I travel	4.356	4.259	0.106
3 I like to know about Chinese culture and history	4.323	4.035	0.000
4 I enjoy being near to nature	4.291	4.317	0.653
5 I like to explore exotic places like the Silk Road	4.189	3.816	0.000
6 I often shop when I go to another country	4.021	3.936	0.221
7 I like to go to museums	3.618	3.680	0.401
8 When I travel I prefer to be near to the beach and the sun	3.220	3.614	0.000

Notes: 1 Statements were measured on a five-point scale ranging from 1 (for strongly disagree) to 5 (strongly agree).
2 Level of significance for t-test.

Source: Kau (2000)

Table 4.25 Psychographic profiles of respondents

between the Asian and Caucasian tourists in expectations about theme park rides and amusements.

Vitterø et al. (2000) looked at the differences in attitudes to six Norwegian attractions by different groups of European visitors. Visitors were asked to give their views on each attraction in relation to whether they found them boring, relaxing, pleasant, interesting, and challenging, so that a flow-simplex could be devised for each.

Figure 4.10 shows how the attitudes to the Norwegian Glacier Museum vary between Norwegians, Germans and other nationalities. Clearly, the

	Caucasian (%)	Asian(%)
Disagree strongly	10.6	8.8
Disagree	22.5	11.4
Neither	32.0	19.8
Agree	21.4	27.3
Agree strongly	13.5	32.6
Totals	100.0	100.0

Source: Kau (2000)

Table 4.26
A theme park
should have
exciting rides and
hi-tech amusement

Germans found the attractions more challenging than the other nationalities. For the other five attractions, the views of all the nationalities were quite similar.

In 2001, Joppe, Martin and Waalen published a survey of the satisfaction levels of Canadian, American and other nationalities of tourists with Toronto as a destination, albeit based on a relatively small sample. The results of this research are summarized in Table 4.27.

Clearly, only some of these factors relate to attractions specifically and they have been marked with an asterisk.

The conclusion appears to be that Canadians, Americans and other nationalities are similar in their views when it comes to what they think is important in a destination, and how satisfied they are with Toronto in general, and specifically in relation to attractions.

However, these two pieces of research only relate to one element each of tourist behaviour. It would be interesting to see more research conducted on all aspects of attraction visiting behaviour. The following issues should be looked at to see if these are cross-cultural differences:

- propensity per head to visit attractions
- preferred types of attractions

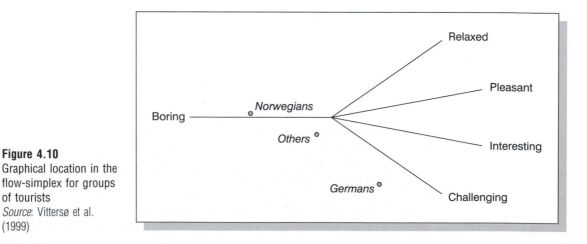

Figure 4.10
Graphical location in the
flow-simplex for groups
of tourists
Source: Vittersø et al.
(1999)

Attribute	Canada (n = 160)		USA (n = 171)		Overseas (n = 28)	
	Importance	Satisfaction	Importance	Satisfaction	Importance	Satisfaction
Transportation	2.86	3.88	3.16	4.3	3.0	3.86
Accommodation	3.61	3.88	3.61	4.27	3.39	3.71
Hospitality	3.18	3.53	3.27	4.31	3.11	4.14
Food service	3.43	3.86	3.43	4.37	3.32	3.89
Value for money	3.45	3.19	3.59	4.39	3.11	3.89
* Things to see and do	3.29	4.32	3.43	4.52	3.14	4.11
Signage	3.12	3.61	3.13	3.75	2.93	3.21
* Shopping	2.93	4.16	2.89	4.36	2.57	4.07
Cleanliness	3.42	3.58	3.37	4.14	3.32	4.04
Safety	3.69	3.65	3.67	4.33	3.64	3.96
* Cultural events	2.61	3.91	2.91	4.20	2.32	3.86
* Attractions	2.96	4.19	3.05	4.25	2.71	3.86
Shopping products	2.82	4.01	2.7	4.21	2.5	3.86
Family oriented	3.54	3.54	2.41	3.95	2.29	3.61
Grand means	3.13	3.81	3.19	4.24	2.95	3.86
Overall experience	3.34	3.93	3.60	4.56	3.29	3.96

Source: Joppe, Martin and Waalen (2001)

Table 4.27 Comparison of importance and satisfaction means for three segments in relation to Toronto

- ability and willingness to pay to visit attractions
- level of willingness and desire to spend money at attractions on catering and merchandise
- attitudes towards, and expectations of, customer service seasonality of visits
- nature of the visiting groups such as school groups, young adults
- 'nuclear families', extended families, group visits
- factors which influence visitor satisfaction.

There is clearly much work to be done before we can draw useful conclusions about cross-culture differences in attraction-visiting.

Gender and attraction-visiting

The tourism industry is rife with stereotypes about gender differences in tourist behaviour, exemplified by the cliché that 'men play golf, while women shop'. But how accurate is this picture today?

Research on gender differences in tourist behaviour is underdeveloped but even less work has been done specifically on gender and attraction-visiting. However, there are a few interesting examples of such research such as a survey conducted by Frew and Shaw in Australia, which was published in 1999. While this project related to personality, gender, and behaviour, we will focus on the gender dimension. Fifty-four per cent of their respondents were women and, therefore, we would normally expect

Attraction	Percentage of females having visited the attraction	Percentage of males having visited the attraction
Sovereign Hill, Ballarat	55	44
Penguin Parade, Philip Island	55	44
Scienceworks Museum, Melbourne	51	49
Bendigo Pottery, Bendigo	55	44
Australian Mint	61	39
Victorian Arts Centre Backstage Tour	62	38
International Festival of Arts, Melbourne	59	41
Melbourne Cricket Ground Backstage Tour	40	60
Powerworks, Morwell	43	57
Australian Grand Prix	36	64
De Bortoli Winery, Dixons Creek	61	39
Australian Stock Exchange Tour	38	62
Victorian Tapestry Workshop, Melbourne	64	36

Source: Frew and Shaw (1999)

Table 4.28 Percentage of females and males having visited selected attractions in Australia

that for any attraction surveyed, around 54 per cent of visitors would be women, if gender factors did not affect demand. However, as can be seen from Table 4.28, this is not always the case.

It is clear, therefore, that there are differences in actual attraction visiting between men and women. However, we need to recognize that these results may not tell the whole story because:

- as Frew and Shaw argued, personality also affects behaviour, and they noted differences between personality types as well as between the sexes
- visiting is not the same as enjoyment and satisfaction, and it would also be interesting to see how satisfied men and women were with their visits to different attractions
- there are clearly cross-cultural differences in the position of women in general, and in the tourism market, specifically, so the picture will vary between countries and cultures.

Again, therefore, this is an area where much work remains to be done.

The future of the attractions market

The future of the attractions market globally and in particular countries will be shaped by a range of factors, notably:

- the volume and nature of supply
- the rate of growth of domestic and international tourism

- the economic situation globally and in particular countries
- changes in lifestyles and general consumer behaviour.

The two main questions relating to the future attractions market are:

- How large will it be?
- What types of attractions will receive most visitors?

Concerning the first question, it seems likely that the overall volume of attraction-visiting worldwide will continue to grow, due to increasing international tourism and growing domestic tourism in recently industrialized countries.

However, it is probable that the growth will not take place, primarily, in the USA and UK where the markets are mature, but in Asia and Australasia, where the markets are still developing. Growth will also be seen in South America, the Middle East and Africa, albeit from a low starting point. In these latter regions this growth will be dependent on political stability as well as economic development.

The author, on the basis of no real empirical data, will now endeavour to suggest which types of attraction will grow greatest in popularity in the next few years. These include:

- attractions which offer hands-on experiences of all kinds where visitors can become participants rather than just spectators
- those attractions which focus on health, both physical and mental, and which integrate exercise and a healthy diet
- workplace visits including craft workshops, farms and industrial sites
- leisure shopping including factory shopping, designer outlets and markets
- fantasy attractions where virtual reality allows visitors to enter an artificial environment where they can enjoy extraordinary experiences
- attractions which allow visitors to learn something new
- places which provide intense experiences for those who feel they have limited time to spare, a trend which is apparently increasing across the developed world
- attractions which incorporate accommodation to allow longer stays, with much of this accommodation being themed to complement the main attraction
- a gradual decline in attractions based on live animals due to animal welfare concerns.

In terms of the demand for attractions and visitor behaviour, the author believes the next decade or so will see other developments, including the following:

- The market for individual attractions will become more international and culturally diverse which poses a challenge for attraction managers.

- As people become more experienced attraction visitors they will demand ever higher standards of service and facilities.
- More and more attractions will focus upon particular market segments rather than trying to appeal to everyone.
- Many attractions will boost their market by hosting more and more special events and features, as the events market continues to grow world-wide at an impressive rate.

Conclusions

In this chapter we have looked at the concept of demand and consumer behaviour in the attractions field. We have also looked at the size and nature of the attraction market in a number of countries. Finally, the author has endeavoured to predict how the attractions market may develop in the future.

Discussion points and essay questions

1 Discuss the application of market segmentation concepts and techniques to the attractions market.
2 Compare and contrast the attraction visiting behaviour in Paris, Copenhagen, New York and Tokyo, based on the data contained in this chapter.
3 Suggest reasons why Tokyo Disneyland has 17.45 million visitors, compared with 12.50 million at Disneyland Paris, 6.90 million at Blackpool Pleasure Beach and 3.40 million at Tivoli, in Copenhagen.

Exercise

You should conduct a small-scale survey in your area designed to discover:

- differences and similarities between men and women in the types of attraction they prefer
- differences and similarities between men and women in terms of what determines their satisfaction levels when visiting attractions.

Your report should highlight the difficulties you experience in conducting this survey.

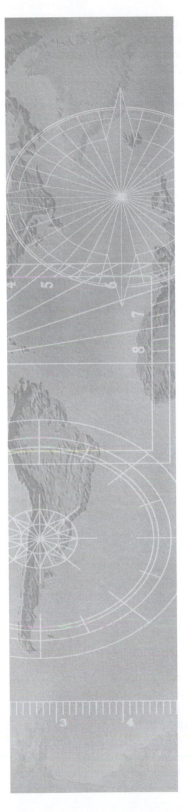

The business environment and visitor attractions

Like any other organization, visitor attractions exist within a business environment, that is, they are affected by a range of factors. The organization can control or heavily influence some of these factors while others are totally beyond its control and it must simply try to respond to them in the most effective way it can.

The business environment has two main components, namely, the *macroenvironment* and the *microenvironment*. The macroenvironment is made up of general societal forces that may be on a national or international scale. They exercise a very strong influence on organizations but cannot be controlled by the organization. They are usually split into four main types, with the initials PEST – political, economic, sociocultural and technological. Looking at these factors is called PEST analysis.

The microenvironment covers the specific key systems and players within the immediate environment of the organization, over which it has either considerable influence or control. These include the structure of the organization itself, its suppliers and marketing intermediaries, existing customers and its competitors.

In reality the business environment is a complex web involving all these factors, and it changes constantly over time. For each organization the most important and influential factors may be different and the pace of change of each factor will vary. Overall the business environment of tourism organizations is considered to be one of the most volatile of all. As we shall see, the business environment of visitor attractions is particularly volatile.

The macroenvironment

Political factors

These cover all the actions of governmental bodies, including organizations like the European Commission, national government and local authorities. They can be broken down into a number of types as follows.

Legislation • • •

Laws passed by governmental organizations can affect attractions in a number of ways. Some affect the management of the human resources in terms of working conditions and health and safety, for example, while others affect the market, such as the UK legislation which placed restrictions on the organization of school trips at the end of the 1980s. Consumer protection legislation affects the management of the attraction product and the way in which the attraction is marketed. Of course, attractions have to operate within the framework of law that covers all organizations, such as the law of contract.

Public sector policy and the attraction market • • •

As well as laws, governmental bodies influence attractions through their policies. As we shall see in the next section, the most important element of policy that affects attractions is economic policy. But other policies are also important, particularly in terms of the attraction market. Transport policy determines how accessible attractions will be, while education policy, such as the National Curriculum in the UK, determines which type of attractions will be popular for school trips. Even decisions like the scheduling of bank holidays influence attractions considerably. Finally, social tourism policies, such as those operated in France, stimulate the domestic attraction market.

Public sector policy and the attraction product • • •

The public sector policy does affect the attraction product. First, there is the role of government in conserving the resources on which the attraction product depends, such as the natural environment or historic buildings. Second, there is the question of the policy of government and local authorities towards the management of the attractions they own, like castles and museums. In many cases publicly owned attractions are the major attraction in a destination. Therefore, how they are managed will have a major impact on the other attractions in the area.

Public sector policy and tourism ● ● ●

Attractions are also directly affected by public sector policy towards tourism itself, for example: whether or not governmental bodies offer grant aid for the development of new attractions or product improvement at existing ones; also to what extent the government markets its country as a tourist destination, domestically and internationally; and what types of attraction it chooses to focus on in its marketing campaigns. Finally, there is the issue of the role of public sector bodies in the education and training of people to work in the tourism industry.

Even this brief and far from comprehensive discussion illustrates the important influence of governmental action on attractions. The public sector shapes the attraction product and market, but it also directly influences the attraction business through its role as an attraction operator. The roll call of publicly owned attractions reads like a 'Who's Who' of top attractions and includes places like the Tower of London in the UK, and the Louvre and Pompidou Centre in France, and also events, such as the Trooping of the Colour in the UK.

An excellent example of political factors and the attraction business has been seen in the UK in recent years, in the public funding of major new attraction projects through National Lottery and Millennium Commission funding. For example, between 1997 and 2002, thirteen Millennium Commission projects were developed in the UK at a total cost of over £700 million, much of it public or pseudo-public sector money. This investment has artificially stimulated the supply side and many of the projects have struggled to achieve their projected visitor numbers.

Economic factors

Governmental bodies also play a major role in the economic factors affecting attractions through their economic policy. The economic factors can again be split into those that affect the market and those that affect the attraction product, as follows.

Economic factors and the attraction market ● ● ●

The attraction market is affected by a number of economic factors given that its success depends on people having disposable income which they are willing to spend, and leisure time. Actual disposable income is affected by the other calls which are made on people's incomes, such as accommodation and food. Therefore, mortgage interest rates and inflation are important factors for attraction operators. Equally important, though, is the issue of perceived disposable income. People may have money but feel they should not dispose of it and so save it in case they become unemployed, or use it to pay off credit they have accumulated.

So far we have focused on the individual but the other crucial economic issue for the attraction market is how income is distributed throughout society as a whole. This is influenced by a number of factors, including:

- the level of unemployment
- the number of people on pensions and social security benefits and the relative generosity or otherwise of these benefits
- taxation policy
- relative wage levels and the differential between industries and between manual workers, white-collar workers, professionals and managers.

Finally, there are a number of economic factors that affect the market such as petrol prices and public transport charges. In terms of the international market, currency exchange rates are also an important determinant of market demand for certain types of attractions with international catchment areas.

Economic factors and the attraction product

The development and management of the attraction product is heavily influenced by economic factors. New product development is adversely affected by high interest rates, and the fall in demand caused by recessions. Likewise, the operation of attractions is affected by economic phenomena like inflation and wage rates.

While it is clear that economic factors are important to attractions, we have to be careful when applying economic theories to the attraction business. Simple laws of supply and demand, profit maximization and pricing are not always appropriate for several reasons. First, not all attractions exist to make a profit; many are happy to just break even and their operators may even be willing to subsidize them. In some cases pricing issues are simply non-existent. Many attractions make no charge for admission. Finally, where charges are made demand is often stimulated artificially through discounts to people who might not otherwise be able to afford to visit the attraction, such as the elderly and the unemployed. This may also be because the attraction has wider social objectives, such as increasing leisure opportunities for disadvantaged people.

Sociocultural factors

A number of sociocultural factors are crucial to attractions, the most important of which are described below.

Demographic trends

A number of aspects of demography are of interest to attractions, including:

- the age structure and class structure, given that certain types of attractions appeal mainly to particular age groups and classes

- the structure of the family and the number of children in households, given that many attractions specifically target the family market
- the number of young people in full-time education, who constitute another important market segment
- the geographical location of people, which determines the potential catchment area of an attraction
- the existence of a diversity of ethnic minorities with their own traditional patterns of leisure activities.

The changing nature of the so-called 'family life cycle' is of crucial importance for attractions. The traditional model was based on the idea that one followed a clear path through life: Child–Young adult–Young couple–Young couple with baby–Growing family–Empty-nesters–Elderly. As we have seen, this highly stereotypical model does not fully reflect the reality of the early twenty-first century.

Cultural trends and consumer behaviour • • •

In recent years there have been dramatic changes in culture and consumer behaviour which are influencing attractions. For example, the interest in healthy eating has made attractions rethink what they offer in terms of catering while many in the last two or three years have been keen to be seen to be responding to the growing concern with green issues.

However, changes such as these have not been isolated and random but have instead been part of the emergence of distinct new lifestyles and subcultures. As we saw in Chapter 4, people are increasingly buying the products and indulging in activities that reflect and reinforce their allegiance to particular lifestyles and subcultures. Purchases are made to strengthen the self-image of the person as an adherent to a lifestyle or subculture and as a way of displaying this adherence to the world at large. Attractions have become part of the phenomenon. Such subcultures and lifestyles have always been evident but now they are probably more sharply defined than ever and are being specifically targeted by marketers.

One such group with an influential lifestyle is health-conscious people. This lifestyle influences food purchases and leisure activities, and may also impinge on other aspects of people's lives and their attitudes such as a concern with passive smoking and opposition to the sponsorship of events by tobacco companies. All these are relevant to an attraction operator who is keen to satisfy his or her customers.

A good example of a subculture is the teenage subculture. This is not a new phenomenon but it is now very highly developed. It has its own leisure activities like computer games and 'raves' and, certainly listening to teenagers talking to each other, many older people feel teenagers almost have their own language. Parents are therefore almost excluded from the world of their teenage children. What is more, young people are increasingly being seen by marketers as consumers in their own right with disposable income of their own to spend as they wish. They are, for example, the core market for training shoes. Attraction operations trying to attract families or groups of young people need to be aware of the characteristics of this subculture.

Many lifestyles and subcultures are very fashion-conscious and are therefore rather fickle markets where the fashions can be very short-lived.

Technological factors

The attractions business is being increasingly affected by technological factors, in three main ways, namely: technology and the attraction product; technology and the management of attractions; and techno-logical development as competition for attractions.

Technology and the attraction products · · ·

Technology has always been important for the attraction product but at the present time exciting new developments are making its role even more crucial. In the 1980s computer games, interactive video, IMAX cinemas and new interpretation technologies in museums, such as artificial smell, changed the attraction product dramatically. The 1990s were forecast to be the era when virtual reality technologies would revolutionize the industry by allowing the spectator to become a participant. Virtual reality can stimulate the senses in a way that has not been possible before. It could change forever certain types of attractions such as zoos. There are, for example, plans for a non-animal zoo called the Worldlife Centre in Leicester which would overcome people's growing concerns about animals being kept in confinement. Much of the ethos behind virtual reality, however, is that it is the activity which is the key attraction not the setting or the more intangible parts of the experience. Its supporters believe that if technology can create the virtual reality of being at the seaside or in an aeroplane, you may no longer wish to try the real thing. This is a highly questionable contention and there is not yet enough evidence to say one way or the other. However, what we can say with certainty is that virtual reality technology is expensive and at present only relatively few attractions can afford to install it on a significant scale, but more and more are trying to do so. It is also true to say that its current appeal is mainly to younger people, particularly males, although this may change.

Technology and the management of attractions · · ·

Technology is increasingly important in the management of attractions to improve efficiency. Computers are now commonly used to handle reservations and stock control, and for the management information systems which are so vital to the effective management of a modern attraction.

Technology as competition for attractions • • •

However, just as technology can be beneficial for attractions, it can also provide competition for them. Technological developments are making the home a veritable entertainment centre, through cable and satellite television, videos and increasingly sophisticated computer games for example. For some types of attraction such home-based entertainment is a direct competitor. Virtual reality technologies also mean that, for some people at least, it is now possible to obtain exciting and satisfying experiences by travelling no further than an arcade in their local high street. As we said above, this new technology appears to appeal particularly to young men so if they are now using these new technologies in their home area, are they no longer visiting attractions, or are the new technologies an add-on to their existing leisure activities?

We have now completed our brief summary of the key political, economic, sociocultural and technological factors that affect attractions. However, there are commentators who would say that there is a fifth set of influences, namely natural factors. All attractions are to some extent dependent on one natural factor, the weather. Some attractions deliberately brand themselves 'all weather attractions' because they recognize how damaging bad weather can be to an open-air attraction which is exposed to the elements. However, we can also extend the concept of natural factors to include the natural environment as a whole. As this is often an attraction in itself, its health and conservation is clearly an important consideration for some attraction operators. Examples of this include wildlife reserves in Africa and woodlands such as the New Forest in southern England.

The microenvironment

There are, as we said earlier, five main components of the microenvironment, in other words, the organization itself, its suppliers, its marketing intermediaries, existing customers and its competitors.

The organization

The effectiveness of the management and marketing of an attraction is heavily influenced by the nature of the organization itself in terms of the following characteristics:

- the management structure and whether or not there is a rigid hierarchy or a flattened hierarchy
- the management style, which may range from highly supportive and encouraging staff participation in decision-making to the idea that managers give orders and staff obey
- the culture of the organization, which can be entrepreneurial or bureaucratic, risk-taking or cautious, open or defensive, driven by enthusiasm or fear
- the way in which functions are arranged within the organization and which are the most influential departments. In some attractions

marketing will dominate and all staff will be told that they are part of marketing. At other attractions financial management will be all-powerful and marketing may be relegated to being a job for just one or two people who live in an office with 'Sales and Marketing' on the door.

The suppliers

Attractions like other sectors of the tourism industry and industry generally are becoming increasingly concerned with the activities of their suppliers for two main reasons. First, the attraction is often judged by customers on the quality of goods and services provided by the supplier. Second, legislation such as the UK Food Safety Act 1991, with its underlying principle of product liability, is making attractions want to control their suppliers to prevent possible criminal charges and civil lawsuits arising from defects in goods and services originating from their suppliers.

Attractions can have a bewildering variety of suppliers, depending on how one defines 'supplier'. Let us look briefly, for example, at the suppliers for an open-air museum such as Ironbridge or Beamish. Any list of suppliers would include the people and organizations who provide the attraction with:

- food to be sold in the on-site catering outlets; these may well be small local suppliers
- souvenirs to be sold in the museum shop, which will often be made by lots of different individuals and companies
- museum artefacts, which could come from other museums, commercial dealers or as donations from members of the public
- goods such as tills and kitchen equipment
- staff uniforms
- specialist services such as the restoration of old machinery; some of these people could be voluntary helpers
- the suppliers of education and training for the museum staff.

Some attractions do try to buy from local suppliers wherever possible to help maximize the local benefits of tourism and to generate goodwill in the local community.

The marketing intermediaries

Organizations are also becoming increasingly concerned with the activities of their marketing intermediaries; in other words, the people who are the interface between them and their customers, the people who distribute the product to the customers on their behalf and those who provide messages about the product to the customer. The reasons for this concern are basically the same as those for the suppliers and could be summed up as quality control and protection against product liability problems.

On the face of it, attractions have few marketing intermediaries but on further investigation it is clear that there are several, including the following examples:

- tourist information centres which display brochures and sometimes offer tickets for sale
- tour operators who include attraction visits in their package holidays which they then sell to their customers
- group visit organizers who have to 'sell' the attraction to the members of the group
- travel writers in the media who provide information about attractions for the public.

Attractions should seek to ensure that these intermediaries are giving the right messages to potential customers. They also need to recognize that some of the most important intermediaries are existing customers who tend to recommend (or not recommend!) attractions to friends and relatives. This makes keeping existing customers happy an even more important task.

As with suppliers, the attractions business is as yet relatively inactive in terms of managing its marketing intermediaries in comparison to many organizations in other industries.

Customers

Following on from the point made about having customers as marketing intermediaries, it is important to recognize that they are part of the microenvironment in their own right. When considering customers as a factor in the microenvironment one should distinguish between existing customers and those who are currently non-users.

With regard to existing customers again there are two main types – regular visitors and first-time visitors. With the regular customer the attraction may wish to use their wide experience of the attraction by carefully monitoring their level of satisfaction and by tackling the problems they identify. Perhaps they should be given rewards for their loyalty such as 'season tickets', and special events, exclusively for regular customers. Finally, they can be encouraged to help play a permanent role in the attraction's marketing effort through 'friends' and 'supporters' organizations.

The challenge with first-time visitors is to impress them so much at the first attempt with the quality of the product and the service that they will become regular customers. Incentives may be required to encourage 'brand loyalty'.

Non-users, too, are of two types – ex-users and those who have never used the product. Ex-users are very important because the reasons they give for no longer being users of the attraction can help attraction operators recognize problems that may not otherwise come to light. Incentives may be needed to tempt these people back to using the attraction. Finally, attention should be paid to those who have never used

Table 5.1 The business environment and different types of attractions

			Type of attraction		
Factor in business environment	**Major theme park**	**Small local authority museum**	**Well-established private zoo**	**Privately owned stately home**	
Macroenvironment:					
Political	Health and Safety law legislation on the rights of part-time workers	Legislation affecting local government including Compulsory Competitive Tendering Control on local authority expenditure	Laws on importing and keeping wild animals	Grant aid for historic buildings	
Economic	The state of the economy Interest rates due to the need for constant new product development	If a charge is made, the state of the economy; otherwise of little importance	State of the economy	State of economy Tax laws on property ownership Currency exchange rates if many visitors are from overseas	
Sociocultural	The percentage of the population in the younger age group The changing structure of the family	The percentage of the population in the middle age groups and in social classes A and B	Concerns with green issues and animal rights	Interest in nostalgia	
Technological	New types of rides Virtual reality Management information systems	Need to keep up with the latest methods of interpretation	Very limited	Very limited	
Natural	The weather, as most theme parks are open air. Therefore bad weather reduces visitor numbers	Weather if under cover or open-air. Most are under cover so bad weather is usually beneficial	State of wildlife in enclosed environment Supply of suitable animals for breeding in captivity	Weather: garden out of doors while house offers shelter from bad weather	

Microenvironment:			
Organization	Usually entrepreneurial Professional culture Mainly seasonal and part-time staff	Often bureaucratic Many permanent full-time staff	Mixture of professional and entrepreneurial culture. Ranges from informal and managing attraction as a hobby, to highly structured and professional	Usually small scale and family-managed
Suppliers	The rides and on-site attractions Catering products Souvenirs Concessionaires and franchises	Artefacts: often from the public Limited catering goods and souvenirs Staff training through museum professional bodies	Animals Catering products Souvenirs	Limited catering supplies Souvenirs
Marketing intermediaries	Tourist information centres Tour operators and coach companies Hotels which display literature Media Existing customers	Tourist information centres Libraries School group leaders Existing customers	Tourist information centres Existing customers	Tourist information centres Existing customers
Customer	Significant brand loyalty but few visits per annum Regional and national catchment area	Often heavy dependence on regular repeat visits Usually local catchment area	Generally high brand loyalty	Generally infrequent visits; once in a lifetime for many overseas visitors
Competitors	Other theme parks Seaside resorts with amusement parks and arcades Other attractions aimed at social classes C and D	Other attractions targeting social classes A and B Visitors in the 25–60 age group Educational groups	Other attractions based on animals	Other attractions targeted at middle-aged people and social classes A and B Other attractions based on heritage

the attraction, to find out why. Incentives may help to convert some into first-time users, but it may be that no amount of effort will persuade some non-users as the attraction simply does not appeal to them. The point comes at which it is not cost-effective to 'chase' non-users.

Only existing customers are generally considered to be part of the microenvironment as only they are really capable of being influenced or controlled by the attraction, rather than non-users over which the attraction has much less influence.

Competitors

An organization's relationship with its competitors is a two-way link, in that you influence your competitors and they influence you. Organizations are either trying to catch up with their competitors or are trying to stay one step ahead of them. Most industries have no difficulty in identifying their main competitors on the basis of identifying who else offers similar products to similar target markets. For attractions, however, it is often far more difficult to identify competitors, for competitors exist on several levels. There are the other attractions, which offer a similar product to a similar market. There are also all the other uses of leisure time and expenditure which are not part of tourism, such as gardening, DIY, reading, home entertaining and so on. It could be argued that competition for attractions is virtually anything that potential customers might be doing with their leisure time and disposable income when they could otherwise be visiting the attraction.

Once competitors have been identified it is important to investigate them with regard to:

- the main product they offer and their target market
- their strengths and weaknesses
- their future plans.

In terms of marketing planning this information should influence the organization's plan in terms of product development, marketing activities and target markets. However, it would be wrong only to respond to the actions of competitors. Attractions should usually do what is best for them first of all, but they should be aware of their competitors and take account of them in their planning.

On a more tactical level, competitors will undoubtedly affect attractions in terms of pricing decisions. They may also influence the attraction through the style and messages of the literature they produce. Attractions often adopt the ideas or initiatives of their competitors in what can appear like a game of leapfrog, in which one person uses the back of a second person to help get ahead of that second person!

We have now looked at the factors in the macroenvironment and microenvironment to which attractions have to respond effectively in order to be successful. However, the precise nature of the business environment varies from one attraction to another and between types of attraction, as does the relative importance of the different functions. Table

5.1 attempts to illustrate this point by reference to four different types of attraction. It cannot, however, convey the full complexity of the situation in that the nature and importance of factors varies over time and is different for individual attractions within a particular category of attractions.

Conclusion

Table 5.1 illustrates how different factors in the business environment affect different types of attractions and that some factors are of more importance to some attractions than to others. However, the most important factors also vary from one attraction to another of the same type, so that Table 5.1 is a gross simplification of a very complex set of relationships.

The key to successful visitor attraction management lies in anticipating changes in the factors and responding to them in a proactive rather than a reactive way. This implies a crucial role for market research and constant scanning of the environment.

Discussion points and essay questions

1 Discuss the ways in which economic factors can affect visitor numbers, development plans, and operations at an attraction.
2 Discuss the importance of suppliers for visitor attractions, using examples.
3 Evaluate the importance for the attractions sector of public and governmental concerns over environmental issues.

Exercise

Select a museum in your region and look at the ways in which:

- technology has influenced its product in recent years
- technological developments may affect its product in the future.

Suggest factors which may speed up or slow down the developments you have anticipated in the future.

Part Two

The Development of
Visitor Attractions

The development process and the role of feasibility studies

Introduction

This chapter looks at the development process. In this context development will be defined as the construction of new buildings and structures for the purpose of attracting visitors.

Types of development

In the field of visitor attractions there are several main types of development:

1 Wholly new purpose-built attractions on sites that were not previously used as attractions, for example, Disneyland Paris at Marne-La-Vallée.
2 New purpose-built attractions developed on sites that were previously used as attractions, such as Legoland, built on the site of the ill-fated Windsor Safari Park, in the UK
3 Major new developments at existing attractions designed to attract more visitors and to allow the attraction to tap new markets. Developments like these are often used in an attempt to relaunch attractions or prevent the onset of the decline stage in the product life cycle. An example of such development could be the installation of a major new ride at a theme park.

4 New developments at existing attractions which aim to improve visitor facilities or encourage increased secondary spending by visitors, for example, new retail outlets and themed catering at many museums.

5 The creation of new events or the staging of events that move from place to place over time such as the Olympic Games, where such events require the development or modification of buildings and structures. Good examples of this are Expo 2000 in Hanover, Germany, and the 2000 Olympic Games in Sydney.

Agents of development

The main agents of development include:

1 Public sector
   (a) central government (ministries and departments)
   (b) quangos
   (c) local government
2 Private sector
   (a) transnational organizations with interests in several sectors of industry, such as Universal and Disney
   (b) major leisure companies such as the Rank Organization UK
   (c) developers who use leisure as part of mixed use developments
   (d) small and medium-sized private companies
   (e) individual entrepreneurs
3 Voluntary sector
   (a) national bodies such as the National Trust
   (b) local trusts covering a geographical area or related to a specific theme, such as industrial heritage, or a particular site or project.

Between these three sectors, and even within them, there are differences in the types of development undertaken in terms of the five types of development outlined above. There are also differences in the types of attractions each sector is particularly concerned with. This is illustrated in Table 6.1.

Motivation for development

As we saw in Chapter 1, different organizations have different motives for being involved in the development of visitor attractions. These also tend to vary according to the sector – public, private or voluntary.

The public sector is generally not motivated by the profit motive, although income generation is important to most public sector bodies. Organizations in this sector are generally motivated to undertake development for the following reasons:

- to conserve the heritage of the country or area
- to provide leisure facilities for the community
- education, usually in relation to history and, increasingly, the understanding of science and technology

Sector	Main types of development[1]	Main types of attractions
Public:		
Central government	1,3,4,5	Museums, galleries, historic buildings, major events
Quangos	3,4	Ancient monuments, historic buildings, museums. Mainly attractions not purpose-built for tourism
Local authorities	1,3,4,5	Museums, country parks, leisure facilities, events
Private:		
Transnational corporations	1,2,3,4	Theme parks
Major leisure companies	1,2,3,4	Theme parks, amusement parks, leisure facilities
Developers	1,2	Waterfront developments
Small and medium-sized companies	1,3,4	Zoos, garden centres
Individual entrepreneurs	1,3,4	Museums, leisure parks, craft centres
Voluntary:		
National bodies	4,5	Stately homes, historic buildings, landscape, major events
Local bodies	1,4,5	Historic buildings, industrial heritage sites, steam railways, events

Note: 1 Numbers 1–5 relate to types of development identified in the previous section.

Table 6.1 Types of development and types of attraction, by sector

- to improve the image of the country abroad or of an area within its own country
- as a tool of economic development or urban regeneration
- to gain political advantage.

This complex range of objectives, which may not be complementary, is one reason why the development and management of public sector attractions is a very difficult task.

In many ways the motives of the private sector are clearer and simpler, although the idea that the only motive is the creation of profit is a misleading generalization. Attraction development in the private sector may have a number of other motives including diversifying the organization's product portfolio, increasing market share, achieving a particular rate of return on capital employed or boosting profits. However, while these are all important longer-term motives for development in the private sector, the short-term objective of profitability within each financial year is usually an essential prerequisite in the private sector.

Traditionally the voluntary sector has had two main motives for becoming involved in attraction development, namely, conservation and education. In both cases, tourism has been a means to an end rather than an end in itself. Bodies like the National Trust use the income generated from visitors to further their conservation work. At the same time many voluntary organizations try to impart an educational message to their visitors, whether it be about the history of the attraction or the importance of their conservation work.

Who carries out the development?

Once the organizations in all these sectors have decided to undertake a development, they may make use of a range of specialists to help them undertake the project. These will usually include architects, engineers, surveyors, building contractors and other specialists. Few attraction developers and operators are able to carry out developments using all their own staff. Much of the skill of project management lies in managing the external specialists to achieve the aims of the organization in terms of the development of the attraction.

Size of development

The scale of developments in the attractions field varies enormously. At one end of the spectrum are the myriad of small-scale attractions, some of which may be only a few square metres and designed to accommodate a handful of visitors at a time. At the other extreme are attractions such as Disneyland Paris which are the size of a small town and can accommodate tens of thousands of people at a time. Events also vary from those which are small scale and require little or no new construction work to those whose scale demands the creation of massive new buildings and structures, such as the Olympic Games.

Just as the scale varies dramatically, so does the amount of capital required to develop attractions, from a few thousand pounds to hundreds of millions of pounds.

Timescales of development

The timescale for visitor attraction development also varies dramatically, often in direct proportion to the scale of the development and whether it is a wholly new development or a modification of an existing attraction. Some developments take only a few months from the original idea to completion while others take many years. For example, the original plan for Disneyland Paris envisaged that the development project would be completed in the year 2017! Events also have different gestation periods, from a few months to several years. For example, the lead-in time for the Olympic Games from deciding to bid to the event actually taking place is about eight or nine years.

The development process

While attraction development is a complex business in terms of types of development, agents, motivation, size and timescale, the development process itself is quite straightforward, in principle at least. It starts with an idea or concept which may be designed either to exploit an opportunity or tackle a threat. There is then a period in which the idea is tested and its potential viability assessed. This may be either through a formal feasibility study or by an informal and non-systematic process. Often this study will result in a decision not to proceed any further. However, if the project is considered viable the next stage is the construction period, followed by the opening of the new attraction.

The feasibility study

The term 'feasibility study' encompasses a wide range of types of study that differ somewhat in respect of their purpose and content. However, the general goal of a feasibility study is quite clear: to test the potential viability of the proposed project as accurately as possible before a decision is made whether or not to go ahead.

Nevertheless, within this general goal, feasibility studies usually have a number of different objectives which reflect the motivation of the organization and the aims of the project. These objectives can include any combination of:

- testing as far as is possible the financial viability of the proposed attraction, which means calculating capital and revenue costs and projecting visitor numbers and income
- clarifying and refining the original concept to reconcile it with issues such as the market, financial viability and site availability
- forecasting the likely nature and size of the target market or markets for the attraction; while formulae exist for this purpose it could in no way be described as a precise science given the large number of variables involved and the uniqueness of each attraction
- providing support and justification for any applications for finance for the project that may be required, such as loans and grants
- helping define the optimum site in terms of size, terrain and accessibility
- supporting planning applications to demonstrate there is a market for the attraction
- attracting potential sponsors, franchisees and concessionaires who may be required
- analysing specific operational issues such as labour availability
- identifying sources of potential financial assistance
- providing useful marketing information.

So far we have considered the feasibility study as a systematic, logical, neutral tool for rational decision-making. However, it is important to recognize that often feasibility studies are not carried out with an open mind. In some cases the study is designed to legitimize a decision that has already been taken, based on other factors such as the views of stakeholders. Furthermore, while a study should start with a clean sheet of paper this is rarely possible in reality. The organization may already own the site or at least be limited in the choice of project location, and the amount of available capital may well be predetermined.

The feasibility study process

Talking about the feasibility study implies that it is one document produced at one point in time. Often, however, the feasibility study will be more of a process than a single exercise. Figure 6.1 is a stylized representation of such a process.

Preliminary concept
|
Rough costings
|
Market feasibility study
|
Revise concept
|
Identify location and site
|
Revise costings
|
Visitor number and spending projections
|
Financial evaluation
|
Identify sources of finance
|
Detailed design and planning including phasing

Figure 6.1
The feasibility study process

Who should undertake the feasibility study?

There are basically two choices, namely, to carry out the study in-house with the organization's own staff or to use outside consultants. Both options have advantages and disadvantages, as Figure 6.2 shows. If the organization decides to use consultants, it must then choose between a plethora of possible companies, which are either large general management consultancies or smaller specialist tourism consultancies. The general practice is to produce a project brief and ask consultancies to tender for the job. Feasibility studies, produced by consultancies are not inexpensive: even one for a modest project might cost in the region of £30 000–£50 000.

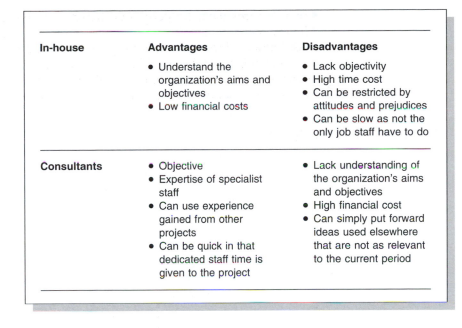

In-house	Advantages	Disadvantages
	• Understand the organization's aims and objectives • Low financial costs	• Lack objectivity • High time cost • Can be restricted by attitudes and prejudices • Can be slow as not the only job staff have to do
Consultants	• Objective • Expertise of specialist staff • Can use experience gained from other projects • Can be quick in that dedicated staff time is given to the project	• Lack understanding of the organization's aims and objectives • High financial cost • Can simply put forward ideas used elsewhere that are not as relevant to the current period

Figure 6.2
The advantages and disadvantages of carrying out feasibility studies in-house or through consultants

The content of the feasibility study

Once one has an idea or concept it is important, first of all, to establish whether or not a market exists for it and, if so, to examine the nature and size of this market. This is achieved through a market feasibility study or market appraisal. Once one knows the size and composition of the likely market one can select a site and estimate possible income figures, which are crucial to the evaluation of the financial viability of the project. Knowing more about the market will also help to refine the concept to help it match the demands of the real rather than the perceived market.

The market study

Attraction operators are interested in four main characteristics of their potential market:

- Who will visit the attraction?
- How many people will visit the attraction?
- Where will they come from?
- When will the visitors come?

We will look at these questions one by one.

In answer to the question 'Who will visit the attraction?' it can be said that there are five main types of visitors:

- domestic holiday-makers
- foreign holiday-makers
- day-trippers

- school and college groups
- local residents.

In addition, many attractions also attract corporate clients for conferences, meetings, exhibitions, product launches and corporate hospitality. In financial terms this is a very important market for many attractions.

However, we can also break the market down in other ways, for example:

- By age: does the attraction appeal to older or younger people?
- By sex: are more male or female visitors likely to be attracted to the site?
- By class: is it an attraction that appeals to social classes A and B or C and D?
- By stage in the family life cycle: does the attraction mainly appeal to families or young single adults?

Thinking about these questions helps the attraction developers think more objectively and forces them to look at target markets given that hardly any attractions appeal to the whole market. However, this is easier said than done and it is very difficult to be sure about target markets in advance of opening. The best approach is perhaps to look at the visitor profile of similar attractions elsewhere. For some attractions, however, based on new concepts, this is not possible.

It is sensible at this stage for the operator to start thinking about those market groups that will be attracted which will require special facilities, such as the wheelchair-bound, and those with hearing and sight problems. A failure to consider these groups at this point will lead to the creation of attractions that are not user-friendly for these groups of potential visitors. Thus the attraction will be deprived of their valuable custom and the prospective visitors will have been denied an enjoyable leisure time experience. This also prevents the socially undesirable idea growing that the disabled are a group out on their own, very different from other visitors.

When planning the attraction it is important to remember that *all* visitors have special needs, not just the disabled. Parents need baby-changing facilities and foreign visitors need signs in their own language, for example.

Perhaps the hardest question to answer is, *'How many people will visit the attraction?'* This depends on a number of factors, including:

- the population of the catchment area within, say, sixty to ninety minutes' drive time of the attraction
- the number of holiday-makers who currently visit the area
- the competitors that exist within the local area attracting similar market segments
- the scale and nature of the attraction itself.

A key figure is the 'penetration factor' which is the actual number of people in each market segment who will visit the attraction. Perhaps surprisingly, the figure is often less than 5 per cent. The figure is generally relatively high for school visits and local residents, lower for day-trippers and very low for holiday-makers (except in established tourist destinations).

These calculations sound very mathematical but in reality it is a mixture of 'guesstimates' as all attractions are different and the market is always changing.

'Where will they come from?' is important because it will influence visitor numbers in that generally the larger the catchment area the greater the number of visitors. Attractions range from those that attract mainly local people to those with an international catchment area such as Disneyland Paris and Legoland. To draw visitors from a regional, national or international catchment area an attraction has usually to be on a large scale and have some novel or unique features.

The final question, *'When will the visitors come?'*, is important because the degree of seasonality affects issues such as staffing, attraction capacity and cash flow management. The degree of seasonality will depend on a number of factors, including:

- the level of reliance on the highly seasonal school-trip market on the one hand, and the family market, which is concentrated in the school holidays, on the other
- the percentage of visitors from the local area, given that the more visitors that are from the locality the less seasonal the demand for the attraction is likely to be.

Clearly, marketing can be used to attempt to even out seasonal demand but its effects are usually limited.

At the end of the study there should be a picture of the likely market for the proposed attraction in terms of visitor numbers, competition and seasonality. This is an essential prerequisite for the financial evaluation, which we will consider after we have briefly discussed the issue of site selection.

Site selection criteria ● ● ●

Choosing the right location and site for an attraction is crucial to its future success. Site selection is an art rather than a science, and the factors that will be taken into account and the weighting given to each factor will vary from one attraction to another, and between developers. However, a number of factors can be identified that will often be taken into account, including:

- proximity to major centres of population
- transport networks and their reliability
- the existence of other attractions in the area
- the socioeconomic profile of the catchment area
- the climate

- the availability of utilities and infrastructure, such as electricity, water and a range of local businesses that might act as suppliers for any new attraction
- the amount of land available that will accommodate the size of the attraction itself but will also provide enough room for future growth
- the type and quality of land in terms of topography: drainage, for example
- the cost of land
- planning policies or statutory controls on the use of land
- the availability of appropriately skilled and experienced labour at an acceptable cost
- public sector financial assistance and 'help in kind' for tourism projects
- the attitude of the local community towards the proposed attraction
- building costs
- labour relations and labour laws.

A good example of some typical factors in site selection is the case of the first UK Center Parcs complex, in North Nottinghamshire, which was studied by Bentley (1989), who believed that the location decision was based on the following factors:

Market-related criteria

Location	Sherwood Forest
Proximity to potential market	8 million people within two hours' drive
Ease of access	Good
Support facilities	Towns, villages nearby
Competing facilities	None
Other tourism development generators	Sherwood Forest itself

Physical criteria

Site aesthetics	Views, varied flora and fauna
Water supply	Center Parcs complements nature
Ability of land to support recreation	Developed man-made lake

Other criteria

Manpower availability and good labour relations	Functional managers attracted from hotels and restaurants
Availability and cost of land, zoning and regulation	Land costs less than nearer to London. Land supply: 440 acres for 629 villas
Government financial assistance	English Tourist Board and local government assistance towards the £34 million investment
Socioeconomic features	Local support: 400 jobs; of host area/local reaction environment enhanced

Financial viability • • •

Financial viability has two elements, namely, capital and revenue. In other words, attractions have to repay their capital cost and produce a profit or surplus on their annual running costs. However, it is important at this stage to recognize that financial viability in the attraction business can mean very different things depending on the type of organization and its objectives. For most private sector attractions viability means a healthy return on capital employed and a profit on yearly trading. But for many public sector attractions capital costs are partly met by external grants and subsidies are provided to cover part of the running costs. For some public and voluntary sector attractions there is a middle road where some may seek to cover their capital costs and break even on their revenue budget.

The market study will have helped clarify the likely capital costs of the attraction because it will have identified the required site location and capacity. Issues such as seasonality will also have helped the attraction planners calculate running costs, such as staffing.

The first job is to estimate the likely annual income of the attraction over a period of, say, five years. This income can come from a number of sources, including:

- entrance charges, although some attractions do not have such charges as a matter of policy, for example some museums
- income from retail and catering outlets
- income from other sources such as franchises, concessions and guided tours, together with room hire and corporate hospitality
- external sources of funding, like grants and sponsorship.

Against these figures must be set a number of costs, including:

- staffing: salaries plus 'on-costs' such as national insurance and extras such as training
- the cost of goods sold in the catering and retail outlets
- heat and light
- insurance
- administration
- maintenance
- rates and taxes
- marketing
- finance charges, namely, the repayments on loans or the amount set aside for the repayment of capital allocated by the parent organization for the development of the attraction
- depreciation.

Because it can take a few years before an attraction reaches its peak visitor numbers and there is a need therefore to 'front-load' market expenditure, attractions often make losses in their first few years. Hence, the reason for developing five-year or even longer revenue and expenditure estimates is to allow assessment of the longer-term prospects of the attraction.

Breakeven analysis is relevant both as part of a feasibility study and as a management control tool once the attraction is in operation. In general terms, breakeven analysis is about calculating how much of a product must be sold in order to cover costs, with no profit or loss. For attractions the key issue is income, which is related to visitor numbers, rather than to sales of a specific product.

In feasibility studies it is important to calculate the year in which the attraction will achieve its breakeven point and move into profit, as this information will be required by potential investors. If the period is too long it may be difficult or impossible to attract funding for the project. Alternatively, if the period is acceptable, it at least allows the operators to plan their cash flow in the period before they can expect to see a profit. A short period before the breakeven point is reached may also encourage finance houses to grant loans and mortgages for the project. Figure 6.3 illustrates how breakeven analysis can be applied to attractions.

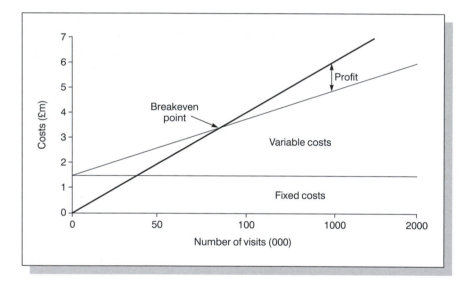

Figure 6.3
Breakeven analysis and attractions

There is, however, a particular complication in relation to attractions, namely that the number of visits is perhaps not the best indicator. This is because calculating the number of visitors an attraction will have to attract to break even is difficult as it is dependent on what kind of visitors they are and how much money they will spend. For example, 1000 schoolchildren paying a concessionary rate of 50 pence for entrance and then buying a pencil for 20 pence will leave an attraction much further from its breakeven point than 1000 adults paying the normal £1 admission charge and buying a book and another souvenir at a cost of £3.

It is also important to recognize that breakeven analysis may not be appropriate for those public sector attractions that are never expected to break even. Nevertheless, these attractions usually do have some kind of financial target so that the techniques underlying breakeven analysis can still be applied to them. Once the attraction is up and running, breakeven analysis can be used as a financial management control technique.

Finally, it must be remembered that an attraction may reach its breakeven point ahead of the planned time and still subsequently fail, so simply reaching the breakeven point is no guarantee of success.

As circumstances can vary dramatically during the gestation period and each year of an attraction's life, it is common to produce several financial projections based on a number of different variables such as staffing levels and the state of the economy. This is a form of sensitivity analysis and results in a series of best and worst case scenarios. Cautious attraction developers may only decide to go ahead with a project if it was viable even under the neutral or worst case scenarios. This is rather oversimplified, however, and we have assumed that calculating the income from a given number of visitors is quite straightforward and that the only thing that matters is the balance of income and expenditure over a complete year. Both assumptions are false. It is actually very difficult to calculate income, even if the overall projected visitor numbers are correct, for two main reasons. First, the income depends on what type of visitors come to the attraction and the types of ticket they buy. For example, if most visitors are school groups or elderly people paying concessionary entrance charges, the income could be up to 50 per cent less than if they were all single adults paying the full adult price. Second, it is also very difficult to estimate in advance what visitors will spend on secondary items such as food, drink and souvenirs. This, too, will be related to the types of people who visit the attraction.

Not only is the balance between income and expenditure over a year important but so is the cashflow. Revenue and spending need to be balanced week by week and month by month, wherever possible, to ensure the cashflow situation is a healthy one. The more seasonal the demand for the attraction, the more difficult it is to manage the cashflow successfully.

We have so far concentrated on the revenue costs and income, but to do the full calculation properly it is essential to forecast accurately the capital cost. This consists of a number of elements:

- the acquisition of the site and any restoration or preparatory work on it that is required
- construction work to create the buildings and structures that house the attraction
- the setting out of the attraction, for example, the displays and artefacts in a museum
- the costs associated with the launch, which are incurred before the attraction starts to earn income, such as staffing and marketing
- any other costs incurred before the attraction opens, such as franchises that have to be purchased or licences and planning permissions that must be obtained.

Problems with feasibility studies

Feasibility studies are very difficult to undertake accurately for a variety of reasons:

1 The market is constantly changing and by the time the proposed attraction opens there could have been major changes in consumer behaviour and tastes. The market can be suddenly subject to external factors outside the attraction's control, such as legislation and government policy in relation to school trips in the UK in 1989 and the early 1990s.

2 No two attractions are the same so it is very difficult to find comparable ones elsewhere that can help operators decide whether or not a proposed attraction is likely to be a success or a failure.

3 The gestation period for the development of attractions is so long that the assumptions on which the study is based relating to variables such as interest rates, building costs and staffing costs may well be out of date by the time work begins.

4 Many attractions, particularly those in the public sector, have complex sets of objectives, some of which are contradictory. There is therefore no simple objective such as profit against which to measure the potential performance of a proposed attraction. For example, a local authority leisure centre may lose money, but it may be considered 'viable' and valuable by local politicians because it provides recreational facilities for the local community, thus enhancing the quality of life and health of local people.

Conclusion

We have seen that feasibility studies are essential to help attraction developers define their concept and support their applications for funding and planning permission. However, we have also seen that producing feasibility studies is extremely difficult for a variety of reasons. Therefore, many operators continue to make decisions based on the results of feasibility studies together with their own judgement arising from their past experience. Often one suspects that given the less than perfect level of knowledge and techniques for conducting feasibility studies, many operators prefer to rely on their own judgement and experience. But the knowledge and techniques are improving, and any operator relying just on their own judgement increasingly appears foolhardy.

Discussion points and essay questions

1 Discuss the factors which determine the breakeven point for visitor attractions.

2 Using examples, identify the most important criteria when selecting a site for an attraction project.

3 Discuss the factors which mean that many attractions take years to develop, from the original concept to the opening ceremony.

Exercise

Produce a simple feasibility study for an attraction concept which you devise. The format of your feasibility study should follow the sequence set out in Figure 6.1. Note all the problems you encounter in preparing the feasibility study.

Factors influencing the success of visitor attractions

Introduction

Every year thousands of individuals and organizations think about developing new visitor attractions. Only a minority of these proposed attractions will ever be built. Most will never be developed for a number of reasons, including funding problems, unfavourable feasibility studies or the lack of a suitable site. Furthermore, many new attractions never take off and either close prematurely or merely survive from year to year. Others achieve early success and then decline due to a lack of investment, visitor management problems or the failure to respond to changes in market demand. Only relatively few attractions achieve constant success over a long period of time.

Experience suggests that while nothing guarantees success, there are a number of factors which contribute to the success of visitor attractions. These factors can be grouped under the following headings:

- the organization and its resources
- the product
- the market
- the management of the attraction.

The organization and its resources

The chances of developing a successful new visitor attraction are greatly enhanced if the *organization has experience of developing and managing attractions*. It will be aware of the opportunities and pitfalls, and will be able to take account of the lessons it has learned from its previous experience. However, the early years of Disneyland Paris show that even experienced, successful attraction operators can make some errors of judgement. An organization with previous experience will also probably have a *human resource team* that will have the skills and knowledge to develop a new attraction successfully.

The most important type of resource, however, and the one which is crucial to successful attraction development, is *financial resources*. Visitor attractions are very expensive to build and run, and those that are successful tend to be developed by organizations with substantial financial resources. The capital cost of developing attractions varies from less than £1 million for a craft centre or small museum to several billion pounds for a project such as Disneyland Paris. Indeed Disneyland Paris is, together with the Channel Tunnel, probably the largest and most expensive construction project of the age in Europe, and perhaps in the world.

As well as the cost of site acquisition and building work, much of the cost comes from fitting out the attraction with expensive museum artefacts or the installation of sophisticated modern technology like lasers and virtual reality experiences. Well-used attractions and those in rapidly changing markets (most of them) also need regular refurbishment, relaunching and remodelling to encourage repeat visits and to keep up with changes in consumer tastes. This is a continuous process that requires investment at frequent intervals. For example, theme parks often believe they need to offer a major new ride every year and these rides often cost over £1 million each.

Attractions also need the financial resources to allow them to provide high-quality facilities and services. Organizations which are short of money often reduce levels of facilities and services and this often leads to a poorer product and, ultimately, fewer visitors. Organizations therefore need to have the resources to maintain standards even in the bad times to ensure the long-term success of the attraction.

Attraction operators also need substantial financial resources to allow them to support the attraction in its early years, when it may be losing money, before becoming profitable. In the public sector, of course, many attractions will never be profitable, so the organization will always need to be able to have the financial resources to continue to subsidize the attraction. This is a problem, certainly in Britain, where pressures on public sector spending have often led to reduced subsidies for attractions.

All attractions must also have the financial resources to allow them to spend considerable amounts on marketing to establish and maintain their market position and to respond to problems such as poor seasons. This is important as many small and medium-sized attractions either fail, or do not realize their full potential, because they do not allocate enough resources to marketing.

Because of the considerable sums of money required to develop major attractions we are increasingly seeing a situation where such projects are mainly being carried out by major companies, or perhaps central government in some countries.

The product

In recent years, most of the most successful attractions have been those based on a *novel approach or a unique idea*. This is crucial at a time when the market is highly competitive and consumers are becoming increasingly sophisticated and demanding. A number of examples of attractions that were successful in the 1980s and 1990s illustrate this point:

- the London Eye Millennium Wheel, in London
- the state-of-the-art moving image technologies at the Futuroscope theme park, in France
- museums with universal themes ranging from erotica to children's toys.

However, simply having a unique idea does not guarantee success. For instance, in the UK the Millennium Dome in London, and the Earth Centre environmental theme park in South Yorkshire, were both very novel ideas but the former had major problems and the latter's future viability is still uncertain.

Of course, novel approaches and unique ideas do not stay so for long and, if the attraction is seen to be successful, competitors will soon be copying, adapting and even improving the approaches and ideas. Therefore attractions based on a new idea cannot rest on their laurels, they must always be seeking the next novel approach or unique idea.

Another important factor in relation to the product is location. The location of the attraction is very important to its prospects of success in three main ways. First, it determines the catchment area, which is based on how many people live within a certain journey time from the attraction, which can be from thirty minutes to several hours. The most successful attractions tend to be those which have a densely populated catchment area as this maximizes the number of potential day-trippers. Therefore, in the UK, an attraction in Greater Manchester has a much larger potential than an attraction in a sparsely populated region such as the north of Scotland or mid-Wales. In the case of certain types of attractions which require a mass market, such as theme parks, regional catchment areas appear to be only able to support one such attraction.

Second, it is easier for attractions if they are developed in existing tourism destinations as they can benefit from visits by people taking holidays in their catchment area. That is why attractions in regions like Cornwall in the UK and the Massif Central in France can attract significant numbers of visitors even though their catchment areas are sparsely populated. Attractions in such areas will, however, usually have a marked seasonal pattern of demand, reflecting the seasonality of holiday-making in the area.

Finally, although a few major attractions such as Alton Towers flourish in spite of being relatively difficult to travel to, the general consensus is that accessibility is vital to the success of most attractions. As most journeys to attractions are made by private car, road access is crucial, particularly in terms of the motorway network. Good road links effectively expand the attraction's catchment area, while being just a few miles off major roads can severely limit the potential visitor numbers of an attraction. Other accessibility issues include the suitability of access routes for coaches, the availability of car parking, and signposting, to make the attraction easy to find. For most attractions rail links are of only minor importance as rail travel is relatively little used for attraction visits. Only rarely is the close proximity of an airport or a ferry terminal significant to attractions: Legoland in Denmark and the Metro Centre in Gateshead are two exceptions.

Many successful attractions have a *variety of on-site attractions* to ensure that there is something for visitors of all types and tastes in all weather conditions. At Wigan Pier in the UK, for example, the attraction has actors, boat trips, a large steam engine and the Opie advertising collection, while the Albert Dock in Liverpool features shops, the Tate Gallery of the North, restaurants and museums. Focused attractions aiming at niche markets may not need or desire this range but most attractions almost invariably need a diversity of on-site attractions. Finally most attractions have recognized the importance of secondary on-site attractions such as shops, themed catering and entertainment.

Variety is also added at many successful attractions through *special events* which are often designed to encourage repeat visits or attract people interested in the theme of the event, who may not otherwise visit the attraction. To be successful, however, they must not be in conflict with the main theme or market of the attraction.

Visitors are increasingly seeking a *high-quality environment* for their day out, so there is a growing demand for cleanliness and an aesthetically pleasing environment at attractions. Customers are beginning to reject attractions which are not kept clean, where vandalism and graffiti is allowed to take hold, and where there is a general air of neglect.

Visitors are also demanding, and rewarding with their custom, good customer service at attractions. The attitude of staff and their competence is of great importance. It is important to ensure, therefore, that staff who come into contact with visitors are enthusiastic, motivated and well trained. This is a major challenge in an industry where salaries are not high and much of the labour comprises seasonal, casual staff.

Visitor facilities are also an important criterion for judging attractions in the mind of the visitor. It is therefore important that attractions provide first-class facilities such as safe car parks, clean toilets, parent-and-baby facilities and information services. Providing such facilities is expensive but is vital for satisfying customers.

The final important point about the product in this brief discussion is *price*. There is evidence to suggest that it is not the price charged for admission to an attraction which affects its success but whether the visitors feel they have received *value for money*. Interestingly, and reinforcing this view, the UK's most visited theme park (Alton Towers) is also the most expensive. The same is also true of theme parks in France and the USA.

Whether or not visitors perceive an attraction to offer value for money depends on:

- the amount of time spent on site
- the quality of environment, service and facilities
- the variety of on-site attractions.

Pricing policies that are not appreciated by customers often include the lack of family tickets, extra charges for car parking and charging separately for on-site attractions rather than offering an all-inclusive ticket that gives unlimited use of all on-site attractions.

It is important to recognize, however, that one of the things that influences a customer's judgement of whether or not the visit has been good value for money are outside the control of operators. Such factors include the cost of travelling to and from the site, visitors' expectations and the weather.

The market

Possibly the most important factor in the success of attractions in relation to the customer is to ensure that the attraction is targeting markets which are *growth markets*. A few examples of growth markets and changes in consumer tastes are outlined below to illustrate this point:

- growth in the older age groups, who increasingly have disposable income as well as leisure time
- a desire among many people to use their visit to an attraction to learn something new, whether it be learning a skill or gaining knowledge
- the wish of many people to participate or become actively involved at the attraction, for example, making a pot of one's own as well as, or instead of, watching a potter make a pot
- a desire among families to find attractions offering something for children to do
- the growing interest in green issues and healthy lifestyles
- the interest in 'leisure', rather than utilitarian, shopping.

Successful attractions will generally be those which tap into these growth markets and consumer behaviour trends.

It is also important to ensure that existing customers are satisfied with their visit as they will give *positive word-of-mouth recommendations* about it to friends and relatives. A survey, discussed in the Leisure Consultants report (1990b), showed that for 68 per cent of people in the UK, such recommendations were a very important consideration in their decision to visit an attraction. That is why the quality of the product offered is so important to the long-term success of the attraction.

The management of the attraction

Successful attractions tend to be those which are effectively managed. Some of the ways in which good management benefits attractions are discussed briefly below. It is important that attractions have *experienced professional managers* across all aspects of the operation. Attractions without such management are often weak in one or more areas, including marketing, financial control, the management of people and strategic planning. Much of the professional management that does exist in the attraction business is found in the private sector in organizations such as the Tussauds Group.

Perhaps the most crucial aspect of attraction management, and often one of the most ignored, is *marketing*. Successful attractions are usually those which have a systematic, professional approach to marketing, which is characterized by factors such as:

- giving adequate attention to market research so that they know their market and its tastes and preferences
- recognizing that marketing is not just about producing brochures and placing advertisements
- taking a longer-term strategic view rather than just a short-term tactical approach
- appreciating that there is not one big 'public' but lots of different market segments with different needs and desires
- spending a significant proportion of turnover on marketing year in, year out, rather than just spending money on an ad hoc basis in response to crises
- accepting the importance of word-of-mouth recommendation and acknowledging the value of giving the existing visitor a first rate experience to encourage positive recommendations
- employing specialist sales and marketing staff while training all staff to realize that they are also part of the marketing effort because to the customer they are all part of the core product

Strongly related to marketing is the ability of good attraction managers to respond faster and more effectively than competitors to changes in the *business environment*. These changes could be as diverse as technological developments, the state of the economy, new laws or changing consumer tastes, but they all have one thing in common: they are all potential opportunities or threats for the attraction and the response of attraction managers will determine whether they will ultimately be an opportunity or a threat. Responding positively to the business environment requires good environmental scanning on a systematic and objective basis.

Following on from the last two factors is the related subject of *competitors*. Successful attractions tend to be those which identify their competitors and set out to achieve competitive advantage over them, attractions that are leaders rather than followers. This is easier said than done as many operators, particularly in the public sector, do not believe they are in competition with anyone. While this is not correct, it is true that it is sometimes difficult to identify the competitor for some attractions. Sometimes they can be different types of attraction or even totally different types of activity altogether.

As well as looking outwards towards competitors, most successful attractions also *monitor their own performance* on a regular basis to allow them to make continuous improvements. These improvements must include the quality of the product they offer, the way they operate, and how they market themselves.

Finally, in a fast-changing market such as the visitor attraction market it is vital that attractions are always anticipating market changes and *planning for the future*. It is all too easy to become obsessed with the present and operate 'crisis management'. To be successful in the long term, attractions need to have a clear vision of where they want to be in five or ten years' time and know how they are going to get there.

The Disneyland Paris experience

Proof of how complex a sector the attractions business is, and how difficult it is even for experts always to be successful, has been clearly illustrated by the Disneyland Paris experience, which it is worth studying in some detail.

For several years after it opened in 1992, there was great debate over its long-term survival. It is interesting, now, to look back at the reasons why Disneyland Paris failed to live up to the expectations of its investors in its early days.

The scale of the problem is clear if one looks at a few figures. First, the attraction was forecast to generate a net profit of some £71 million in 1993 while in reality it lost some £600 million in the same period. Expected revenue in 1993 of £781 million turned out to be much lower at just £560 million. The problem was not so much caused by low visitor numbers but rather by the fact that visitors spent less than expected per head during their visit.

Perhaps we can identify a number of reasons why Disneyland Paris was not as successful initially as its owners hoped or, indeed, many people expected. The main reasons put forward for the relative failure of the attraction included the following:

1 Its opening coincided with a major recession in Western Europe that had dampened tourism demand in all the main target markets.
2 The location near Paris means that the attraction suffers cold, wet weather for part of the year. This led to demand being greatly reduced at these times of the year. This was in contrast to the Disney attractions in Florida and California where the climate is good enough to ensure that there is all year round demand for the attraction.
3 Prices were perceived to be high for the European market, particularly for the hotels and food.
4 Visitors resented the fact that alcohol was not available with meals, which is alien to European consumer culture in general, and French traditions in particular.

5 Potential visitors were put off visiting the attraction by the rule forbidding visitors to bring food into the park with them, so visitors are forced to buy the expensive food which was provided by the attraction's own outlets.

6 The product offered by Disneyland Paris lacked appeal for some market segments, for example, the lack of 'white-knuckle' rides makes it less attractive to younger, more adventurous visitors.

7 The complex was seen by many Europeans as an insensitive piece of almost economic imperialism by a major US corporation at a time when many in Europe have become concerned at American influences on European culture.

8 There was a perception that the quality of service at Disneyland Paris is perhaps not as good as that in the American parks because of the difficulty of getting European staff to behave in the US tradition. This may well have disappointed many early visitors who had previously visited the American parks and they may well have passed on these negative impressions to potential visitors. Staffing was undoubtedly a problem and many ex-Disneyland Paris staff were clearly unhappy about their experience of working for a Disney theme park.

Disneyland Paris was sucked into a vicious circle. Its early problems resulted in negative media coverage which, in turn, persuaded many potential visitors not to visit the attraction. It is always difficult to break out of such a vicious circle.

Since its early days, Disneyland Paris has changed its management team and is now seen to be successful, both financially and in terms of customer satisfaction. Neverthless, the early problems at Disneyland Paris show that even an experienced attraction operator can make mistakes.

Conclusion

There is no guarantee of success for an attraction that follows any set of principles. Furthermore, as well as all these tangible factors there is no doubt that many successful attractions also have something special, an intangible 'magic' about them which is impossible to create artificially. Nevertheless, it is more likely to be present at attractions which are professionally managed and are based on an innovative concept.

Discussion points and essay questions

1 Discuss what you consider to be the three most important factors in determining the success or failure of visitor attractions.
2 Evaluate the reasons why its location is often thought to be the key to success for attractions.
3 Discuss the reasons why Disneyland Paris has been transformed from a relative failure into a success story in the past five years or so.

Select what you consider to be a successful attraction. Analyse the attraction, including its history, and identify the factors which have led to its current success. Suggest what could happen to turn the attraction into a failure.

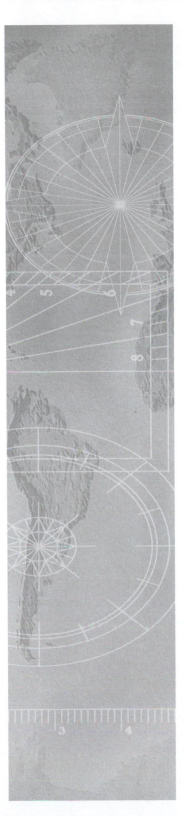

Financing visitor attraction projects

Introduction

This chapter examines the ways in which visitor attraction projects can be funded and the issues surrounding the financing of attraction projects. It focuses on the capital funding required to set up the attraction rather than the running costs and revenue once the attraction is up and running. This latter subject is covered in the later chapter on financial management. However, while this present chapter concentrates on the development of new built, human-made attractions, it does also look at major new projects at existing attractions, which require capital funding. These could include new rides at theme parks, or large new exhibitions and displays at museums and galleries.

The purposes for which capital funding is required

Capital funding is required for:

- site acquisition and the work necessary to prepare the site, including landscaping, for its new use as an attraction
- the cost of constructing new buildings and structures or adapting those already existing on the site
- fitting out and decorating new buildings and structures, and the installation of equipment

- expenditure relating to the launch and public opening of the attraction that is incurred before any income from visitors is generated. This includes pre-launch marketing and the cost of staffing which is required in the development period
- a sum of money to cover the costs of the attraction in its early days of opening before it starts to generate significant amounts of income.

This list is highly generalized and therefore perhaps it is helpful to illustrate it by considering a hypothetical project such as a new industrial heritage attraction based on an existing complex of semi-derelict canal-side warehouses and a textile mill. In this situation capital funds would be required for the following purposes:

- the purchase of the freehold or a long leasehold on the existing land and buildings
- structural repairs to the buildings to make them sound and safe
- internal modifications to adapt the buildings to their new use, for example putting extra floors in the warehouse which may consist of just a single tall chamber
- the construction of new buildings and structures such as toilets and car parks
- the refurbishment of existing mill machinery which will be an exhibit in the new attraction
- the acquisition of artefacts for the museum exhibitions and displays
- historical research
- the design and creation of the exhibition and displays in terms of graphic panels, dummies, audiovisual shows and so on
- the equipping of the ancillary facilities and support services, such as catering and retail outlets
- the purchase of stock required for the opening of the attraction, such as merchandise, guidebooks and food
- the salaries of staff who must be recruited before opening, which is most staff, together with the costs of training
- the cost of establishing communication and management information systems, for example, the cost of telephones and computers
- pre-launch marketing including advertising, mailshots, literature production and distribution, and the development of databases
- professional fees for architects and surveyors, for example, together with display designers and engineers
- a sum of money to cover contingencies and to cover the opening costs in the early days before income reaches significant levels.

Some of these elements are specific to the type of attraction in our example, while others are standard for all types of attractions.

To some extent the cost of some of the items will vary depending on whether the project is being carried out by the public, private or voluntary sectors. For example, in the case of voluntary organizations, costs could be reduced by the use of voluntary labour.

Table 8.1 gives an idea of the cost of attraction development in the UK, based on an updating of 1992 estimates.

Sources of funding

Funding for attraction projects can come from three sources, namely, the public, private and voluntary sectors. It also comes in two forms:

1 Direct financial contributions, for example loans and grants.
2 Indirect financial 'help in kind' that, while not giving the developer money, provides goods and services which reduce the capital cost of the project. Examples of this include land provided free of charge or at very low cost by the public sector and the provision of infrastructure such as roads, which are built by the public sector. Such action by the French government greatly reduced the capital costs of the Disneyland Paris project for the Disney organization. Other examples of such indirect aid include leasing and franchising.

Direct funding: private sector

Most direct funding comes from the private sector in the form of:

- overdrafts
- loans: short, medium and long term
- commercial mortgages
- venture capital
- equity
- business expansion scheme.

For most developers the clearing banks may well be their main source of funding.

Overdrafts are a common source of short-term finance which can help provide working capital to cover expenditure such as the purchase of stock for retail outlets. This type of finance is not usually used for major capital purchases, but can help with cash flow in the period before the attraction begins to earn income on a significant scale.

Short-term loans are generally taken out over three years or less and are often used for a specific purpose, for example to buy a particular item such as a new ride at a theme park. They can be quite expensive to service and the interest rate may be up to 5 per cent above the base rate. However, some banks may grant interest payment or capital repayment holidays of several months' duration to help newly established attraction projects.

Medium-term loans usually run from three to ten years and are usually secured. They are often used for buying fixed assets, such as property, or extending an attraction. 'Repayment holidays' of up to two years can be negotiated and sometimes repayments can be seasonally weighted for tourism businesses where cashflow is highly seasonal.

Table 8.1 Estimated sample costs of different types of attraction

Function	Description	Cost per square metre (£)	Functional unit	Cost per functional unit (£)
Museums	New displays to existing museum including redecorations and new layouts	200–400	–	–
	Conversion of warehouse into museum, including shop/café and public toilet	750–1200	–	–
	Heritage centre, including exhibition areas, shops, cafeteria, viewing galleries, lecture rooms, public toilets, display areas and car parking	1600–1850	–	–
Zoos	Creation of children's zoo, including landscaping animal shelter, paddock areas and enclosures	75–200	–	–
	Animal house including viewing galleries, display areas and animal quarters	1200–2000	–	–
	Aviary centre	600–750	–	–
Leisure parks	Children's outdoor adventure/theme fun park, including landscaping and individually designed play/adventure equipment	–	Play equipment	12 000–20 000
	Conversion of warehouse into children's indoor fun house, including play equipment	–	Play equipment	13 000–20 000
Rides	Boats for canal/river sightseeing trips	–	Seat	–
Visitor centre	New visitor centre, including cafeteria, public toilets, reception/meeting area and office	600–900	–	–
	Extension to provide offices and exhibition areas	550–900	–	–
	Conversion of outbuilding into visitor centre, including shop and tea room	400–600	–	–
Tourist information centres	New centre	600–800	–	–
	Refurbishment of existing centre	350–550	–	–

Category	Description			
Catering	New cafeteria, including public toilets and display area	650–850	Person	700–900
	New cafeteria, including public toilets, office, patio area, shop and car parking	800–950	Person	1900–3000
	Conversion of existing building to provide public toilets and catering facilities	450–600	Person	600–850
Theatres	New theatre and arts centre, including public toilets, restaurant, bars and lounges, backstage facilities and car parking	1200–1800	Seat	8000–10 000
	Refurbishment of existing theatre	900–1500	Seat	6000–8000
Cinemas	Single screen cinema, including public toilets, bar lounge and car parking	1300–2000	–	–
Exhibition halls	Halls, including public toilets, cafeterias, bars, shops and car parking	1000–1350	–	–
Aquaria	Sea life centre, including exhibiting galleries, dolphin pool and arena, cafeteria, public toilets and car parking	1500–2000	–	–
Leisure pools	Fun pool, laned pool, viewing areas, changing facilities, catering/bar area and car parking	1000–1300	–	–
Flumes	Fun pool and laned pool, wave machine, flumes, machine, flumes, water features, terrace areas, changing facilities, catering and bar areas, shops and car parking	1500–2200	–	–
Sports halls	Main sports hall and changing facilities	500–700	–	–
	Main sports hall, gym, changing facilities, catering and bar/viewing areas and car parking	850–1000	–	–
Ice rink	Indoor ice rink, including changing facilities, catering and bar/viewing areas, shops and car parking	900–1200	–	–

Source: adapted and updated from English Tourist Board and James Nisbet and Partners (1992)

Long-term loans are usually provided for a period of more than ten years. They are usually used for fixed assets with a long lifespan, such as buildings. They are secured loans, usually using the freehold or leasehold of the property as security. Normally it is possible to choose between fixed interest rates and variable rates related to the base rate.

Commercial mortgages are available to finance property purchases. They are very flexible because of the opportunity to choose between repayment or endowment mortgages. Sometimes a short capital repayment holiday can be arranged to reduce an attraction's expenditure in its early days. These mortgages can have fixed or variable interest rates and are available from building societies as well as banks.

Venture capital is another possibility for prospective attraction developers who are new or young companies. It provides them with the capital funding they need to realize their full potential. In return for their investment the venture capitalists will require a stake in the attraction operator's company, a say in decision-making and a high rate of return on investment. A variation on this is *development capital*, which is provided to enable existing established companies with good prospects to expand. Thus, this might be an appropriate source of funding for attraction operators wanting to change the nature of an existing attraction or expand it to attract new markets. Such funding is provided by pension funds, merchant banks and insurance companies, as well as by the high street banks.

Equity, or the sale of shares, is occasionally used to fund major attraction projects such as Disneyland Paris. Investors are attracted to such projects by the chance to achieve a good rate of return on the investment. Raising finance in this way means the initial capital cost for the developer is reduced but it does have a negative side in that it means profits will have to be shared with the investors and, ultimately, control of the attraction could be lost to other shareholders.

In reality, most attractions will use a combination of the above funding methods to finance new attraction projects. Whatever methods they use, their chances of receiving financial support from private sector sources will be greatly enhanced if their application to prospective funders has the following four characteristics:

1 The attraction developer has a successful track record in the tourism industry.
2 There is an experienced management team with a good record of achievement in the attraction business.
3 The developer is perceived to have substantial financial resources of their own together with collateral on which loans can be secured.
4 A very precise estimate is offered of the costs of the proposed project.

We have focused on external sources of funding, but for many attraction operators new projects will often be funded by their own capital or through profits generated within the business. This may be sufficient for projects which are on a modest scale but is unlikely to be sufficient to finance major new projects. There is of course an 'opportunity cost' involved in using internal funding and therefore most operators use external funding sources as well as utilizing internal funds. One of the main attractions of using internal funding is keeping debts and gearing ratios as low as possible.

Direct funding: public sector

The public sector, including the European Commission, central government and local government, provide a variety of types of direct financial assistance for attraction projects. However, the number of schemes and the agencies involved makes for a very complex situation. We will explore this issue by focusing on the situation in Europe.

European Commission • • •

The European Commission provides grants and loans for all kinds of attraction projects based on where they are located and their objectives. Assistance is available for projects in:

- urban areas where industrial industries are in decline, with resulting unemployment
- regions where average incomes are low by European standards and where there is a need for projects to help stimulate tourism development and the economic benefits it brings
- rural areas where the rural and agricultural economy is in decline and there is a need to develop rural tourism to compensate for this decline.

Most of the project funding is controlled by strict criteria.

European Commission funding has had a major impact on attraction development in Europe in recent years, with new heritage centres in Ireland, improvements at archaeological museums in Greece, rural attractions in Spain and new flagship attractions in the urban areas of the UK for example.

This funding will, of course, in the future also be available to the countries which look likely to join the European Union (EU) in the forthcoming years, including Malta, Cyprus, Poland, Hungary, the Czech Republic and Turkey. This development will reduce funding in existing EU member countries as resources are diverted to the new member countries.

Central government • • •

The 1995 edition of this book noted eleven different central government schemes in the UK, which were providing direct government funding for attraction projects. These have now reduced and the government is less keen on directly supporting attraction projects. Its enthusiasm for them is unlikely to have been increased by the problems with the Millennium Dome in London.

Instead the UK government has preferred attraction projects to be funded indirectly via the National Lottery. However, it is still a political decision as to how Lottery funds are spent. As we have seen elsewhere in this book this Lottery funding has been seen as a case of unfair competition' by existing private attractions.

In other countries some governments continue to invest heavily in attractions, while in others, such as the USA, the emphasis is still on private sector funding.

The problems with the financial performance of some UK attractions, developed with National Lottery funding, perhaps proves that the American approach is the best, at least from a financial point of view. The emphasis on private funding has also been at the heart of attraction development in Asia.

Local government

Local government in the UK lacks the resources to provide much financial assistance to new attraction projects. However, in countries where decentralization has strengthened local government in recent years, such as France and Spain, local government has played a major role in funding attractions. We have seen this in the cases of Futuroscope and the developments in Barcelona for example.

In this section we have split the public sector finance into three different sources. However, with major projects, normally all these sources will be combined with private sector funding, to create a funding package. Often each piece of the package is dependent on the others being in place. Attraction developers, therefore, have to keep all the potential funders content, or risk the whole project failing to secure funding.

For example, the Eden Project, an £80 million project in Cornwall in the UK, which opened in 2001, received funding from the following sources:

	£ (million)
Millennium Commission	40.0
English Partnerships (government agency)	3.9
European Regional Development Fund	10.0
Miscellaneous grants	1.3
Charitable donations	0.5
Loans and private sector funding	20.5
Sponsorships and donations in kind	3.8
Total	80.0

Source: *Locum Destination Review* (Spring 2001)

Direct funding: voluntary sector

Voluntary organizations often play a limited role in the funding of attraction projects and some voluntary trusts provide modest grants for certain types of projects, particularly those with a strong conservation or educational flavour. Fundraising by voluntary bodies can also provide direct funding for attraction projects which have these two main objectives.

Having looked at the scope of direct funding for attraction products, it is now appropriate to look at the indirect sources which reduce the capital costs of projects in a variety of ways rather than contributing money directly to them. These, too, can be looked at in terms of the private, public and voluntary sectors.

Indirect funding: private sector

Attractions are increasingly using leasing to reduce the capital costs of projects. The attraction can make use of an asset or a piece of equipment in return for payment of a rental over a period of time. The leasing company continues to own the asset, which usually never becomes the property of the attraction, although arrangements can be made for the attraction to buy the asset at an agreed price once the lease expires. Leasing can give attractions the use of equipment that would otherwise require upfront capital funding while paying for it out of revenue. Many items of equipment may now be leased by attractions, including cars, computers, theme park rides and catering equipment.

Traditional *hire purchase* may also be used to reduce the capital cost of projects. The attraction pays a deposit for a piece of equipment and then pays regular amounts until ultimately the attraction owns the equipment. The advantage is that the attraction enjoys the use of the equipment from day one but it can spread the payment over a period. However, for this advantage there is a cost, in that the total purchase cost under hire purchase is higher than the cost of purchasing the article with one initial payment.

Sale and leaseback arrangements are also becoming increasingly popular with attraction developers and operators. Property and major capital equipment is sold to a third party to raise finance and is then leased back from the third party on a long-term basis.

Some attractions reduce the initial costs of their investment by the use of on-site *concessions and franchises*. Third parties are invited to set up and operate units such as retail units and catering outlets on site. These third parties pay the costs of setting up their units and then pay either a rent or a percentage of profits. The attraction operator usually ensures that the concessionaires and franchisees meet certain quality standards to ensure that they do not compromise the reputation of the attraction. While this type of arrangement reduces the initial capital costs of attraction projects it means that often the operator will not receive the full financial benefits of a successful attraction.

Finally, *sponsorship* can often help to reduce the capital costs of attractions by providing 'help in kind', in terms of labour and materials, for which the operator pays nothing or a reduced price. Organizations provide sponsorship in return for some perceived marketing benefit, of which the three main ones are:

- an improved image of the sponsoring organization
- a greater awareness of the organization's products and services
- direct sales of the organization's products and services.

Gaining sponsorship is difficult and success is usually based on the following factors:

- precise targeting of potential sponsors
- matching the desires of the potential sponsor with the attraction product
- providing opportunities for the sponsors to promote and publicize their products and services
- attracting positive media coverage to help maximize the sponsor's exposure to its target audience.

While indirect funding from the private sector tends to be based on one or more of these five main types, indirect funding from the public sector is based on a bewildering range of possibilities.

Indirect funding: public sector

The public sector – central government and local authorities – can help reduce the capital cost of attraction projects in a number of ways, including by providing:

- land and buildings free of charge or at less than the true market value, sometimes in return for a stake in the enterprise
- tax 'holidays' and tax allowances on capital expenditure
- expensive infrastructure such as transport links and drainage
- duty concessions on the import of materials
- labour availability through job training schemes funded by the public sector.

Again, in the UK central government ideology and local authority spending constraints have limited the extent of such assistance in recent years, while in other countries, notably France, the opposite has been the case.

Indirect funding: voluntary sector

The main way in which the voluntary sector can help reduce the direct capital costs of attraction projects is through the provision of voluntary labour. Volunteers are very important in the development of certain types of attractions such as heritage centres and steam railways. This reduces the cost of labour for construction work, fitting out, decoration and the installation of exhibits, which for some attractions can be the largest single item of capital expenditure.

Although a complex subject, some general conclusions can be drawn about attraction funding. Private sector attraction developers tend to rely on private sources of direct and indirect funding together with public sector grants, loans and indirect funding. Public sector operators usually rely on their own resources together with public sector grants. They make very little use of private sources and only limited use of voluntary assistance. Finally, voluntary bodies tend to rely on their own resources and public sector funds, although wealthier groups may also use private sector sources.

The criteria used by each sector to decide whether or not to support particular projects are even more clearly distinguished. Private sector funders tend to look for projects that have a good prospect of financial success and will provide a good rate of return on their investment. On the other hand, the public sector tends to judge projects in terms of their job creation potential and their ability to help stimulate economic development and the regeneration of urban areas. Finally, the voluntary sector usually looks for projects which have conservation and/or educational objectives.

Attracting external funding

It is important to recognize that just as the sources of funding are numerous and differ between projects, likewise the ways of obtaining finance also vary. They differ in terms of procedures, criteria, paperwork, rules, conditions and the length of time taken to make decisions, to mention just a few of the factors.

When trying to attract funding from any source, attraction developers need to decide how much money they need, when they need it, how long they need it for and what security they are able to offer. They also need to ensure that they approach the right organizations and that they present a good case.

Business plans

Business plans are designed to demonstrate to potential funders that the proposed project is financially viable. But it must also persuade the financial institutions that the developers are a good risk and that the attraction will be professionally managed. The business plan must cover all the factors that are relevant to the success or failure of the project, not just finance. Such plans have a lot in common with feasibility studies, although they tend to be wider in scope and are designed to persuade a third party that the project merits investment. Whereas the feasibility study is supposed to be a neutral document that objectively helps the attraction operator decide whether or not the project is viable.

There is no standard format for a business plan but it is usually expected to include a number of elements:

- the *objectives* of the project and of the organization which is behind the scheme
- the *experience and skills of the senior management* in the organization and whether or not there are gaps that need to be filled

- the *corporate structure of the attraction operator*, for example whether they are a limited company, a sole trader or a voluntary trust
- the *core product and services* the attraction will offer and the costs involved in providing these goods and services
- the size and nature of the *market* and the trends in the market, together with the costs involved in attracting the market to visit the attraction
- the way in which *price* will be determined and the price that will need to be charged to achieve a satisfactory profit margin
- who the *competitors* will be and how the proposed price relates to the prices charged by these competitors
- the *proposed site* and its suitability for use as an attraction; information should also be provided relating to the costs of converting the site, buying the necessary equipment, whether that is theme park rides or museum displays, and the cost of maintenance
- the proposed *suppliers* of goods and services to the attraction and issues such as quality control and credit terms for suppliers
- estimates of the *staffing* numbers, including how many will be permanent or seasonal, full-time or part-time. Potential funders will expect to see figures on staffing costs including the costs of recruiting staff and training as well as wages and salaries
- the *management information and control systems* that the developer proposes to use
- *financial forecasts*, including both profit and loss accounts and cash flow projections. While the former is an accounting concept that is not strictly 'real', cash flow is very real. It looks at the actual way in which money will come into and go out of the attraction. Forecasting is a problem for attractions and will be discussed in more detail later in the chapter.

Nevertheless, potential funders will expect attraction developers to show a thorough understanding of the capital and revenue costs of the project, together with the likely income over a period (usually five years or more). They will also expect the developer to know, realistically, when the attraction is likely to become profitable, when it will be able to repay loans and the rate of return it will offer for investors.

Before submitting the business plan for consideration by financial institutions it is a good idea to look at it critically to identify any weaknesses that may give the institutions a bad impression of the project. These could include a lack of experienced local labour, a site with no room for future expansion, or highly seasonal demand.

Finally, in addition to the written business plan those seeking loans or investment from financial institutions should prepare a good verbal presentation of their case and should ensure that they can answer any questions the potential funders are likely to ask.

Financial forecasts and projections

The core of the business plan will be the financial forecasts and projections, which will have four main elements:

- the capital cost
- revenue expenditure, year by year, including the cost of servicing loans and providing a return for investors
- income, year by year
- profit and loss figures, year by year.

It is normal to produce projections for a number of years (usually at least five).

The capital costs are not too difficult to forecast as many of the costs are known in advance, for example the cost of buying premises, and others can be reasonably accurately forecast by professionals, such as the fitting out of museums. However, costs can escalate if unforeseen problems arise, for example if the site has unexpected problems. Likewise, *revenue expenditure* is not too difficult to project with a reasonable degree of accuracy. The elements that have to be included under the expenditure category include:

- staff, including on-costs such as National Insurance and employers' pension contributions
- the cost of goods to be sold in the retail and catering outlets
- heating and lighting
- maintenance
- communications – telephone and postage for example
- loan repayments, debt charges and interest payments
- ground rents
- replacement of furniture, fittings and equipment
- depreciation
- taxes
- insurance.

Many of these are either known in advance (ground rent, for example) or can be forecast on the basis of professional advice or the previous experience of the organization (for example staffing costs).

However, while many of the costs are fixed and therefore not too difficult to forecast, it is very difficult to project the variable costs because they are totally related to visitor numbers and type. For example, the cost of food and souvenirs to be sold on site will depend on how many visitors come and what they will want to buy. Even experienced attractions operators recognize that all attractions are different and, therefore, it is difficult to predict the precise size and value of the market for a new attraction. The projected expenditure figures can also be seriously disrupted by unforeseen circumstances, for example if an expensive piece of equipment breaks down and needs to be repaired or replaced.

The hardest set of figures to estimate are the income projections as they are largely dependent on the size and nature of the market for the attraction and factors outside the control of the attraction operator, as can be seen from the following list of some of the main categories of income:

- entrance fees and charges
- retail sales
- catering sales
- meeting room hire
- payment from concessions and franchises
- sponsorship
- grants.

The first four categories will depend totally on the numbers and type of visitors, while the next two will also be influenced by the nature of the demand for the attraction.

As attractions tend to offer reductions for certain categories such as schoolchildren and senior citizens, the proportion of visitors who pay such lower entrance charges is crucial to attraction income. For example, let us imagine an attraction charges £3 for adults and £1.50 for senior citizens and school parties, and that overall it receives 100 000 visitors a year. If 90 000 of these were adults who paid the full fee and not reduced rates, its income would be £285 000. If, on the other hand, the visitor numbers were reversed so 90 000 were concession-paying visitors, the income would be £165 000, a massive difference. It is also likely that adults will spend more on food and drink and souvenirs than senior citizens and schoolchildren.

Cash flow projections and management

The forecasts we have just been considering are based on the income and expenditure, year by year. However many attractions are highly seasonal businesses where income and expenditure vary dramatically between seasons and have distinct peaks and troughs. It is therefore important that attraction developers also forecast their month by month or even week by week cash flow to ensure that they always have sufficient revenue coming in to meet their expenses at any one time. Many attractions have high costs in their early days, such as the purchase of goods to be sold in the retail outlets and catering units, while they may have to wait for the peak season for the bulk of their annual income. If an attraction opens in March in time for the Easter period, it will have to spend considerable money on stock but wait until the months of July and August to receive up to three-quarters of its annual income. It is therefore usual for attractions to project their income and expenditure at least on a month by month basis to allow them to see where cash flow problems may occur. They will then try to reschedule some elements of their expenditure to relate them more closely to their peak periods of income generation. Furthermore, because of the heavy 'front-loading' of expenditure in the early days of an attraction's life before income levels become substantial, it is common for many new attractions to build a sum, to cover this expenditure in the early days, into the capital costs of the attraction.

Sensitivity analysis

All financial projections and forecasts are based on a set of assumptions, such as visitor numbers and expenditure, income and interest rates, in terms of the effect they will have on the cost of servicing debts, for example. However we have seen earlier in the book that the business environment of attractions is highly complex and volatile. It is therefore only logical to realize that these assumptions will often turn out to be wrong, so it is necessary to produce a number of possible projections based upon different assumptions and scenarios. This is the basis of sensitivity analysis, which examines the impact on the projections of changes in the basic assumptions.

The factors that could be taken into account in a sensitivity analysis for an attraction project could include:

- changes affecting demand, such as the state of the economy, trends in consumer tastes and preferences, and modifications to the transport network that may make the attraction more or less accessible to its potential market. Even changes in the weather can have a vital impact on demand; for example a wet national public holiday can be disastrous for an open-air attraction
- changes affecting the operating costs of the attraction, including new legal requirements, modifications to interest rates and increases or reductions in taxes.

Many developers operate a simplified and manageable form of sensitivity analysis by producing 'best possible' and 'worst possible' case projections in addition to their projections based on the set of assumptions, which are currently accurate.

Project evaluation and investment appraisal

Having prepared financial forecasts which are as accurate as possible, it is necessary for the potential funder to evaluate the project and appraise it as an investment opportunity. That is what we will now consider by looking at the three methods of investment appraisal which have traditionally been used:

1 *Return on capital employed*. This is the ratio of the average annual profit of the attraction expressed as a percentage of the original capital investment. This is a relatively simple and straightforward method which is widely used. For example, if the profit is £50 000 and the capital cost was £500 000 the rate of return on investment would be 10 per cent.
2 *Payback period*. This is also a popular method of investment appraisal and is based on the number of years it will take to recoup the original capital investment. However it does have a weakness in that it does not take into account the reduced value of the original capital over time because of inflation.
3 *Discounted cash flow* (net present value or internal rate of return).

Furthermore, in the case of projects where at least part of the investment comes from the sale of shares, a number of other methods are used to evaluate projects. These include the price/earning ratio, the dividend cover ratio, earnings per share and the dividend yield.

However, it would be wrong to give the impression that the project evaluation and investment appraisal is based only on financial information. Potential funders will take a number of other factors into account when evaluating a proposed project. A brief list of some such factors might include:

- the confidence which potential funders have in the attraction developer and the experience and expertise of its senior management team
- the financial assets of the organization and its ability to withstand losses in the early days of the attraction's life
- the amount of security and collateral that can be offered by the organization
- the objectives of the potential funding institution, in other words, perhaps it wishes to branch out into the attraction field or, conversely, it may want to leave the leisure sector altogether.

The problems of attracting private sector finance for attraction projects

First, attraction projects are seen to be a high-risk investment. There have been spectacular failures (Millennium Dome) and major projects that have failed to leave the drawing board, all of which have made potential funders nervous of investing in attraction projects. Furthermore, attraction sites are highly specialized and inflexible, so, if an attraction failed, it would be very difficult to find a buyer for the site unless by chance someone wanted to use the site for its original purpose, which is very unlikely. Otherwise the cost of converting the site to a new use would be very high, whereas offices and shops are much more standardized and their conversion to meet the needs of a new owner is usually relatively easy and inexpensive.

Second, because of the rapid changes in consumer preferences and the resulting shortening of the attraction product life cycle, attraction projects not only have high start-up costs, but also need regular expensive new developments to maintain their competitiveness. This means they need regular substantial injections of capital, with no guarantee of success. Furthermore, the shortening life cycle means the payback period for investment can be short, perhaps just three or four years. This puts great pressure on the attraction to generate high annual profits that may be unrealistic in a volatile market which is influenced by factors outside the control of the attraction operator.

For these reasons investing in attractions has not been popular with many financial institutions and most attractions find it difficult to raise private sector capital.

The previous section has focused on obtaining external private sector capital funding for private sector human-made new-build attractions.

There are, of course, a number of possible exceptions to this model of capital funding. For example, there are *private companies seeking direct public sector funding and indirect financial assistance* such as grants, loans, free land and tax 'holidays' for example. This usually involves negotiating with the funding bodies and meeting conditions whether they relate to the location of the project or the number of jobs that will be created. Public sector funding will usually only cover a proportion of the costs of the project, and the decision-making period is often too long for private sector developers.

Another possibility is *an attraction project developed by the public sector*, whether it be central government or local authorities. Funding tends to be through their own resources (income from taxes and activities) or through public or voluntary sector grants and loans offered by the European Commission or, in the case of local authorities, by central government. Again the applicants must meet the conditions relating to the grant and loans. One problem for local authorities in the UK, apart from recent government constraints on their spending, is the fact that by law they are often unable to use money collected from one source to invest in a different activity. Public bodies in some other countries do not appear to have similar problems. Finally, as the public sector does not usually attempt to make a profit, the main criteria for funding a project will be its social and economic benefits rather than the 'profit' it might make. This means that public sector projects are rarely attractive to private sector financial institutions.

A third possible exception to the capital funding model is *attraction projects developed by voluntary sector organizations*, which are mainly funded through public and voluntary sector grants together with money raised from the fundraising activities of the organization itself. Wealthier voluntary bodies may also raise funds from the private sector.

Management buy-outs

In recent years a new phenomenon has been seen in the leisure industry which, while not a way of funding projects as such, does have an impact on project funding, namely the management buy-out. In the rationalization caused by the recession in the UK in the 1990s many organizations sought to divest themselves of non-core businesses, sometimes through sales to former management teams, who acquired equity in the business. It is thought that this equity gives a strong incentive to managers to maximize profitability, which can make such enterprises attractive to potential investors. The equity may also be extended to the workforce who may be encouraged to invest their own money in the enterprise. An example of management buy-out in the attractions field is Wookey Hole caves in Somerset, which was divested by the Tussauds Group, the owners of Alton Towers, Warwick Castle, Chessington World of Adventures and Madame Tussauds. Other management buy-outs have also been created by the contracting out of local authority services such as leisure complexes and sports centres.

Conclusion

We have seen that yet again the attractions world is a highly complex one, this time in terms of how projects are funded. Furthermore, we have seen that there are significant differences in the financing of projects between the public and private sectors. One thing that is certain, however, is that in a highly competitive and volatile environment attractions that are undercapitalized and lack the funding to regularly update and relaunch themselves will usually be the attractions that fail.

Discussion points and essay questions

1 Using examples, discuss the reasons why many investors seem reluctant to invest in attraction projects.
2 Discuss the contention that government grant aid for attraction projects amounts to unfair competition for other attractions, and encourages the development of non-viable attractions.
3 Critically evaluate the importance of cash flow in the attractions business.

Exercise

Devise a concept for a hypothetical new attraction. Then develop a detailed business plan for the attraction, following the format outlined in this chapter.

CHAPTER 9

Designing visitor attractions

Introduction

This chapter looks at the process of designing visitor attractions. It focuses on tangible human-made attractions and considers design from a number of angles:

1 What we design at visitor attractions.
2 The reasons why we take such time and trouble to design these features of attractions.
3 Who does and who should design visitor attractions.
4 The different objectives that designers have to attempt to meet.
5 Design and external audiences.
6 The constraints that are placed on attraction designers.

What do we design?

Attractions generally consist of a whole range of elements which all need designing, whether the attraction is completely new or is adapted from existing buildings and structures. These elements include:

- the main buildings and structures in terms of their size, form, appearance, colour and materials
- the ways in which the interiors of the buildings and structures are subdivided and their fitting out and decoration

- the layout of the site as a whole and the location of buildings and structures in relation to the spaces between them
- the design of the open spaces on the site and their appearance (landscaping and paving for example)
- the route footpaths on site will take and the materials that will cover their surfaces
- the location and form of site 'furniture' such as signposts and litter bins
- the siting, form and appearance of on-site support services such as car parks, shops, toilets and catering outlets
- the entrances to the site and possible new access roads
- on-site transport systems such as tramways.

This is just a short list and, clearly, the precise mixture of elements will vary from site to site and from attraction to attraction. However, whatever the specific mixture, one principle remains true always, namely, that although the site consists of a variety of elements it must be designed as an integrated whole.

Successful attraction design is based on the synergies which are created by the way all the elements of the attraction interact with each other. This is true in terms of how efficiently the site will operate just as much as the aesthetic pleasure visitors will derive from the attraction. This highlights one of the key problems of attraction design – that attractions must meet a number of objectives some of which are not always compatible.

When designing attractions the people involved must be aware of the fact that they are not just designing physical buildings and spaces. Their design also sets the parameters for the visitor experience. In other words, the way they design the tangible elements of the attraction will shape the intangible visitor experience. For example, poorly designed entrances which act as bottlenecks, long walks between on-site attractions and a lack of cover for visitors would all greatly reduce the enjoyment of a family visit on a wet day.

Why do we design?

Design is the way in which we give form to our ideas and the design process allows us to refine our original concept. There are clearly a number of obvious reasons why attractions are consciously designed:

- It gives guidance to the people who have the job of turning ideas into physical reality such as builders and landscape gardeners.
- It ensures that the best possible use is made of resources, including the site itself as well as money and labour.
- It is the way in which an abstract idea is turned into a tangible form that will attract visitors.
- The design itself is important in terms of obtaining planning permission and helping persuade potential funders to invest in a project, as visual representations are powerful tools of persuasion (or dissuasion!).

Who designs attractions?

Attractions are designed by a variety of people. Some companies specialize in designing the complete attraction, including the buildings and structures, their fitting out and decoration, together with the spaces and the support services. In other cases specialists will be brought in to design particular elements of the attraction such as museum displays and landscaping.

For some organizations such as local authorities, all or most of the design expertise they require may be available in-house while for others most of it will have to be bought in either from one organization or a series of specialists. This latter situation obviously means there is a great need for skilful project management to ensure there is co-ordination and integration.

Many operators of smaller attractions will often undertake the design function themselves, with limited professional advice, even though they may not be specialists in the attractions field. While this is a low-cost option, it can cause problems in that an attraction may not perform as well as it could have done had it been professionally designed.

Design objectives

As we said earlier, attractions have to be designed to meet different, and sometimes apparently incompatible, objectives. This inevitably involves a degree of compromise. In this section we will look at some of the more common design objectives in relation to attractions, beginning with two types of financial objectives.

Profit and income generation

The design of an attraction needs to be geared to generating income to ensure that financial targets are met. Design can help income generation in a number of ways:

1 The creation of a visually striking entrance that will encourage people driving or walking past the site to visit the attraction, in other words so-called 'passing trade'.
2 The development of efficient kiosks where visitors pay the entrance charge to maximize the throughput of visitors.
3 The location of revenue-earning units on site in the right place to ensure that their income generation potential is optimized. For example, placing shops towards the end of the route that visitors take so that they do not have to carry their purchases around the site with them, possibly for several hours. This convenience, together with the natural desire to buy souvenirs at the end of a visit, ensures that the retail units generate as much income as possible. Likewise catering units need to be located in relation to how people use the site. Visitors rarely eat substantial meals at the beginning of a visit so most cafés and restaurants need to be situated in the middle or towards the end of the

normal visit route. However, other visitors like to 'graze' on snacks rather than having a sit-down meal. Therefore fast-food kiosks need to be strategically placed around a large site, selling items such as drinks and ice creams.

4 The design of income-generating units themselves, as well as their location, helps to ensure the maximization of income by making the unit attractive to consumers. Shops need to be bright with attractive displays, and should be laid out so that visitors need to look around all the displays before they reach the exit, thus increasing the likelihood that they will find something they want to buy. Just like in supermarkets, there should be some inexpensive items at the cash desk to tempt people to pick them up as they wait to pay for their purchases, such as confectionery and pens. Catering outlets also need to be attractive to visitors, with good décor and displays of the food on sale.

5 To optimize their income potential, retail and catering outlets also need to be designed to be efficient so that queues are minimized and customers do not give up and go away because it is takes too long for them to be served.

Economy of operation

As well as helping attractions earn more income, it is also important that they should be designed in a way which minimizes their operating costs. Good design can reduce costs in three main areas: labour, energy and merchandise stocks.

Labour is usually the largest single item in the budget of an attraction but the costs can be reduced through design. For example, catering outlets can be laid out so that the time taken to serve each customer is as low as possible. Furthermore, costs can be reduced by designing features such as the desk where the entrance charge is paid, and the shop designed so that one set of staff can service both functions, usually by locating them in the same place. Displays can be designed so that they require minimal maintenance while information panels can significantly reduce the need for guides and attendants. Design can be used not only to reduce labour costs but also, as these examples illustrate, to increase the efficiency and productivity of labour.

Another substantial cost for many attractions is *energy*, and this expenditure can also be reduced by design. For example, clever use of natural light reduces the need for artificial light. Attractions can also be designed so that heat generated by activities in one part of the attraction may be used to reduce the cost of heating elsewhere.

Finally, sensible design can also prevent *stock* loss through pilfering. This is particularly true in relation to shoplifting in retail outlets. Locating pay desks near to exits and installing mirrors, for instance, will help to reduce the theft of stock, as will layouts which allow visitors to be easily monitored by pay-desk staff, or at least to feel as if they can be observed if they are thinking about stealing goods.

Flexibility

As consumer tastes and the business environment of attractions are constantly changing, it is important that attractions are designed to be flexible so that they can respond to these changes. Otherwise they can quickly become obsolete with little prospect of long-term survival. Designing for flexibility is made more complex because the nature of the changes that dictate the need for flexibility are almost infinitely varied. They include legal requirements, technological developments, consumer preferences and competitors' actions, to name just four.

The flexibility of attraction design can take a number of forms, including:

- The ability of the attraction to accommodate new physical structures such as theme park rides and new museum displays. This means the old structure will have to be capable of being removed and the new one installed with all the related support services.
- The ability to operate the site on a reduced scale, perhaps by closing part of the site in the off-peak season to save money. In this situation the attraction must have been designed so that it can function even when part of the site is closed.
- On a smaller scale, elements of attractions need to be flexible enough to be able to temporarily change their use to exploit a market opportunity. For example, in a museum areas might be converted from display areas to seminar rooms in the daytime or for sherry receptions or buffets in the evenings. In these circumstances the attraction design must ensure that the transformation can be accomplished quickly and with minimal labour while, at the same time, other attraction users are not inconvenienced.

While flexibility is highly desirable, however, it can never be limitless and the flexibility that can be designed into an attraction will always be limited by factors such as budget and legal requirements such as fire regulations.

Safety and security

Legislation and the need to protect visitors and staff means that safety and security must be a major consideration in the design of any new attraction. The following is a list of attraction design issues in terms of safety and security:

- The location of dangerous machinery so that it does not pose a threat to visitors, particularly children, or to the operating staff.
- The need to reduce the risk to visitors from on-site traffic and perhaps from waterways that may run through a site.
- Ensuring that fire exits are easy to find and use.
- Making sure that stairs and footpaths are designed and built in materials that will make it less likely that people will slip on them.

- Laying out the attraction so that potential fire risks are not located next to each other or adjacent to naked lights and sources of heat.
- The protection of visitors' cars in car parks and the need to design car parks that discourage car thieves. This means providing lighting, for example, and not having the car park split up into bays by landscaping so that thieves cannot be seen.
- Locating pay desks and safes so that staff do not have to walk about carrying large amounts of money, thus making them a target for thieves.

These are just a few examples of designing for safety and security but we must recognize that the need for safety and security can be disadvantageous in other ways. For example, museums may not be able to realistically re-create mine environments because they are intrinsically dangerous, while the need to prevent car theft can lead to large easily observed but desolate car parks with no landscaping that might otherwise make them aesthetically attractive.

All-weather operations

To be successful, most attractions need to be able to attract visitors in all weather conditions. In Northern Europe this tends to mean designing attractions that offer on-site attractions and services under cover to overcome the problems caused by bad weather. It is also important to bear in mind the need to locate car parks and design walkways around the site in such a way that they are not too inconvenient for visitors who come to the attraction on days when it is wet or icy or just very cold. The ability to operate, and be attractive to visitors, in bad weather is crucial if attractions in Northern Europe are to attract visitors in the off-peak season when the weather tends to be at its worst. However, it is important to note that design also needs to tackle the problems that can be caused in hot weather, by installing air conditioning for example.

User-friendliness

Visitors tend to respond best to attractions that have been designed to be user-friendly. Designing an attraction to be user-friendly means looking at every aspect of the visit from the journey to the attraction to setting off on the journey home. Visitors want attractions which are easy to use and where as little of their precious leisure time as possible is wasted on mundane tasks such as queuing.

Some of the key elements in the design of user-friendly attractions are outlined below:

1 Signposting of routes to and from the attraction whether they be on roads or footpaths. Visitors are not likely to be impressed if they are unable to find the attraction easily – some may even give up and go elsewhere.

2 Making it easy to gain access to the attraction through good, well-located car parks, and efficient entrances for example.

3 Helping visitors orientate themselves once they are inside the attraction and providing information to help them decide how to spend their time on site. This means signs and information boards as well as leaflets.

4 Attractive, easy to use, good quality support services such as toilets and catering facilities in the right locations.

5 Easy to follow routes around the attraction that show visitors the best parts of the site with the minimum effort.

6 Ensuring that the attraction is designed to cope with likely peak crowds so that queuing and congestion is kept to a minimum.

7 Making it easy for visitors when they want to leave the site to find the exit and to allow them to leave the site and set off home as quickly as possible.

Welcoming visitors with special needs

Designers have to bear in mind that many potential visitors have special needs of one kind or another, and attractions should be designed accordingly. Otherwise these people will be unable to visit the attraction and will miss the opportunity to enjoy it and, as a result, the attraction will lose the potential income that could have been earned from these visitors. Some of the special needs that should be thought of in the design process are:

- For people in wheelchairs or those who, while not in wheelchairs, find it difficult to walk, the design of walkways, methods of on-site transport and the way visitors travel from floor to floor in buildings are crucial if they are to fully enjoy the site like other visitors.
- For visitors with hearing difficulties graphic displays of information are particularly important. Furthermore if part of the appeal of the attraction is oral, such as actors or sound effects, systems such as induction loops need to be incorporated in the design to allow these visitors to gain as much enjoyment as other visitors.
- For visitors who are visually impaired, provision has to be made so they can gain pleasure from their visit. For these visitors the senses of smell and touch are important so that gardens with aromatic plants and museums with artificial smells are attractive, as are those where visitors can touch the exhibits.
- For parents with babies it is essential that there are facilities for changing babies and heating bottles.

Aesthetic appeal

Most successful attractions are those that have an aesthetic appeal to visitors. This appeal can be based on size, form, colour or materials. For designers the problem is that aesthetics are a subjective matter and people's views of what is attractive vary. For example, some people dislike the glass pyramid which was built in the early 1990s at the Louvre museum in Paris, while others find it very pleasing. It is therefore important that designers try to appeal to the aesthetic tastes of the attraction's target market or markets rather than just designing attractions that please their own personal aesthetic ideas or will impress other designers.

Environmental friendliness

Given the growing public concern with green issues, attractions need to be seen by their visitors as environmentally friendly and design has a key role to play here, by:

- minimizing waste and ensuring that as much of the waste generated by the attraction as possible is recyclable
- designing the attraction to make it energy-efficient
- making use of environmentally friendly materials in the construction of the attraction.

Design and external audiences

As well as needing to be satisfactory for the attraction operator, the design of the attraction in terms of site layout and the appearance of buildings, structures and spaces is also of interest to a number of external audiences, of which three are particularly important – planning authorities, funders and potential customers.

In most countries all new physical attractions will usually require some form of planning permission, usually from a local authority, before they can go ahead. The following aspects of the design will often determine whether or not the planning authority will approve or reject the application:

- The scale of the project and whether it is an appropriate size in relation to neighbouring buildings and structures.
- The materials it is proposed to use, the appearance of the attraction and whether this is acceptable in aesthetic terms. This is particularly important in areas of high-quality townscape or landscape.
- The suitability and safety of methods of access to the site, such as roads and car parks.
- The quality of landscaping on the site and the use of landscaping to screen the less attractive parts of the site from people on adjacent sites.
- Noise generated by the attraction and how design can be used to reduce disturbance for the attraction's neighbours.

Planning authorities often publish guidelines based on their policies to show potential developers what they are looking for in terms of design for their area in general and for particular sites which are ripe for development. The views of planning authorities on design can be seen through decisions they have made on other applications. However, as attraction applications are few and far between and attractions are all different, it is very difficult to use these sources of information to help design an attraction in a way that will maximize the chances of receiving planning permission. Perhaps the best approach is to consult local planners from an early stage to ascertain their attitude to the project and to see whether the attraction could be designed differently to make it more acceptable to them.

The institutions funding the project will also be interested in the design of the proposed attraction. Their evaluation of the design will affect their perception of the project and it is important for the attraction developer that investors and potential funders approve of the design. Financial institutions may be more subjective in their appraisal of the design and their judgement may rest on factors such as:

- whether or not the design looks as if it will be expensive or relatively cheap to implement
- whether or not the institutions believe the appearance of the attraction will be aesthetically pleasing to visitors
- how expensive it appears to be in terms of likely maintenance costs
- how simple the plan is, so that unforeseen problems that would be expensive and time-consuming to solve will not be experienced during the construction phase.

The last, but probably most important external audience, is the potential visitors. It is unlikely that the design of the attraction alone will motivate them to visit it. However, when they visit the attraction the design will greatly affect their enjoyment of the day and will influence whether or not they decide to come again. They will judge the attraction design more on its user-friendliness than on the aesthetics of its appearance. Given the importance of site design to visitors, it is perhaps surprising that many attraction designers and developers do little or no market research on their proposed designs for attractions.

Design constraints

So far we may have created the impression that the design of attractions is about designers meeting internal organization objectives and pleasing external audiences by designing the ideal attraction. However, all designers work within constraints, and attraction designers are no different. The most common constraints include:

- the budget available for the project
- the culture of the organization which is developing the attraction and the views of its senior managers on attraction design. Its experience of successful attractions elsewhere and their design will also act as a constraint on the designer
- problems relating to the site itself, including its size, topography, drainage systems and the nature of the subsoil

- legal aspects, including health and safety and fire regulations
- local planning authority policies
- the climate.

The design compromise

Therefore we can see that the design of new attractions is always the result of a compromise between a number of forces, some of which may be contradictory. These forces are illustrated in Figure 9.1.

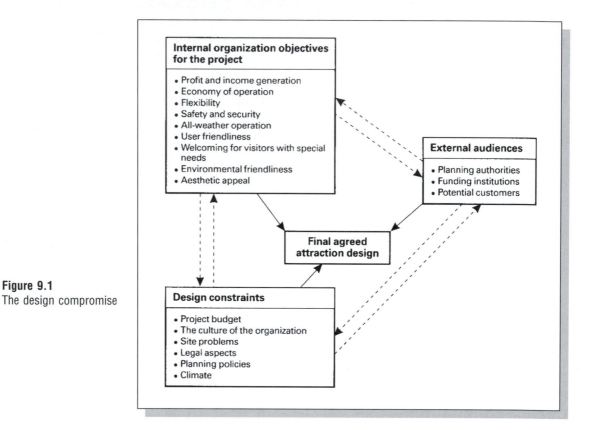

Figure 9.1
The design compromise

Of all the factors that influence attraction design, probably the most important is the project budget. However, design compromises that aim to save capital funding and maintenance costs may have an adverse effect on the long-term financial performance of the attraction by reducing its income generation potential.

A case study: Vulcania, France*

It might be helpful to give the reader an example of an attraction that has been well designed to meet its objectives.

*The designs are presented here with the kind permission of Vulcania™

Figure 9.2
Vulcania, France

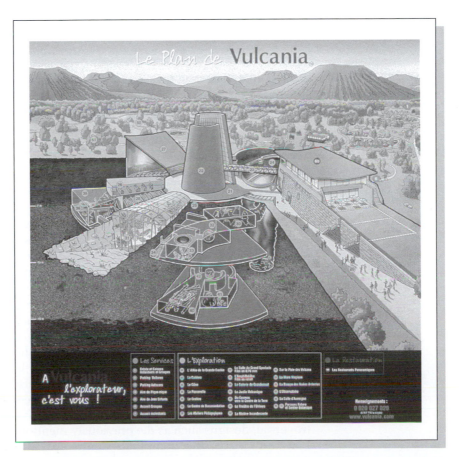

Figure 9.3
Vulcania, France

Vulcania is a brand new attraction in the Auvergne region of France, designed to tell visitors about volcanoes in a region of former volcanic activity. Developed on a 57-hectare site, 13 kilometres from the regional capital of Clermont-Ferrand, the attraction has been developed by the regional council.

It is described as a 'scientific exploration park' and given the nature of the attraction theme of volcanoes, about 75 per cent of the attraction is underground.

To achieve its objectives the designers had to produce a design which:

- re-created the shape of a volcano and provided spaces where visitors could learn about the aspects of volcanoes, in as realistic an environment as possible
- allowed visitors to move freely around the attraction
- offered easy access for visitors arriving by bus, in cars or on foot
- featured a volcanic garden with a 'climate' designed to illustrate through vegetation and species of the Southern and Northern hemisphere, the territorial recovery by life, once the volcano activity has stopped
- provided services such as restaurants in convenient locations
- included facilities for educational groups who come to do project work at the attraction.

The designers have produced imaginative, practical designs to allow the attraction to achieve the objectives shown above. Their designs are illustrated in Figures 9.2 and 9.3.

International perspective

While the basic principles of attraction design remain the same worldwide, there are three differences between the UK and other countries in attraction design.

First, while Britain has great experience of heritage attractions there is still relatively little experience in the UK of designing major theme and amusement parks. Most British parks have been developed in a piecemeal fashion over a period rather than being created at one point in time to a blueprint. By contrast, designers in the USA have great expertise in designing new theme parks and have achieved high levels of sophistication in the design of this type of attraction.

Second, designers in the UK have traditionally been rather conservative when it comes to designing buildings and structures at attractions. While in terms of museum displays UK designers have been very imaginative, British attractions have rarely been the scene of innovative architecture and design. In France, on the other hand, attractions have been a test-bed for imaginative, and sometimes controversial, designs such as the previously mentioned glass pyramid at the Louvre in Paris, the Pompidou Centre in Paris and the Futuroscope theme park near Poitiers. Perhaps this reflects the fact that architecture in France is seen more as an art form than it is in the UK.

Third, UK attractions are designed with the cool, damp British climate in mind. The design of attractions in other countries needs to take account of dramatic variations in climate between countries. Some climates are hot and dry while others are hot and humid, perhaps with pronounced monsoon seasons. Attraction designs have to reflect local climatic conditions.

As the tourism industry becomes ever more global and is increasingly dominated by international corporations, it will be interesting to see how successful companies are when they try to use design concepts that are successful in their home country in a new country. The Center Parcs all-weather dome, which was developed in Holland, has migrated success-fully to the UK and France. However, the Disney theme park design concepts that have worked so well in the USA and Japan have been less successful in France.

Conclusion

As we have seen, designing a visitor attraction is a matter of reconciling the needs of the developers with the desires of the users. However, design does not exist in isolation; it interacts with aspects of attraction development and management, such as human resource management, operations management, financial management and marketing, to shape the visitor experience. The difference is that whereas the latter can all be changed over time to reflect changing circumstances, the design cannot easily be modified and changed once the attraction has been built. It is therefore vital that attraction designers get it right the first time.

Discussion points and essay questions

1 Discuss the ways in which visitor attractions can be made more environmentally friendly.
2 Based on your experience of attraction-visiting, evaluate the performance of the attractions sector in terms of user-friendliness.
3 Discuss the extent to which the design of attractions can influence visitors' experiences.

Exercise

Visit a visitor attraction in your own country and then produce a report, critically evaluating its design in terms of the design objectives discussed in this chapter.

Project management

Introduction

Once the decision has been taken that a proposed attraction development is feasible and should go ahead, the project has to be managed from that moment until the day it opens to the public. This period can range from a few months for small attractions to a number of years for a major attraction.

Project management has a number of objectives. Its first job is to ensure that the attraction opens on time through the co-ordination of all the different resources involved in the development process, including people and materials. Second, it is the responsibility of the project manager to see that the project is completed within the agreed budget, through the efficient management of the same resources.

Rogers and Slinn (1993) have identified a four-stage project development process:

1 Planning
   (a) goals
   (b) time and cost estimates
   (c) team building
2 Scheduling
   (a) resourcing
   (b) sequencing activities
3 Controlling
   (a) monitoring
   (b) revising plans and targets
4 Implementation and operation.

Who is managing the project?

Most attraction projects will have a single person in overall control of the management. This may be the person who will be the manager of the attraction once it is completed and has been appointed early to oversee the construction process. For major projects, specialist project managers may be employed who will leave the attraction once it opens.

What are they managing?

Managing attraction projects is a complex activity because it involves managing a whole range of elements including resources, time and quality, and these three are connected by intricate interrelationships.

Managing resources

The resources that need to be managed are of two main types.

1 People: either directly employed by the attraction operator or those employed by other organizations who are brought in to fulfil particular tasks. The people involved in the creation of attractions are of many different types and include:
   (a) architects, designers, and surveyors
   (b) builders and tradesmen such as plumbers and electricians
   (c) the suppliers of materials
   (d) decorators and shop-fitters
   (e) landscape gardeners
   (f) marketing staff
   (g) local authority regulators such as building inspectors and environmental health officers
   (h) public utilities such as gas, water and electricity.
   Failure to co-ordinate the people on site effectively results in delays and extra costs.
2 Materials: this means all the goods that are needed as part of the development process. Again, there are a myriad of them as can be seen from the following brief list:
   (a) building materials like bricks, concrete, glass, doors and windows
   (b) landscaping materials such as soil, rocks, plants and shrubs
   (c) materials for surfacing car parks and footpaths
   (d) pipes that will carry water and gas to the site and electricity cables
   (e) site 'furniture' such as signposts and waste bins
   (f) the core element of the attraction such as theme park rides, animals for zoos and displays at museums
   (g) the equipment needed in the on-site shops and catering outlets such as tills and ovens.

Poor management of materials can cause delays and increase costs.

Managing time

All attraction projects have timescales which they try to work to, usually based on an opening date which is widely publicized in advance. Clearly, a failure to open on time or even opening when not fully finished could cause business to be lost and might lessen public confidence in the attraction. It is therefore vital that time is effectively managed. This means ensuring that tasks are completed in the right sequence so that contractors are not kept waiting because they cannot get on with their job until other people have finished their work. Thus it is important that realistic estimates are made at the beginning of how long jobs will take to complete. Finally, the schedule must allow for slippage due to unforeseen circumstances. In other words, a cushion of time needs to be built in to protect the schedule against possible problems such as bad weather or delays in the delivery of materials to the site.

Managing quality

Project managers must ensure that attractions are developed to the appropriate quality standard. The quality level that is achieved is usually the result of a compromise and a trade-off between the constraints of resources, time and budget. Nevertheless it is important that the level of quality is acceptable to the target market or markets. The concept of quality at attractions covers a number of aspects such as appearance, safety and durability, for example. The project manager is responsible for quality control during the development process and for ensuring that the attraction is built to the agreed design and that no one on site 'cuts corners' to save money unless it is with the approval of the project manager. A failure to control quality at this stage might adversely affect the long-term viability of the attraction by making it less attractive to visitors.

Project management techniques

For many attraction operators project management is an art rather than a science and is an ad hoc activity based on experience and judgement. However, there are now a number of techniques available to allow developers to manage the complex development process in a systematic and efficient way. These techniques are briefly considered below.

Critical path analysis (CPA)

Critical path analysis is a time-based technique for managing projects which recognizes and plans the need for interaction between the various players involved in the development process. First it identifies all the tasks involved in the project from start to finish. It then puts them in a chronological sequence, and applies timescales to each job. It looks at the 'networking' that is required between the key players, and when it needs to take place. Importantly, CPA allows project managers to see the interrelationships between the tasks. It works back from the opening date for the attraction so that managers can easily see that task X will have to be completed by Z weeks before the opening day otherwise the attraction will not be finished on time. It also allows the manager to see that task X cannot start until another team has finished task Y. Thus, on a day-by-day basis project managers can monitor progress towards the goal of the attraction being completed on time.

Programme evaluation and review technique (PERT)

This technique also disaggregates attraction projects into a number of tasks and jobs. These tasks are then analysed in terms of the likely time it will take to complete them but, instead of one duration being calculated, three possible timescales are completed – the shortest possible, the most likely and the longest possible. Managers can then estimate likely completion dates, which is particularly important in situations where a grand opening is planned and late completion would be a massive problem.

Linear programming

Linear programming is a mathematical technique which is used to help managers plan the most effective use of their resources such as personnel. A number of variables can be introduced into the programme and it will show the alternative ways of achieving the desired outcome.

The skills of the project manager

The good attraction project manager needs a number of skills, including:

- attention to detail, as one slight oversight can lead to major problems later
- the ability when dealing with contractors and suppliers who may be in a strong position vis-à-vis the project manager to respond in a way that will not upset relations with these people to the detriment of the project
- firmness when dealing with contractors and suppliers who may, for example, be trying to increase their charges above the amount originally agreed
- the ability to think quickly and make sound judgements when under pressure
- a good grasp of the technical aspects of construction so they can negotiate knowledgeably with contractors
- a sound appreciation of the principles of budgeting and financial control
- the ability to communicate with different types of people, including investors, who come to check on progress, professionals such as architects, and builders and their labourers
- the skill of solving problems logically and quickly, and not panicking when problems arise.

Problems that may arise

The main types of problem most commonly encountered include:

- bad weather which slows down building work and can make underfoot conditions so bad that construction and landscaping work may have to stop altogether for a while
- regulations and legal problems such as restrictions on work on health and safety grounds following an accident or additional work required following visits by building inspectors
- the failure of suppliers to deliver essential materials or delays in the delivery of materials
- key personnel being off work sick or on holiday
- contractors and suppliers trying to increase their charges once work has begun and it is crucial that their tasks are completed quickly otherwise the project as a whole will be delayed
- changes to the original design being made by architects once construction work has commenced
- problems with payments being made by the attraction operator to contractors and suppliers such that work is stopped until bills are paid.

Some of these problems are predictable and can be anticipated, in which case they should never occur. Others are almost impossible to foresee, and always have to be responded to efficiently and as quickly as possible.

Contingency plans

All project managers should have contingency plans based on the question, what if? Managers should have a good idea of what the implications of a particular problem would be, how it would affect overall progress, and what could be done to minimize the negative impact on the project. Sensible project schedules will also build in a safety margin of time as a contingency against unforeseen circumstances that slow down the project. If contingency plans are to be successful, project managers need to have the power to make decisions about allocating more staff or spending more money to solve a problem at very short notice.

Managing construction work

Much of the rest of this chapter will look at the issues involved in the management of construction work, which is usually the largest single element in an attraction project, particularly in terms of cost.

Let us imagine that the design for a new building or structure has just been agreed. Where do we go from there? Once the design is approved the quantity surveyor, who is responsible for keeping the construction work to budget, will meet the design team to prepare a detailed cost plan for the work. At this stage the surveyors and designers will want the client to confirm all the design details as alterations made subsequently may cost a great deal of time or money, or both.

Most contractors for building works have one or two aims, either to minimize time or to maximize cost control and quality control. Most well-planned attraction projects should fit into the latter category. There tend to be two ways of purchasing construction work:

1 Those where a lump sum price has been agreed before work commences.
2 Those where a basis has been agreed for calculating the final cost of the building.

Clearly the former is usually best, as it provides an incentive for the contractor to be efficient and gives developers a good idea of the final cost. However, it is important to note that, in exceptional circumstances, even a lump sum contract can be varied up or down.

Lump sum contracts themselves are of two types. First there are so called 'design and build contracts' where the contractor is invited to tender for the design and the construction of the building. Second, there are the 'conventional contracts' where the design team prepare full working drawings with a detailed specification and contractors are invited to tender for the construction work based on these drawings and specifications. With the latter type the client (the attraction operator, represented by the project manager) has more control but accepts greater risk, and vice versa. Conventional lump sum contracts can either be with quantities of materials specified or without quantities, where the contractor will have to calculate the quantities of materials required.

Generally contracts are put out to tender and contractors are invited to submit a price for the contract as specified. The number of tenders sought should depend on the value of the project – the more expensive the project, the greater the number of tenders that should be sought. Price is clearly the main determinant of which tender to accept but project managers should also make checks on the successful tenderer in terms of history, experience, reputation and financial situation.

Before work begins a number of checks are in order to prevent future problems:

- Ensure that everyone involved (architects, surveyors, builders, attraction operator) is clear about their duties and responsibilities under the contract.
- Check that all the necessary insurance policies have been taken out.
- Make sure that all the necessary permissions and licences have been obtained, such as planning permissions, building regulations and fire regulations.
- Ensure that funding is in place to cover the cost of the work so that work is not delayed because of unpaid accounts.

Once work has started it is essential that the project manager monitors progress and keeps an eye on timing, cost and quality control. The agreed programme and the specification, which should be included in the contract, form the basis for such monitoring, as the project manager can compare actual with agreed programme and specifications and identify variances. Regular cost checks relating real costs to agreed costs also help to keep the project on track from the client's (attraction operator, represented by the project manager) point of view.

In case of problems it is important for the client or project manager to agree parameters within which the contractors, architects and surveyors are free to make decisions when problems arise. These parameters may be in terms of financial limits on what can be spent without reference to the client, or the types of items that can be bought without consulting the project manager.

The client will be expected to pay money during the construction period, before work is completed, to allow the contractors to pay wages and buy materials for example. Clearly it is important to ensure that these payments are not unreasonable in relation to the work which is under way.

Even when the building is complete the role of the project manager is not over. Usually contractors and architects will separately issue documents saying the building is finished and is of a satisfactory standard. There is a set period which, in effect, is the guarantee period during which problems must be put right by the contractor. Project managers should check that all problems are sorted out during this period to prevent the need for expensive remedial work later. It has to be said that, while the process seems straightforward, trying to have defects put right in this period can be a case of 'easier said than done'. Defects can be highly subjective and contractors are understandably reluctant to spend more money than they need to on the work, as it obviously reduces their profit margin on the job. There are legal procedures available in the event of a dispute but in reality it is easier to avoid a dispute in the first place.

The prevention of problems and disputes cannot be guaranteed but it is more likely if the client follows some simple guidelines, including the following:

- Only use experienced and qualified architects and surveyors.
- Give designers a clear brief and do not keep changing this brief.
- Let the professionals get on with their job but keep an eye on them.
- Pay bills on time.
- Do not rush the designer or contractor so that they are forced to 'cut corners'.

Project management and the opening of the attraction

While the management of the construction phase is separate from the management of the attraction when it has been opened to the public, the management of the project development phase includes the opening or launch of the attraction. Project managers have to ensure that the attraction is ready and looking its best for the day of the launch. They may also be involved in providing special facilities for the opening ceremony, such as a platform or dais together with services for the media such as power supplies for the equipment required by television outside broadcasts. The role of the project manager is over only after the opening day when the attraction begins its operational life.

Conclusion

We have seen that project management has a crucial role to play in the development of new visitor attractions and that the job of project manager is a demanding one which calls for a person with many different skills, not the least of which is the ability to work with all the other professionals involved in the process such as architects, surveyors and builders. How well the project is managed before the attraction opens to the public largely determines how successful the attraction will be after it opens.

Discussion points and essay questions

1 Discuss the skills which a project manager working in the attractions sector needs to possess.
2 Critically evaluate the scope and nature of project management in the attractions sector.
3 Discuss the factors which can upset the management of visitor attraction projects.

Exercise

Devise an attraction concept and then construct a simple critical path analysis, to guide the project from the concept to the opening day. You will need to consult the literature on CPA to undertake this exercise.

Part Three

The Management of Visitor Attractions

The role of the manager and management styles

Introduction

The management approach or style adopted at a particular attraction is important in several ways. It determines the formal structure of the organization and the informal culture. The approach taken will influence staff attitudes and job satisfaction, and will therefore have a direct impact on the visitor experience at the attraction. However, although it is an important subject for these reasons, very little has been written on management approaches specifically at visitor attractions.

The role of the manager

The views of some management theorists on the role of managers have been neatly summed up by Crossley and Jamieson (1989) using the mnemonic, POSDCORB, which stands for:

Planning
Organizing
Staffing
Directing
Co-ordinating
Reporting
Budgeting.

This view sees the manager as a strategist, operating in a compartmentalized world, with time to reflect and consider, before issuing instructions and initiating action.

In 1973, Mintzberg argued that this idea of the manager as a scientific and systematic planner was often, in reality, a myth. His view of management would probably ring true to most past and present attraction managers. It consists of the following three ideas:

1 Managers work at an unrelenting pace, are action orientated and dislike reflective activity.
2 Managers favour verbal communication and engage in an unending variety of brief unscheduled interchanges of information.
3 Managers process much information and then make most decisions based on judgement and intuition.

This set of ideas sees management as more of an art and the manager as more of a pragmatic tactician than a strategist.

Before going on to look at management styles, we should say a few more words about the role of managers, specifically in relation to attractions. Managers need to realize that their position gives them responsibilities which are theirs and theirs alone. Their staff can only function effectively if they carry out these responsibilities. First, it is the unique role of the manager to take an overview of the attraction as a whole, while other staff will take a narrower, partial view based on their role at the attraction and/or their particular area of expertise. Second, whereas most staff are concerned with the day-to-day operational management of the attraction in the present, it is the job of the manager to think about the future of the attraction. Furthermore, while the staff manage the 'home front' they rely on the manager to represent the interests of the attraction to key external audiences such as funding bodies, parent companies in the case of attractions owned by major corporations, and politicians in the case of public sector attractions. Finally, staff rely on their manager to remove any obstacle that prevents them from doing their job to the best of their ability, such as inadequate administrative systems or lack of resources.

To effectively carry out these roles, managers need to see themselves as managers, who make decisions, guide changes and develop policies, rather than as administrators who merely operate systems. Given that most attraction managers become managers because they were good at a specific job, for example marketing in the case of theme parks or research and conservation in the case of museums, it is important that they can adapt to the wider responsibilities of being a manager, rather than still thinking as a specialist.

Management styles at visitor attractions

When we focus on management styles we are fundamentally looking at the attitudes adopted by the manager towards the job itself but also more importantly towards particular groups of people, namely the staff, trade unions, more senior managers, other 'stakeholders' such as shareholders, councillors and voluntary helpers, and last, but not least, customers. These attitudes are influenced by a number of factors including:

- the personality of the manager
- good and bad experiences of management styles the manager has had at other attractions, either as the manager in question or as a member of staff
- the level of confidence the manager has in his or her own position as a manager and his or her view of how much power and influence he or she has.

Perhaps we need to start by looking at the attitude of the manager towards the job itself, which will reflect what they think are the main aims of the attraction operation. These might include reducing costs to a minimum, achieving a particular rate of return on investment, maximizing visitor numbers, enhancing the visitor experience, improving the image of the attraction, maximizing quality, providing an educational experience for visitors and pleasing particular stakeholders such as shareholders or local authority councillors.

However, management styles are really about how these ideas about the job in general are translated into attitudes towards key groups of people such as staff, superiors in the management hierarchy, customers and external organizations such as suppliers.

Management styles and staff

The approaches to staff that managers can choose to adopt at attractions include:

- trying to improve performance by instilling fear in people or by being supportive
- giving people more responsibility over their individual jobs or keeping power centrally in their own hands
- staying in their office, remaining somewhat aloof, or managing by 'walking the site', and talking to staff
- increasing their credibility with staff by showing they can do all the jobs involved in running the site by 'mucking in' and helping at busy times, or staying in their office even when operational staff are under great pressure
- trusting that people will do their job without strict constant supervision or believing that people only work when they are under constant supervision
- giving staff information on how the attraction is doing or being secretive and deciding that people do not need, and should not be given, such information.

Clearly, these examples represent extreme positions at either end of the spectrum. In reality most managers sit somewhere on a continuum between these extremes, and a manager who favours one position that could be described as 'liberal' on something like trusting people with information may take a much less liberal view on another issue, such as the decentralization of decision-making power.

It is also important to recognize that, to some extent, managers are not totally free to choose which approach to take in relation to staff. On the one hand, their choice may be constrained by corporate policy, while on the other it will be influenced by the manager's own personality.

Management styles and superiors in the management hierarchy

Attraction managers also have to decide what approach they are going to take in their dealings with their own line managers. Some of the choices they have to make are:

- Should the manager try to lead their superiors into making particular decisions, or should the manager merely carry out the ideas of their line managers?
- Should the manager take credit from line managers for the successful initiatives taken by their staff in order to improve the manager's own career prospects, or should the manager ensure that it is the relevant staff who receive the credit?
- Should the manager need to try to change the mind of a line manager, and should they do so bluntly and directly or in a more indirect and tactful way?
- When should the manager consider bypassing a line manager and going 'above the line manager's head' to a higher level of management?
- How much involvement should the manager have in the day-to-day management of the site, which is primarily the responsibility of other members of staff?
- To what extent will the manager defend staff if they are criticized by more senior managers elsewhere in the organization?

The approach managers choose to take to their superiors may well be less a conscious choice and more a matter of responding, only half-consciously, to the traditions and cultures of the organization and the personalities of the manager and her or his superiors. Furthermore, managers will often adopt different approaches at different times in response to different situations. The way managers deal with their superiors does have an effect on their reputation among their staff. A strong manager who is seen to stand up for the attraction and the staff against senior management is likely to be highly respected, and vice versa.

Management styles and customers

The link between management styles and customers has two main elements:

1 The degree of contact the manager intends to have with customers. Some choose to walk around the site, talking to customers, while others choose never to go out of their way to see a customer.
2 The systems that managers develop that affect the visitor experience, including how complaints are handled.

In both situations, the approach taken by managers has an impact, not only on visitors, but also on the attraction's staff. In the first case, too much contact between managers and customers can lead staff to believe that managers are checking up on them and do not trust them to look after the customers' needs. Conversely, managers who do not spend time talking to visitors may be accused by their staff of being 'out of touch'.

When we look at the second case, the key to success is for managers to develop the systems in co-operation with their staff, and to communicate the approach these managers favour to their staff so that they follow the approach too. Otherwise a situation can arise where there is a real gap between what should happen in theory and what happens in practice.

Finally, staff are likely to follow the example set by managers in terms of their attitudes towards customers. Managers must therefore be aware that if they are seen to behave arrogantly or condescendingly toward visitors, their staff are likely to follow their example.

Management styles and external organizations

Managers also have to decide how they are going to handle relations with a range of external organizations that might include:

- suppliers
- market intermediaries such as tourist information centres
- grant-making and funding bodies
- regulatory agencies such as fire authorities and environmental health departments
- the media.

There is often a fundamental difference between these types of organizations in terms of their relationship with attractions. In the case of suppliers, the attraction is generally in the more powerful position as it is the buyer in the relationship. On the other hand, when we look at the four other types of bodies in the list, the attraction is often in a weaker position as it is a seller, trying to persuade the external organization that it should promote its product, give it money or not take action against its interests. The approach taken by managers will clearly need to be different depending on whether the attraction manager is in the position of a 'buyer' or a 'seller'.

In relation to suppliers, managers must decide whether they are going to develop long-term relations with them or show no loyalty to suppliers and simply 'play one off against another'. This will probably depend on the nature of the product, and how easy it is to find good suppliers.

Management approaches and corporate culture

The management style adopted by those responsible for running attractions combines with other factors to create a corporate culture at the attraction. These factors include:

- the attraction's history and traditional ways of doing things
- the attitude, experience and opinions of staff
- the size of the attraction
- the state of the business environment in terms of issues such as legislation, the economic situation and the actions of competitors
- the policies of parent organizations if the attraction has one.

Attraction cultures, like those of other organizations, can be of many types, including:

- entrepreneurial or bureaucratic
- risk-taking or cautious
- open or secretive
- confident or defensive
- dynamic or inert
- extrovert and externally focused or introvert and internally focused
- team-based or individually competitive
- thrives on change or resists change
- self-critical or complacent
- ethical or dishonest
- empowering or highly centralized
- focused or lacking in direction.

These are just a few possible characteristics of culture. Clearly, these are extremes and most attractions will be some way between the two. Furthermore, attractions may appear to have a modern type of culture in some respects, while appearing old-fashioned in other ways.

Traditionally, approaches to corporate culture have been thought to be different in different sectors. Private sector attractions have been seen to be more entrepreneurial and dynamic, for example, while those in the public sector can often seem to be bureaucratic and inert. However, many public sector attractions are now behaving in a more entrepreneurial manner due to their need to generate more income to compensate for reductions in government funding. At the same time many smaller private sector attractions appear to be rather inert and slow to respond to changes in the business environment.

While it is not too difficult to analyse cultures, creating or changing them is a very complex and difficult process. Managers who wish to modify cultures may face obstacles including the traditions of an organization and the resistance of individual staff to change of any kind. It is therefore important that change is negotiated rather than imposed. Where possible, a transition period should also be planned. However, in some cases, such as a sudden loss of funding or a change in the law, cultures may have to be changed almost overnight which may make negotiation and a period of transition difficult or impossible to implement.

Culture is becoming increasingly important, not just in terms of the operation of the attraction, but also in terms of marketing, for increasingly organizations in the service industries are trying to use their internal culture as a marketing ploy. For example, the Virgin Atlantic airline stresses its ethical open approach to business while Disney 'sells' its clean-cut family values. More and more attractions will, in future, realize that they can use their corporate culture, if it is in keeping with what the market finds attractive, as a valuable tool to help them achieve competitive advantage.

Management ideas and the structure of organizations

While culture is a 'soft', abstract concept, the structure of organizations is the 'hard' solid manifestation of management styles. There is clearly a two-way relationship between the cultures and structures of organizations, with each influencing the other.

Organizational structures have a number of components:

1 The decision-making structure, which can be highly hierarchical, in the form of a pyramid, or can be relatively flat. In many organizations middle tiers of management have been removed to flatten the hierarchy. Most attractions are too small to have ever had a tier of middle managers so it is relatively easy for them to have a flat hierarchy if they so desire.

2 The structure through which management and staff relate to each other, which includes the formal recognition, if such exists, of trade unions and how they are involved in the management of the organization. At most private and voluntary sector attractions unions as such do not exist or are very weak. However, at public sector attractions unions may be very influential, and can constrain the ability of managers to introduce change. (Should Britain ever adopt the EU's Social Chapter the role of unions and workers generally at attractions could become more important.)

3 The formal systems in relation to human resources, including recruitment, motivation, rewards, appraisal and staff development.

4 The mechanisms by which managers communicate with staff, such as staff meetings and newsletters, and by which staff communicate with each other.

5 The way in which the functions of management are allocated to particular departments and individuals. For example, who is responsible for human resource management, and is marketing the job of a department with one or two staff, or is it seen to be the responsibility of all staff?

It is important to note that while any attempts to change the structure of an attraction may well meet resistance on the grounds that 'we have

Table 11.1 The difference between 'new managers' and 'old managers'

The new manager	The old manager
Sees himself/herself as a team manager in a relatively flat hierarchy	Sees himself/herself as a leader, at the apex of a pyramidal structure
Is likely to be a graduate, specialist, trained manager with a management qualification	Probably lacks any qualifications and has become a manager by working their way up from the bottom
Is a strategist concerned with the future as well as the present well-being of the attraction	Is a tactician who tends to concentrate on the present
Believes in planning and forecasting and developing plans to guide day-to-day action	Believes planning is impossible because of the volatility of the business environment, and therefore tends to be reactive
Relies on market research when making marketing decisions	Relies on his/her experience and judgement
Focuses on the wants and needs of customers	Focuses on the attraction product and making things as easy as possible from an operational point of view
Sees marketing as a process in which promotion is just one stage	Sees promotion in terms of brochures and advertisements for example, as the core of marketing
Is outward looking and scans the business environment constantly	Looks inward and rarely looks at what is happening in the business environment
Recruits staff in a systematic and open way	Recruits staff in an ad hoc manner and may rely on friends and relatives of existing staff
Consciously tries to operate equal opportunities policies	At best, simply complies with law on equal opportunities, at worst, ignores equal opportunities altogether
Operates staff development schemes to motivate people and improve their job satisfaction	Relies on chatting to people on site and taking ad hoc decisions to motivate staff and give them job satisfaction, if he/she thinks about it at all
Offers staff training after completing individual training needs analysis	Offers training as a perk or to keep staff happy
Rewards and promotes staff on the basis of merit and performance	Rewards and promotes staff on the basis of length of service and because they like the person

Table 11.1 continued

The new manager	The old manager
Prefers to boost income rather than make cuts in difficult times	Simply cuts costs in difficult times, regardless of the impact on service quality
Constantly tries to improve the attraction's performance	Only takes action when a particular problem emerges
Shows imagination when trying to solve problems	Relies on past ideas and experience when tackling problems
Communicates with staff through systematic channels and via their team leaders	Communicates with staff in an ad hoc manner, in other words, when they see them, by accident, rather than through their line managers
Provides information on how the attraction is performing and makes it clear to each member of staff what their roles at the attraction are	Keeps most information on the attraction's performance secret and leaves staff to decide for themselves what their role is at the attraction or believes they intrinsically know their role
Provides properly worked-out training programmes for students on work experience placements and honours them	Views students on placement as 'cheap labour' or as the people who should carry out the monotonous tasks that no one else wants to undertake
Manages his/her time effectively	Wastes some of their own time and that of other staff
Delegates good and bad jobs to other staff and trains them to do the jobs	Finds it difficult to delegate and when he/she does they tend to delegate the monotonous tasks, and then constantly monitor the person who is doing the job, having not properly briefed them on the task
Tries to carry out all work within working hours, without the need to take work home. Having to take work home would be seen as a failure	Takes work home or at least says they do, and believes this is a positive thing to do
Follows the latest fashions in management theory and practice, such as total quality management	Is sceptical of all management theories and what he/she sees as passing fads
Is action orientated	Is bureaucratic

always done things in such and such a way', it is still probably easier to change a structure than it is to modify a culture. But unless managers can change cultures, changes in structure will only have a limited impact.

'New managers' and 'old managers'

The terms 'new' and 'old' are used in relation to managers in a very judgemental manner. In other words, the word 'new' is now equated with 'modern' while the term 'old' is equated with 'old-fashioned'. As we shall see, this represents a gross oversimplification, but let us start by looking at the perceived differences between the two types of manager, as illustrated in Table 11.1.

Table 11.1 patently gives a simplistic view, that may not reflect reality in a number of ways, including the following:

1 Managers rarely fit into one category or another. It is far more likely that an individual will be a 'new manager' on one issue but an 'old manager' on a different matter. For example, an attraction manager may be a strong believer in the idea that he or she is a team manager in a flattened hierarchy but may not believe in strategic management and planning.
2 The manager of an attraction may believe in the concept of the 'new manager' but may in reality behave more like an 'old manager'. Perhaps he or she thinks that marketing decisions should be based on good market research but, as such data will probably not be available, he or she will rely on past experience and judgement to make such decisions. This difference between theory and practice may be the result of a number of factors, including:
   (a) lack of resources
   (b) too many pressures from external sources, such as superiors in the management hierarchy
   (c) lack of confidence in their own ability.
3 Some of the characteristics of the 'new manager' which commentators believe indicate a good manager, may not be seen as such by staff or stakeholders. Staff, for example, often like the old-style manager who works their way up from the bottom, chats to staff on site and helps out at busy times. A new-style manager, by contrast, who arrives as a graduate, develops formal communication systems and does not help at busy times, could be viewed in a very negative manner by the staff. Second, stakeholders such as shareholders or those who provide the funding for attractions may favour managers who cut costs in difficult economic times over those who try to boost income, which may involve risky speculation using financial resources that are in short supply.
4 Attraction managers may believe in the principles of the 'new manager' but they cannot behave as one because their freedom of action is constrained by the beliefs and policies of their superiors and major stakeholders. These might include the managing director of a major commercial operation or their shareholders, local authority councillors and government ministers, who control public spending in

the case of public sector attractions, and the trustees of charitable bodies that run voluntary sector attractions.

Conclusions

As we said at the beginning of this chapter, the role of managers and the management style they adopt are important in that they affect the operation of the attraction, the staff and the customers. In reality, different management approaches are appropriate for different types of attractions at different times. Some of the ideas discussed above are undoubtedly easier to adopt at large privately owned attractions than at small commercial attractions or local authority museums, for example.

It has to be said that most of the content of this section has been based on applying ideas developed by organizations in other sectors of the economy. Given that the visitor attraction business is relatively young and has grown up rapidly, it has not yet had time to develop its own specific concepts of management style, corporate culture and organizational structure. Therefore, if the sector is to continue to grow and develop, it needs to create its own body of management theory and learn from examples of good management practice at other attractions.

Finally, however, when developing these theories and principles, attractions must beware of the fact that management theory and practice as a field is subject to fashions and fads and is constantly changing. Attraction managers should perhaps use whatever management approaches work for them rather than trying to follow fashionable ideas.

Discussion points and essay questions

1 Discuss the application of the Crossley and Jamieson concept of POSDCORB, as outlined in this chapter, to the attractions sector.
2 Critically evaluate the idea of the 'new manager' and the 'old manager' identified in Table 11.1.
3 Discuss the merits and problems of different management styles.

Exercise

Select an attraction in your own country and interview the senior manager and a selection of staff to:

- identify the style(s) of management at the attraction and the nature of the corporate culture
- gain the opinions of staff about the management style and its effectiveness or otherwise.

CHAPTER 12

The marketing concept

The marketing concept

In recent years, marketing has become fashionable and has taken centre stage in industry. Its growing influence has been particularly spectacular in the public sector. Marketing texts and training courses have proliferated and most recent developments in management theory have focused on, or have been highly influenced by, marketing. There are a number of possible reasons for this growing interest, including:

- the dramatic changes in the structure of many economies, with the decline of traditional manufacturing industries and the rise of service industries which tend to have been more innovative and marketing orientated than the traditional industries
- the changing nature of the market and consumer behaviour, and the identification of new niche markets such as the health-conscious and 'green' consumers, for example
- recessions which have forced organizations to look critically at how they operate, including their marketing activities
- privatization of previously state owned organizations which now need to be more responsive to the wants and needs of their customers, in order to make a profit
- pressure on publicly owned undertakings to behave more commercially and reduce their reliance on subsidies.

This brief list is based on the UK experience but it is also relevant in many other European countries and on other continents. Therefore, perhaps, we should look at what marketing is all about, starting with some definitions:

1 Marketing is a 'Social and managerial process by which individuals and groups obtain what they need and want through creating and exchanging products and values with others' (Kotler, 1994a).
2 'Marketing is the management process responsible for identifying, anticipating and satisfying customer requirements profitably' (Chartered Institute of Marketing, 1984).
3 'Marketing is both a philosophy and a business function . . . a state of mind concerning the optimum approach to business and the activities whereby such ideas are translated into practice' (Baker, 1985).
4 'Selling focuses on the needs of the seller; marketing on the needs of the buyer' (Levitt, 1960).
5 'Marketing is not only much broader than selling, it is not a specialized activity at all. It encompasses the entire business. It is the whole business seen from the point of view of its final result, that is, from the customer's point of view. Concern and responsibilities for marketing must therefore permeate all areas of the enterprise' (Drucker, 1954).
6 'The aim of marketing is to make selling superfluous. The aim is to know and understand the customer so well that the product or service fits . . . and sells itself' (Drucker, 1973).
7 'Marketing is to establish, maintain, and enhance long-term customer relationships at a profit, so that the objectives of the parties involved are met. This is done by mutual exchange and fulfilment of promises' (Grönroos, 1990).

These definitions tend to focus on the customers and their needs and wants. As well as these definitions it might be helpful to look at some general principles and ideas relating to marketing. These can be summarized as follows:

1 Marketing is all about helping the organization achieve its aims and objectives and it therefore needs to be tied in to the corporate strategy process.
2 Marketing is not just about selling. Selling is simply one of the latter stages in the marketing process and if marketing is customer led it is not a matter of trying to sell people products but, rather, simply giving them the chance to buy something they want.
3 Marketing is not just about promotion (advertising and brochures); promotion is a means to an end not an end in itself.
4 Marketing should permeate the whole culture of an organization rather than just existing in a single department or in the job descriptions and titles of specific members of staff.
5 Marketing is not just about money and profit. There can be many other objectives for marketing including, for example, encouraging the use of a service by socially disadvantaged people, conservation, education and improving the health of the population.

6 Successful marketing is customer led in that it finds out what its potential customers want and develops products to meet those needs and wants. It is not about developing products and then trying to find customers for them. Marketing cannot solve the problems of products that people do not want. This customer-centred approach implies a crucial role for marketing research.

7 Marketing is a continuous process involving constant monitoring, performance evaluation, and modifications to strategies rather than just being a one-off exercise.

8 Marketing exists at both the strategic and tactical level although the two must be interlinked if marketing is to be successful. It also involves long-term and short-term planning.

Approaches to marketing

Traditionally there have been four approaches that organizations could take to marketing:

1 *Production approach*. This approach is based on the idea that customers will favour products that are available and highly affordable. Therefore in this approach managers should concentrate on low cost production and efficient distribution.

2 *Product approach*. The underlying principle is that customers will choose products that offer features, performance and levels of quality that differentiate them from other products. This means an emphasis on product improvement on the part of the manufacturers and service providers.

3 *Selling approach*. This is based on a belief that customers will not buy enough of the product unless the organization carries out substantial promotional and selling activity.

4 *Marketing approach and market-led approach*. This says that the key to achieving the organization's goals lies in identifying customer wants and needs in target markets and delivering to these people products that satisfy them more effectively than one's competitors.

This latter approach is the one which is in fashion at the moment while the production and selling approaches, in particular, have been discredited in recent years. However it would be wrong to suggest that this means that organizations have now adopted a market-led approach. Many still operate one of the other approaches or a mixture of two or more of them. Indeed, it is arguable whether or not a truly market-led approach can ever be fully achieved because organizations often cannot rapidly change their product to meet changes in market demand. They have existing staff and plant which cannot always be quickly changed or modified. Clearly, organizations will only seek to satisfy those customer needs and wants that allow them to meet their own corporate objectives, within their financial resources.

Being market-led is not just about improving the way a company markets its products. It is also about being used as a marketing tool in itself by organizations which think that being seen to be market led or customer centred will lead customers to view them more favourably and will make it more likely that they will purchase the product. This idea is reflected in many of the slogans being used by organizations in their advertising. The following three examples will suffice to illustrate the point:

- 'Everything We Do is Driven by You' (Ford Motor Company)
- 'Have it Your Way' (Burger King)
- 'You're the Boss' (United Airlines).

Marketing visitor attractions

All the ideas discussed earlier in this chapter are clearly relevant specifically to the marketing of visitor attractions. However, most of the theories have fundamentally developed from the field of manufacturing industries primarily. Visitor attractions, on the other hand, are fundamentally a service product and therefore their marketing needs to be considered in terms of the fact that they are service organizations in general and tourism organizations specifically.

Visitor attractions as services

As we saw in Chapter 3, service products, as opposed to manufactured goods, have a number of distinctive characteristics which have implications for how they are marketed. These are highly relevant to the attraction product and are outlined below.

1 The *staff* involved in the production and delivery of the product are part of the product itself as they come into direct contact with customers, and staff attitudes and behaviour directly affect the customers' enjoyment of the product. Staff are therefore a crucial consideration in the way attractions are managed and are a vital element in attraction marketing. Disney is a good example of an organization that has recognized this.

2 The product is *intangible* so that customers cannot experience it and try it out before they decide to buy it. Therefore, marketing must encourage people to buy a product on the basis of an image and information received rather than on the basis of personal experience. This means brochures are very important, as is editorial coverage in the media, hence the importance of press and public relations for attraction marketers. Given that many people who have not visited attractions before rely on word-of-mouth recommendations from friends and relatives, it is important that the experience of visitors is a good one so that they will give a positive impression to potential visitors.

3 As the product is *perishable* and cannot be stored, there is a tendency for last minute discounting to ensure that some income at least is received for a product that will have no value once it has perished. This is the rationale behind last minute package holiday deals for example. As few

attractions require pre-booking this phenomenon has only limited relevance to attraction marketing.

4 *Customers are part of the production process* and their attitudes and behaviour affect their experience and that of other customers. The problem for attraction marketers is that these variables are largely outside their control and are difficult to predict. However, we do know that certain types of visitors such as schoolchildren and the elderly can have very different attitudes and behaviour patterns, and that bad weather tends to change attitudes and behaviour for the worse.

5 The *service product is never a standardized product* because of the uncontrollable variables that affect it including the different attitudes and moods of the staff who deliver the product. Quality control is difficult to achieve therefore, but is no less important than it would be in a manufacturing company. Many other factors affecting the product are outside the control of the 'producer', such as the weather, so that a standardized product cannot be guaranteed by the producer or attraction.

Visitor attractions and tourism marketing

As part of the tourism industry, visitor attraction marketing also shares some of the characteristics of tourism marketing in general, both in relation to the nature of the product and the market. These similarities between tourism generally and attractions specifically are discussed below.

First, the tourism product is an experience that begins in advance of the actual consumption of the product and in some ways continues after the consumption. The experience of visiting an attraction has a number of phases, which are all part of the overall experience:

- the anticipation of the visit – the period of looking forward to the enjoyment that you expect will result from the visit
- the journey to the attraction where the aim is to get to the attraction as easily and quickly as possible
- the time spent at the attraction
- the journey home
- the memories of the visit, both good and bad, and more tangible reminders such as photos and souvenirs.

Attraction operators can only control part of this process but the experience is seen as a whole by the visitors and they will rarely distinguish between what is the responsibility of the attraction and that which is outside the control of the attraction operator. The nature of the total experience therefore is what ought to concern attraction marketers.

Second, tourism products offer only *shared use rights* in that you cannot usually buy exclusive rights to use them. For attractions this means it is important, wherever possible, that groups who may be in conflict with each other, such as school groups and the elderly, are not mixed together.

Likewise tourism products only offer *temporary use rights* after which the purchaser has no further rights in relation to the product. For most attractions this period is one day, although it can be longer or if there is a prescribed tour that all visitors undertake it can be a shorter period of as little as one hour or less. For many events the period will relate to the length of a performance such as a play or an activity such as a football match. The period spent at an attraction tends to determine the level of spending per person (the longer the stay the higher the spending) and the daily capacity of the site. In both ways, the length of stay therefore influences the financial performance of the attraction.

Fourth, the *customer has to travel to the product rather than the product being delivered to the customer.* This means that accessibility is a crucial factor in the likely success of an attraction and means that signposting, for example, and good directions and brochures are very important marketing tools for attractions.

The next factor is that the *demand for tourism products is highly seasonal,* with the bulk of demand coming in July and August. Weekends are also usually much busier for attractions than weekdays. Attraction marketing is therefore often concerned with trying to stimulate off-peak demand to improve the utilization of the attraction at quieter times.

Finally, the *price* charged is not always dictated by supply and demand. Some of it is related to social objectives such as increasing use by disadvantaged groups. This is probably more true of attractions than any other sector of the tourism industry.

Key issues in visitor attraction marketing

In addition to those characteristics which attraction marketing shares with other services generally and tourism products specifically, there are others that are particularly relevant to attractions. These are discussed briefly below.

The *marketing objectives* of attractions are very varied depending usually on the sector in which the attraction operates, namely the private, public or voluntary sectors. For private attractions the objectives are often profit, market share, expanding the product portfolio of the organization or achieving a satisfactory rate of return on investment. On the other hand, public sector attractions may have wider and less financial objectives, including widening leisure opportunities for the community and encouraging participation by people who are socially disadvantaged. However, spending controls are making public sector attractions concentrate more on generating income. Finally, the voluntary sector attractions tend to use tourism as a means to an end in that the money received from visitors is poured back into the main work of the attraction operator, which tends to be education and conservation.

Attractions are *marketed by other people as well as by themselves.* For example tour operators use them in their brochures to encourage people to take particular holidays, while governments promote major attractions to encourage people to visit their country. Finally, local authorities and tourist boards use attractions as a major part of their marketing of tourism destinations.

A third important factor is that the *level of competition* varies dramatically between types of attractions. For example, the theme park and seaside amusement arcade business is highly competitive, while local authority museums and sports centres tend to be mutually exclusive in that councils only operate them within their own area. Therefore, the only competition tends to be internal competition where the only museums in an area may all belong to the same local authority and will therefore, in effect, be competing against each other. The nature of competition is complex and some 'competitors' can simply be other uses of leisure time and disposable income, such as gardening and home entertainment.

A fourth point is that the attraction market is particularly *volatile and fashion led*.

Many key factors in the visitor experience are *outside the control of attraction operators*, such as the weather. It is therefore important that attraction operators are aware of this and take action accordingly, such as providing facilities for bad weather or promoting the fact that they are under cover.

Visitor usage rates vary dramatically from occasional purchases, perhaps just once in a lifetime, to people who may visit the same attraction many times a year. For example, an American paying their only ever visit to Northern England might visit a heritage centre once while a local resident interested in local history may be a frequent visitor.

Attractions tend to have *high fixed costs* so that sudden increases in visitor numbers do not increase their costs significantly while low visitor numbers do not allow them significantly to reduce their costs. This fact has implications for marketing, and particularly pricing and sales promotions.

Finally, many attractions have *small marketing budgets and no specialist marketing staff*.

New developments in marketing

Marketing is a relatively new subject and it is constantly developing. Two of the most recent developments have significant implications for attraction marketing.

Relationship marketing is highly fashionable today. It is based on the idea that it is easier to retain existing customers than to have to go looking for new ones. Organizations therefore seek to communicate constantly with customers and give them incentives to stay loyal. A good example of this is the frequent flyer programmes of the airlines. As yet attractions have made relatively little use of this idea although a few do have season tickets or 'friends' schemes, but this will undoubtedly increase in the future.

The author has written elsewhere about *demarketing* and remains convinced that this concept will grow in importance in the future. It involves using marketing techniques to persuade people *not* to buy or do particular things. This could be important to attractions in terms of trying to:

- reduce visitor numbers at overcrowded attractions
- reduce visitors at peak times
- discourage particular groups of visitors such as noisy tour groups in cathedrals.

Having introduced the marketing concept, in relation to attractions, it is now time for us to move on to look at the application of the principles and techniques of strategic marketing planning to attractions.

Discussion points and essay questions

1 Compare and contrast the four approaches to marketing – production, product, selling and market led – in relation to the attractions sector.
2 Discuss the implications of seasonality of demand for attraction marketers.
3 Discuss the implications for marketing of the fact that the attractions product is largely intangible and bestows only shared use rights on visitors.

Exercise

Look at the work of several marketing theorists such as Drucker, Kotler, Levitt, and Gronroös. Compare and contrast their ideas on marketing. Finally, examine the application of these ideas to visitor attractions.

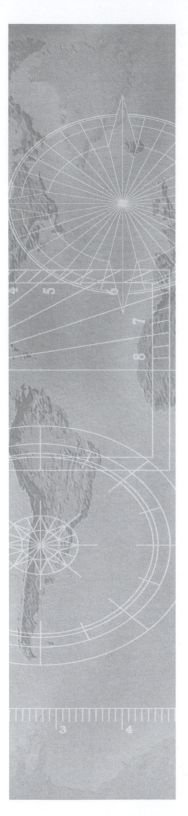

Strategic marketing planning

Strategic marketing planning is concerned with the systematic organization of marketing to ensure that it achieves the wider objective of the organization. It incorporates marketing planning at the strategic, longer-term level and the tactical, short-term level. In simple terms, strategic marketing planning sets out to answer the following four questions:

1 *Where are we now?* This means analysing the organization's current situation and direction.
2 *Where do we want to be in the future?* This involves establishing mission statements, and setting goals and objectives.
3 *How are we going to get there?* This means devising strategies and tactics to help the attraction achieve its goals and objectives, and looking at implementation issues.
4 *How will we know when we get there?* This involves monitoring progress, evaluating the performance of the marketing function and setting up systems for modifying the marketing activities and/or the strategies and plans in response to this monitoring.

This implies that the strategy process starts with a blank sheet of paper. This is clearly not true for organizations, which usually have an existing strategy plus a number of constraints including their financial and staff resources, their history and culture, and their existing product portfolio.

Strategic marketing planning involves the use of a range of techniques that will be discussed later. It usually works to a specific time period which could typically be five years so that there is a five-year strategy geared to helping the attraction attain a certain position at the end of that period. There will usually be one-year tactical marketing plans developed each year to help move the attraction towards this ultimate goal.

The rationale for strategic marketing planning

Strategic marketing planning is valuable to organizations for a number of reasons, including:

- the effective allocation of resources
- pinpointing the organization's strengths and weaknesses
- identifying market threats and opportunities
- forcing organizations to clarify their mission and look to the future
- ensuring that methods of evaluating performance are developed
- making sure attractions consider their competitors
- guiding day-to-day marketing activities
- allocating responsibilities to individual members of staff.

The strategy hierarchy

It is important to recognize that marketing strategies exist at different levels, as follows:

- organization-wide strategies, for example the Tussauds Group or an individual attraction if it is not part of a larger organization
- strategic business unit, or individual attraction, strategies within a larger organization, for example, Alton Towers or Warwick Castle
- individual product strategies, for example educational services or corporate hospitality.

Where are we now? Analysing the current situation

The strategy relies on an objective and comprehensive analysis of the current situation of the attraction. A number of techniques are available to help with this task including SWOT (Strengths, Weaknesses, Opportunities, Threats) analysis, Boston Consulting Group matrix, product life cycle, market segmentation and product positioning. These techniques must not be used slavishly or in isolation; it is better to use them in a way that works for the attraction than in a way which simply follows the textbook model.

SWOT analysis

This is perhaps one of the most badly understood and used techniques in marketing, so it is worth spending some time discussing the principles on which it is based. It is designed to look at the gap between where the attraction itself is now, at the beginning of the plan period, and the direction in which its market or markets are moving now and the way they will change over the plan period. The aim then is to ensure that the strategy bridges the gap so that by the end of the plan period the attraction and its markets are matched and in harmony.

To this end the strengths and weaknesses are internal to the attraction and are based on the situation as it is at one point in time, namely, the beginning of the planning process. Furthermore, these are the factors over which the attraction has control or considerable influence. Conversely, the opportunities and threats relate to factors which are external and outside the control of the attraction, and they are considered in terms of not only the situation today but also how they will change over the plan period. They are posed as opportunities or threats because it is believed that most of these factors could become either, and which one they eventually become depends on the way the attraction responds to them.

It will by now be apparent that SWOT analysis is strongly related to the concept of the business environment (see Chapter 5) with the strengths and weaknesses generally corresponding to the microenvironment and the opportunities and threats being similar to the forces in the macroenvironment. However, as we shall see, it is slightly wider than the factors that make up the business environment, and the distinction between internal and external does not totally correspond to the microenvironment and macroenvironment.

The elements that might be taken into account in an evaluation of an attraction's strengths and weaknesses would be the following:

1 The *organization*, including its financial and staff resources, its culture, the influence of marketing in the corporate decision-making structure, existing strategies, and the way quality is managed.
2 The *marketing system*, in other words the way in which the attraction is currently marketed. This includes issues such as the size of the budget, performance measures and which staff are involved in the marketing function.
3 The *product or products* which the attraction offers. This means the core product together with the tangible and augmented products, and includes the quality of service offered by the staff. It also covers the physical characteristics of the attraction and the support services such as shops, catering outlets and car parks. Finally it is important to look at the image and reputation which the attraction has and the benefits it offers to its customers.
4 The *existing market* of the attraction in terms of variables such as place of residence, reason for visiting, benefits sought, usage rate, age, sex and stage in the family life cycle, for example.
5 The *suppliers* and the quality of goods and services they provide for the attraction.
6 The *marketing intermediaries* and the image and messages they give about the attraction to potential visitors.

At the end of this exercise there should be an inventory of strengths and weaknesses. Wherever possible, the result should be presented so that like can be compared with like. In other words, the strengths of the organization should be placed alongside the organization's weaknesses and so on.

It is questionable how objective managers can be in analysing the current performance of the organization they manage. Sometimes consultants can play a useful role in this part of the process. Furthermore, it is important to obtain the views of customers on these issues as it is their perceptions that are potentially most important. Some attempt should also be made to prioritize the strengths and weaknesses in order of importance.

Turning our attention to the *opportunities and threats* that are facing the attraction, and will face it in the future, these should be considered under the following headings:

- *political* factors, including legislation and government policy
- *economic* factors, including the state of the economy and the distribution of wealth
- *social* factors, including demographic change and trends in consumer behaviour which will influence the size and nature of the future market
- *technological* factors, in terms of technology that can help attractions, such as virtual reality, and those that pose a threat, like home-based entertainment systems
- factors in the *natural environment* such as pollution and other types of damage, given that the natural environment is often a crucial resource for attractions
- *competition*; this means identifying competitors and analysing their strengths and weaknesses and their likely future strategies. This should help attractions see how they might use their strategy to gain a competitive advantage over these competitors.

Again there should be some indication of the weight of importance of each individual opportunity or threat.

The decision to put any individual item under either the opportunity or threat column will depend on the nature of the current strengths and weaknesses of the attraction. What is seen as a threat now can be transformed into an opportunity by changing the organization itself in a way which allows this transformation. For example, if a zoo decided to invest in improvements to give it a reputation for conservation work and looking after the welfare of its animals, it could possibly overcome the potential threat caused by the rise of public dislike of the idea of zoos. It would be seen as a market leader and could sell itself as a new kind of 'post-zoo' animal attraction. It could even exploit new technology such as virtual reality to take this idea further, perhaps by replacing animals altogether.

The problem with SWOT analysis is that it happens at one point in time – it is a 'snapshot' which forms the basis of a plan that will last for a number of years. During this period it is likely that the internal and external circumstances on which the SWOT was based will change. It could be, therefore, that modifications might need to be made to the strategy in response to these changes.

The Boston Consulting Group matrix

Whereas SWOT analysis looks at the organization as a whole, the Boston Consulting Group (BCG) matrix focuses on the range of products offered by an organization, in other words, its product portfolio. It examines products in the portfolio, one by one, in terms of their share of the market for that particular type of product and the rate of market growth in the market for this particular product. The model is illustrated in Figure 13.1.

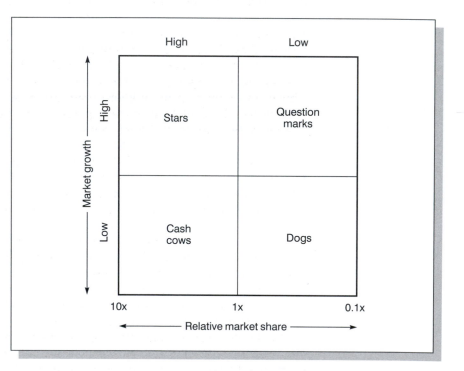

Figure 13.1
The Boston Consulting
Group matrix

This technique can be used in two ways.

1 To look at whole businesses within a group such as the properties owned by the National Trust or individual attractions such as Alton Towers within the Tussauds Group.
2 To examine business activity in individual products offered by a company or attraction. In the case of attractions this could mean corporate hospitality or educational services, for example.

The matrix splits businesses or products into one of four categories which each have implications for the generation and selection of strategy options:

1 *Stars*: these businesses and products enjoy a high market share in a rapidly growing market. They should be providing stable profits for the organization but there is a danger of competitors coming into the market to challenge the star's position in these high-growth markets. The strategies for these products therefore need to focus on maintaining competitive advantage.

2 *Question marks*: these businesses and products have a relatively low market share in a rapidly growing market. This may be because they are old products that are being overtaken by competitors or they may be new products which have just been launched into the market. The aim therefore will be to prevent them turning into 'dogs' or increasing market share to convert them into 'stars' respectively.

3 *Cash cows*: these businesses and products have a high market share in a market which is growing at a modest rate only. They are steady generators of cash flow and are thus vital to organizations.

4 *Dogs*: these businesses and products have a low market share in a market with only modest growth rates. Often the best option here is to terminate the business or stop providing the product or to sell the business or product to another organization. Alternatively, they may sometimes be kept to provide a platform for future stars or to put pressure on competitors' 'cash cows'.

It is clear from the above that 'stars' and 'question marks' require investment to allow them to maintain their position or realize their potential respectively. On the other hand 'cash cows' and 'dogs' may provide investment through steady cash flow or the profits from the sale of a business or product respectively.

The aim therefore is often to achieve a balanced portfolio that may include businesses or products in all four categories. This means using strategies to move businesses or products from one box to another over time. This may seem surprising, but think for a minute what would happen if all an organization's businesses or products were 'stars' and 'question marks'. There would be a great need for investment but there would be few internal sources of such funding. External sources such as bank borrowing or the selling of shares would have to be considered which would be far less satisfactory. If all the businesses or products were 'stars' the organization could find itself being attacked by competitors on all sides and could see its overall market position decline dramatically.

We can see that the matrix not only helps organizations assess their current marketing situation and look at their future marketing opportunities and threats. It also focuses attention on a number of other areas of management strategy, such as the following:

- the management of cash flow and the planning of investment
- acquisition and diversification policies
- the organization's human resources in terms of their expertise and experience so that potential future strengths and weaknesses can be identified.

However, there are a number of problems in trying to apply the BCG matrix in the attraction business. Some of the main ones are:

1 The model assumes there is a competitive market which, as we have seen, is not always true, as, for example, in the case of local authority museums and sports centres.
2 It also assumes that it is possible to measure market share for a particular business or product. This is often difficult or impossible in the case of attractions, as markets are often ill-defined and cannot be measured.
3 Finally, the model is based on the idea of rational decision-making within the context of the private sector where organizations seek to maximize their financial performance. However, many attractions exist within the public or voluntary sectors, where any strategy decisions are taken on the basis of political or social objectives. The model is incapable of handling this level of complexity.

Product life cycle

When analysing their current situation, organizations may wish to know where their attraction is in terms of the product life-cycle. In marketing terms this is important for two main reasons:

- The type of customers is different at different stages in the product life cycle, which means the marketing media used to reach them and the marketing messages they will respond to will likewise be different at each stage.
- Organizations need to recognize when they need to relaunch their product as this is a major exercise in product development that implies significant investment over and above the normal cost of marketing.

The product life cycle is discussed in detail in Chapter 3.

Segmentation

In terms of deciding where we are now it is important that attractions do not just focus on their product, but also on their existing market. This means producing a profile of those who already use the attraction in terms of the major methods of market segmentation that were discussed in Chapter 4. This means looking at the existing visitors in terms of criteria such as their age, sex, place of residence and social class, together with their lifestyles and personalities, perhaps. The aim is to see how the current market segments relate to market trends to see what gaps exist between the current situation and the way the market is moving. It is then possible for strategies to be devised that will help bridge the gap. For example, a theme park segmentation exercise may show that it has a largely youthful market at a time when demographic trends indicate that most growth will take place in the older age groups. This may suggest to an attraction that it needs to develop marketing strategies that will help it attract more older visitors.

Product positioning

The final technique we will consider in this section also focuses on the market. Product positioning means looking at where customers perceive you to be in the marketplace. Figure 13.2 shows some hypothetical examples of a product positioning 'map' that an attraction marketer might adopt. Managers could then see whether customers' perceptions either mirror their own view of the attraction's position in the market or their aspirations for where they wanted to be seen in the market.

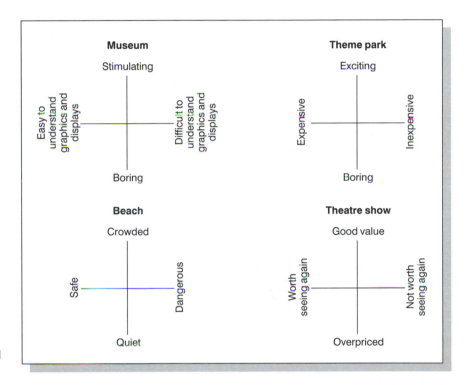

Figure 13.2
Product positioning and attractions

In marketing terms, any disparities between the customer and the manager's viewpoint imply a choice. The attraction's market and product have to be changed to reflect the views of customers, along with the product, or else the marketers have to try to attract new customers whose perceptions will match those of the attraction managers.

The importance of marketing research and management information systems

Clearly all the techniques we have discussed are only practical if good marketing research and management information data are available. This includes:

- visitor numbers and a profile of existing customers, ex-customers, and non-users

- visitors' perceptions and opinions on the attraction
- objective information on the organization and how it operates
- up-to-date information on competitors and their performance
- a thorough appreciation of the position of the attraction in the marketplace as a whole
- an understanding of likely changes in the macroenvironment.

Furthermore, using them as a basis for strategic development also implies a knowledge of other things, such as the likely costs involved in turning a 'question mark' into a 'cash cow', or of relaunching an attraction that is in decline, for example.

Tables 13.1 and 13.2 illustrate the main types of methods of marketing research that are relevant to attractions. It has to be said, however, that for many attractions, particularly those in the public and voluntary sectors, and some attractions in the private sector, such data are simply not available.

Research category	Used in	Typical marketing use
1 Market analysis and forecasting	Marketing planning	Measurement and projections of market volumes, shares and revenue by relevant categories of market segment and product types
2 Consumer research	Segmentation and positioning	(a) Quantitative measurement of consumer profiles, awareness, attitudes and purchasing behaviour, including consumer audits (b) Qualitative assessments of consumer needs, perceptions and aspirations
3 Products and price studies	Product formulation, presentation and pricing	Measurement and consumer testing of amended and new product formulations, and price sensitivity studies
4 Promotions and sales and research	Efficiency of communications	Measurement of consumer reaction to alternative advertising concepts media usage; response to various forms of sales promotion, and sales force effectiveness
5 Distribution research	Efficiency of distribution network	Distributor awareness of products, stocking and display of brochures, and effectiveness of merchandising, including retail audits and occupancy studies
6 Evaluation and performance monitoring studies	Overall control of marketing results and product quality control	Measurement of customer satisfaction overall, and by product elements, including measurement through marketing tests and experiments

Source: after Middleton (1994)

Table 13.1 The main types of marketing research

A. Desk research (secondary sources)
1 Sales/bookings/reservations records; daily, weekly, etc. by type of customer, type of product, etc.
2 Visitor information records, e.g. guest registration cards, booking form data
3 Government publications/trade association data/national tourist office data/abstracts/libraries
4 Commercial analyses available on subscription or purchase of reports
5 Previous research studies conducted; internal data bank
6 Press cuttings of competitor activities, market environment changes

B. Qualitative or exploratory research
1 Organized marketing intelligence, such as sales-force reports, attendance at exhibitions and trade shows
2 Group discussions and individual interviews with targeted customers/non-users to identify perceptions and attitudes
3 Observational studies of visitor behaviour, using cameras or trained observers
4 Marketing experiments with monitored results

C. Quantitative research (syndicated)
1 Omnibus questions of targeted respondents
2 Syndicated surveys, including audits

D. Quantitative research (ad hoc and continuous)
1 Studies of travel and tourism behaviour and usage/activity patterns
2 Attitude, image, perception and awareness studies
3 Advertising and other media response studies
4 Customer satisfaction and product monitoring studies
5 Distribution studies amongst retail outlets

Source: after Middleton (1994)

Table 13.2
The range of available marketing research methods

If managers decide that the only way they can obtain vital data is through surveys they need to decide:

- who will carry out the surveys
- when and how often they will be carried out
- how many people will be surveyed and how they will be chosen to ensure that the sample is representative
- what questions to ask
- how they will analyse the results of the survey.

Finally, managers need to remember that there are other sources of marketing research data; and while these may not be statistically sound, they still give a good indication. Such data can include visitor complaints and competitors' literature, for example.

Looking at the attraction from the customer's point of view

When conducting marketing research it is all too easy for busy attraction managers to see their attraction only from their own point of view. However, if the attraction is to be successful it is important to remember that it is the view of the customers which is most important. From time to time, therefore, managers might consider trying to put themselves in the shoes of their customers by looking at the attraction from the visitor's point of view.

Managers should imagine they are visiting their own attraction as a customer for the first time. They should compile a list of the strengths and weaknesses of their attraction from the point of view of such a customer. They might then decide how to promote the strengths as part of their marketing, and what action they could realistically take to tackle the weaknesses.

For most attractions it is important to recognize that their market consists of a number of different distinct types of visitors with their own particular needs and desires. They may want to produce lists of strengths and weaknesses for each of these groups which typically might include school parties, families, foreign visitors and those who have difficulty in walking.

However, it is very difficult for managers to look at their attraction in such an objective manner. They might therefore enlist the help of other people in this exercise, namely their staff and customers, to ensure that the results are as objective as possible. Staff can help draw the manager's attention to problems and the complaints made most frequently about the attraction by visitors. Meanwhile, managers may also wish to elicit their visitors' views directly either by talking to them or by 'shadowing' or 'tracking' specific visitors on a particular day to see for themselves the good and bad things they experience when visiting the attraction.

At the end of this phase of the process, an attraction should have a good idea of where it is now and what opportunities and threats it will face in the future. It is then in a position to start to look at where it ought to be going, how it will get there and how it will know when it arrives. This is illustrated in Table 13.3, which shows the sequence of action that should unfold from this point.

It is important to recognize, as stage 10 implies, that attractions will normally not start this process with a clean sheet. Instead they start with the previous strategy or a set of problems and issues if there is no existing strategy.

Where are we going? The setting of goals and objectives

Answering this question involves a sequence of steps. The attraction must begin by *defining the future business* they want to be in; in many cases this will mean continuing within their existing parameters. In other words, a theme park may decide it wants to continue to be a theme park offering 'white knuckle' rides to a youngish market, but just wants to do it more profitably. However the attraction may wish to alter the whole nature of its

Stage in the process	Action
1 Define the business	Setting the parameters within which the attraction will operate including the nature of the product that will be offered
2 Mission statement	A brief statement covering the main direction and purpose of the attraction during the period covered by the plan
3 Setting goals and objectives	These will relate to the overall aims and mission of the attraction
4 Generating strategy options	Looking at the different ways in which the objectives might be achieved
5 Evaluating the strategic options	Deciding which option fits in best with the attraction's current situation, history, culture, resources, mission, objectives and other corporate policies
6 The marketing strategy covering the full plan period	Agreed set of chosen routes to help achieve the objectives
7 Marketing plans	Tactical plans covering shorter time periods that guide the tactical action that is needed to implement the strategy
8 Resource statement	Outlines what resources will be required to implement the strategy and marketing plans. It also allocates implementation responsibilities to individuals
9 Evaluation and control	The monitoring and review of the implementation of the strategy and the process which is used to ensure that the strategy is kept on course and responds to changing circumstances
10 Current situation analysis	At the end of the plan period the process starts all over again

Table 13.3
The strategy development and implementation process

business, either by diversifying or divesting. For example, Chessington World of Adventures decided, on the basis of a current situation analysis and in view of changes in consumer demand, to diversify away from being simply a zoo to being seen as a theme park with more than just animals. Alternatively some attractions may decide to focus on their core business and sell off or stop offering some of their other products. A hypothetical example of this might be a museum that decided it would no longer offer facilities for school visits because the education market was too volatile and dependent on government legislation or because its subject matter did not follow topics covered in the National Curriculum.

Having defined the business, attractions need to develop a *mission statement* that encapsulates what the attraction wants to achieve, the direction it wishes to take, and how it wants to be seen by the market and its competitors. Mission statements tend to be short and broad but they provide the framework for the setting of goals and objectives. Several possible mission statements, or parts of mission statements, that attractions might adopt are outlined below to give readers an idea of their content:

- 'To become the market leader in the UK theme park market.'
- 'To offer the highest standards of service to customers at all times.'
- 'To maximize profits through satisfying the needs and wants of customers more effectively than competitors.'
- 'To use the economic benefits of tourism to further the educational and conservation work of the organization.'

As well as giving a picture of the organization's aims to outsiders, the mission statement should act as a unifying force for the attraction's staff, so that whatever their job, they all understand what the attraction is trying to achieve.

The traditional distinction between *goals and objectives* is a blurred one, although the conventional wisdom is that the former tend to be more general and the latter more specific. It is perhaps better to talk about objectives and targets, in the context of attractions. Typical objectives for attractions might include the following:

- To win a greater share of the market.
- To achieve competitive advantage over specific competitors.
- To maximize revenue while minimizing costs.
- To improve awareness of the product.
- To increase profits.
- To increase visitor numbers.
- To improve the balance and stability of the product portfolio.
- To improve cash flow.
- To attract more visitors from disadvantaged groups.
- To improve the quality of service.
- To improve the rate of return on capital invested.

These objectives should then be turned into more detailed targets wherever possible to make it easier to evaluate the success or failure of the strategy. In the case of the objectives outlined above, these targets might be as follows:

- To increase the attraction's share of the theme park market from 10 per cent to 15 per cent within five years.
- To introduce a new product feature that the main competitor does not have, such as a new type of technology, like virtual reality, a new ride, a set of unique artefacts, or a very prestigious exhibition.
- To increase retail sales by 20 per cent within five years, without increasing overhead costs.

- To create a clear brand image for the attraction.
- To increase gross profit by 10 per cent every year during the plan period.
- To attract an extra 10 000 visitors in year one, 15 000 in year two, 20 000 in year three, 25 000 in year four and 30 000 in the final year of the five-year plan period.
- To introduce a new product into a growth market and withdraw a 'dog' from a stagnant market.
- To reduce the seasonality of demand so as to even out cash flow over the year as a whole.
- To attract more visitors from ethnic minorities so that by the end of the plan period the percentage of visitors from ethnic minorities will reflect the proportion of the population which is from ethnic minorities.
- To reduce customer complaints by half within five years.
- To improve the rate of return on capital investment employed from 7 per cent to 12 per cent within five years.

Attraction managers might also define their objectives and targets in relation to the techniques discussed in the section on current situation analysis. For example, they could be framed in terms of the Boston Consulting Group matrix or product life cycle profile the organization would wish to have for its product portfolio at the end of five years. Likewise, it could set itself the target of achieving a specific product positioning in the mind of its customers or a specific customer profile made up of the most desirable mixture of market segments. If these ideal, future desired actions are superimposed on the current situation it graphically illustrates the gaps that exist and which the strategy will need to try to close.

How are we going to get there? Devising the strategy

There are several stages in the development of strategies to achieve the goals and objectives. Strategy choices have to be generated and evaluated. An agreed strategy can then be developed for the full plan period with marketing plans to guide the tactical action that is required to implement the strategy. There needs to be a clear statement of the resource implications of the chosen strategy to help integrate it into the overall corporate planning of the organization.

The generation of strategic options

Strategies are all about attractions using the resources and variables they control (for example the organization and the product) in such a way that they achieve their goals and objectives. It is all about exploiting opportunities and neutralizing threats or turning them into opportunities. This means being proactive and dynamic. There are a number of ways in which organizations may try to achieve these aims; the skill is in choosing the strategy that is most appropriate for the particular attraction at the time.

The generation of strategic options

Strategies are all about attractions using the resources and variables they control (for example the organization and the product) in such a way that they achieve their goals and objectives. It is all about exploiting opportunities and neutralizing threats or turning them into opportunities. This means being proactive and dynamic. There are a number of ways in which organizations may try to achieve these aims; the skill is in choosing the strategy that is most appropriate for the particular attraction at the time.

There are a number of techniques available which offer organizations a range of choices. *Ansoff's matrix* (see Figure 13.3) looks at how the product and market can be manipulated and gives managers four options:

1 *Market penetration*, which involves increasing the usage of the existing product by the existing market. For attractions this might mean offering season tickets as incentives for more frequent repeat visits.
2 *Product development*, which means offering new products to the existing market either to increase usage and spending or to retain brand loyalty. This could involve introducing new 'white knuckle rides' at theme parks or better shops and catering facilities at museums or new types of shows for theatres which have a core of regular users.
3 *Market development*, which means finding new markets for the existing product. A good example of this was when Club Med started marketing its product to the English-speaking market – in the UK, Ireland and the USA. Other examples could include industrial heritage attractions with a local or regional catchment area trying to encourage overseas visitors to visit them while on a holiday in the UK. Or it could mean local authority sports centres trying to attract users from other local authority areas.

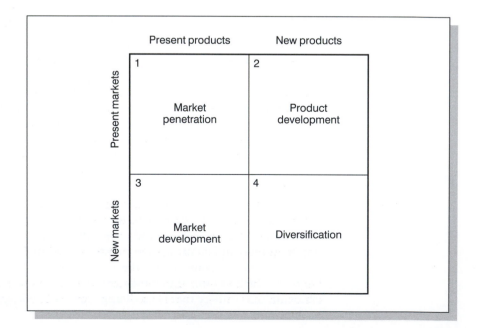

Figure 13.3
The Ansoff matrix

4 *Diversification* is a highly risky strategy that involves offering new products to new markets, in other words a move away from the core business. This could include an attraction like Granada Studios Tour when it opened the Victoria and Albert Hotel, or a museum that started to offer consultancy services for example. However, probably the most common example is attractions that develop new corporate hospitality packages for the business sector. Clearly, diversification can operate at different levels from a slight change to a massive shift in product and market.

The importance of these four options is that they tend to have different implications for marketing strategies. Market penetration is a low-cost alternative that mainly involves the use of promotional techniques. Product development can be very expensive in terms of buying new on-site attractions such as rides or artefacts. Market development implies an enormous effort in promotion with considerable expenditure on advertising and literature. Finally, diversification means large amounts of investment and a high level of risk.

Moving on to the second technique, Michael Porter, in 1985, identified three types of generic marketing strategy which an organization might adopt to achieve competitive advantage:

1 *Cost leadership*. This means using economies of scale and cost efficiencies to become the lowest-cost producer so that you can either undercut competitors or charge similar prices to competitors but achieve better profit margins. As we saw earlier in the book, for many types of attractions a value-for-money image is more important than price alone in determining the success of attractions. It would appear therefore that the method is of relatively little relevance to most attractions. In any event the existence of high fixed costs at attractions reduces the opportunity for economies of scale and cost reductions. Some commentators also believe that cost leadership is a relatively crude strategy that eventually gives way to one of the other two types of strategy.

2 *Product differentiation*. This means developing and marketing the product so it is different from that of other competitors, so that price is no longer the main consideration because the product on offer is no longer the same. For example, if a theme park has a spectacular ride that no one else has, price becomes less of an issue. Attractions often look to achieving product differentiation but it can be expensive – and your competitors often quickly copy what you have done so that your product is no longer differentiated.

3 *Market focus*. This is where an organization decides it will focus on a particular market segment and try to achieve its objectives by becoming the market leader in a niche market. Some spas, for example, specialize in treating people with a particular type of disorder.

These techniques are useful but they are only two of a number of ways in which options can be generated. Attractions will often look at the strategies adopted by their competitors. It would also be wrong to give the impression that the approaches outlined above are mutually exclusive; they can be, and often are, combined.

Evaluating the strategic options

There are a number of ways of evaluating strategic options, a number of tests that can be applied to see which ones are most appropriate for the attraction in question. These normally relate to the likely outcomes and the resource implications of adapting particular options. The outcomes will be measured in terms of how far the options will take the strategy in the direction of achieving the organization's objectives. The resource implications will include:

1 *Financial resources*: what expenditure will be required and when it will be spent?
2 *Human resources*: what implications are there for recruitment and training?
3 *Physical resources*: what new equipment or buildings will be required?

In addition to these relatively objective considerations, the evaluation process, like the generation of options, will be influenced by subjective factors such as the attitudes and prejudices of managers, for example.

The final strategy

We now have a strategy that will guide the attraction's marketing for five years. However, it must be flexible and capable of responding to changes in the basic assumptions on which it is based. It is worth building into the strategy ideas on how it might adapt to the most likely changes such as those relating to the state of the economy.

The strategy should include timescales for action within the five-year period and should talk about who will be responsible for different aspects of its implementation. Many strategies fail because they are strong on analysis and ideas, and weak on implementation.

Strategies are fine for giving a broad-brush picture but they are of limited value to those who are responsible for day-to-day marketing at the attraction. They are too general and their timescale is too long. Tactical marketing plans, usually covering one year, are therefore used to operationalize the strategy and guide marketing activity on a day-to-day basis.

A critique of strategic marketing planning

Most people accept the logic of strategic marketing planning, even if in practice they find it difficult to operate. However, some people question whether the whole concept is relevant to service organizations like attractions that exist in highly volatile business environments. They argue that strategies can become rigid blueprints that are incapable of adapting to changing circumstances and exploiting unforeseen opportunities.

These commentators tend instead to follow the ideas of writers like Tom Peters (1989) in his book *Thriving on Chaos*. They say organizations should concentrate on being dynamic and flexible so that they thrive on the challenges posed by change rather than finding change an irritant to be resisted. This implies that marketing is less about strategies than it is about the culture of the organizations and the attitudes of staff.

There is clearly much to be said for this philosophy, although it is perhaps based on a mistaken view that strategies have to be rigid or inflexible. Furthermore, there is a danger that this idea of 'thriving on chaos' can be used as an excuse for a lack of direction and ad hoc crisis management, so that for customers and staff it can seem more like 'drowning in chaos'. Nevertheless it should be possible to combine the best elements of both approaches to produce strategies which provide clear direction for attractions and guidance for day-to-day marketing without losing the ability to be flexible, dynamic and responsive to changes.

In addition to this objection to the concept of strategic marketing planning, other criticisms of a more specific nature are made about it. These include that:

- the process is too time-consuming, particularly for smaller attractions
- it requires market research data which are well beyond the means of most attractions
- it is a technical process and few attraction managers have the necessary training or experience
- 'hunches', judgement and experience are more effective than pseudo-scientific methods of marketing planning – the well-known 'seat of the pants' approach.

Perhaps the main value of strategic marketing planning is the fact that it makes marketers think in structured and systematic ways about what they are doing.

Discuss points and essay questions

1 Discuss the strengths and weaknesses of existing marketing research in the attractions sector, based on the types of research identified in Tables 13.1 and 13.2.
2 Evaluate the potential application of Ansoff's matrix to visitor attractions.
3 Discuss the contention that strategic marketing planning is of little value in a rapidly changing market like the attractions sector.

Exercise

Select an attraction and conduct a detailed SWOT analysis of the attraction, with each part being supported by evidence.

The implementation of marketing strategies

Marketing strategies are generally implemented through marketing plans. In this chapter we will look at how the 'marketing mix' is manipulated through marketing plans to achieve the aims of the attraction's marketing strategy. It also includes a consideration of marketing organization issues at visitor attractions.

Marketing plans

Marketing plans are programmes of action which should incorporate answers to the following questions:

- What will be done?
- When will it be done?
- What will it cost?
- Who will do it?
- How will it be measured?

The plans are usually based on manipulating the marketing mix to help the attraction implement its strategy. For, as Kotler said, the marketing mix is the set of controllable marketing variables which the firm blends to produce the response it wants in its target market. Traditionally the marketing mix has meant the four Ps, namely, Product, Price, Promotion and Place. We now look at these four Ps in more detail.

Product

Product covers the following elements:

1 Designed characteristics and packaging: for example, for a museum this includes the building, the artefacts, methods of interpretation and support services such as shops and cafés.
2 Service component: including the number of staff and their appearance, competence and attitudes. Disney attractions are renowned in this respect and much effort is put into recruitment and training.
3 Image and reputation: for example, is a museum considered to be exciting or dull?
4 Branding: does the attraction have a well-recognized brand name, such as Alton Towers and Madame Tussauds?
5 Positioning: is the attraction seen as being at the top or bottom end of the market and is it seen as a market leader?
6 Benefits bestowed: museums and galleries offer the chance to learn while some special events offer status, and theme parks provide excitement.
7 Quality: the quality management systems used by attractions and the level of quality they achieve, perhaps measured by the number of complaints.
8 Guarantees and after-sales service: in other words, what is done to help customers if something goes wrong or how customers are looked after and communicated with after they have visited the attraction.

Price

Price is a very complex issue for attractions. It covers a range of aspects, including the following:

1 List price or normal price: the standard admission and usage charge, usually the individual adult rate.
2 Discounts: these are used for marketing purposes to attract more visitors at quiet times or to attract market segments who are thought to be highly desirable such as families (because of their spending) and groups (because of their numbers). Discounts can be of two types, namely, reduced cost (50 pence off, for example) or added value (such as 'two for the price of one' offers).
3 Concessions: these are reductions on the normal price which are made on the basis of social objectives, the idea being to allow 'disadvantaged' people to visit attractions who might not otherwise be able to afford to visit. This approach is particularly common at public sector attractions, which have wider social goals than commercial attractions, and tend to be aimed at people such as students and the unemployed. There are dangers in this approach, however, for when such concessions are given to disabled people for example, it reinforces the view that they are different to other people and are by definition poor. The same is also true of elderly people, some of whom are affluent and do not need such concessions to encourage them to visit attractions.

Marketing managers must understand the differences between discounts and concessions as they are based on different principles and are offered for different reasons:

1 Value for money: as we have seen this is perhaps more important than the actual price paid. However, this is clearly a subjective area that will depend on people's personal opinions.
2 The cost of travelling to and from the attraction: this is important because it is all part of the cost of a trip to the attraction. Again this will vary depending on who is the customer, how far they have travelled and what method of transport they have used.
3 Methods of payment: in other words, whether you can pay in advance or only on the door and does the attraction accept credit cards.
4 Credit: for group bookings, the credit terms are important.
5 Price/quality trade-off: this covers the important relationship between the price charged and the quality of the product.

Promotion

A bewildering range of promotional tools are available to marketers but attractions tend not to use all of them. The main ones are outlined below.

Literature ● ● ●

As customers cannot inspect the product before purchase, the attraction brochure is vital. The success of attraction literature tends to depend on its design and content, the size of the print run, and how well it is distributed. While nothing can guarantee success, following a few simple guidelines often improves the effectiveness of literature. For example:

- There should be *different brochures for different purposes*, such as those for ordinary visitors, and those for group visits.
- The *size and format* of each piece of literature should be chosen so that it is convenient for customers to pick up and carry around with them. An A4 sheet folded twice, for example, is a common format for attraction brochures.
- The *design* should grab the attention of the target market.
- The *content* should provide the information required by the potential customer, such as facilities and location, together with the right editorial to make them want to visit the attraction.
- An *appropriate print run* must be chosen so that there are neither too many nor too few to meet the needs of the attraction.
- An *effective distribution system* will ensure that brochures are not wasted by being on the wrong shelves at the wrong times of the season (or not on any shelves at all).
- *Brochures must not become dated*: for example, if price information is put on a brochure it may become out of date when prices are changed.

An example of an attraction leaflet, for Buckingham Palace, is illustrated in Figure 14.1.

Figure 14.1

Attraction leaflet for Buckingham Palace

Table 14.1 The advantages and disadvantages of different advertising media for attractions

Type of medium	Advantages	Disadvantages
1 Television	Visual and moving image	Expensive to buy advertising space
	Reaches wide audience	High production costs for advertisers
	Customers tend to remember television advertisements and be influenced by them	Cannot be stored for future reference by consumers
2 Radio	Relatively inexpensive in terms of air time and production costs	Cannot be stored for future reference by customers
		Relatively low impact on listeners – sometimes used as 'wallpaper', in other words, the listener's attention is often not concentrating on what is being said on the radio
3 Newspapers	Visual image	Stationary image
	Can be stored for future reference by customers	Often tied to when a newspaper is produced, which could be weekly in small towns
	Often daily, so message can be changed frequently	
	Modest advertisement and production costs	
4 Periodicals	Visual image	Stationary image
	Can be stored for future reference	Relatively infrequent production means information can be come dated
	Good for reaching target audience of people interested in topic covered by the periodical	

Type	Advantages	Disadvantages
5 Annual guides and yearbooks	Visual image Often consulted by people who are really interested in a particular subject	Stationary image Annual publication means information can become dated Often relatively high cover price may reduce readership
6 Posters (a) Transport (e.g. airports and rail stations)	Visual image Colourful	Stationary image Relatively inexpensive site rental but passers-by pay relatively little attention as they are engaged in other activities
(b) Other sites (e.g. roadside hoardings)	Visual image Colourful Large size Prominent locations, e.g. major road junctions	Stationary image Expensive site rental
7 Placement (getting the product featured within programmes rather than in advertisements)	Reaches mass audiences May be more influential if it is not a paid advertisement as people may take in the message subconsciously	Difficult to arrange Can be expensive in the case of mass market television programmes and films

Advertising • • •

Some major attractions such as theme parks and important special events can afford expensive television advertising while other attractions may use it on a one-off basis to promote special events like craft fairs at stately homes. Otherwise the press are the main paid advertising medium for attractions, including local and regional newspapers and magazines and guides aimed at people who take day trips. Relatively little use is made of radio and poster sites for attraction advertising. Successful advertising depends on designing the right advertisement and placing it in the right media at the right time. It has to be said that most attractions, particularly those in the public sector, tend to have relatively small advertising budgets. Table 14.1 outlines the main advantages and disadvantages of the major different advertising media for visitor attractions.

The cost of advertising media is usually related to a combination of factors including the number of people who the advertisement will reach (newspaper circulation and viewer figures, for example) and how influential the medium is thought to be in persuading customers to buy particular products.

However, as most attractions are not mass-market products, but rather are niche-market products, there is usually no need to utilize the expensive mass-market media. Highly targeted advertising strategies are usually more relevant. This targeting can take a number of forms including:

1 Targeting media which are aimed at appropriate niche markets. As these media will have smaller circulations/viewing figures than their mass-market equivalents, their costs will be lower. For example, a dry ski slope may choose to advertise on television only on a late-night ski programme, while industrial heritage attractions may use specialist magazines aimed at enthusiasts.
2 Advertising at certain times of the year only, such as theme parks advertising at the start of school holidays.
3 Targeting potential customers in a particular geographical area that can be targeted through local newspapers, for example, which are less expensive than the national newspapers. As most attractions have predominantly local or regional catchment areas this is often a sensible approach. For example, the local weekly newspaper may be the best advertising medium for a council-owned museum in a small market town.

Television is only used rarely by attractions due to the high cost involved. In the UK, when it is used it tends to be in one of the following situations:

• by large family market attractions such as theme parks, at the beginning of the summer and Easter school holidays
• just before and during public holidays, of which, major garden centres are a good example

- when a new product is being launched
- a 'one-off' single advertisement promoting special events, such as a theatrical performance at a historic house.

Ultimately advertising decisions are usually a trade-off between the available budget and what managers would ideally like to do. If the budget is large enough it may be worth using an advertising agency to help make the advertising effort more professional and effective. They may be able to buy advertising space at lower rates and will be able to advise on the target markets of different media, so managers can see to what extent the audiences they want to reach read a particular publication. They can also help with advertisement design. However, their advice is not inexpensive and they need to be carefully chosen and briefed if they are to be a valuable addition to the team.

Press and public relations

Unlike paid advertising, press and public relations can give attractions free editorial coverage in the media. This depends on providing the media with good stories in the form of press releases, although whereas with advertising you control the content of the advertisement and when it appears, with press releases there is no guarantee they will be used and journalists can change and edit them in ways the attraction may not like. Nevertheless it is potentially a free method of promotion which can be very useful for attractions with limited marketing budgets.

Sponsorship

Attractions may sponsor events, people or organizations to give people a positive image of the attraction and to make people aware of its name. For example, zoos might sponsor an animal conservation campaign. The key to success in sponsorship is to choose things to sponsor that appeal to your target market.

Direct marketing

Increasingly marketers are communicating directly with customers, through, for example, direct mail to people's homes. Attractions use this method quite infrequently but they do use direct mail in relation to the group and school-visit markets. To do it well requires good databases but these can be very expensive to acquire.

Sales promotions

These are temporary offers or discounts that are used to attract business at quiet times. An example would be a scheme whereby children are allowed into the attraction free when accompanied by an adult who has a coupon from a particular newspaper.

Personal selling • • •

This is not commonly used by attractions but there is an element of personal selling when staff represent attractions at exhibitions and trade fairs where they talk directly to potential customers.

Signposting • • •

This is a crucial way of making potential visitors aware of the attraction's existence, given the high reliance of many attractions on persuading 'passing trade' to visit the attraction.

Internet marketing • • •

Since the first edition of this book was published in 1995, the Internet has revolutionized distribution in many sectors. As yet its role in the attraction sector is limited. However, it still has the potential to:

- encourage the development of pre-booking and direct marketing
- allow two's – promotion and place – to be combined, so that potential visitors can gain information [promotion] and make reservations [place] in the same single transaction.

It is inexpensive and therefore allows great potential, particularly for small attractions.

Place

Place, the fourth P, means the place of purchase and includes distribution. In other words it is how the customer is given an opportunity to purchase the product. It is an important issue in manufacturing industries where the norm is to use retail outlets to help deliver the product from the factory to the consumer. In the case of attractions, however, the distribution situation is interesting for two reasons:

1 The customer travels to the product, rather than vice versa.
2 Pre-purchase or pre-booking of the product is rare. Most attraction visitors simply turn up and buy a ticket at the attraction gate. Nevertheless, distribution channels do exist and the main ones are outlined below, although due to the nature of the product and the way it is purchased, it can be difficult to distinguish between place and promotion.

Attraction booking agencies • • •

Traditionally, it has been rare for people to buy tickets in advance for attractions, and where such advance booking has taken place, it has generally involved direct contact with the attraction itself. In recent years a number of agencies have entered the market, operating as marketing intermediaries, including tourist information centres, for example. In general, however, these agencies tend only to operate in the domestic market. An exception to this is the *Keith Prowse* organization. This offers tickets for a range of attractions, including:

- USA: Walt Disney World, Sea World Adventure Park, Busch Gardens, Disneyland, Universal Studios Hollywood, Seaworld California, Legoland California, Six Flags Magic, Mountain Berry Farm
- Canada: Niagara Falls
- UK: Legoland Windsor
- France: Disneyland Paris
- Spain: Universal Studios Port Aventura.

Keith Prowse also offers passes to sets of attractions in the USA and Canada. Furthermore, the organization offers tickets for cultural events and shows, sporting events, and city tours in places as diverse as New York, Toronto, Prague, Dubai, and Sydney.

The brochure lists nine good reasons to buy tickets from Keith Prowse:

1 You are guaranteed *no price increases* after you book.
2 You avoid any price increases at the gates.
3 You can take advantage of *great tickets* – some not available at the gates.
4 For the major theme parks and attractions you get *the actual ticket* of admission. *No queueing* at the ticket kiosk or at the voucher exchange window.
5 *Avoid* the risk of *devaluation of your currency*.
6 *You don't have the worry* of taking extra cash on holiday.
7 You can *plan your holiday fun time and spending* before leaving home.
8 You can *guarantee your seat* at the show or performance of your choice before you travel.
9 You *can plan your holiday itinerary* – make the most of your holiday fun time.

Since the first edition of this book was produced, other such ticket agencies have opened, such as Seligo and Flightdesk. These agencies are part of larger tourism organizations which provide a range of services for the independent traveller.

Additionally, some tourist information centres now sell attraction tickets, sometimes even offering customers a discounted rate if they purchase them from a tourist information centre. Some tickets are sold via packages arranged by tour or coach operators or group visit organizers. Some major attractions can be pre-booked by telephone or direct mail, and computer reservations systems operate for attractions where capacity is limited and pre-booking is the norm, such as theatres.

These are the main distribution channels for the purchase of the product. But there are also channels that exist in terms of how customers gain access to information about the attraction, particularly where pre-booking is not the case. These include literature distribution outlets such as libraries, and attraction consortia that encourage people visiting one attraction to visit other members of the group. Then there are destination marketing brochures which contain information about attractions as part of their mission to encourage people to visit the destination. Clearly, in these cases there is a strong overlap between place and promotion.

The seven Ps

In 1981, Booms and Bitner decided that for service products a seven Ps marketing mix was more appropriate. The extra three Ps are as follows:

- People – in other words the staff in terms of their training, appearance, behaviour, commitment, activities, customer contact and so on.
- Physical evidence – the environment in which the service is delivered, including layout, noise and furnishings, for example.
- Process – namely corporate policies and procedures, including employee empowerment and customer involvement.

Some commentators have said that in many ways these extra Ps are an extension of the product category, but they do emphasize the importance of those three factors in the service sector and they are clearly relevant to attractions.

The resource statement

The marketing plan should include a statement of the resources – financial, human and physical – that will be required for its implementation. It also allocates responsibilities between individuals and sets deadlines for the completion of tasks. There are many ways of writing a marketing plan and there is no right or wrong way. The following example is a hypothetical marketing plan, for an imaginary heritage attraction in North West England. Hopefully, it will illustrate the nature of marketing plans and how tactical action is used to achieve objectives.

A case study

Northtown Canal Basin is an industrial heritage attraction, located in a medium-sized industrial town in Lancashire. The attraction consists of a number of old mills and canal-side buildings which have been converted into museums of social and industrial history. There is also a shop, pub, restaurant, exhibition hall, concert hall and meeting room. It was set up in the late 1980s and was an instant success. In its early days visitor numbers exceeded expectations and within two years it was attracting over 400 000 visitors. Since then the number of visitors has fallen and the managers are endeavouring to achieve an increase in visitors over the period 2001–2.

The marketing objectives for this period have been identified as follows:

1 To attract more first-time visitors from the adjacent regions of West Yorkshire and the West Midlands given that these regions are currently under-represented in the visitor profile.
2 To attract more overseas visitors from selected countries where the attraction is already well known.
3 To use special events to attract more repeat visits by people within the attraction's own region.
4 To attract more group visits, education visits and conference business at off-peak times.
5 To increase per head spending by visitors.
6 To find out more about existing customers and potential visitors.
7 To improve the attraction's reputation for customer service.
8 To monitor the effectiveness of the marketing activity that is undertaken.

All of this has to be achieved within a total marketing budget – excluding staff costs – of £80 000. There are no staff specifically employed to carry out marketing activities at present, so the job tends to be carried out by the general manager.

The marketing plan which was eventually adopted to achieve these objectives is set out in Table 14.2. It ran from April 2001 to March 2002.

It may be that part of the way through the year the assumptions on which the plan is based could change and the plan may need to be modified as a result.

Finally, in reality the question of 'when will we know when we get there?' is never answered, for organizations never arrive at a point where they have achieved their aims and can stop marketing. Changes in the attraction and its business environment mean that the aims and objectives will constantly need to be modified. Furthermore, as one plan period ends another one begins so that there will always be a target to strive to achieve. As we said earlier, marketing is a continuous process.

How will we know when we get there? Evaluation and control

Many organizations do not pay as much attention to this stage as they should; they assume that once they have a strategy, that is the end of the story. But the strategy is only valuable if it works, and evaluation and control are how we ensure the strategy is implemented. It is important therefore that there is a system for monitoring the progress of the strategy so that tactical action can be taken either to get the strategy back on course or to take advantage of new opportunities.

Evaluation requires that the strategy contains measurable targets, and that there are management information systems that ensure that managers have all the up-to-date information they need to see whether or not these targets are being achieved. These systems should include

Table 14.2 Marketing plan 2001–2

	Action	When	Who	Cost
1 Literature	Produce 100 000 copies of a new colour brochure to be distributed via tourist information centres, hotels, other attractions etc. Produced as A4, folded twice	Autumn/winter for when stocks of the existing brochure run out	General manager to oversee with the help of an outside graphics company	£20 000, including distribution
	Produce 2000 copies of a folder into which other literature can be placed	April/May	General manager with help of graphics company	£4000
	Produce 2000 copies of a guide to the attraction for group visit organizers	May/June in time to generate business for the off-peak season	General manager with help of graphics company	£1500, including distribution
	Produce 1000 copies of a guide to the attraction for coach companies to be distributed through a trade journal	June/July in time to generate business for the off-peak season	General manager with help of graphics company	£2000, including distribution
	Produce 1000 copies of a simple guide to conference and corporate hospitality facilities at the attraction	June/July in time to generate business for the off-peak season	General manager with help of graphics company	£2000, including distribution
	10 000 copies of general brochure translated into German and French and distributed via British Tourist Authority offices in Paris, Brussels, Frankfurt and Zurich which appear to be the best non-English speaking markets for the attraction. Copies of the English language brochure will be distributed by the British Tourist Authority in other key markets such as the USA, Canada and Australia	March 2002	General manager with graphics company, translator and British Tourist Authority	£3000

	Description	Timing	Responsibility	Cost
2 Advertising	Advertise in the 'What's On' columns of newspapers in North West England, West Yorkshire and the West Midlands during the school holidays in the summer	July/August	General manager with advertising agency	£11 000
	Limited advertising in trade journals at appropriate times and around the time of key trade exhibitions	April, July and November	General manager with advertising agency	£4500
	Entries/advertisements in annual guides to days out in the region	Throughout the year	General manager with advertising agency	£3000
3 Press and public relations	Press releases to local newspapers, newspapers in other regions, and the trade press with good news stories that will raise the profile, and enhance the reputation of the attraction	Throughout the year	General manager with advertising agency	£1000, mainly postage and stationery
	Competitions in newspapers and magazines in target markets where the attraction offers free entrance tickets in return for free coverage in the press	In time for the school holidays	General manager	No real cost
	Sponsorship of relevant good causes that will improve the attraction's image and raise its profile	Throughout the year	General manager	£3000 plus 'help in kind', free tickets, etc.
	Arrange visits to the attraction by leading travel journalists and broadcasters that will lead to favourable media coverage	Summer/autumn when the attraction is busy and looks its best	General manager	£1000

Continued overleaf

Table 14.2 Continued

	Action	When	Who	Cost
4 Sales promotions	Special offers to boost off-peak business from North West England, West Yorkshire, and the West Midlands. These offers will be made via newspapers. The offers will be added-value offers such as a free gift or cup of coffee with each ticket purchased, or offers such as 'two for the price of one'	Autumn/winter/spring	General manager and advertising agency	No cost for the tickets but £4000 for related advertisements in addition to the general advertising budget
	The promotion of 'children are free when accompanied by an adult' offers to attract business at the start of the school holidays for people in West Yorkshire and the West Midlands, promoted via newspapers	July	General manager and advertising agency	No cost for the tickets but £2000 for related advertisements, in addition to the advertising budget
5 Mailshots	Targeting separate mailshots to organizers of group visits, coach operators, conference organizers and corporate hospitality buyers using databases purchased from the regional/national tourist boards and/or commercial organizations	Late spring/summer	General manager with help of student on placement and/or temporary/casual staff	Distribution costs covered under literature costs. The databases should cost about £2000
6 Exhibitions	Being represented at trade and public exhibitions and trade fairs by the regional tourist board	Throughout the year	General manager	Package available from the tourist board covering representation at all exhibitions at a cost of £4000

7 Membership of regional tourist board	Become a commercial member of the regional tourist board	April	General manager	£4000
8 Market research	Daily surveys of visitors and their opinions about the attraction	Throughout the year	General manager and the attraction staff	Little if any
9 Special events	Providing a venue for special events in the off-peak period that might attract further visitors, including concerts, entertainment and special food promotions in the attraction restaurant	Off-peak season	General manager	No net cost. Indeed it should contribute income to the attraction
10 Customer service	Customer care courses for all staff	Off-peak season	General manager and local college	£1500
	Foreign language courses for key staff to help them communicate with overseas visitors	Off-peak season	General manager and local college	£1000
11 Monitoring	Install a simple monitoring system for testing the effectiveness of the marketing activity including performance indicators	Developed in April/May but operating all year round	General manager	No real cost
12 Staffing	Students on unpaid placements and casual staff at peak times	Late spring/early summer	General manager	£1000
13 Contingency fund	A modest sum of money to allow the attraction to take advantage of unforeseen marketing opportunities	To be used as opportunities arise	General manager	£3000

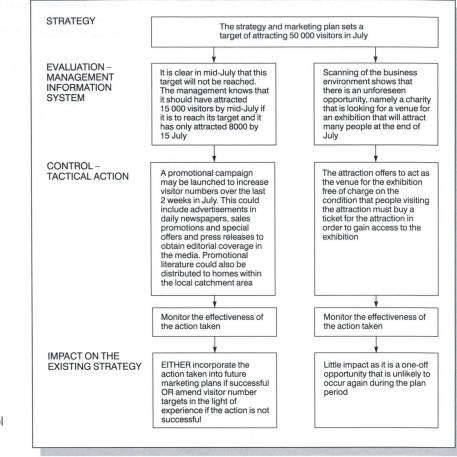

Figure 14.2
Evaluation and control
mechanisms: a
hypothetical example

internal data on the performance of the attraction and external information on changes in the attraction's business environment. There then need
to be control mechanisms to allow corrective action to be taken if the
strategy is off target. Let us look at this using a hypothetical example,
which is illustrated in Figure 14.2. As Figure 14.2 shows, the corrective
action which is taken should ultimately be fed back into the strategy so
that the strategy is modified in response to experience.

Marketing organization

As well as the marketing activities that are actually undertaken, a crucial
aspect of marketing is how the marketing function is organized within an
organization, and how it relates to other aspects of the organization
structure. Traditionally, marketing was a separate department which may
have been orientated specifically towards sales. It was often relatively
powerless against departments like finance and production. However,
with the rise of service industries and the customer-centred approach,

marketing has become more powerful within most organizations and it is now seen as the responsibility of all staff.

The marketing functions that have to be managed include:

- *planning and control*, including marketing research, marketing planning, marketing mix design, product development, marketing campaigns, budgeting, evaluation and control
- *execution and implementation*, such as attending exhibitions, managing advertising campaigns, writing press releases and sales calls
- *co-ordination*, namely, liaison with other departments such as operations, finance and human resources to ensure that the product is related to the customer desires in terms of quality, price and availability.

In large organizations these functions may be the responsibility of different people, in which case, co-ordinating their activities becomes a major preoccupation.

In many ways, large attraction organizations are following the fashions in management theory of decentralization and empowerment. In terms of marketing this implies that strategy will not only be dictated by head office or the chief executive but will also have a bottom-up element as its implementation will involve giving added discretion and responsibilities to front-line operating staff.

So far we have focused on larger attractions but most are in reality small or medium sized. In this situation the general manager often performs the role of marketing manager as part of her or his duties. In this case marketing organization is a matter of how much time a general manager can devote to it when there are often more pressing and time-consuming operational and financial problems to be tackled.

Whatever the size of the attraction organization, the nature of marketing organization is likely to be a reflection of a number of factors, including the size of the attraction, its staff resources, the marketing budget, history, corporate culture and the attitudes of managers. History, in particular, is a powerful force; how often has someone questioned the way an organization manages its marketing, only to be told 'we have always done it that way'?

All the issues discussed above are internal factors but attractions are interesting in that some of their marketing activity is affected by initiatives which are external to, and wider in scope than, the attraction itself. This includes attraction-marketing consortia which practise co-operative marketing. A good example in the UK is the Treasure Houses of England group whose members are Beaulieu, Blenheim Palace, Broadlands, Castle Howard, Chatsworth, Harewood House, Warwick Castle and Woburn Abbey. The consortium produces a glossy colour brochure that features all eight properties. In the past this brochure has featured vouchers offering a sales promotion, namely, 'one adult admission at child rate if accompanied by at least one person paying the full adult rate'. It has also featured a photographic competition with £2500 in prizes, called the 'Treasure Houses of England and Kodak Amateur Photographer of the Year Competition'. Other examples of consortia operating such co-operative marketing include groups based on a particular geographical area such as the Cornwall Association of Visitor Attractions.

As the attraction market becomes increasingly competitive, more and more attraction-marketing consortia are being established. Their aim is to help each member achieve better use of their, usually limited, marketing budget. Members of these consortia tend to carry brochures of other member attractions and combine to take joint advertising which no member on their own could afford. They may also produce a brochure that covers all of the member attractions.

These consortia tend to be of two types:

1 Those made up of similar types of attractions, such as stately homes or farm attractions.
2 Those bringing together attractions in a certain geographical area such as a county (Cornwall, for example) or an area with a well-established 'brand' name, such as Herriot Country or Shakespeare Country.

Furthermore, these attraction consortia are either the result of co-operation between the attractions themselves, or are created by local authorities or regional tourist boards.

An example of such a consortium which developed in the late 1980s is the 'Heritage Six', a group of six industrial heritage museums in North West England. The members included:

- Wigan Pier, Greater Manchester
- Ellesmere Port Boat Museum, Cheshire
- Styal Mill, Cheshire
- Helmshore Textile Museum, Lancashire
- Greater Manchester Museum of Science and Industry
- Merseyside Maritime Museum.

The group was brought together by the North West Tourist Board which provided administrative support for the consortium.

The consortium undertook a range of promotional activities:

- producing a joint brochure that featured a sales promotion, in other words, a money-off offer in relation to the admission charges at the member attractions
- a competition open to people who visited all six member attractions
- a jointly funded advertising campaign in conjunction with the North West Tourist Board
- a joint press release campaign to raise the profile of both the consortium and its individual members.

In the future, marketing consortia may widen their activities to include such possibilities as becoming purchasing organizations to allow individual members to take advantage of the economies of scale in purchasing that a consortium might achieve, or setting quality standards and operating as a self-regulating body to maintain quality standards.

Another type of external marketing organization is public sector destination marketing, where attractions are used as a tool by local authorities or government to market an area or a country as a tourist destination. A good example of this in the UK is found in the Potteries area of Staffordshire where the city of Stoke-on-Trent tries to attract tourists by promoting a range of attractions related to the ceramics industry under the title of the 'China Experience'. This consortium has continued, supported by the local authority, and an up-to-date case study of it is to be found in Part Four of this book.

Proactive attractions will ensure that they become involved in such campaigns, and use them as part of their marketing plans. It is important that managers are always looking for ways of making their marketing organization more cost-effective and efficient, and more responsive to changes in their business environment.

Constraints on marketing

Some of the major constraints are listed below:

- the budget available
- the strengths and weaknesses of the marketing staff, including their training, experience and attitudes
- the corporate culture of the organization and its history
- unforeseen changes in the business environment
- the legal framework, such as consumer protection legislation and health and safety regulations
- ethical considerations
- the actions of competitors.

The diversity of attraction marketing

Attraction marketing is, as we have seen, not a homogeneous activity. Its nature varies between different types of attraction and from one organization to another. This variety includes differences in objectives, marketing activities and marketing organization. One of the main distinctions tends to be between large and small organizations, in which case these distinctions are generally related to resources. In other words, larger attractions tend to have more money and specialist staff to devote to marketing. The other major distinction tends to be between attractions in different sectors, namely, the public, private and voluntary sectors. Here it is mainly the objectives that will vary between sectors.

Many marketing objectives in the public sector tend to be social, while those in the private sector are usually related to profit and financial performance. There are also differences between the sectors in terms of the freedom of action of managers, in that public sector managers operate within constraints that do not affect their private sector counterparts by and large, such as decision-making based on party politics for example.

The role of marketing research

It is widely accepted that in an era of consumer-led marketing, marketing research is of crucial importance. We need to know more about attraction visitors if we are to market attractions more effectively. We need to understand more about the following aspects of the market:

- how visitors decide which attractions to visit
- the factors that influence customer satisfaction at attractions
- the reasons why people do not visit particular attractions
- customer perceptions of attractions.

At the same time we have to recognize that marketing research is not just market or consumer research. It is also about:

- identifying and analysing competitors
- predicting important changes that will take place within the business environment of the attraction
- measuring the effectiveness of the attraction's marketing activities.

It is clear, therefore, that attractions need to devote more resources to marketing research.

The future of attraction marketing

Attraction marketing is likely to change dramatically in the future in response to a number of changes in the wider business environment. Some of the most important likely changes are outlined below:

1 The *nature of the product* will change due to technological developments such as virtual reality.
2 The *market* will change in terms of its demographic structure and its behaviour. There will be more older people with money and the concern with green issues may start to have a real impact on attractions.
3 Technology may also influence the choice of *media* available for use by marketers. For example, direct marketing may become more important if British houses begin to gain access to home-based database networks like the French Minitel system which is linked to the telephone.
4 Any changes in the *law* such as law relating to consumer protection and data protection, to name but two areas, will be relevant to attractions.
5 *Political factors* such as the growth of the EU and the changes taking place in *Eastern Europe* may create wider international markets for attractions. Perhaps in the future we will see the rise of the 'Euro-attraction consumer'. This change will also mean that attractions have to become more skilled at marketing their product internationally.
6 The future will bring change in the nature of *competition*, both from other attractions and from other uses of leisure time and disposable income.

Attraction marketing will also be influenced by changes in marketing and management theory, which is a field that is subject to fashion cycles. For example, will De Bono's concept of 'Sur-Petition' replace the idea of competition, and will attractions seek to achieve competitive advantage by selling themselves on the basis of 'value monopolies' where they sell their ethics and values as an integral part of the product? Such an approach appears to be successful in other industries if the Body Shop experience is anything to go by. If the next fashion is going to be business ethics and social responsibility as many commentators believe, 'value monopolies' could replace traditional models of competitive advantage such as those put forward by Porter.

These chapters have looked at attraction marketing both as a concept and as a practical activity. They have looked at marketing activity as a process and at the techniques which are part of this process. We have seen how strategic and tactical marketing relate to each other, and have discovered that the nature of marketing varies between large and small attractions and between public, private, and voluntary sector attractions. These chapters have shown that strategic marketing planning is a useful tool to guide decision-making and day-to-day marketing but it is not a panacea and it should never be seen as a way of producing blueprints that should be followed exactly.

Marketing is also a creative activity, and successful marketing means combining structured and systematic ways of thinking and working with imagination, judgement and experience to ensure that the attraction is in harmony with its target market. Ultimately, it is the response of the market that will determine whether or not an attraction is successful.

Discussion points and essay questions

1 Discuss the advantages and disadvantages of marketing consortia in the attractions sector.
2 Devise performance indicators to help monitor the effectiveness of the hypothetical marketing plan case study set out in this chapter.
3 Discuss the application of the Booms and Bitner seven Ps to attractions.

Exercise

Collect the brochures of a number of attractions and analyse them in terms of their size, format, style, and content. Discuss the extent to which the brochure would persuade you to visit the attraction and why.

Human resource management

Introduction

The management of the human resource at attractions could arguably be considered to be the most important aspect of the management of visitor attractions for two reasons. First, as a service industry the attitudes and abilities of the staff will have a crucial impact on the way the service is delivered to the customer and will therefore directly affect their enjoyment of the visit and their perception of the attraction. Second, for most attractions labour costs are likely to be the largest single item in their revenue budget.

Human resource management is concerned with obtaining, organizing, training, motivating and rewarding the people needed by the organization so that they perform in a way which allows the attraction to meet the needs of its customers. In recent years, particularly related to the rise in service industries where staff are a key part of the product, human resource management has become a fashionable area of management theory, and has lost its old name of 'personnel management'. In the past, personnel management was a relatively narrow area involving mainly mechanical tasks such as recruitment advertising, organizing interviews, advising managers on the technical aspects of personnel matters and, often, dismissing staff. By contrast, human resource management is a much wider activity that takes a holistic view of the organization's human resources and adopts a positive, developmental approach to their management. However, it must be said that while this concept of human resource management is now widely accepted in theory by managers its implementation in practice is perhaps more limited.

Three main ideas underpin the growing interest in human resource management:

1 Organizations have to seek to maximize the effective use of their staff just as they have always sought to optimize the use of their financial resources and physical resources.
2 The organizations that are likely to achieve the best performance from their staff are those which are concerned with helping their staff develop themselves, in the widest sense, as individuals.
3 Human resource management is exactly what its name suggests, in other words it is a management, not an administrative, task.

Furthermore, it is now widely recognized that human resource management is not solely the job of someone who has the words on the door of their office, but rather that it is the responsibility of anyone who has management or supervisory responsibilities. It is also inextricably linked with other areas of management such as marketing (given that staff are part of the service product) and financial management (as staffing is likely to be the largest single item of expenditure in the budget).

Even more fundamental is the fact that human resource management is now seen as being crucially important in the development and implementation of corporate strategy in the broadest sense. The buzzwords of recent years, such as corporate culture, quality and change management, all imply a pivotal role for human resource management. Corporate culture means the attitudes, beliefs and values of the staff; quality includes the quality of service delivered by the organization's people, and it is surely the staff who have to change most in any change management process.

Indeed the major challenge facing tourism organizations (and organizations in other industries) in recent years has been the need to change in response to the rapidly changing business environment. This challenge has only been met successfully by organizations that have given more attention to, and developed fresh ideas in relation to, human resource management.

The problems of human resource management at visitor attractions

It has to be said that in general the tourism industry does not have a particularly good reputation in the human resource management field, although there are many exceptions to this generalization. Perhaps this situation has arisen due to the fact that the tourism industry generally and attractions in particular have a number of characteristics which make effective human resource management very difficult. These include:

1 *High turnover of staff*, which may be a result of the relatively low pay, long hours or the monotonous nature of many jobs. This is a commonly voiced set of complaints about tourism jobs but it is not always a true picture. Nevertheless, whatever the reason, turnover is often relatively high, particularly at some types of attractions such as seaside amusement parks.

2 *Seasonality of demand* means that much labour is casual and temporary, which can result in little commitment to the job and a very limited amount of time available for training.

3 *Poor status* of jobs, which means it is difficult to attract and retain good staff.

4 *Lack of career structures* and 'ladders of progression' at many attractions, particularly the smaller ones, means there is a lack of opportunities for intelligent and well-motivated staff.

5 *Unusually demanding jobs*, in that staff are constantly exposed to visitors, and are expected to be smart and cheerful at all times. Furthermore, they have to handle sensitively the complaints of people who feel that their visit, of which they have probably expected so much, has not lived up to their expectations. People who can perform well in this stressful environment are difficult to find.

6 *A lack of management expertise* in the human resource field at many attractions where there is no specifically designated human resource manager and the managers have little formal training in the management of people.

7 *Lack of widely recognized qualifications and training schemes* for attraction staff that could make recruitment easier and more reliable for employers, and give the industry a better image in the minds of prospective employees. Perhaps this is a function of the fact that the attraction business is relatively new and such qualifications and schemes have not yet had time to become fully established, although there have been some significant developments in recent years.

It is important to note that most of the problems discussed above relate to private sector attractions rather than those operated by the public sector. Attractions operated by central government and local authorities tend to have their own particular set of problems, some of which are in direct contrast to those in the private sector. They include:

• *low turnover*, which means that with tight budgets and fewer opportunities for creating new posts, little 'new blood' can be brought into the attraction

• *inflexible working practices* that are not compatible with operating in the tourism industry, such as not working on Sundays

• *fixed-wage rates* that are not related to performance and are often above the market rate for similar jobs in the private sector; this can often be the case with catering supervisors and shop staff, for example, at public sector attractions

• *standardized recruitment procedures and disciplinary procedures* that were not developed with attractions in mind and are not appropriate.

The last three problems make it difficult for public sector attraction operators to compete with their private sector counterparts on a level playing field.

So far we have focused on the problems of human resource management at attractions. However, it is imperative that we put these problems into context and balance them by looking at some of the good points about the management of people at attractions. Taking private and public sector attractions as a whole, their problems are probably less than those of other sectors of the tourism industry such as hotels and travel agencies. Furthermore, there are many examples of good human resource management and stable, contented and productive workforces at attractions in both the public and private sectors.

Human resource management at the strategic level

There are a number of ways in which human resource management is an issue for attraction operators at the strategic level:

- *management styles* and the attitudes taken towards the role of managers, staff relations and how these relate to the corporate culture
- *management structures and hierarchies* and the level of autonomy and responsibility given to staff and their role in decision-making
- staff planning and the cost-effective use of human resources
- the role of staff in the implementation of changes in corporate strategy, in other words *change management*
- the part played by the workforce in a service sector organization in the *quality* of the product generally and in systems such as quality control, quality assurance and total quality management specifically.

Management styles

The management style which attractions adopt, consciously or unconsciously provides the climate in which human resource management operates within the organization, while structures and hierarchies provide the formal framework. Management style shapes the experience of what it is like to be a member of staff in a particular organization and there are many different styles. The two extremes are perhaps best summed up by what are called the 'old manager', who is often equated with the traditional manager, and the 'new manager'. In reality most managers fall between the two extremes. This is discussed at length in Chapter 11.

It is obvious that the style adopted by managers is crucial to how staff feel about their job, their line manager and the organization as a whole, and this in turn will influence the way the members of staff deal with the visitors.

Management structures and hierarchies

Management styles are reflected in the structure of organizations. The management structure adopted by an organization has a number of functions:

- It provides the framework for co-ordinating the work of the organization.
- It lays down the channels of communication.
- It establishes the links between different departments and different levels within the organization.
- It identifies line management responsibilities and determines the decision-making process that will operate.
- It allows individuals to see where they fit into the organization as a whole, and to whom they are responsible and for whom they are responsible.

There are a number of ways in which attraction organizations can be structured. Some of these are outlined below:

1 *Centralized or decentralized*. In some cases power or responsibility is centralized in the hands of one or two people while in others everyone has a share.
2 *Informal or formal*. Some organizations operate on the basis of personal contact and word of mouth, while others rely on formal methods of communication and control such as memos, standing orders and procedure manuals. Most organizations operating the informal system tend to be small but when organizations grow they usually feel the need to adopt more formal structures.

While these two choices of approach relate to the organization as a whole, managers also have to decide on what basis they will sub-divide the organization. They have four main choices:

1 *Function based*. This is the traditional way of structuring organizations in which they are split up according to management functions such as marketing, human resources and finance.
2 *Product based*. This means dividing the organization up on the basis of the product offered. Within a single attraction this could mean having divisions for retailing, catering, conferences and education services for example.
3 *Market based*. This would mean focusing on the different market segments served by the attraction, such as schoolchildren, coach parties, corporate users and overseas visitors.
4 *Spatially based*. Here the organization is sub-divided on the basis of the geographical spread of its activities. Clearly for individual one-site attractions this would not be appropriate. However, large organizations which have a number of attractions often do organize themselves on this basis, for example the National Trust and English Heritage.

However, it is normally the case that no single approach will be satisfactory and that there will need to be a combination of more than one. This means adopting a *matrix structure*, a hypothetical example of which is illustrated in Figure 15.1 for a museum, using a mixture of function and product. Clearly this is just one possible approach, there are

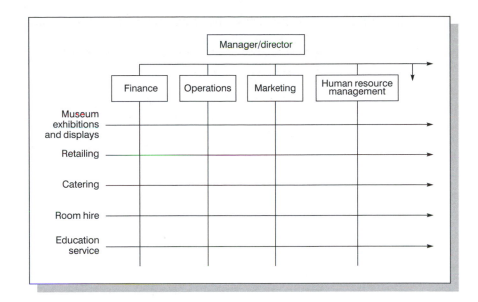

Figure 15.1
A matrix structure for a visitor attraction

many others. As we said earlier, the type of structure will depend on variables such as the size of the organization and the sector in which it operates. Small private attractions often have no formal substructure and most of the staff will perform a number of functions. In major corporations such as the Tussauds Group the organization will be split into the individual attractions which may be run as separate entities such as Warwick Castle, Madame Tussauds, Alton Towers and Chessington World of Adventures. Within these organizations, staff will often be highly specialized in contrast to those at the small attractions. Finally, within the public sector, structures tend to be traditionally function based with a strong emphasis on administration, although this is changing. In many cases, local authority attractions are part of departments with much wider responsibilities and interests and within which they are just a minor activity. This can cause real problems as the senior managers in the department may not understand, or be sympathetic to, the management of attractions.

In common with other aspects of management theory, much attention has recently been paid to the subject of organizational structure. For service organizations in volatile business environments theorists have said structures should above all be flexible to allow organizations to respond quickly to change. There has also been a move towards 'flattening' hierarchies so there are less tiers. This has been related to the idea of 'empowering' individual staff and it has often resulted in the removal of middle management. The concept of being market led, which is now very fashionable, implies a move away from function-based structures to those focused on markets and products.

Staff planning

Staff planning is concerned with optimizing the use of the organization's human resources, now and in the future. Staff planning has a number of components, including:

- an analysis of existing staff and their strengths and weaknesses
- forecasts of the future numbers and types of staff that will be required, and when they will be required
- training and staff development needs
- career paths for key staff.

In reality few attractions indulge in staff planning on any scale, but if the use of human resources is to be made as effective as possible it is an important task that all attractions, large and small, should undertake.

The human resource process

Having looked at human resource management at the strategic level it is important to look at how the ideas we have explored can be put into practice on a day-to-day basis. We will now examine how attractions can recruit and retain good staff. We will look at the human resource process, from the first recognition that a new member of staff is required, to the time when the new person is well established in their job, to the time when the person leaves the organization for whatever reason. This 'human resource system' is illustrated in Figure 15.2.

The recruitment process

Having taken the decision to recruit a new member of staff, rather than modifying other people's jobs or the operation itself to prevent the need to recruit a replacement, it is first necessary to design the job.

Job design

Job design means deciding what the purpose of the job will be and where it will fit in with other people's jobs. It will set the objectives for the postholder and will determine the content of the job. The job design is vital because it will ultimately determine the level of job satisfaction the person in the job will have and will dictate how effectively the postholder will be able to contribute to the success of the organization.

Managers may decide to keep the job as it was before or they may change it slightly or dramatically in one of the following ways:

- increase or reduce the responsibility and level of autonomy
- enrich the job by adding variety
- maximize the flexible use of the workforce by increasing the range of tasks involved (so-called 'multiskilling' to ensure that staff in different jobs can cover for each other in the event of sickness, holidays or even strikes).

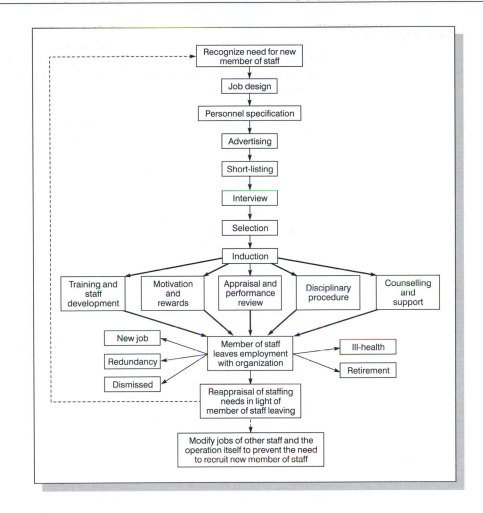

Figure 15.2
The human resource system

Often at attractions little conscious job design is carried out and jobs often stay the same for months and years even after their original purpose has changed or even disappeared. In some cases, however, particularly in the public sector, there are restrictions on the ability of managers to change job designs because of formal procedures or union agreements. When designing a job the views of many people should be sought, including the previous holder and other staff who will come into contact with the postholder.

Job description ● ● ●

Once the job has been designed a job description can be produced. This is essential, not only as part of the recruitment process but also to help with training, reward systems and performance appraisals. However, in the first place its role is to make potential applicants aware of the nature of the job. There is not a single correct way of writing job descriptions but they must be honest, lawful and as detailed as possible. Perhaps a hypothetical example will help illustrate the role and content of the job

Heading	Comments	Hypothetical example
1 Job title	Should indicate the nature of the job	Head of Retail Services
2 Department	–	Retail Services
3 Salary/wage range and remuneration package	This will be related either to the market rate for the post or, in the public sector, it may be determined by national pay scales and locally negotiated agreements. Other aspects of the remuneration package should also be included under this heading	£14 000–£18 000 depending on experience plus other benefits including health insurance and a pension scheme, together with the possibility of bonuses
4 Duties and responsibilities	An outline of the main duties and responsibilities of the post wherever possible. There should usually be a 'catch-all' phrase covering any other duties that may be required of the postholder occasionally	To maximize the profit of the retail operation, both on-site and through mail order Managing the retail operation staff in the most cost-effective manner possible The ordering of merchandise Ensuring the secure storage of stock Stock control and the maintenance of accurate records Budget preparation and financial control Ensuring the highest standard of service for customers Being a member of the attraction management team Other relevant duties that may be allocated from time to time
5 Report to	The postholder's line manager	The General Manager
6 Responsible for	Postholder's subordinates – how many there are and their job titles	3 permanent full-time sales assistants 2 permanent part-time sales assistants 10 seasonal sales assistants 1 part-time finance clerk The postholder is also responsible for managing the concessionaire who operates the mail order business on behalf of the attraction
7 Decision-making power	The limitations on the decision-making power of the postholder should be outlined	The postholder has the power to hire and dismiss all staff employed by the retail operation, subject to the agreed budget, and can spend up to £1000 without needing to obtain the approval of the General Manager

8 Working relationships	People within and outside the organization the postholder will be expected to work with together with an outline of the nature of the relationship	Working with other departmental managers and the attraction management team
		Liaising with the finance department on budgets and financial control
		Working with the marketing department to ensure that the goods stocked are appropriate for the target market(s)
		Buying from suppliers at the best possible price
9 Terms and conditions	Further details of the terms and conditions that go with the post	5 weeks paid holiday per annum
		Period of notice: 2 months
10 Date job description written	Alerts applicant to the fact that the details may change in response to changes in the organization's structure and activities	February 1995 (subject to review)

Figure 15.3 The job description

description. Let us imagine we are recruiting a manager for the retail operation of a large attraction. Figure 15.3 shows a hypothetical job description for such a position.

Personnel specification

While the job description talks about the job, the personnel specification focuses on the type of person who might be the ideal postholder. Some of the headings that might be found in a personnel specification include:

- Age range
- Physical attributes
- Qualifications/education
- Personal skills and qualities
- Experience in a similar post
- Technical knowledge.

These requirements often will be listed in order of priority or may be split into those which are essential or desirable when it is unlikely that any one person will meet all of them.

Many employers are now adopting a competence approach to recruitment; in other words, they are focusing on what applicants can do and at what level. This means breaking skills down into single attributes, some of which may be important while others are irrelevant. For example, communication skills are often put down as a requirement for jobs. However, in the case of a marketing assistant at an attraction who

253

will be doing mainly telephone selling, confidence on the telephone and listening skills are obviously the most important requirement. Furthermore, whereas the term 'communications skills' is rather vague and difficult to assess, the latter attributes are easier to evaluate. This is very important because the main role of personnel specification is to develop criteria which can be used in shortlisting and selection. Competence-based qualifications like National Vocational Qualifications (NVQs) or their Scottish equivalents (SVQs) may in future be a useful tool of recruitment, although their use by attractions currently is limited.

At this stage it is important to note that personnel specifications and job descriptions must be developed with equal opportunities in mind, both in terms of general principles and the law. Duties and competences should not be included unless they are non-discriminatory. Furthermore, in relation to personnel specifications, the attributes should be relevant and necessary for the specific post otherwise good candidates may be excluded because they do not meet a particular, unnecessary requirement. For example, most catering staff rarely need GCSE English when all they need to write down are simple orders, and such a qualification requirement may discriminate against people from countries with different education systems where English is not the first language, and where GCSE qualifications are not available.

Advertising

The role of advertising is to attract suitably qualified people who might be interested in the job to consider the post on offer and perhaps to make an application. This objective must influence the content of the advertisement and the choice of media in which to advertise the post.

The advertisement has to fulfil several roles. It must:

- attract the attention of potential applicants
- accurately outline the purpose and content of the job
- provide enough information to encourage the right candidates to apply
- give a good impression of the attraction to all those who see the advertisement; in other words, advertisements have a wider public relations role.

Most jobs in attractions are advertised in the printed media but the selection of a particular newspaper or journal will depend on the nature of the job. The choice includes local, regional and national newspapers, trade journals and the journals produced by professional bodies. Specialist managerial posts will tend to be advertised through national newspapers, trade journals and professional body publications, while low-skilled, modestly paid posts will often be advertised only in local papers.

It is important to understand that the content of advertisements and where they are placed will affect the types and number of people who will apply. It is vital therefore that advertising is carried out in a way that does not discriminate against particular types of people.

Finally, we must recognize that many attraction jobs are never advertised but are instead filled through friends of existing staff or people existing staff have met in a work context. While this is an attractive option which potentially reduces the risks of recruitment, there are dangers and it is also very much against the spirit of equal opportunities.

Short-listing

Given the large number of applicants there are for attraction jobs, short-listing can be a long, labour-intensive and difficult task. However, the requirements set out in the personnel specification can provide criteria against which to judge applicants, so that many may be discounted at an early stage. Several people should ideally be involved in the short-listing to prevent one person's prejudices and preferences from dominating the process.

Interviews

Traditionally most people who are selected for attraction jobs have been chosen on the basis of a brief interview which might last a few minutes. In recent years the process of interviewing potential managers has become more sophisticated and can now last more than a day and include tests and exercises. However, many of the manual jobs are still filled through very informal, almost casual, interviews. This is understandable in some ways but is very undesirable given that many attraction staff can cause death and injury if they do their job badly. At a more routine level inappropriate staff can damage an attraction's reputation through their poor performance and attitude. The situation is particularly problematical in the public sector where it is often very difficult to dismiss unsatisfactory staff once they have been recruited.

The desire for a quality reputation and efficiency is leading many attractions to devote more attention to the process of interviewing. There is also a growing recognition that the traditional interview is no longer a satisfactory way of selecting people. It is an artificial situation with both parties playing roles rather than being themselves, and the time is often too short to allow the interviewer to fully get to know the candidate. However, the interview does have a role to play and following a few simple rules can help maximize its effectiveness.

- Hold interviews in surroundings which allow interviewees to relax and be themselves.
- Prepare some questions beforehand, based on a thorough reading of the candidate's application form.
- Make the interviewee feel comfortable at the start of the interview.
- Listen to the interviewee and respond to their answers rather than just reading out prepared questions.
- Probe and follow up in areas where the interviewer has concerns about the applicant.

- Take notes to ensure that each applicant can accurately be remembered at the end of a long day's interviewing.
- Give the interviewee ample opportunity to ask questions.
- Allow adequate time for the interview and ensure there are no interruptions.

However, the interview can also be complemented by other activities to help attractions ensure that they recruit the right person. These include:

- individual practical exercises
- formal presentations
- group projects to assess how people work in a team
- personality tests
- group interviews
- social events to see how people behave when they relax.

The type of technique used should reflect the attributes set out in the personnel specification and they will therefore vary from post to post. The aim should be to test the candidate against the desired attributes and the nature of the 'interview' should reflect the nature of the job, so that a formal interview may not be the best way to evaluate a potential theme park ride operator, or a chef, for example. Instead, they should be invited to show what they can do in practical terms.

References

At some stage those responsible for the recruitment exercise will want to consider the applicant's written references. They may also wish to telephone referees for a less formal 'off-the-record' discussion of the candidate's strengths and weaknesses. Deciding when to check references is a matter of opinion. Some managers do it before short-listing or interviewing while others only check the references of the candidate to whom they wish to offer the post.

Selection

In theory, the selection itself should be an objective activity, preferably carried out by more than one person to prevent bias, based on who best meets the personnel specification. In reality most selection decisions are subjective and are based on emotion rather than fact. People choose people they feel 'will fit in' or 'they can work with'. Not only is this against the principles of equal opportunities, as people tend to choose people who are like them or they find physically attractive, but given how cursory many interviews are, it can also lead to problems once the person is in post. Nevertheless, human nature being what it is, the tension between objectivity and subjectivity is always present in the selection process but at least managers should be able to recognize when they are being subjective.

Finally, it is important in public relations terms to act professionally when recruiting staff and that means writing positive letters to all unsuccessful applicants.

Casual and seasonal staff • • •

Many attraction managers would agree with what we have said in relation to permanent staff but would say it is impractical and unnecessary in relation to casual and seasonal staff. While one appreciates the practical problems involved with seasonal and casual staff, it has to be said that the same principles should apply to their recruitment given that the problems that can result from the recruitment of bad casual and seasonal staff are just as serious. Casual staff could in some instances cause injury through their negligence or incompetence, while their poor performance and attitudes could change an attraction's reputation just as easily as that of permanent staff.

Retaining good staff

Retaining good staff requires good systems and effective, sensitive human resource management. It has to begin before the new member of staff's first day at work through a good programme for introducing them to their new job before they arrive.

Induction • • •

An induction programme should have the following components:

- further information about the job and the organization, and if necessary, advice on housing, education and so on if the new member of staff is moving from another area
- the identification of a 'buddy' or 'mentor' who will take responsibility for helping the new staff member to settle in
- a staff handbook containing details on matters as diverse as working hours, health and safety guidelines, staff discounts in the attraction shops and catering outlets, and even the location of staff toilets
- a talk with a senior manager to help show the new recruit where they fit into the organization
- an early meeting with the line manager and those with whom the postholder will be working closely
- a tour of the site to orientate the new recruit
- time to learn about the attraction, the product it offers, and the markets it serves
- any other information that relates to the specific post.

Motivation • • •

Most people are very enthusiastic when they start a new job and the challenge for managers is to maintain this enthusiasm by motivating the staff. One of the main roles of managers, albeit a relatively ignored one, is the motivation of their staff through their actions and their attitudes. In an industry where the work is hard and the pay is modest, managers who can motivate their staff are very valuable.

There are a number of ways in which managers can motivate staff and keep up their enthusiasm, and some of these are outlined below:

- Manage people in a sensitive way and making them feel that their managers understand them.
- Praise people when they perform well and constructively criticizing their mistakes and helping them learn from them.
- Support staff when they are in trouble and protect them from criticism by managers who are not their line managers.
- Allow staff to take risks and learn from their mistakes rather than punishing them for making mistakes.

As well as the actions of individual managers there are a number of more general ways of motivating staff.

Financial incentives can take the form of bonuses and commissions and can either be given to individuals or to teams or to the whole staff. For example, shop staff could be offered a percentage of any increases in profits which they can achieve. A whole range of *non-financial incentives* are available including gifts, trips to conferences and trade shows, and formal recognition such as 'Employee of the Month' award schemes. The latter can be nominated by customers or can be used to encourage improvement from staff whose performance has been below par.

With all such incentives there are, however, two main problems: the criteria that will be used to select people and the fact that some people may be in a better position to gain recognition than others, for example shop staff rather than administrator if income-generation is used as a criterion. Another problem with incentives is that people can come to expect them as a right, in which case they no longer fulfil the role of encouraging improved performance.

Training can often be used to motivate people, particularly if it takes place away from the attraction in attractive surroundings. Being selected for a training course can be used as an incentive or reward, and as it involves the attraction spending money on the member of staff it makes them feel valued by the organization.

The downside of such incentive schemes is, of course that those who are not rewarded may become demoralized, in which case the schemes can be counterproductive.

Job satisfaction can be improved in a number of ways including:

- 'empowerment', in other words, giving individual staff more power to make decisions in their everyday area of work
- variety and job rotation to prevent the boredom caused by doing monotonous tasks all the time
- the existence of promotion on merit rather than length of service and a clear career structure so that people can develop and grow within the organization

- minimizing the constraints and bureaucracy under which the post-holder works
- working in groups so that individuals feel they belong to a team.

Monitoring and improving performance

Staff like to feel that managers know what they are doing so performance monitoring can not only improve the effectiveness of the organization but can also help increase job satisfaction. Most organizations (but not many attractions) have formal performance monitoring systems.

Appraisal and staff development • • •

These two phrases are often used interchangeably but they are subtly different. Appraisal is often seen as judgemental and somewhat threatening as well as being normally concerned purely with the job. Conversely it is usually thought that staff development is broader in scope and is concerned with the development of the member of staff as a person rather than just an employee carrying out tasks. The staff development philosophy is that someone who feels the organization is helping him or her develop as a person is more likely to perform well and remain with the organization.

Most staff development schemes are designed to be a two-way dialogue between staff and their line managers, once or twice a year. Their aim is to produce an action plan for the member of staff that contains targets for achievements and performance improvements over a given period of time. In return the managers undertake to provide the necessary resources, time or training to help the staff member to implement their personal action plan. At the end of the period the plan is reviewed and the person's performance is evaluated. This may or may not be used as a basis for performance-related pay. In the light of the review of the old plan a new action plan will be agreed, and so on.

For staff development to be successful, however, there needs to be trust, honesty and commitment on both sides and both managers, and staff must prepare well for their meeting and it must be a two-way discussion.

Training and education • • •

One of the more common elements in action plans is the identification of the need for training or education to help people perform better in their job and to develop their potential in general. However, training and education can take a number of forms for attraction staff:

1 Mentoring, where an experienced member of staff passes on their experience to a newer member of staff, and encourages and supports the development of the latter.
2 On-the-job training under the supervision of an experienced person. This is how many people learn to operate rides or use tills.

3 Reading manuals or textbooks and then doing practical exercises to put the theory into practice. This is appropriate for people learning to use new computer programs for example. It is also the basis of the current boom in so-called 'distance learning' for those who want to learn without having to leave a job to go on a course.

4 Group problem-solving, such as 'quality circles' where people learn from each other's ideas. For example, the attraction café staff could form a quality circle to look at problems such as queueing and food wastage. Participation in these circles would in itself be a learning experience.

5 Short on-site courses run by the organization's own trainers which could, for example, outline new company safety procedures, or on-site courses run by people from outside the organization. Some attractions are now using outside trainers to teach staff some language skills if they attract many overseas visitors whose first language is not English.

6 Off-site courses which can last from a few hours to many months. In the latter case attendance could be part time or full time. These courses can either relate specifically to visitor attraction management or to relevant general functions and skills such as marketing, assertiveness, computing, or financial management.

Traditionally there have been very few qualifications specifically for attraction staff. The situation is now changing, although the industry has been slow to recognize the importance of qualifications and still often values experience rather than qualifications. Many further and higher education courses now offer modules at different levels on visitor attraction management.

The need is to create courses which are relevant to the needs of industry which will help improve the qualifications of attractions staff which, in turn, will help the attraction business to be taken more seriously and be more respected as a sector of the tourism industry.

Training is, of course, expensive and is only successful if people's individual needs are accurately identified and met. In difficult times, as with most industries, training budgets at attractions will often be among the first to be cut. However, in a service activity where the performance of staff is an integral part of the product, cost-cutting on training is likely to adversely affect the organization's trading position and lead to disenchanted staff. For attractions to succeed it is important that the ideas in this section are applied throughout the attraction, to senior managers and junior staff and to casual and permanent staff alike.

Handling human resource problems

Although good management should minimize problems, there will always be some human resource problems that have to be dealt with, usually relating to situations where staff performance is not acceptable for one reason or another. When such problems occur they need to be dealt with quickly and effectively. Avoiding or ignoring problems with individuals can cause wider difficulties. For example, a lazy person can demotivate other workers who have to work harder to cover for them.

Organizations need procedures to protect the interests of both the organization and the staff. These usually take the form of disciplinary and grievance systems respectively. They tend to be more formal in the public sector, where they are usually part of trade union–management agreements. On the other hand, in the private sector the procedures tend to be more informal. Nevertheless, all attractions also have to live within the legal framework provided by employment law, including the fear of being taken to an industrial tribunal if the organization acts unlawfully.

Disciplinary action is likely to be taken in response to unacceptable behaviour by staff or inadequate performance. Usually there will be a sequence of actions beginning with verbal warnings then written warnings, and finally dismissal. It is important that at all stages the legal rights of workers are respected and good records are kept in case managers have to defend their actions before an industrial tribunal.

There should also be grievance procedures to allow staff an opportunity to seek redress if they feel they have been unfairly treated in any way. It could be a matter of being overlooked for promotion, a perceived lack of support from a line manager, or a disagreement about bonus payments. The system must be seen to be fair and impartial, although in reality many staff will be reticent to complain about their treatment for fear of reprisals, whether this fear is justified or not.

In most industries the disciplinary and grievance procedures would have been agreed with the worker's trade union or unions, and union representatives should support staff at hearings. However, as in much of the tourism industry, unions are quite weak in attractions except in the public sector. Few workers belong to unions and there is no union which specializes in attractions. Some attraction operators would probably not even recognize trade unions or allow their workers to join a union without the risk of being sacked. This lack of union organization makes it more difficult to operate such procedures and less likely that they will be introduced by attractions.

There are other human resource problems that managers must tackle in a sensitive way that is fair to the individual worker but also protects the interests of the attraction. These include workers with serious health problems and people with severe personal difficulties. Managers in this instance need to adopt a counselling role and act in a supportive manner. Failure to do this will probably result in bad feeling on behalf of the colleagues of the person with the problem.

Termination of employment

Sooner or later, every member of staff leaves the employment of the attraction, for any of a number of reasons, some of which we will now consider.

Dismissal

This is usually the result of some form of misconduct on the part of the employee. Managers must be sure of their facts and the law before dismissing a worker or they may face a legal challenge.

Redundancy

This is usually a result of the attraction changing its operations so that the person is no longer required, or the fact that the attraction has problems and can no longer afford to employ the worker. In this case, choosing whom to make redundant is a crucial decision. Managers may choose on the basis of a number of criteria including age, length of service, quality of work, health record and the material circumstances of the workers.

Managers must also be careful not to contravene equal opportunities and employment law when choosing whom to make redundant. For example, it is unlawful to choose people for redundancy just because they are pregnant or are union officials. It is thought to be good practice to help staff who are made redundant to try to find new jobs through careers counselling, help with preparing CVs and so on.

Retirement

Many staff fear retirement and good employers will provide counselling and help to prepare staff for the day when they will no longer be employed at the attraction.

Ill health

Many people have to give up their job each year because of ill health. Either they can no longer work or they can no longer do a particular job. For example, someone employed to carry heavy equipment may develop back problems. Where possible such people should be found new duties which they can manage, but sometimes they may have to leave work. In these cases they should be helped to find a new more suitable job or they should be offered a generous severance package.

New job

When staff leave for a new job managers should conduct 'exit interviews' to see why the person has accepted a new job. People leaving will often be very candid in their views about the organization and such views can be valuable in helping managers appreciate problems they may not have been aware of previously.

Whenever people leave, for whatever reason, except dismissal, the organization should formally recognize their contribution with a gift and/or an event of some kind. Otherwise it gives the staff who remain the message that the efforts of employees are not appreciated by the management.

Someone leaving is an opportunity to review the staffing structure and decide whether to replace the person or modify operations and the duties of other staff so as to prevent the need to recruit a replacement. Attractions may choose not to replace someone for a number of reasons, such as lack of money or the fact that the job may have become obsolete because of changing circumstances. If it is decided to recruit a replacement, then the human resource system starts all over again.

The ideas discussed above represent the ideal but, clearly, they must be implemented in a way which is commensurate with the situation in a specific attraction. They are relatively easy to introduce at large attractions with a specialist human resource manager. On the other hand it is harder to operate such sophisticated systems at small attractions, where one person has to fulfil all the management functions, including marketing and finance as well as human resource management.

Developing groups and teams

So far we have concentrated on individual workers, but human resource managers must also create the climate in which effective groups and teams of staff can develop. Tuckman, as long ago as 1965, identified four stages through which teams or groups pass. First, there is the forming stage, when group members first meet each other and start to take on roles. Second, comes the storming stage when members challenge each other's views on how to carry out the task in hand. Third, there is the narrowing stage when rules and procedures are agreed. Finally, in the performing stage, cohesiveness is achieved and the group begins to work effectively.

Belbin (1981) suggested that in any group members take on roles, and he identified eight types:

- The chair: the social leader who guides and co-ordinates the group.
- The shaper: the person who takes the lead in tackling the task.
- The plant: the imaginative ideas person who needs to be nurtured.
- The monitor: the analyst who keeps a check on the group's progress.
- The company worker: the organizer.
- The resource investigator: the fixer.
- The team worker: the mediator and conflict resolver.
- The finisher: the person who keeps the group on target to meet their deadlines.

Quality circles

Very few attractions have yet adopted the techniques of quality circles that have proved successful in other industries. This involves groups of staff who work together, meeting at regular intervals to discuss issues of mutual interest and to generate solutions to problems. The scale of such problems is usually small and the solutions normally require a modest level of resources. Many commentators believe that for quality circles to be successful the staff teams needed to be empowered to act on their ideas without needing specific management approval, and they should have a small amount of money that they can use at their discretion. It is important, therefore, that issues tackled by quality circles are discrete to the team's own area of responsibility so that any solutions they implement do not adversely affect the other areas of the operation, and other workers.

At attractions suitable topics that might be considered by quality circles might include:

- reducing the level of pilfering from the attraction shop, which could be tackled by the shop staff
- finding ways of reducing queuing at the entrance to the attraction, which might be discussed by kiosk staff
- café staff could look at ways of reducing food wastage.

There is no reason why the quality circle concept may not be used to solve broader issues that affect more than one work team. For example, staff from all over the site, and with different roles, could be brought together from time to time to look at ways of reducing the causes of some of the commonest visitor complaints.

Constraints on human resource management

Until now we have talked about human resource management at attractions as if human resource managers have a free hand to do whatever they want. This is of course not true, and they have to operate within a complex web of constraints, some of which are internal to the organization while others are external (Table 15.1). The factors listed are generally more relevant to private sector attractions, and while they do affect public sector attractions, the latter also face some specific constraints. First, their activities are controlled by government legislation and constraints on expenditure. For example, the legislation on compulsory competitive tendering has meant that at some sports centres and museums many staff may be employed now by outside contractors rather than being recruited and managed by the attraction itself. Thus the human resource managers no longer control certain staff who are crucial

Table 15.1
Internal and external constraints on human resource managers

Internal	External
Budgets	The state of the labour market
The difficulties of predicting labour demand due to the problems of forecasting visitor numbers	Employment law
	Existing provision of training courses and educational qualifications
Corporate culture and history	
Existing staff resources	Accepted ideas on what constitutes good practice among the human resource management profession
Established personnel procedures and practices	

to the quality of the product, such as cleaners. Second, the spending constraints placed on local authorities by central government lead to restrictions on staffing at attractions. Unfortunately these restrictions do not relate in any way to visitor numbers or the financial performance of the attractions. Therefore managers at attractions owned by local authorities, whose spending is being restricted by central government, could find themselves having to run the attraction with fewer staff at a time when visitor numbers are rising. This has enormous implications for both the quality of service offered and staff morale.

Finally, local authority pay rates are set nationally, are part of union agreements and are not related to the market rate. This reduces the freedom of movement of public sector attraction managers and means that often they pay too much for some of their labour. Furthermore established custom and practice makes it difficult for local authority attraction managers to achieve flexibility in the way they use labour. For example, Sunday has never been seen as a normal working day, even though it is usually the busiest day for attractions, and there are often strict demarcation lines between jobs such as museum attendants, cleaners and maintenance staff.

There are also constraints which are specific to attractions run by large companies and others that apply to small private attractions. In attractions which are part of large organizations that own a number of attractions or have interests in other industries, human resource policies may be laid down centrally, giving relatively little freedom to managers at individual attractions. In the case of small private attractions the problem is often that the attraction has one manager who has to fulfil all management functions such as marketing and finance, as well as the management of people. It is likely in this situation that the manager will have little time to spend on human resource management and may well have little or no experience in the field.

Equal opportunities

Some attraction managers see the legislation relating to equal opportunities as a constraint and an imposition. However, the discipline which compliance with this legislation dictates in terms of recruitment procedures, and having to think consciously about everything that is done, can only improve the quality of human resource management at attractions. But there is more to equal opportunities than just compliance with the law. It is a way of thinking, and it means not only equal opportunities for people regardless of sex or race but also ensuring that other groups, such as the disabled and older people, are not discriminated against. As well as the ethical and legal reasons for pursuing equal opportunities there are practical hard-headed reasons for taking equal opportunities seriously. First, staff who are suffering discrimination at work, such as women who are being sexually harassed, are unlikely to be performing to their full potential in their job. Second, failure to offer opportunities to the disabled and older people as workers deprives attractions of people who may be a major asset to the organization's workforce. Finally, attractions with no staff or few staff who are disabled or from ethnic minorities, for example, are less likely to attract many visitors from these groups as they may not be able to identify with the attraction and its staff.

The importance of good practice in human resource management

Equal opportunities are just one example of good practice in human resource management. Other examples include:

- objective recruitment procedures
- good induction
- effective staff development schemes
- comprehensive and flexible training provision
- motivational management
- consistent and fair disciplinary and grievance procedures
- appropriate levels of remuneration that reflect workers' contribution to the success of the attraction
- sensitive support for people with problems.

Good human resource management practice not only benefits attractions in terms of improving the performance of staff, it also can help to give attractions a competitive advantage in the marketplace. In the first place contented staff deliver a better product to existing customers, thus making repeat visits more likely. Second, once an attraction develops a reputation for good staff it is more likely to attract new first-time visitors. The Disney organization has successfully exploited this fact so that now one of the first things visitors will say when asked what they like about Disney World, for example, is the quality of the staff.

International perspective

It is often said that recruiting and retaining good staff in the tourism industry in the UK, and possibly Europe, in general is difficult because of the low status of service jobs. Similarly, commentators have suggested that the attitudes of French staff are not suitable for Disneyland Paris. There is a view that the Americans are the best exponents of human resource management in the service sector generally, and at attractions in particular, based on the success of their theme parks. Disney, for example, recruits on the basis of social skills and attitude as well as qualifications, and provides a thorough induction for new staff and sets strict guidelines for staff behaviour. However, some opposition is beginning to be voiced concerning the resulting standardized and regimented approach of staff at such attractions, although most customers appear to approve.

Clearly, there are also variations between countries in terms of employment law, labour markets and human resource management custom and practice, which means that the management of people at attractions can never be truly standardized across the world. As many transnational corporations in other industries have discovered, and perhaps as Disneyland Paris is now discovering, there is a need to 'think globally but act locally' if they are to succeed.

The future

Returning to the UK, the future of human resource management at attractions looks likely to be exciting and uncertain. The Single Market has increased labour mobility in Europe so that the attractions may be competing with attractions elsewhere in Europe for good staff. This will continue in the future. Second, the social policy and legislation of the European Commission will increasingly influence the working conditions and terms of employment of attraction staff. Finally, the so-called 'demographic time-bomb' means there may be fewer of the young people that attractions have relied on to make up their workforce. This may result in higher labour costs at attractions or the need to find new sources of labour, such as the growing number of older people. These uncertainties will continue to challenge attraction managers for many years to come.

Conclusion

We have seen that human resource management at attractions is a complex activity that exists at both the strategic and tactical levels. There are clearly general issues that affect all attractions but there are others that are specific to certain types of attractions, such as those owned by the public sector, large corporations or small-scale entrepreneurs. Finally, it is important to recognize that good human resource management not only improves the performance of staff but also enhances the quality of the product and improves its reputation in the minds of visitors. It thus plays a direct part in determining the success or failure of attractions.

Discussion points and essay questions

1. Discuss the difficulties involved in implementing the 'human resource system' shown in Figure 15.2.
2. Critically evaluate the application of the concept of equal opportunities in the attractions sector.
3. Discuss the most effective ways of retaining good staff and how this can be achieved at attractions.

Exercise

Think about three typical jobs at an attraction at different levels. Then devise a job description for each one based on the ideas set out in this chapter.

Financial management

Introduction

The aim of this chapter is to make the reader aware of the main issues relating to financial management that face the attraction manager. There is no intention to discuss the many technical aspects of financial management in detail. That is the preserve of the accountant.

What is financial management?

At most attractions, financial management is at the core of all corporate strategy. Most of the organization's objectives will be phrased in financial terms such as profit, or will have financial implications. For example, increasing market share implies increased expenditure on promotion, while improving the quality of service may involve more training or financial incentives for staff.

In the broadest sense, financial management is concerned with ensuring money is available to allow the attraction to function on a day-to-day basis and making sure that these funds are used in such a way that it allows the organization to achieve its financial objectives. However, the term 'financial management' is something of an umbrella phrase which covers a number of separate functions that contribute to the overall management of financial resources. These functions include financial planning, financial control, management accounting, cost accounting and financial reporting.

Financial planning decides how the financial resources of the attraction will be utilized in the future.

Financial control is concerned with ensuring that the attraction's financial resources are used in an efficient way so as to prevent waste. It is also about security, ensuring that money is properly accounted for to reduce the opportunities for theft. It usually operates in a mechanized way through a series of systems and procedures.

Management accounting is concerned with management information systems that provide the data, such as costs, turnover and cash flow, that form the basis of decision-making.

Cost accounting, as its name suggests, focuses on the analysis of the attraction's cost structure, both fixed and variable. It is also concerned with the apportioning of costs equitably between cost centres.

Financial reporting is the formal process of presenting the financial performance of the attraction over a year to its stakeholders whether they are a board of directors or a council committee. For private sector attractions this will normally take the form of the annual report and accounts. There are usually two main statements included in a financial report:

- the *balance sheet*, which summarizes the attraction's financial position at the end of the accounting year, in terms of its assets and liabilities
- the *profit and loss account*, which outlines the attraction's income and expenditure over the same period.

Financial management objectives

Ultimately, all these functions are designed to help achieve the attraction's financial objectives. All attractions will vary somewhat in the nature of their financial objectives but there are certain areas in which they are fairly standard. However, it is important to recognize that financial objectives tend to vary between attractions in the private, public, and voluntary sectors. This is illustrated in Table 16.1.

Budgeting

Whatever the objectives of the attraction, its main financial management framework will be its budget, which will usually cover a financial year. Budgets have a number of functions, of which the following three are the most important:

- They guide everyday financial management.
- They provide a basis for evaluating performance and taking decisions on corrective action.
- They are used to impress stakeholders such as banks and grant-making bodies.

Private	Public	Voluntary
Profit, namely generating enough income to cover surplus to plough back into the attraction and/or provide a return for stakeholders	Liquidity, in other words, generating enough income to pay bills if possible, but if there is a subsidy for the attraction the objective may be to try to cover as high a proportion of the costs as possible	Liquidity plus a surplus generating enough to plough back into the main work of the organization whether that be conservation or education
Achieving the highest possible price for the product to maximize revenue	To charge a price which is socially and politically acceptable even if it is lower than the market might stand	Charging a price that will allow the organization to generate the desired surplus
Forcing costs down to the lowest possible level	Cost reduction through efficient operation	Minimizing costs, wherever possible
Maximize utilization, providing it is profitable utilization of the attraction's resources	Maximizing utilization within resource constraints. Even potentially profitable plans may have to be rejected if they would need resources that cannot be provided, such as extra staff	Maximizing utilization providing it does not interfere with the main work of the organization
Meeting financial targets	Living within the budget	Living within the budget

Table 16.1 Financial objectives for attractions in the private, public and voluntary sectors

Budgets are of two types – capital and revenue. Capital budgets are concerned with the purchase of large items of equipment and/or the carrying out of major pieces of work; in other words, with spending that tends to be what one might call one-off payments. Examples might include buying a new theme park ride or repainting an entire attraction. Capital budgets tend to be long term, covering perhaps up to ten years, while revenue budgets tend to be limited to one financial year.

Revenue budgets cover expenditure and income that tends to take place intermittently over the year rather than at one particular time, that is, only the running costs and income of the attraction. It will also be concerned with the level of profit or surplus (or loss) that the attraction will achieve at the end of the year.

The revenue budget will have to cover a wide variety of headings, such as:

Income	Expenditure
Entrance charges	Salaries
Extra income from on-site attractions and rides	On-costs such as employer national insurance contributions
Food and beverage operation	

Income	Expenditure
Souvenirs and other shop sales	Training
Hire of meeting rooms	Travel and subsistence
Guided tours	Recruitment
Special events	Purchase of goods for sale
Rents and tenancies	Equipment
Franchises and concessions	Clothing and uniforms
Grants	Services such as window-cleaning and laundry
Sponsorship	Transport
Facility-use fees such as television filming	Marketing
Consultancy services based on areas of expertise the attraction managers may possess	Maintenance
	Fuel, light, heating
	Cleaning
	Water
	Administration
	Telephone and postage
	Rents
	Licences
	Servicing of debts and repayment of loans
	Taxes
	Insurance
	Depreciation
	Professional fees

To improve the quality of decision-making it is common now for managers to want to monitor the financial performance of parts of the attraction rather than just the total operation. Otherwise a part of the attraction that was performing badly could be hidden by the satisfactory financial performance of the entire attraction. To this end many attractions now make use of the concept of *profit centres* and *cost centres*, which are then monitored on an individual basis. Profit centres are the main aspects of the attraction that attract income, including entrance charges, the shop and meeting room hire. Cost centres are the main areas of the attraction that incur costs.

While it is relatively easy to apportion income to profit centres it is more difficult to decide what proportion of the overall costs of the attraction should be apportioned to particular cost centres. If we take an attraction shop as an example, there are specific costs related to it which are easy to identify, such as the cost of purchasing stock, and staff. However, there are also general overhead costs such as administration and loan repayments which are more difficult to apportion to specific cost centres such as the shop. In this case there are three crude mechanisms which may be used to determine what proportion of these costs the shop should be allocated:

1 Based on the proportion of the attraction's staff or area which are devoted to the shop. For example, if the shop employs a quarter of the

attraction's staff it would be allocated a quarter of the general overhead costs.

2 Based on the proportion of attraction income earned by the shop.

3 Based on the amount of usage the shop receives as a proportion of total usage of the attraction. Clearly the decision on apportioning costs will be different if the shop is only visited by about a tenth of the attraction's visitors or if it is open to people who are not even visiting the rest of the attraction.

Apportioning costs is also complicated by the existence of fixed costs and variable costs. Fixed costs are those such as insurance which are the same regardless of visitor numbers. There are also semi-fixed costs such as lighting. Variable costs on the other hand are those which depend on the number of visitors, for example the purchase of souvenirs and food for sale in the retail or catering outlets. Fixed costs are relatively easy to forecast and apportion but variable costs are not, as they are susceptible to sudden change.

It helps if the profit and cost centres can be one and the same, so that their performance can be monitored as if they were mini-attractions in their own right.

So far we have focused on an annual budget but in a market like that for attractions, which is highly seasonal, cash flow management on a week by week or month by month basis is highly important to ensure that the attraction always has enough money to cover its costs at any one time. Attraction budgets should therefore also include a cash flow statement that says when money will come in and when expenditure will be incurred on a week by week or month by month basis. An example of such a statement is shown in Figure 16.1. Such a statement enables organizations to see when they will be 'cash rich' or 'cash poor', which may influence when they buy goods or services where they have a choice when to purchase a particular item or service.

The budgetary process

The budgetary process consists of a number of stages:

1 Evaluating the existing budget for attractions which are not new, as most budgeting is based on history in that existing budgets are modified and rolled forward to form the basis of the budget for the next year.

2 Discussions within departments and between departments on changes that might be required on the basis of previous experience or future plans.

3 Testing the proposed budget in relation to the prevailing constraints such as the rate of return on investment required for stakeholders or the need for budget reductions caused by government control on local authority budgets.

4 Approval of the budget.

5 Implementation of the budget through budgetary control.

6 Monitoring of performance against the budget, identifying variances, taking corrective action, or modifying the budget.

	April	May	June	July	August	September	October	November	December	January	February	March	TOTAL
Net revenue	30 000	40 000	50 000	70 000	100 000	80 000	40 000	20 000	20 000	10 000	10 000	30 000	500 000
Expenses	40 000	50 000	50 000	60 000	70 000	50 000	20 000	15 000	15 000	25 000	25 000	30 000	450 000
Monthly cash flow	(10 000)	(10 000)	0 000 0	10 000	30 000	30 000	20 000	5 000	5 000	(15 000)	(15 000)	0	
Cumulative cash flow	(10 000)	(20 000)	(20 000)	(10 000)	20 000	50 000	70 000	75 000	80 000	65 000	50 000	50 000	
Cash at beginning of month	80 000	70 000	60 000	70 000	100 000	130 000	150 000	155 000	160 000	145 000	130 000		
Cash position at end of month	70 000	60 000	60 000	70 000	100 000	130 000	150 000	155 000	160 000	145 000	130 000	130 000	
Profit/ loss at the end of the year													50 000

Figure 16.1 A cash flow statement for an attraction opening in a highly seasonal market

Problems with budgeting at attractions

Preparing and implementing attraction budgets is difficult because of a number of specific problems:

1 The usual practice of basing budgets on past experience and precedent is not very useful in the attraction business which is rapidly changing, so that it is highly unlikely that the future will be a rerun of the past.
2 In such a volatile market the forecasting of things like admission income on which budgeting depends is very difficult. Contingency plans are therefore required to allow the budget to cope with differences between the original forecasts and reality.
3 Many factors which influence the budget may well be outside the control of the attraction's operation, such as legislation that may impose expensive duties on operators or reduce the market size, while sudden breakdown of major plant can dramatically increase maintenance costs at a stroke.

The ideal response to these problems is zero budgeting, which each year starts with a clean sheet, although in reality freedom of action is limited by the existence of fixed costs and debt servicing, for example.

Management information systems

Management information systems are designed to provide managers with the information they need to make sensible decisions. The types of information that may be required include the following:

- visitor numbers in total and by types of visitor
- visitor expenditure and where they are spending their money on site
- staff costs
- major unexpected bills
- the credit situation in terms of what the attraction owes others and what the attraction is owed
- income from rents, franchises and concessions
- stock levels
- budget variances.

It is important that such data are up to date so that action can be taken quickly to tackle problems. Some of the data may need to be provided on a daily basis, for example visitor spending and daily stock levels, which can be obtained from computerized tills.

Keeping records

A basic form of management information system is the keeping of records that not only aid management but also fulfil a number of other purposes, such as:

- seeing how the attraction has developed over time
- providing historic data as a guide for future predictions
- providing information for potential funders
- as evidence in lawsuits and disputes
- complying with company law and the need to provide information for government agencies, such as tax returns
- informing stakeholders of the progress of the attraction.

A range of records should be kept, of which the following are a brief selection:

- income records, including monthly cash flow records, sales sheets and cash register rolls
- expense records, including bills, invoices and receipts
- payroll records, including pay slip data and information on sick leave
- equipment records, including information on maintenance expenditure and leasing contracts
- legal records, including copyrights and trademarks
- tax records, including property, sales and income taxes
- record of debts and debtors
- accounting records, including accounts, ledgers and bank statements
- administration records such as annual reports, audit documents and board or committee minutes.

Decisions have to be taken as to how long to keep this material, to what extent it will be confidential and to whom it will be accessible.

External information sources

As well as these internal records, financial managers at attractions also need to keep up to date with events outside the attraction, and they therefore need a system for obtaining external information. Such information might include:

- changes in taxation policy in terms of Corporation Tax and employer's national insurance contributions for example
- changes in the law relating to things like health and safety and employee rights and terms and conditions of employment
- likely economic changes, such as interest rates and inflation, that may affect the cost of running the attraction and issues such as unemployment and the distribution of wealth which affects the visitor numbers and expenditure
- technological developments, which could mean new developments in management information systems or new types of attraction products that the organization may need to purchase to maintain its position in the market
- changes in accounting practice and financial reporting procedures.

Such data need to be collected in a systematic and structured way. Most will come from the scanning of trade journals and specialist reports, which may not be easily accessible to the average attraction financial manager.

Performance indicators

Monitoring performance requires good information systems as we have seen, but it also requires performance indicators that are phrased in financial terms. A number of possible such indicators for attractions are set out below:

$$\frac{\text{Payroll cost}}{\text{Revenue generated}} \times 100 \text{ per cent}$$

$$\frac{\text{Income from profit centre}}{\text{Staff involved}}$$

$$\frac{\text{Net operating expenditure}}{\text{Number of visitors}}$$

$$\frac{\text{Net cost of marketing}}{\text{Number of visitors}}$$

$$\frac{\text{Admission income}}{\text{Total operating costs}} \times 100 \text{ per cent}$$

$$\frac{\text{Total visitor expenditure}}{\text{Total visitor numbers}} = \text{Visitor spend per head}$$

$$\frac{\text{Income}}{\text{Operating expenditure}} \times 100 \text{ per cent} = \text{Recovery rate}$$

$$\frac{\text{Individual profit centre income as a fraction of total attraction income}}{\text{Individual cost centre expenditure as a fraction of total attraction expenditure}}$$

where profit and cost centres are one and the same part of the attraction. If the top fraction is higher than the lower the centre is performing well, and vice versa.

Profit maximization

For most commercial attractions profit maximization will be the main financial objective. This objective can be summarized in a simple equation:

Profit maximization = Increased revenue generation + cost control and reduction.

Revenue generation

Attraction income can be increased in a number of ways, some of which we will now explore.

Attracting more visitors

There are three main ways in which more visitors can be attracted in the relatively short term:

1 Increased promotional activity to raise awareness and encourage people to visit.
2 Using sales promotions such as season tickets to persuade existing customers to visit the attraction more often.
3 Arranging special events on specific themes so that people who might not otherwise visit the attraction will be encouraged to visit it because the theme of the event appeals to them. The hope is that having visited once because of this event, they may become regular visitors.

Pricing

Attractions manipulate their prices in a number of ways that are designed to attract more visitors, as can be seen from the following examples:

1 Reducing entrance charges in the off-peak season to encourage more people to visit, in the hope that they will spend more money in the shops and catering outlets. This price reduction may reflect the fact that some on-site attractions are not available in the off-peak season, particularly if they are in the open air.
2 Offering concessions to attract people on low incomes who might otherwise be unable to attend the attraction, such as students and the unemployed.
3 Offering reduced price group rates to encourage coach parties and school groups to visit.
4 Sales promotions that offer discounts including 'two for the price of one' or 'children go free when accompanied by an adult'.
5 Using family tickets that reduce the overall cost of a visit.
6 Offering people more benefits in return for the entrance charge they pay; in other words, enhancing the 'value for money' element of pricing. These could include special events or displays, free car parking, or a free cup of tea or coffee.

Clearly, pricing only works in this way if the demand is elastic to some extent. Fortunately this is the case with most attraction demand.

A key pricing decision for attractions is whether to charge an all-inclusive price that includes all on-site attractions, or to charge an entrance price and then make additional charges for on-site attractions such as individual rides or for services such as car parking. There are arguments on both sides but there is a growing recognition that customers find the latter approach irritating; whether it would stop them visiting an attraction is another matter.

The important point in relation to pricing is that it is generally not used to increase visitor numbers overall, but rather to boost demand at quiet times or from market segments, such as families, who are seen to be attractive because of their propensity for 'secondary spending' on site.

Increasing visitor expenditure

For many attractions entrance charges now represent only a minority of their overall income. More revenue often comes from the other opportunities that are offered on site for visitors to spend money. Some of these opportunities are discussed in this section.

Shops

Shops are a major way of increasing visitor spending providing they offer what visitors want to buy. Often items on the theme of the attraction such as replicas of museum exhibits and prints of paintings at galleries will be popular. Otherwise it is a matter of looking at what the customer would buy elsewhere and offering this, for example speciality foods, crafts and gift stationery. There needs to be something in the shop to suit the taste and pocket of every market segment, from the overseas visitor willing to make an expensive purchase to the schoolchild with 50 pence in their pocket looking for a souvenir pencil. The key to success in attraction retailing in terms of maximizing income is only stocking items which move quickly rather than gathering dust on the shelves and choosing items with the highest profit margins.

Catering outlets

As far as catering outlets are concerned, they must relate to the length of time people are likely to spend on site and the time of day when most people will be on site. Usually attractions will need a café or restaurant where visitors can have coffee or tea, snacks in the morning and afternoon, and a full meal at lunchtime. The food served must be selected so that it is attractive to the market segments which the attraction serves. Special provision must be made for those who are vegetarians and those who are health-conscious. Furthermore, the aim should be to provide a quality catering product and to focus on food and drink which offers the best profit margins. Some attraction operators in isolated areas may decide they can charge a premium price as they have a captive market. However, this is a risky strategy that can result in people bringing their own food, or leaving early to find somewhere else to eat. In addition to cafés and restaurants, large attractions may also need kiosks and mobile catering units to provide for people who want to eat and drink in the style which Americans call 'grazing'. This type of catering can include things like cold drinks, ice creams and pizzas for example. The types of catering offered will need to be tailored to the desires of the attraction's specific markets.

Guided tours ● ● ●

These are another potential source of income, although they are labour intensive and expensive to operate. Many attractions use two other methods to achieve the same results as guided tours but without the heavy labour costs. These are the sale of guidebooks that allow people to go round on their own, and 'Walkman' tours where a taped commentary is provided for visitors, to which they listen using a personal stereo headset. However, administering and controlling a 'Walkman' tour operation can also be a time-consuming activity.

Corporate users ● ● ●

Another source of income for attractions which is becoming increasingly popular is the use of attractions by corporate users. This can take a number of forms:

1 The hiring of rooms and spaces for seminars, conferences and exhibitions.
2 The use of attractions for corporate hospitality such as themed conference dinners or evening sherry receptions.
3 The use of unusual attractions as 'sets' for the launch of new products. They can provide exciting visual backgrounds to enhance the appeal of photographs of the product that will be used in advertisements.
4 Facility fees received from television companies for filming.

All these sources of corporate income are more likely to be available to attractions which are either unusual or prestigious, or both. Their advantage is that generally corporate users spend more highly on food and drink than ordinary visitors and they often wish to use the attraction at quiet times such as weekdays and the off-peak months.

Obtaining revenue from other sources

There are a number of other sources from which attractions can receive revenue, including the following.

Rents and tenancies ● ● ●

These come from businesses which occupy premises on the attraction site, such as shops, and usually involve the payment of an agreed fixed sum by the tenants to the attraction.

Franchises and concessions • • •

Ride operators in amusement parks or on-site catering outlets may operate on this basis. In the latter case these are often not fixed payments to the attraction but are based on the financial performance of the concession. It is vital therefore that the attraction receives accurate accounts from the concessionaire to ensure that it is receiving all the money to which it is entitled. Attractions must exercise strong control over franchisees and concessionaires to ensure that they are maintaining the same quality standards as the rest of the attraction.

Consultancy services • • •

The attraction may offer consultancy services to other attractions. A good example of this is the Ventures consultancy business which grew out of the management of the Beaulieu attraction in Hampshire. The consulting services offered by other attractions are usually on a limited scale but may include advice in areas such as retailing and training.

Grants • • •

Grants may be one-off payments or a regular annual grant. They may be general or intended for a specific purpose.

Sponsorship • • •

Sponsorship of the attraction may be general or may be related to a specific aspect of the attraction. Sometimes this sponsorship may be motivated by the desire to increase awareness of the sponsor or it may be designed to improve the sponsor's image with the attraction's visitors.

Maximizing the use of people, premises and financial resources

Attractions have high fixed costs which means that most of their costs are incurred whether the attraction is visited by ten or a thousand people in a day. Therefore, it is important that the attraction makes the best possible use of its resources, particularly the staff and the premises.

The main problem for most attractions is the off-peak period when, often, visitor numbers are small, staff are far from fully occupied and the premises are underutilized. The challenge for managers, therefore, is to attract more visitors at these times. A popular way of achieving this is to run special events that appeal to people who would not otherwise visit the attraction.

Furthermore, given that most attractions are very expensive to develop and run, it is amazing that many of them are only open from perhaps 10.00 a.m. to 5.00 p.m. Thus, for some seventeen hours a day, they are unused. Many attractions are now realizing this and are offering evening activities or are making themselves available for social functions in the evenings.

These initiatives not only maximize the use of staff and premises but also optimize the use of the attraction's financial resources. Special events and evening opening, for example, can make a major contribution to the attraction's fixed costs. There can be a beneficial side effect to such initiatives in that for the staff many of these initiatives add variety to their working life and increase their job satisfaction. Such moves can also cheer up staff in the off-peak season, which can be a depressing and demoralizing time. They can therefore be valuable staff motivation tools.

Mix of business

Successful attractions tend to be those which have a well-balanced mix of business. In other words, they are not overdependent on one particular market or susceptible to changes in the market which are beyond their control. A good business mix is one which reduces the risks by having a diversified product portfolio that maximizes the income of the attraction and the utilization of its resources.

The idea of reducing risk through diversification is particularly important. In the late 1980s and at the start of the 1990s in Britain, many attractions which depended on the school market were badly affected by government policy and legislation that changed the nature of the education market in the short term and led to a reduction in the value of the market.

Obtaining the most profitable business mix is a delicate matter. It means focusing on the most lucrative business such as corporate hospitality and family visitors at peak times, and attracting less lucrative visitors such as school groups and coach parties of elderly people at the off-peak times. This requires very sophisticated marketing, and clever use of pricing policy.

Credit control

The final way in which attractions can maximize their income is to ensure that they receive all the money they are owed, as quickly as possible, through credit control. For attractions this will often mean the money they receive from visitors of whatever type. Many attractions do not extend credit for group bookings beyond the day on which they visit the attraction which solves the credit problem for this type of visitor. However, the attraction will need good credit chasing systems for many corporate users who will often want to pay after the event and for tenants, franchisees and concessionaires. In extreme cases this may mean employing private debt collection agencies.

In summary, the main ways in which attractions can maximize their revenue include:

- increasing visitor numbers
- encouraging secondary expenditure by visitors on site
- obtaining the best possible business mix on the site which optimizes the use of the site, the staff and the physical resources so that, whenever

possible, the attraction is hosting profitable activities, every hour of every day

- maximizing external sources of income, such as grants and sponsorship
- effective credit control.

However, it is always vital that, except in the case of loss leaders, the time, effort and money which is put into trying to maximize income generation is cost-effective. Clearly it should not cost more to generate the revenue than the amount of revenue that is generated.

Cost control and reduction

Cost control and reduction is a vital element in the maximization of profit at attractions. However, as we will see, it is rather more complicated and problematical than income generation.

Staffing

In terms of staffing, cost control and reduction has two elements, namely increasing productivity and reducing the amount of staff required wherever possible. Productivity can be increased by multiskilling, where staff are trained to perform several jobs rather than just one, as would have been traditional. They can then be moved around either to cover for holidays or to move from areas of the attraction which are quiet to areas which are busier. Alternatively, people could be trained to perform all the tasks involved in a particular geographical area of the site, including maintenance. For example, the people who receive the entrance charge from visitors could also be trained to work in the shop or serve in the café while other staff could be trained to do routine maintenance work thus reducing the need to employ as many specialist maintenance people. The key to productivity lies in ensuring that staff are always busy, even on days when there are few visitors.

There are a number of ways in which labour costs can be reduced which may or may not be acceptable to managers:

- employing fewer people
- employing casual staff rather than staff on permanent contracts so that in quiet times they can be laid off or their hours reduced
- spending less on training
- reducing wage rates
- contracting out jobs so that you only pay for a specific job to be done when it needs to be done, rather than employing somebody all the time in case it needs to be done.

All these ideas carry the danger that implementing them may demoralize and demotivate staff and/or lead to a worsening of the service which is offered to customers.

Goods purchased

Action also needs to be taken to control and reduce the cost of goods purchased for resale in retail and catering outlets. This can be achieved in a number of ways, including:

1 Bulk purchase of fast-moving items to achieve the best possible purchase price.
2 Regular reviews of suppliers and the use of competitive rivalries between suppliers to ensure that the best possible price is always obtained.
3 Wherever possible, goods should be bought on a 'sale or return' basis so that if the goods are not sold, the attraction incurs no cost other than the cost of returning the goods to the suppliers and the hidden costs of storing the items.
4 Operating 'just-in-time' delivery systems so that valuable storage space is not taken up with items that will not be required for sale for weeks or even months. However, this requires excellent and sophisticated stock control systems, otherwise sales could be lost because stocks run out.
5 Delaying the payment of supplies until the last possible moment can help cash flow but it can also reduce the goodwill which an attraction enjoys with its suppliers.
6 Pilfering must be minimized through security measures such as mirrors and the location of checkouts which make it difficult for people to steal the merchandise.
7 Reducing food wastage through sensible buying, good storage and preparing the right quantities of fresh food each day.

In addition to these two major cost elements, of staffing and goods purchased, there are a number of other overheads that need to be controlled or reduced:

1 Tackling the *costs of communication* such as telephones and postage by aggressively monitoring staff usage and letting everyone know they are being monitored.
2 Reducing the cost of *utilities* such as water, electricity and gas by making people aware of the need to be careful in the use of light and heating.
3 Introducing *energy conservation* measures to redress the overall energy costs of the attraction. The importance of such action is clear given that in the early 1990s major museums and galleries in the UK were estimated to be spending in excess of £100 million per annum on energy (National Audit Office, 1992).
4 *Selling off unproductive assets* that are a liability.
5 *Leasing* equipment when that might prove to be less expensive than outright purchase, for example company cars.
6 *Contracting out services* that the attraction needs to the supplier who offers the best price. This might cover things like the provision of laundry services, window-cleaning and insurance.

7 Using *sponsorship in kind* whereby in return for publicity in some form, businesses supply attractions with goods or services free of charge or at a reduced cost.

8 *Putting off planned routine maintenance and decoration*, providing that this does not compromise the safety of staff or customers.

9 *Rescheduling loan repayments.*

10 *Reduced opening hours* in the quiet times, or the operation of the site with a reduced number of on-site attractions in the off-peak season.

There are four very important points relating to cost control and reduction which attraction managers need to always bear in mind. First, *reducing costs can adversely affect the quality of service* which attractions offer to their visitors. This can result in a reduction in visitor numbers in due course as people who were disappointed with their first visit will decide not to go back. For example, reduced staffing at the pay booths may lead to larger queues, while delaying the redecoration of part of the attraction can lead to its looking shabby and uncared for.

Second, because most attractions *have relatively high fixed costs* the scope for cost reduction is fairly limited. Staff have to be available, rides have to be operated, food and services have to be available whether twenty visitors turn up on a particular day or 2000. Furthermore, because attraction visits are generally not pre-booked and are affected by uncontrollable things such as the weather, it is impossible to forecast accurately demand in advance, which makes resource planning very difficult indeed.

Third, many of the costs relating to visitor attractions are *outside the control of the attraction operator,* for example:

- taxes
- the on-cost of employing labour, such as National Insurance Contributions
- the cost of complying with legislation such as health and safety regulations and the Food Safety Act
- interest rates which affect loan repayments
- depreciation which is a substantial element in a business which is subject to fashion and fads so that on-site attractions need to be replaced before they would normally need to be because they are no longer attractive to visitors.

Finally, the *expense involved in cost reduction must itself be cost-effective.* It would be foolish to spend hours and hours of staff time monitoring telephones if the savings on telephone bills amounted to just a few pounds. Likewise it would not be sensible to control people's work activities so totally that they became demoralized and stopped taking initiatives that could either earn income for the attraction or reduce its costs.

As we have seen, it is often difficult and risky to cut costs substantially at attractions, so managers may prefer to be prudent in the way they control costs, while putting most emphasis on income generation as the way to maximize profit.

The special case of public sector attractions

Public sector attractions (those owned by central government or local authorities) in contrast to those in private ownership, tend to have different objectives rather than just pure profit. These were outlined earlier in the chapter. Furthermore, public sector attractions operate different financial systems and have different sets of constraints within which they have to operate. In general, they have less freedom of action than private attractions in the field of finance. The best way of illustrating this is to look at the issues covered in this chapter in the same sequence but then relate them to a public sector attraction whether it is a local authority museum or a castle owned by the state.

However, it is important to note that by definition this section must be based on generalizations that will not reflect the situation in all public bodies and at all public sector attractions. For example, the constraints are probably greater for local authorities due to the severe spending controls placed on local councils by central government in the UK in recent years.

Perhaps we should start by looking at the five elements of financial management we identified at the beginning of the chapter. Financial planning is more difficult in the public sector because many of the assumptions on which financial plans must be made are outside the control of the attraction and are subject to change at very short notice. Spending levels and rules are set on the basis of political desires and can be changed at a stroke because of political expediency. In this sort of environment, future planning of any kind is very difficult.

Financial control will often be dictated by standard procedures which are not always appropriate to the attraction business, while management information systems may be limited due to a shortage of money. Cost accounting is of limited value only, as many costs are not capable of being modified for political or social reasons. Finally, the financial reporting system is very different, although if done well it should still supply useful data for decision-makers. However, for political reasons there may be a temptation to report the financial situation in a way which covers up problems.

The objectives of public sector attractions tend to be more complex than those of their private sector counterparts. They are political and social as well as financial. These objectives may not always be compatible, which makes financial management a very difficult task.

The budgeting process is usually a political rather than a financial exercise as departments vie with each other to see who will achieve the best outcome in the budgeting process. Most attractions exist in departments which themselves have other responsibilities, so they may be seen as a service whose budget can be cut to help another service which may be a higher priority for the politicians. For example, a leisure department may see an art gallery as being less of a priority than a swimming pool or a sports centre. Therefore, budgets can be cut at a time when in business terms they may need to be increased.

This lack of a link between the needs of attractions and the taking of budgeting decisions is a real problem for public sector attractions. It is made worse by the fact that the allocation of budgets to public bodies as a whole is based on political criteria rather than the needs of the body and its services.

The standing orders of local authorities often prevent them from being able to move money between budget headings in response to changing circumstances. This lack of flexibility is a real problem that does not exist for private attractions. Furthermore, while public sector attractions tend to experience seasonal demand like other attractions, their ability to minimize its impact through cash flow management is limited by the fact that the financial procedures often restrict their ability to schedule payments at the best time from a cash flow point of view.

Meanwhile, the financial burden on public sector attractions is artificially high because they are usually expected to make a contribution to 'central establishment costs' which represents the sizeable administrative structure of the authority. This will probably be calculated as a percentage of their budget and may as such bear no relation to the use they make of the services provided by the authority centrally. It is therefore an artificial set of costs over which they have little or no control.

Moving on to the subject of monitoring performance, because of their complex objectives and the traditions of the public sector, many public sector attractions lack clear performance indicators. They therefore can lack the ability to be constructively self-critical which, in turn, prevents them from achieving their full potential.

Finally, the control placed on their budgets, the financial procedures and rules they work within, and the lack of freedom of action for managers means that the opportunities for revenue generation and cost reduction are more limited than they are in private sector attractions. Income generation can be affected by the following:

- unwillingness to charge market prices at attractions for political and social reasons
- inability of managers to invest large sums of money, at short notice, in ways which will ultimately increase income
- some potential corporate users and organizations may not be allowed to use the attraction for political reasons, because of the nature of their business or disagreements with their political beliefs
- budget cuts may make it impossible to provide the level of service or product improvements that would be necessary to increase income.

The restrictions under which public sector attractions operate can also affect their ability to reduce costs, as follows:

- Union agreements and the personnel policies of the authority as a whole can reduce the ability of managers to reduce labour costs or increase productivity through the more flexible use of labour.
- The attraction must comply with rules relating to relationships with suppliers and contracts entered into by the authority as a whole.

This often results in attractions not getting the goods and services of the right quality or at the right price.

- Selling off unproductive assets or contracting out services may be against the beliefs of the political decision-makers. In recent years, however, it is more likely to have been the case as, in the UK, government agencies and local authorities have been forced to sell off assets or contract out services whether they like it or not. Either way, the needs of the attraction and the freedom of action of its manager are restricted in a way that would not usually happen in the private sector.

While the picture painted above is definitely based on the worst possible scenario, most public sector attraction managers would find at least one or two points in it that reflect their own experience. However, there are public sector bodies which have fought hard, and with some success, to overcome these problems. Likewise there are many private companies that do not operate in anything like the way we described earlier in this chapter. It all goes to show, yet again, that it is very difficult to generalize about visitor attractions.

The special case of small attractions

We have to recognize that most of what we have said about private attractions relates to the larger ones, but many attractions are small scale. In these cases, their ability to operate the kind of sophisticated financial management systems that have been discussed in this chapter are severely limited or non-existent. Often there will be just one manager who has to do everything, although there may be a part-time book-keeper. They will therefore need to develop systems that are suitably simple and easy to operate, although the same principles should apply as those on which the more sophisticated systems are based.

Furthermore, small-scale attraction entrepreneurs may not feel they have the freedom to, or may not wish to, invest money to increase income. They may prefer to focus on cost control and the maintenance of existing profit levels. Some will simply not want to expend the extra effort that would be required to optimize profits, instead settling for an acceptable return on investment and a less stressful lifestyle.

Conclusion

In this chapter we have focused on the key issues in the financial management of attractions – human-made attractions, primarily in the UK. However, the principles and techniques we have discussed are also relevant to special events. Furthermore it is unlikely that they would have been much different if we had been talking about the attractions business in other countries, although details such as financial reporting systems and costs such as taxes and interest rates may have been different.

Discussion points and essay questions

1 Critically evaluate the performance indictors for attractions which were suggested in this chapter.
2 Discuss the risks involved in reducing costs at visitor attractions.
3 Critically evaluate the ways in which attractions can increase their revenue generation.

Exercise

Construct an annual operating budget for a hypothetical visitor attraction. Then identify the factors which could adversely affect the budget.

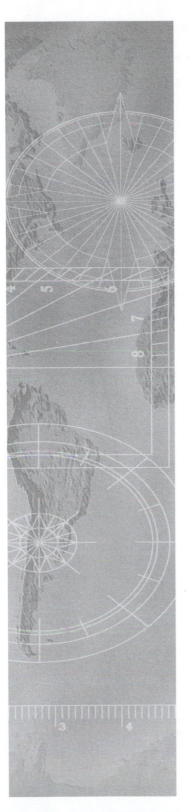

Operations management

Introduction

Rogers and Slinn (1993) have said that operations management is 'concerned with the design, operation and control of the system that matches the organization's resources to customer service needs'. In this system the input (the resources of the organization) are transferred into the output (the services offered to the customer) through a process in which value is added to the input to produce the output.

On a more basic level, operations management is the day-to-day management of the site. It is about marshalling the attraction's resources, notably the staff and physical equipment such as machinery, to provide a satisfactory service for the customer and an acceptable rate of return on the use of these resources. The goal of operations management at attractions is the smooth and efficient operation of the site.

In a sense it could be said that everyone on site is involved in operations management as, in a service activity, everyone is part of the operation. Furthermore, the activities of financial, human resource and marketing managers also have an effect on how the site operates.

At small attractions one person may fulfil all the management roles, including operations, while at large attractions a number of specialist operations managers may be employed. In a relatively new area such as attractions management it is rare to find people specifically called 'operations managers'. More often the role is part of a wider brief or the job is split between several staff.

The objectives and functions of operations management

The objectives and functions of operations management at attractions tend to vary depending on whether one looks at the subject from the point of view of the organization or its customers. This point is illustrated in Table 17.1. As we can see from the list in this table, which is far from comprehensive, there are contradictions in the objectives. First, some of the organization's own objectives are potentially conflicting, for example making provision for visitors with special needs can impose additional costs on the attraction operator which would conflict with the objective of minimizing operating costs. Perhaps more important are those areas where the objectives of the organizations appear to conflict with those of the customers, for example, in relation to the quality/cost trade-off and problems that may arise. This illustrates the dilemma of the operation manager's position. He or she has to reconcile the resources of the organization with the needs and desires of the visitors.

The scope of operations management

Operations management of an attraction site covers a multitude of variables. Perhaps it is helpful to split these variables into those which are controllable or influenced by the attraction operator and those which are

The organization	The customer
Maximizing throughput and opportunities for visitor spending	Minimizing delays, crowding and queuing
Safety of visitors and staff	Safety of visitors
Minimizing operating costs (labour, energy, and so on)	Maximizing quality of service and optimizing visitor enjoyment
Looking after the needs of those groups of visitors who are described as 'visitors with special needs', such as the disabled	Treating every visitor as if they are unique and special
Ensuring quality standards are as high as possible within resource constraints	Optimizing quality regardless of costs
Problems solved quickly and as cheaply as possible	No problems occurring in the first place but if they do, being solved quickly without regard to the cost to the organization
Compliance with the law	

Table 17.1
Operations management from the viewpoints of the organization and customers

Controllable	Influenceable	Uncontrollable
Staffing levels, and staff training and utilization	Staff motivation and behaviour	Staff prejudices
	Capacity of the site – influenceable through changes in the route around the site, provision of more pay desks, restaurant places and so on	Customer attitudes and expectations of the attraction
The volume and quality of stock purchased for retail and catering outlets		Customers' tastes and prejudices in general
Systems such as stock control, ticketing and reservations		Weather
	Activities of franchisees and concessionaires	
	Accidents which may or may not be unavoidable	
	Number and types of visitors on site at any one time	

Table 17.2
Controllable, influenceable and uncontrollable variables in operations management at attractions

not. Some of the major variables are listed in Table 17.2, which makes it clear that operations management is a matter of controlling and influencing variables wherever possible, and responding quickly and effectively to those which are uncontrollable. However, it is not always easy to distinguish between these three types of variable. For example, through lobbying it is technically possible to influence new legislation. However, as the attractions lobby is relatively weak, it is highly doubtful whether such lobbying would be effective; in reality it is probably an uncontrollable factor.

The skills involved in operations management

Operations management is a complex task that requires a number of skills and attributes. The main ones are listed below:

- a thorough knowledge of the site and the staff and an appreciation of how visitors use the site
- the ability to see the site as a whole while also paying attention to matters of detail
- being able to plan systems and procedures in advance and foresee likely visitor flows, for example, but being flexible enough to change these systems and procedures in the light of changing circumstances
- communication skills when briefing staff on systems and procedures and when dealing with dissatisfied customers
- the ability to work under pressure and to act logically and effectively in crises
- a good understanding of the principles of management control and financial management
- being tactful but firm and decisive

- having confidence in his or her own abilities and judgement
- seeing things from the visitor's point of view and understanding the perspective of other staff
- always being self-critical, constructively critical of the existing systems and striving for constant improvements.

Operations management and problem-solving

Managers have to deal with a number of unforeseen problems in the day-to-day operational management of the attraction. These problems come in a number of shapes and forms, including:

- visitors' cars being damaged in, or stolen from, the attraction car park
- mechanical breakdowns in terms of either the attractions on site, such as theme park rides, or the equipment on which the operation of the attraction is based, like computerized tills in the retail outlet
- minor vandalism which might involve broken windows or graffiti
- part of the site becoming impassable due to bad weather
- staff not turning up for work due to sickness.

However, many of the operational problems found at attractions do not arise suddenly but are instead long-standing and continuous. Here the aim is often not to solve the problem but merely to ameliorate its effects. Such problems might include:

- long queues or 'bottlenecks' on the site
- slow throughput in catering outlets caused by poor design of the catering facilities
- finding the balance between keeping relatively small stocks of merchandise to minimize outlay and not running out of goods
- the need to reduce waste, whether it be energy or staff time, or unsold food in the catering outlets.

Problems at attractions tend to be of two types:

1 Minor ones, where individual members of staff can be empowered to devise and implement solutions, where those solutions will not have knock-on effects elsewhere within the attraction.
2 Major ones, which affect all or most of the attraction where solutions require a holistic view and can only be achieved through teamwork.

Operations management and crisis management

Whereas problem-solving at attractions is largely about trying to resolve difficulties that are of little real interest to the outside world, crisis management is concerned with dangers that could lead to loss of life and/or phenomena that would bring the attraction to the attention of people and organizations outside the attraction. A range of such possible crises can arise at attractions. A few examples are given below:

- an outbreak of fire
- a bomb explosion or a bomb hoax
- a major accident such as people being injured on a theme park ride or visitors to an animal attraction being attacked by animals
- an outbreak of food poisoning at the attraction's food outlet
- attraction takings being stolen by armed robbers.

When such crises arise, two types of action are required:

1 Action to tackle the crisis, which may include evacuating the site or closing certain operations until the crisis is over.
2 Handling the media who will become interested in the attraction because of the crisis.

Whereas problem-solving relies on creating and developing ad hoc solutions to one-off problems, crisis management needs to be more formal and pre-planned. Major crises totally disrupt attractions so it is vital that everyone knows what to do automatically in the event of a crisis. This means a set of standard procedures which should be followed in the event of an emergency. These will normally be contained in some form of emergency procedures manual. Such a manual would outline who should do what in the event of a particular emergency. It should also say who should deal with the media and what should be said.

Perhaps surprisingly, many attractions do not have such emergency procedures manuals, which is worrying given that many attractions are, by their nature, potentially dangerous places. Industrial heritage attractions may have working machinery, safari parks have wild animals and theme parks have their rides.

Furthermore, many attractions are crowded at busy times so any attempted evacuation would be a major undertaking. Given these considerations, it should be clear that all attractions need procedures manuals to guide action in the event of crises and it is important that staff *read them* and understand their role in the event of an emergency.

Operations management and risk management

Risk management is all about looking at what might go wrong, how often it might go wrong, and how serious the consequences might be. Writing in 1982, Nilson and Edginton identified four types of risks in relation to the frequency with which they might occur and their severity. They then suggested what action managers should take in relation to these risks. Their four categories are described below.

Low risk, low severity

These are incidents which happen infrequently and are not serious in their consequences. Managers must accept these risks, as the cost of trying to prevent them would outweigh the benefits of preventing them. Such problems are so rare and incapable of being predicted that it is difficult to plan what to do if they do occur.

Moderate risk, low severity

In the case of relatively common problems which are not very serious but which occur fairly frequently, the aim is to manage them. This may mean drawing up a list of guidelines so that staff know what to do in the event of the problem occurring. Again the cost of prevention would exceed the benefits of preventing the problem occurring in the first place.

Moderate risk, high severity

There are some risks which are moderate in terms of the frequency with which they may occur but which also have severe consequences. In this situation, attractions would normally try to take out insurance policies to cover them in the event of the risk becoming reality.

High risk, high severity

These are problems which may occur frequently, and with serious consequences, if preventative action is not taken. The aim here is sensibly to avoid the situation arising, although managers may also wish to develop guidelines and take out insurance policies in case the risk turns into an actual event.

This model is a general one, perhaps more relevant to recreational activities than to attractions, but it can be adapted to make it more appropriate for attractions. Some examples of the four categories in relation to attractions are as follows:

1 Low risk, low severity: this could mean the risk that a few people might become a little distressed or offended by a particular exhibition at a museum. Clearly, if the exhibition were to be removed for the sake of this tiny minority, it would deprive the majority of the pleasure of seeing the exhibition, so that the cost of removing the risk would outweigh the benefits.
2 Moderate risk, low severity: might mean the risk of minor vandalism on the attraction site. Here, guidelines should be produced so staff know what to do when they discover such minor vandalism but the enormous cost of preventing such damage might well outweigh the actual financial cost of the damage.
3 Moderate risk, moderate severity: this might include fires that destroy an individual small theme park ride. In this case insurance is probably the most relevant form of action.
4 High risk, high severity: there are numerous examples at attractions of situations where, unless action is taken, major incidents could take place anytime with severe consequences. For example, if a theme park ride is not maintained properly, at some stage it may well collapse while being

used by visitors with the result that many people could be killed or injured. Clearly, in this situation, avoidance is the best strategy.

It is also important to recognize that there are two types of related risks, namely risks to people – visitors and staff – and to things (equipment and buildings, for example). There are also risks to the reputation of the attraction.

Operations management and the visitor experience

Good, effective operations management at attractions can greatly enhance the quality of the visitor experience and vice versa. The main ways in which the management of the operation has a major impact on the visitor might include:

1 How queues are managed, if they cannot be prevented. This means making sure people know how long they may have to queue and perhaps providing entertainment to take people's minds off the fact that they are queuing. Of course, it is even better if operational management can ensure that queuing does not develop in the first place.
2 Handling complaints in an effective manner so that visitors feel that their complaints are handled sympathetically and that action is taken as a result of their complaints. This means attractions developing procedures that all staff should follow in the event of complaints, together with giving staff the authority instantly to solve minor complaints themselves without having to consult senior managers, which might well take time.
3 Solving problems quickly, as visitors tend to have only a limited amount of time they can spend at the attraction. If a problem arises which adversely affects the quality of the visitor's experience, it is important that it is resolved rapidly or it may ruin the visitor's day and make them feel that their visit has not given them value for money.
4 Managing the attraction's environment in a way that makes it look well kept and maintained, as this increases visitors' enjoyment and makes them feel good about their decision to visit the attraction.
5 Managing the attraction in a way that makes visitors feel safe and secure, which will mean that they relax and enjoy themselves rather than worrying about the things that might go wrong.

Creating operational management systems that are user-friendly and enhance the visitor experience is quite a challenge. It is important to prevent a situation where visitors believe that the way the operation of the attraction is managed represents an obstacle to their enjoyment of their visit.

Operations management and competitive advantage

In the increasingly competitive attraction market, managers are always seeking anything that will give them a competitive advantage in the market. While at one time operations management was seen as a domestic matter at the attraction itself, which held little interest for the outside world, it is increasingly being seen as a potential marketing tool. The Disney Corporation has long promoted the way it manages its attraction as a unique selling proposition (USP) to create competitive advantage. The impression that they are well managed, clean and safe, and are staffed by well-trained, friendly and motivated staff has been successfully sold to people who have not even been to a Disney attraction. A major part of Disney's success is the result of the positive attitudes and opinions people have about the way the attraction operation is managed.

Other attractions are now trying to use various aspects of the way they manage their operations to improve their reputation in the market. Some of the approaches that can be taken include the following:

1 Trying to appeal to people who are concerned about the environment by promoting the fact that the attraction's operations are managed with green issues in mind. Some may even seek some formal recognition of this, such as the British Standard BS 7750 (in the UK), to support their claims. This standard covers environmental management systems.
2 Communicating the fact that the attraction is operated in a way that recognizes the needs of disabled visitors.
3 Emphasizing the concern of the attraction with the safety of visitors and the security of their property, particularly their cars, when they visit the attraction.
4 Focusing on the skills and commitment of the staff and the quality of service they deliver.

Obviously, it is important that attractions make sure that they live up to their promises for if visitors find the attraction does not offer what it claims to, then they will not visit again and will give a bad impression of the attraction to friends and relatives. This could result in the attraction not only failing to achieve competitive advantage, but perhaps suffering competitive disadvantage!

Operations management and quality

Operations management is clearly the cornerstone of whether or not customers will perceive the attraction to be of high or poor quality. In terms of quality, there are two aspects to operations management. First, there are the processes of operations management, in other words, how the attraction goes about the task of operating. This means focusing on operations management systems and procedures. Second, there are the outcomes of operations management, namely, how well the systems and procedures work in reality and the results of their implementation. Things may look good on paper but not be practical, or they may be practical but the desired outcomes are not achieved because staff are not following the systems and procedures. This emphasis on processes and systems is at the core of the BS 5750/ISO 9000 standards but for attraction managers it is ultimately the outcomes that are most important.

Operations management: special cases

So far we have looked at the subject of operations management in general, but there are certain types of attractions that have their own specific operations management issues. Some of these are briefly discussed below.

Public sector attractions

Here, operations managers often have to work within rules and regulations which are imposed from outside and may not be conducive to the management of attractions. Sometimes, key elements of the attraction operation such as cleaning and catering may be outside the direct control of attraction managers due to the results of compulsory competitive tendering (CCT). Finally, many decisions relating to the operational management of attractions in the public sector will be taken on political rather than operational grounds.

Small-scale attractions

Most of this chapter has been based on the assumption that there are specialist operations management staff. However, in the case of small-scale attractions, it may be that they lack staff who are experienced in operational management. Indeed it may be that there is only one owner or manager, for whom operations are only a minor part of their job, together with financial management, marketing and human resource management.

Constraints on operations management

Constraints on operations management come in a number of forms, including:

- the operations manager's abilities, experience and attitudes
- the traditions and culture of the attraction organization
- resources, skills and attitudes of the staff, and the freedom they are given by the organization's structure to take the initiative on operational problems
- the availability of financial resources to solve operational problems
- the pressures where the attractions hardly ever close, so that there is little downtime in which to carry out remedial action
- legislation and regulations
- the social acceptability or otherwise of operational management systems.

Conclusion

We have seen in this chapter that operations management is in many ways the key to customer satisfaction, and optimizing the financial performance of the attraction. Effective operations management requires precise objectives and clear guidelines on which member of staff is responsible for which aspect of the attraction's operation. It also means setting performance targets for operational management such as how quickly particular problems will be solved and what level of complaint is acceptable. Furthermore, good operations management means being prepared for predictable problems and being flexible enough to cope with sudden, unexpected emergencies.

As well as dealing with problems, effective operations management can also improve an attraction's image and can be a positive marketing tool.

Given the importance of operations management for attractions it is surprising how little management attention is devoted to developing proactive, systematic, quality operations management systems. Instead, far too often operations management is about being reactive, coping with crises that could have been foreseen, panic, chaos and 'papering over the cracks' of inadequate operations management. Many attractions still do not appear to understand the long-term cost of this situation in terms of market image and future visitor numbers.

Discussion points and essay questions

1 Discuss the implications of the contents of Table 17.2 for operational managers at attractions.
2 Discuss the techniques which could be used to reduce queues and improve visitor experiences in queues at attractions.
3 Discuss the skills required for effective operations management at attractions.

Exercise

Select an attraction with which you are familiar. For your chosen attraction you should devise a crisis management plan, based on the points made in this chapter.

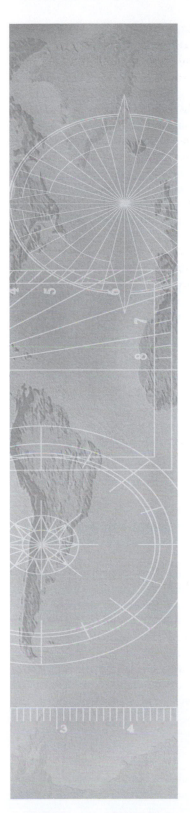

Ethical challenges in attraction management

Introduction

In recent years, there has been a growing interest in ethics in business, as in politics. Managers in all industries face ethical dilemmas every day and the visitor attraction sector is no exception.

The ethical challenges in the visitor attraction sector fall into two groups:

- those which affect all types of attractions, such as environmental issues and sustainability
- those which exist within particular types of attraction such as heritage attractions and wildlife attractions.

In this chapter, we will look at these aspects of ethical challenges in a little more detail. However, it must be recognized that this is not a comprehensive coverage of the ethical issues facing attraction managers; it is just a selection of three of the most high profile issues.

Environmental issues and sustainability

In the first edition the author used the term 'green issues' and then went on to take a broad view of this subject that included social and economic, as well as environmental, issues. For the second edition this is replaced by the more appropriate and sophisticated terms of environmental issues and sustainability.

Nevertheless 'green issues' is still a very wide and rather vague overarching term for a broad range of topics. However, we can say that sustainability means developing and managing attractions which are as environmentally friendly, socially equitable and economically viable as possible. This definition clearly means that the challenge is to every management function within the attraction as we shall see later in this chapter.

In recent years considerable attention has focused on how consumers and organizations can become greener, or more environmentally friendly, for it is accepted that no economic activity can be totally 'green'. This action can take a number of forms and might typically include the following:

- symbolic action in relation to the day-to-day operation of the organization, such as the use of recycled paper
- making production processes more environmentally friendly
- reducing packaging that wastes resources and fulfils no useful purpose
- lowering energy consumption
- sponsoring conservation projects.

Much debate has focused on the motives behind such action and it has to be said that the most powerful reasons for organizations to adopt more environmentally friendly practices have been selfish rather than altruistic, including:

- cost reduction
- improving the public image of the organization
- seeking to achieve competitive advantage in the marketplace by responding, and being seen to respond, to consumers' concerns over environmental issues.

Many organizations have also wished to appear to be concerned and to be taking action so that governments would not feel the need to bring in legislation to force them to adopt certain practices, in the interests of the environment. For governments, too, have felt the need to respond to public concerns with a wide range of measures, including expert reports and codes of practice, although rarely legislation.

This trend reflected that seen in tourism as a whole, where a growing interest in 'green issues' led to the creation of the concept of sustainable tourism. We will now look at how this concept of sustainability can be applied to attractions.

Towards more sustainable visitor attractions

In Chapter 2 we saw that attractions have negative and positive impacts, in terms of economic, environmental and sociocultural impacts. In this section, we will look at how attractions can be made more sustainable by maximizing the positive impacts and reducing the negative impacts.

The development of attractions

The development of a new attraction poses a number of potential problems for the environment and the host community, including:

- Damaging or destroying the habitats of the existing flora and fauna.
- Creating an eyesore through the development of buildings and structures that are of an inappropriate scale, are aesthetically in poor taste and use unsuitable building materials.
- Polluting the local environment as a result of the construction of the attraction.
- Putting a strain on local infrastructure, such as roads and the water system, during the construction phase.
- Using outside labour rather than local people to help build the attraction. Not only does this deprive local people of employment opportunities but the outsiders may also have cultures which are at odds with those of the local population, which may result in resentment and tension.
- The theme of the attraction itself may be at odds with the culture of the area in which it is developed.
- Adjacent land prices may be forced up beyond the reach of local people as speculators buy up land near the new attraction in the hope that its value will be increased because of its proximity to the new attraction. Of course, this will not be seen as a problem by the local people who own such land!

This lists only some of the negative impacts that can be caused by the development of a new attraction. In many parts of the world, planning systems exist to prevent some of these problems, particularly those relating to the physical environment. These include:

- controls on the scale of development and the building materials that can be used
- giving protection to habitats and landscapes by designating them as protected areas and preventing development taking place within them
- forcing developers to provide their own infrastructure as well as, or instead of, using the one developed to meet the needs of the local community.

However, in many countries such systems do not exist and even where there are such systems, they often lose the battle when their adversary is a major corporation providing many jobs or is the government or a local authority which may not even be subject to the system.

For any such system to work properly it must be able to predict in advance what the impact of a proposed development on the environment is likely to be, and that is where *environmental impact assessments* (EIAs) can be helpful. According to Rogers and Slinn (1993) these have four main elements, in that they:

- review the context in which the development is being proposed; the nature, scale, form, timing and so on
- forecast the benefits and costs, and identify by whom they will be enjoyed or shouldered
- appraise alternative scenarios
- set out the opportunities for impact alleviation and/or compensation that will be undertaken if the project is given approval.

Such assessments are valuable and important aids to decision-making.

For attractions to operate in a 'greener' manner in respect of the environment, they must address the issues outlined above, if only to ensure that they will obtain planning permission. However, perhaps, if they are willing to go beyond what the planners demand, they may gain local goodwill which might prove useful in the future. A good example of such a proactive approach to environmental matters are the actions of the developers of the Center Parcs UK complex in Sherwood Forest, Nottinghamshire, UK.

Center Parcs UK had detailed discussions with local planners about the design of the complex. They also talked to a number of specialist environmental agencies about this development, including the former Nature Conservancy Council. Once the site had been selected, an ecological survey was carried out, and the subsequent design and layout reflected the results of this investigation.

Villas were carefully sited and roads and other services were blended into the landscape to cause the minimum of disturbance to the environment. A lake was created together with streams and waterfalls which provided an excellent habitat for natural flora. Some 500 000 new native trees and shrubs were planted, while grassy areas were also established. A special reserve was created for black fallow deer and bird-nesting and bat-roosting boxes were provided to help conserve the existing wildlife in the area. In addition, areas of heathland were restored and a decision was taken that chemicals would only be used on site as a last resort. Within five years of opening the site was being officially recognized for the quality of its wildlife.

Environmental friendliness was, however, not just considered to be a matter for the outdoor areas. Within the buildings, energy conservation was a major consideration and collection points were set up for the recycling of products like bottles, cans and paper. The attraction operator used recycled stationery for their correspondence.

Center Parcs UK has demonstrated that large tourism developments can be sensitively designed and can even help enhance an area's wildlife. However, there are of course ethical issues about the extent to which it is right artificially to create new wildlife habitats.

However, Center Parcs UK has continued to show great sensitivity to the question of wildlife, at its original site in Nottinghamshire and at its later sites at Elveden (Suffolk) and Longleat (Wiltshire). An interesting paper by Johnson and Collins, published in 2001, showed how the planting of woodland on the sites has led to a great interest in the number of flora species, and birds such as blackbirds, song thrushes, linnets and bullfinches.

The authors suggest that Center Parcs UK is an example of good practice based on four principles:

- selecting sites where the existing flora and fauna is not of great value
- designing and building sensitively for minimal impact
- managing the sites to encourage the growth of target species and habitats
- ongoing monitoring of the state of the ecosystems on site.

The work of Center Parcs UK has been recognized with various awards, as well as with ISO 14001.

This leads us on to a wider consideration of how the relationship between developer and local community may be made greener, given that EIAs are usually more concerned with the environment than the local economy and community. Perhaps we need a new form of wider EIA that looks at the sociocultural and economic impact as well as the environmental impact of proposed projects.

There is clearly a need for developers to involve the local community more in the process of developing a new attraction from the original concept, through construction, to the opening day and beyond. This might take a number of forms including:

1 Public meetings to make people aware of what is planned and to answer their questions and allay their fears.
2 Working with local groups, such as schoolchildren and amenity groups, and involving them in the development of the attraction. Such groups may also be given, for example, a small amount of space at the attraction for a project of their own choosing which is complementary to the needs of the attraction, perhaps a small nature reserve.
3 Keeping people informed of progress through the local media.
4 Using local labour and suppliers, wherever possible.
5 Taking the advice of local people on issues such as traditional local architectural styles and building materials.

In these ways, and the many others that might be identified, the needs and desires of the community may be reflected in the way the attraction is developed, while from the developer's viewpoint, opposition may be reduced.

However, there are dangers in such action. It may be seen as manipulation rather than participation by local people and may increase rather than reduce local opposition to the project. Second, expectations may be raised in the minds of the local community which the developer cannot meet for financial or other reasons. Finally, the process of involving more people may lead to an increase in costs and/or the time taken to develop the attraction.

In any event, any attempt to increase community involvement in the development of new attractions will often come up against two problems:

1 Many people will simply not be interested enough to get involved as they have other priorities in their daily life. This means there is a danger that the process of increasing involvement may be 'hijacked' by a few groups or individuals who may not reflect the opinions of the whole community.
2 In most instances, the concept of community, in other words people sharing similar attitudes, lifestyles and aspirations, is a myth. Most villages, towns, cities and regions are made up of a number of 'communities' with very different views on any issue. These communities may be defined in terms, perhaps, of age, or sex or race or religion. It is therefore a matter of choosing which community or communities one will listen to most.

The management of attractions

The last section concentrated on human-made attractions that are purpose-built for tourism. However, when we consider how the management of attractions can be made more sustainable we can also look at two other kinds of attraction:

- natural features such as caves and forests
- human-made features that were not originally designed as tourist attractions, such as cathedrals and castles.

However, although the types of attraction may be different, many of the principles of sustainable attraction management remain the same. Furthermore, many of the issues are very similar to those outlined in the last section, and continue to be relevant once the attraction has opened. These include pollution, the demands made on the local infrastructure and the employment of local labour.

In this section, we will focus on how attraction management could be made more sustainable in terms of the different management functions, namely, operations, human resource management, financial management and marketing.

More sustainable operations management

If we take a broad view of operations management, it could contribute to more sustainable attraction management in the following ways:

1 Reduce energy consumption through insulation and switching off heating and lighting, whenever this can be done without reducing the quality of the visitor experience. Perhaps visitors would be willing to

tolerate an attraction if it were a little cooler and darker than usual if they knew it was for the sake of the earth's energy resources.

2 Reduce waste and ensure that recyclable materials are used wherever this is practical.

3 Minimize pollution whether it be water, air, or noise pollution.

4 Buy from local suppliers wherever possible.

5 Only buy from suppliers who also behave in a responsible manner towards the environment.

6 Be a 'good neighbour' and minimize inconvenience to those who live around the attraction, by not operating noisy machines at night or on Sundays, for example, or by ensuring that delivery lorries do not make deliveries at times when local roads are already congested.

7 Place controls on visitor flows where unlimited visitor access to parts of the attraction would cause environmental damage such as the erosion of footpaths or increased water pollution.

8 Zone potentially conflicting uses of an attraction so that they are kept separate, or separate them by allowing each to take place at different times.

9 Maintain the environmental quality of the attraction rather than possibly responding to financial constraints by cutting spending on measures that improve and enhance the environment, such as regular cleaning and refurbishment of buildings and the replacing of plants and trees that die.

10 Ensure that the attraction is accessible to all sectors of the community, including those people who have disabilities.

More sustainable human resource management

In a broad sense making human resource management more sustainable might include the following elements:

1 Recruiting local people wherever possible, even if this means spending more effort trying to find suitable staff from the local area than it would take to obtain experienced staff from outside. It may also mean having to practise positive discrimination in terms of recruiting local people even if they are not as skilled as those who might be available outside the area. This clearly has implications for service quality and for the amount of training that might be required.

2 Adopting human resource policies that are in keeping with local culture and employment practices. In some countries this may cause real problems for organizations; for example, it may mean having to take a different view of what constitutes equal opportunities or even ignoring altogether some aspects of equal opportunities. This is clearly a very contentious and controversial concept.

3 Training local managers so that one day they will be able to take over from the managers who may have come in with the company to manage the attraction.

4 Training staff to understand the importance of green issues and to operate in a greener manner on a day-to-day basis.

5 Taking care when staff have to be made redundant, for whatever reason, that it is handled sensitively and that all possible efforts are made to make it as painless as possible for the person concerned.

More sustainable financial management

We rarely think of financial management as being a management function that can lead to more sustainable attraction management, but it can. For example, wherever possible, attractions should not be managed to achieve unreasonably high rates of return on investment in the short term, as this often means having to manage the attraction in a way that is exploitative and not sustainable. However, given the problem of funding attraction projects, such an approach may not be possible.

A possibly more practical way in which financial management can help is through ensuring that small local suppliers are paid promptly, which will help them stay solvent and will also increase goodwill towards the attraction within the local community.

More sustainable marketing

There are many ways in which marketing can contribute to making attractions more sustainable, including:

- being honest about the attraction in literature and making visitors aware, through its brochures, of how they can help make the attraction 'greener' through their own behaviour
- targeting those visitors who are likely to be most sensitive and amenable to the concept of sustainability at attractions
- trying to market the attraction so that seasonality of demand is reduced and to lower visitor numbers at peak times, so reducing the overuse of attractions that may occur at the height of the season
- setting out to attract higher-spending visitors so that the attraction may be able to achieve its financial objectives from a smaller number of visitors; this prevents some of the problems that arise from over-crowding and congestion
- operating pricing policies that discriminate in favour of local people or providing concessions for particular groups such as the unemployed and schoolchildren
- ensuring that the product is acceptable to local culture and that any special events at the attraction are not offensive to the opinions of the local community
- encouraging visitors to use public transport to travel to the attraction rather than private cars to reduce congestion and air pollution.

In the above discussion we have taken a very broad view of sustainability issues. However, the fact remains that for most people at least, sustainability means the physical environment. This is particularly important for visitor attractions as, in many cases, their physical environment – whether the structure or fabric of a historic building or an element of the natural environment – constitutes the attraction itself. In this situation, managing visitors properly is crucial, otherwise the very attraction itself may cease to exist or at least may be seriously damaged. How to prevent such an outcome is the subject of the following section.

Visitor management at attractions

In 1991, as part of the 'Tourism and the Environment' initiative referred to earlier, a report was produced by leading consultants Pieda plc, entitled 'Maintaining the balance: visitor management case studies'. Some of the case studies were of attractions such as Salisbury Cathedral, Warwick Castle and Land's End. Many of the possible ways of tackling the many visitor management problems faced by such human-made heritage and natural attractions were explored in these case studies, which were published in the English Tourist Board publication (1991), *Tourism and the Environment: Maintaining the Balance*. They included:

1 Use visitor donations to repair the damage done by visitors and to conserve the attraction.
2 Create facsimilies of delicate features so that visitors can see what they look like without damaging the original. This has been tried with some art collections in the UK and has also been used successfully in other countries, the Lascaux II caverns and copies of works of art and furniture in some Loire chateaux, in France, for example.
3 Erect fences around easily damaged structures to restrict access and thus reduce wear and tear. A good, if rather controversial, UK example is, of course, Stonehenge.
4 Appoint staff specifically to monitor the activities of visitors, although these can make the attraction seem somewhat less than welcoming for visitors.
5 Reduce 'bottlenecks', for example by introducing one-way visitor flows and improved signposting.
6 Close attractions when they are perceived to have reached their carrying capacity or saturation point. The carrying capacity could be based on the number of people that can be accommodated before unacceptable damage begins to take place. On the other hand, it could be a perceptual capacity which is concerned with the point at which the number of visitors begins to damage the visitor experience, the ambience of the attraction, its sense of place. However, closing attractions in this way can upset visitors who may have travelled many miles to visit it. One alternative might be to ask visitors to book in advance so they will know in advance whether they will be able to gain access on a particular day.
7 Restrict access by car and encourage visitors to arrive by more environmentally friendly forms of transport such as buses, trains, horseback, bicycle or foot.
8 Develop new attractions on-site or adjacent to existing attractions to take pressure off existing 'honeypot' attractions.

9 De-market attractions or encourage people to visit fragile attractions outside the peak season and on less busy days of the week.

Constraints to making attractions more sustainable

It is only fair to point out, however, that managers do not have total freedom of action and there may be limits on their ability to implement sustainable policies, for example:

- the manager's own lack of expertise in the field and the general lack of specific, practical advice for attraction managers
- the belief of some key stakeholders that the current concern with green issues is a fad that will soon pass
- many staff may not wish to undertake the radical changes in attitudes that becoming greener implies
- a lack of capital funding that may be needed to pay for energy conservation measures, while greening the process of attraction development may raise costs to an unacceptable level.

In some instances it might actually be wrong for attractions to try to be very green. For example, if the mission of an industrial heritage attraction is to reproduce the working conditions of yesteryear as accurately as possible, measures to reduce pollution and noise, and to save energy, might actually make the attraction less successful in terms of its aims!

International perspective

Most of this chapter has focused on the UK, and while many of the general principles discussed here are relevant to all countries, there are key differences in other countries that need to be recognized. These include:

- differences in the interest of consumers in environmental issues, from countries where people appear to have little interest to countries like Germany and Austria, where people are used to already behaving as consumers in ways that would seem quite 'dark green' to the British
- varying degrees of environmental and social legislation and regulations in different countries
- differences between countries in terms of the general attention paid to environmental and social issues by corporations
- areas where the key attractions are fragile, natural or human-made attractions that are in danger of disappearing and where action to save them is apparently taking place too slowly.

Summary

In this section we have taken a broad view of sustainability issues and have seen how attractions can become more sustainable both in terms of their development and management. However, we have also seen that this could be used as a cynical ploy to achieve competitive advantage on the basis of a few tokenistic actions. Furthermore, we have observed that the current concern with sustainability issues could be a passing fashion that might disappear or decline dramatically, in which case investing in it could turn out to be a waste of time and money, although it must be said this does not seem very likely.

Whatever happens, it is likely that at least for the foreseeable future sustainability issues will be an important element in the business environment for attraction managers and will require action, whether it be proactive or reactive.

We will now look at the ethical issues in two specific sectors of the attraction business, heritage and wildlife.

Ethics and heritage attractions

The number of heritage attractions has grown rapidly in recent years, worldwide, and the concept of heritage has changed to embrace modern popular cultural heritage, social history and recent history. However this sector contains a number of ethical challenges for managers including the following:

1 The idea of authenticity and commodification where heritage may be exaggerated, censored, or packaged in ways which are not authentic but which increase the market appeal of the heritage in question. This is a very controversial area of debate within the field, particularly with the rise of 'living history reconstructions' which are clearly artificial but purport to be realistic. Halewood and Hannam, in 2001, published an interesting paper about Viking heritage attractions in Europe including museums, heritage centres, theme parks, village reconstructions and special events. They concluded that most managers and tourists are aware of the artificiality of much of what is being presented but that both seem happy with the experience provided.

2 Usually the choice of stories and interpretation media at heritage attractions is made by professionals rather than by the wider communities, even when these attractions are funded by the local community. There is a strong argument for saying that if the subject of an attraction is a particular community or place then, surely, the people of that area should have a say in which stories are told, and how the stories are told.

3 In some heritage attractions it seems that history is selectively viewed or censored to avoid controversial or sensitive subjects. Yet, surely, a heritage attraction should offer the whole story as objectively as possible. Aspects of history that can be excluded from museums can include everything from slavery to wars, the role of ethnic minorities to social issues such as drugs, sexual behaviour to corruption.

4 Recently, heritage attractions have made enormous efforts to make themselves more entertaining and more attractive to non-specialist visitors, through interactive exhibits, for example. However, there is a danger here that the medium becomes more important than the

message, with visitors remembering the interpretative technology rather than the story it was telling.

Ethics and wildlife attractions

Until the last twenty years or so, wildlife attractions were both socially acceptable and popular. However, recently, traditional wildlife attractions have come under great pressure in the USA and Europe, in particular:

- zoos have been increasingly criticized for keeping wild animals captive in cages, for the amusement of visitors
- circuses have been attacked for getting creatures to perform unnatural tricks for the entertainment of their customers.

However, zoos and circuses with animals are still popular in many parts of the world where animal welfare concerns are not so highly developed, or where cultural attitudes towards animals are different.

In the USA and Europe, the reaction to the criticism of zoos, for instance, has led to three developments:

- changing the emphasis in publicity from entertainment to education and conservation
- modifying zoos to improve the environment for animals together with the creation of safari parks
- switching the emphasis to aquariums, where fish are the main attraction. Apparently people are less concerned about fish in captivity than they are about mammals and reptiles and birds!

In all three cases, the changes do not fundamentally deal with the underlying issues of using animals for entertainment, and keeping creatures in captivity.

Later in the book there is a case study which looks in a little more detail at the evolution of wildlife attractions. The attractions sector also contains a major ethical issue in relation to funding, which will now be briefly discussed.

The ethics of attraction funding

One ethical issue that applies to many types of attraction is the question of funding. In many countries, attractions are wholly or partly funded by the public sector. This raises several ethical concerns:

- Public sector capital funding can create unfair competition for other attractions in the commercial and voluntary sectors.
- Public sector capital funding can lead to the development of new attractions which are not financially viable in the longer term. If attractions need public funding to allow them to be built, rather than being able to raise the funding commercially, then it must raise questions about their viability. This point has clearly been seen with

some of the projects in the UK that were funded by the National Lottery and Millennium Commission, and have failed financially.

- Public sector funding is often given to attractions, with little or no consultation with local taxpayers, where the money is being given away to what could be large affluent companies.
- Public sector subsidies towards the revenue costs of attractions allows them to charge less than market prices which again constitutes unfair competition. For example, the government in the UK is making the major national museums free to visit while small voluntary and private sector museums have to charge fees to allow them to pay their bills.

The concept of ethical business and corporate citizenship

Across all industries, in recent years, there has been a growing interest in ethical issues in business and management. This has arisen for the following reasons:

- High profile political and business scandals have focused media attention on ethical standards in business. This has led to a growth of consumer interest in ethical issues.
- Some 'ethical' actions, such as environmentally friendly measures like energy conservation, can help a business reduce its costs.
- Companies and whole industries want to be seen to be acting responsibly to persuade governments that they do not need to introduce legislation and regulations to improve corporate ethical standards.

When challenged on ethical issues, however, organizations, including attractions, can respond in a number of ways, as are illustrated in Figure 18.1.

This analysis can clearly be applied to the visitor attraction sector. For example, zoos 'put the other side of the case' by talking about their conservation work as a counterbalance to their entertainment dimension, while museums may practice 'tokenism' with a small temporary exhibition on a previously neglected subject.

However, as yet, we have seen relatively few examples of attractions seeing ethical issues as potential opportunities rather than as threats. So far, few attractions have seen more ethical operations as a positive tool for achieving competitive advantage. However, we have seen how Center Parcs has achieved wide recognition for their environmental sensitivity, which has not harmed their market reputation.

The growing media, customer and government interest in ethical issues may lead more and more attractions to endeavour to use ethical concerns as opportunities to enhance their reputation and increase visitor numbers. This could include:

- adopting the concept of 'Corporate Citizenship' where the attraction gives attention to its social and environmental impacts and recognizes its duties towards the wider society. This concept is becoming

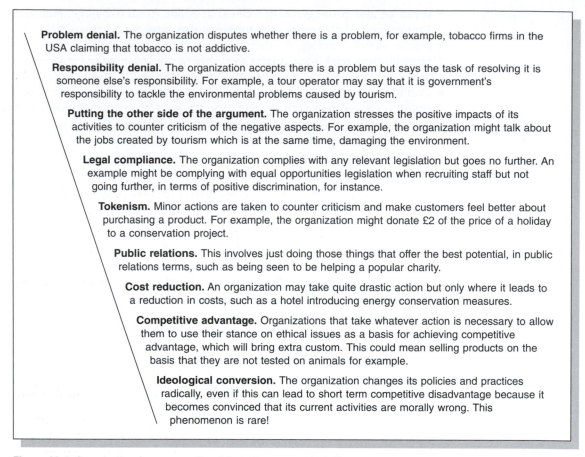

Problem denial. The organization disputes whether there is a problem, for example, tobacco firms in the USA claiming that tobacco is not addictive.

Responsibility denial. The organization accepts there is a problem but says the task of resolving it is someone else's responsibility. For example, a tour operator may say that it is government's responsibility to tackle the environmental problems caused by tourism.

Putting the other side of the argument. The organization stresses the positive impacts of its activities to counter criticism of the negative aspects. For example, the organization might talk about the jobs created by tourism which is at the same time, damaging the environment.

Legal compliance. The organization complies with any relevant legislation but goes no further. An example might be complying with equal opportunities legislation when recruiting staff but not going further, in terms of positive discrimination, for instance.

Tokenism. Minor actions are taken to counter criticism and make customers feel better about purchasing a product. For example, the organization might donate £2 of the price of a holiday to a conservation project.

Public relations. This involves just doing those things that offer the best potential, in public relations terms, such as being seen to be helping a popular charity.

Cost reduction. An organization may take quite drastic action but only where it leads to a reduction in costs, such as a hotel introducing energy conservation measures.

Competitive advantage. Organizations that take whatever action is necessary to allow them to use their stance on ethical issues as a basis for achieving competitive advantage, which will bring extra custom. This could mean selling products on the basis that they are not tested on animals for example.

Ideological conversion. The organization changes its policies and practices radically, even if this can lead to short term competitive disadvantage because it becomes convinced that its current activities are morally wrong. This phenomenon is rare!

Figure 18.1 Organizational responses to ethical dilemmas and challenges

fashionable with companies and organizations who want to be seen as 'good guys'. The author believes it will become a major competitive advantage tool in the years to come

- developing 'Ethical Marketing' where the organization focuses on making its product, price, promotion, and distribution, fairer and more honest, and then uses this to attract new market segments and/or retain existing customers.

It remains to be seen how many attractions will follow this path but it will be used increasingly by companies in other industries and other sectors of tourism.

Conclusions

This chapter has reflected on changes which have taken place since the first edition appeared in 1995, in that:

- it has talked about 'sustainability', a wider, more sophisticated concept than the original concept of 'green' issues

- it has looked at the growing interest in ethical business, in general, and the concept of corporate citizenship and ethical marketing.

The author has suggested that in the years to come the whole question of ethics will grow in importance in all sectors and this trend will affect attractions. Successful attractions will be those which anticipate this development and proactively prepare for it, rather than those which ignore it and only react when the 'writing is on the wall'.

Discussion points and essay questions

1 Discuss the ways in which the development of new visitor attractions can be made more environmentally friendly.
2 Critically evaluate the reasons why attractions should endeavour to operate in line with the principles of sustainability.
3 Discuss the arguments, for and against, wildlife attractions from an ethical point of view.

Exercise

Visit a museum or heritage centre in your area. Identify the ethical issues raised by the stories being told and the ways in which history is being interpreted. If possible, bring these issues to the attention of the management of the attraction and discuss them with the management, noting their views.

Managing quality

Introduction

Quality appears to be the buzzword of our time, in manufacturing and service industries, and in the public and private sectors. Marketing theorists have convinced us that being perceived to be a quality organization offering quality products is the key to success. However, the whole subject is still in its infancy in service industries such as tourism, and is surrounded by confusion and muddled thinking.

What do we mean by quality?

The International Organization for Standardization (ISO) has defined quality as 'the totality of features and characteristics of a product or service that bears on its ability to satisfy stated or implied needs'. According to this definition, quality is about 'fitness for purpose' where the purpose is the needs of the customer. However, allied to this is the concept of reliability, in that it is not a quality product if, although being fit for its purpose when it functions properly, it does not work properly very often.

There is a myth that quality means a 'Rolls-Royce' type product, namely premium prices and small-scale production for an exclusive market. This is simply not true. Quality simply means offering a product of the right grade for the chosen market or markets, at the appropriate price. This latter point is important because quality is not an absolute, but is a trade-off between the product the customer wants, and the price they are willing to pay.

Finally, it has to be said that quality can mean different things to different people involved in the production and consumption of a product. To the customer it may be a product that provides the maximum benefits for the minimum cost, while for the company producing the product it may be its ease of production and sale. For financial shareholders in the company it may be the products that achieve the highest profit margin or rate of return on investment. These will not necessarily be one and the same product.

Quality and customer satisfaction

Quality is a product-led concept in that it focuses on the features and attributes of the product. However, marketing today is all about being customer focused. The customer-focused way to look at quality is through customer satisfaction where quality is perceived in terms of the extent to which the product or service satisfies the needs and wants of the customer.

The historical development of the concept of quality

The concept of quality was developed in manufacturing industries, particularly those involving engineering, and was geared to reducing wastage during the production process and faults in the final product. In recent years, however, the idea has grown that quality is not just about outcomes like these but, rather, is about the whole process that takes place to achieve these outcomes. This has led to an increasing emphasis being placed on quality management systems, some of which are outlined below.

In the past few years the view has also grown that quality management is not just part of a management function such as production or operations management and the responsibility of just a few members of staff who have quality as part of their job description. Instead, following Japanese management ideas, there is a belief that quality has to percolate through the whole corporate culture and that it is the responsibility of all staff.

Furthermore, many companies are now seeing quality as an essential part of their marketing strategy as they seek to achieve competitive advantage in the marketplace by obtaining the reputation of being a quality organization offering a quality product. Some companies see quality as a vehicle for achieving wider management goals such as the achievement of cultural change and the motivation and empowerment of staff.

This latter point, relating to staff, has become increasingly important in recent decades with the rise of service industries, where instead of a physical product, the production process produces an intangible product, the main feature of which is the attitudes and competencies of the staff delivering the service. Hence the rise in recent years of customer care programmes.

Quality management approaches

Over time four main quality management approaches have emerged: quality control, quality assurance, total quality control and total quality management, in ascending order of sophistication and width of scope.

Quality control

Quality control is about monitoring product or service quality, identifying quality problems and addressing them. It is about problem-solving and traditionally has been carried out by quality control inspectors in factories. In this case the responsibility for identifying problems and solutions rests not with the member of staff making the product or delivering the service, but with the inspector.

Quality assurance

Quality assurance is concerned with the prevention of quality problems in the first place, and the onus is on the member of staff concerned to get it right first time rather than waiting for an inspector to spot problems. This is often thought to have the advantage of being cheaper than a system which allows problems to arise in the first place.

Total quality control

This approach takes a wider view of the production or service delivery process than the previous two systems and looks at all the possible factors that might influence the final product or service, rather than just the narrow final production process itself.

Total quality management

This system, commonly known as TQM, is concerned with trying to achieve constant, continuous improvement in product manufacture or service delivery quality to meet both the organization's objectives and its customers' needs. It involves the whole organization, all departments, every activity of the organization, and every member of staff at all levels. Total quality management is by far the most fashionable system at the moment, although it is easier to adopt it in principle than in practice.

Government regulation and quality

In 1979 the UK government, for example, introduced British Standard 5750 (BS 5750) which set standards for quality management for organizations in the manufacturing and service sectors of the economy, including attractions. The international standard for quality, ISO 9002, can also be applied to attractions albeit with some difficulties.

In recent years the UK government and the European Commission have introduced legislation which has affected quality management in another way, that is, consumer protection laws based on the principle of product liability and the idea that everyone involved in offering the product (suppliers, producers, distributors) is responsible for the quality of the final product. Recent examples of such legislation include the Food Safety Act 1991 in the UK and the European Commission's Package Travel Directive. This type of legislation has led producers such as food companies, and will lead producers such as tour operators, to take a far greater interest in the quality management systems of their suppliers (farms or hotels respectively, for example) and their marketing intermediaries (supermarkets or travel agents). This is because they are now linked together and are reliant on each other to ensure that they do not contravene this legislation.

Quality management and services

As we mentioned earlier, most quality techniques have evolved from manufacturing industries but, as we saw in Chapter 3, services have very different characteristics from manufactured goods and products. Some of these characteristics make quality management in the service sector particularly difficult, including:

1 The service product, unlike manufactured goods, is not a standardized product. It is affected by a number of variables such as the attitudes of the staff delivering the service and the expectations of the customers who are themselves part of the production process, so that in effect the product is different for every customer.
2 The intangibility and perishability of services mean that, in contrast to tangible products, 'faults' in the product cannot easily be seen and it is not as easy to replace a 'faulty' product.
3 Many services are complex products which involve a high degree of interdependence and inseparability of the elements of the product, which further complicates the management of quality.

Quality management and the tourism industry

Some sectors of the tourism industry have developed, perhaps unfairly, an unfortunate public reputation in relation to quality. An example that comes to mind is of some tour operators working in the lower priced end of the market. However there are some good reasons why quality management is particularly difficult in tourism. These include:

- People only buy shared use rights to tourism products such as package holidays, in other words, they must share their resort or their accommodation with other people whom they have not chosen to spend their holiday with. These other people's behaviour can adversely affect the tourist's experience of their holiday, for example, noisy people in a hotel can ruin a holiday for families with young babies. However, the tour operator has little or no control over who else uses the resort or hotel and therefore has little control over this aspect of the quality of the product.

- People pay very different prices for their holidays and the UK industry has developed a reputation for providing low-cost summer sun holidays in response to what is seen as the unwillingness of the consumer to pay more for a basic 'sun, sand, sea and sex' package holiday. Perhaps therefore, prices and profit margins are sometimes so low that it is impossible to meet even the most modest threshold of quality. This may explain the large number of complaints that are often received about such package holidays.

- Customers often have unrealistically high expectations of holidays, which perhaps it is impossible for the product ever to live up to. For example, holidays represent dreams for many people, are saved up for and dreamed about for a whole year, while for others holidays are a way of bringing back life into unhappy marriages or overcoming grief following a bereavement.

Other sectors of the tourism industry also face criticisms in terms of their quality from time to time. For example, it is argued that most British seaside resorts fail the 'fitness for purpose' quality test for they do not offer a product that meets the needs of most modern holidaymakers. Furthermore, some traditional chain hotels are sometimes criticized for being expensive in relation to the quality of product they offer their customers.

Quality and visitor attractions

The attractions sector does not in general suffer an image problem in terms of quality, although there are quality issues relating to certain types of attractions. Quality at attractions can be looked at in two ways: as a set of outcomes, in other words, the 'product' which the customer receives, or as a process, namely how the attraction operates and the process by which the product is produced and delivered to the customer.

Looking at quality as a set of actions relating to the final product means focusing on issues such as:

- the physical environment of the attraction
- the price the customer pays to use the attraction and the extent to which this is perceived to offer value for money by customers
- the service offered to visitors by the attraction staff
- the reliability of the product, and how often the full product is not available to customers, because of mechanical breakdowns or staff shortages for example
- the safety of customers visiting the attraction
- the number of complaints received from customers by the attraction operators.

Alternatively, if one concentrates on the process which leads to the outcome, one has to take a wider perspective altogether, which may mean considering the following issues:

- human resource management policies, including recruitment, motivation, training, rewards and disciplinary action
- the organization's culture, hierarchy and the style of management
- the marketing function and the impressions of the attraction which is projected to potential visitors, together with the relationship with marketing intermediaries
- purchasing policies and the link between the attraction and its suppliers
- procedures for anticipating and responding to changes in the business environment.

This development of seeing quality as a matter of process as well as just outcomes reflects the growth of the idea that quality is about the organization as a whole and the way it operates rather than just being about its products. In many cases, in the minds of customers, the attraction operators and their product or products are synonymous. It is therefore important that attraction operators pay attention to both the process and the outcomes in their quality management systems.

Finally, there are two other important general points that need to be made in relation to quality at attractions. First, ideas on what constitutes quality at attractions will change over time and, so, attractions that are perceived to be of good quality now but which fail to respond to changes in the business (and physical) environment may come to be seen as of a lower quality at some point in the future. Second, as with other types of industry, there is always the question of to what extent quality should be comparative. In other words, should we look at quality in terms of attraction A being of better quality than attraction B, even if they are very different types of attraction in very different locations and owned by different types of organization.

Quality management systems at attractions

When designing their quality management systems, attractions have to consider three main questions:

- What definition of quality they will use?
- What performance standards should be used and what measurement system to utilize?
- What management systems they need to adopt to achieve quality?

As relatively little has yet been written on quality management at attractions, managers have usually applied principles developed in other sectors of the economy. However, the English Tourism Council in the UK has produced a voluntary 'Visitors Charter' or 'National Code of Practice for Visitor Attractions' which sets out some guidelines that are thought to indicate the difference between high quality attractions and other attractions. This is reproduced below:

> *Visitors' Charter* (National Code of Practice for Visitor Attractions)
> The owners and management have undertaken:
>
> 1 To display this Visitors' Charter prominently, and to include the symbol wherever possible in promotional material, to signify compliance.
> 2 To describe accurately in any advertisement, brochure or any other printed means, the amenities, facilities and services provided and to indicate on all such promotional material any significant restrictions on entry.
> 3 To display clearly at public entry points (a) any charges for entry (including service charges and taxes where applicable) and whether there are additional charges for individual attractions, and (b) hours of operation (opening and closing).
> 4 To manage and, where appropriate, staff the attraction in such a way as to ensure visitor safety, comfort and service by maintaining a high standard of customer care, cleanliness, courtesy and maintenance. All staff who meet visitors should be distinguishable as employees or voluntary staff.
> 5 Where appropriate to the nature, scale and location of the attraction, to provide adequate toilet facilities, coach and car parking and catering arrangements.
> 6 To give due consideration to the requirements of disabled people and people with special needs, and to make suitable provision where practicable.
> 7 To deal promptly and courteously with all enquiries, requests, reservations, correspondence, and complaints from visitors. To advise visitors how comments may be recorded, and to whom they should be addressed.
> 8 To provide public liability insurance or comparable arrangement and to comply with all applicable planning, safety and other statutory requirements. (English Tourism Council, 2000)

To be effective, quality management systems must cover every aspect of the management of the attraction. These include:

1 The tangible elements of the product (buildings and structures, for example) in terms of aesthetic appeal, cleanliness, maintenance levels, reliability of operation, safety, comfort and security.
2 The characteristics of service delivery which might include:
   (a) the competencies and attitudes of the staff performing the service
   (b) the time taken to answer telephone enquiries or the amount of time visitors have to spend in queues

(c) the frequency with which equipment or systems break down so that the normal product is not available to customers

(d) what guarantees or warranties are offered to customers

(e) the effectiveness of complaints procedures.

3 Human resource management in terms of how staff are recruited, trained and motivated to ensure that their performance is optimized.

4 Quality in relation to marketing attractions, includes charging fair prices, being honest in the content of literature and giving the right messages to the right target market at the right time.

5 Financial management in terms of the effectiveness of budgetary control, for example.

6 Relationships with the suppliers who provide the attraction with goods and services and with the marketing intermediaries who act as the 'go-betweens' that link attractions with their customers.

7 The provision for visitors with special needs.

8 Relations with the local community.

9 Behaving in a way that is perceived to be socially responsible, for example being seen to be 'green'.

10 The effectiveness of management systems and procedures.

11 Planning for the future.

Measuring quality and satisfaction

We can only develop quality management if we can measure quality. Let us now, therefore, look at two approaches to measuring quality and satisfaction which have been applied to attractions.

Bench-marking and attractions

The technique of bench-marking has been around for some time but only recently has it been applied to attractions specifically. A major project on bench-marking at attractions has been conducted in Hampshire in the UK, beginning in 1998. This project defined bench-marking as: 'an ongoing process of measuring and comparing the performance of organisations in order to encourage continuous improvement towards a standard that is regarded as good practice' (Young and Ambrose, 1999).

Bench-marking allows an organization to monitor its performance against that of other organizations in the same sector. It also allows the organization to monitor its own performance over a period of time.

The Hampshire experiment covered nine attractions, all of which charged an entrance fee. It covered five aspects of the operation of the attraction:

- marketing
- retailing
- catering
- financial management
- other income generation activities.

The pilot project had three main stages:

- customer satisfaction research at all attractions
- the development of a good practice bench-marking manual which required attraction managers/staff to give numerical scores to their attraction for a range of criteria
- the preparation of individual action plans for each attraction, based upon the results of the bench-marking manual exercise and the customer satisfaction research.

For marketing, for example, the following criteria were measured:

- Marketing function – addresses issues such as the over-arching marketing plan, marketing budget, marketing staff and organizational commitment to marketing.
- Market research – addresses good practice process for on- and off-site market research.
- Customer base – addresses the attraction's understanding of their customer base.
- Competition – addresses the attraction's understanding of local and regional competition.
- Communication – addresses the issues of internal and external communication.
- Brochure/leaflet – addresses the quality of the attraction's promotional literature.
- Promotion and publicity – addresses such issues as the attraction's PR and events programme, web site and promotional strategies.
- Mailing list – addresses the attraction's approach to establishing and monitoring customer mailing lists to support marketing activities.
- Monitoring and evaluation – addresses the attraction's approach to monitoring and evaluation of marketing activities (Young and Ambrose, 1999).

Let us imagine that overall, based on all these criteria, the mean score for all nine attractions was 75 per cent, with a range of 55 per cent to 95 per cent. One of the attractions, Attraction X scored 60 per cent. They, therefore, know that they are below average performance, in relation to, marketing and they need to improve. Theoretically, therefore, they could look at attractions which scored better than them and learn lessons from these attractions to help them improve their own performance.

The scheme is based on co-operation and trust between the members of the 'bench-marking club' and on the willingness of the better performing attractions to share good practice with the weaker performers.

Surely, it will be difficult to sustain such co-operation in attraction markets that are highly competitive. Which attraction is going to help weaker direct competitors become as strong as them? It is, perhaps, better for government agencies or at least independent organizations to manage bench-marking and create sector-wide standards to overcome this problem.

Bench-marking schemes can have other problems which need to be overcome if they are to be effective, notably:

- the need for simplicity and ease of operation
- the need for objectivity and honesty when measuring one's own attraction's performance.

Nevertheless, bench-marking can be a good way of improving performance across a sector.

However, at a time when attractions are looking for competitive advantage not competitive parity, bench-marking can lead to a 'lowest common denominator' approach. It could also lead to more homogenization rather than differentiation which would be a pity because diversity is one of the strengths of the attraction business.

SERVQUAL and HISTOQUAL

SERVQUAL was developed by Parasuraman et al. in 1985 as a way of measuring product and service quality numerically. It has been extensively used in hospitality for example. Frochot and Hughes, in 2000, published a paper which sought to apply this concept to heritage attractions in the UK, specifically, with a tool called HISTOQUAL. Table 19.1 illustrates the results of this exercise, based on a survey of a particular sample of visitors, at three heritage attractions in the UK.

Designing quality management systems: a hypothetical example

Having looked at some general points about the nature and scope of quality management systems it is now time to focus on how to design systems, using the three principles we outlined at the beginning of the first section, and a hypothetical case study.

Let us imagine we are designing a quality system for a medium-sized theme park, owned by a large corporation, that has a regional catchment area. The first task is to define quality in relation to the theme park. Such a definition could be seen in terms of a number of elements, as follows:

- the reliability of the product, in other words, how frequently it breaks down or fails to operate properly
- the level of customer satisfaction
- the effectiveness of management functions such as human resource management and marketing
- optimizing financial performance
- the reputation of the theme park with important external audiences such as its parent company, trade bodies and the national tourist board.

These definitions of quality could be translated into the following *performance standards and measurement systems*:

Factors	Items	Mean scores	Standard deviations
Responsiveness		*4.67*	38
	Staff are always helpful and courteous	4.69	58
	Staff are willing to take time with visitors	4.73	50
	Visitors are made to feel welcome	4.64	62
	Level of crowding is tolerable	4.63	59
	Staff are well informed to answer customer requests	4.70	52
	Visitors feel free to explore, there are no restrictions to access	4.52	72
	The property and grounds are opened at convenient hours	4.72	67
	Staff are always available when needed	4.78	51
Tangibles		*4.19*	43
	The property is well kept and restored	4.21	75
	The general cleanliness and upkeep of the property and grounds is satisfying	4.39	67
	The grounds are attractive	4.17	76
	The site has remained authentic	3.98	78
	Direction signs to show around the property and grounds are clear and helpful	4.18	61
	The garden and/or park contain a large variety of plants	4.20	50
	The interior of the house offers a lot of interesting things to look at	4.21	65
Communications		*3.84*	63
	The written leaflets provide enough information	3.75	91
	The information on the property and grounds is detailed enough	3.92	86
	Visitors are well informed of the different facilities and service attractions available at the property	4.04	64
	Foreign language leaflets are helpful	3.63	64
Consumables		*3.88*	57
	The restaurant offers a wide variety of dishes and refreshments	3.95	81
	The shop offers a large variety of goods	3.94	70
	The restaurant staff provide efficient service	3.64	74
Empathy		*2.64*	87
	The property considers the needs of less able visitors	2.53	77
	Facilities for children are provided	2.79	78
Total scale		4.13	27

Source: Frochot and Hughes (2000)

Table 19.1 Mean scores of HISTOQUAL across the final sample

1 The 'white knuckle' rides should be functional on at least 95 per cent of the days when the attraction is open, and when they break down they should be back in action within less than two hours. Reporting systems need to be developed to allow these performance indicators to be measured.

2 At least 75 per cent of visitors should be very satisfied with their visit and that on no day should complaints exceed 1 per cent of the number of visits. These would be measured through visitor surveys and records of complaints.

3 Reduce staff turnover by half and improve the qualifications of staff, which could be measured by using personnel records.

4 Increase the conversion rate of enquiries to actual visits by 10 per cent; this would require records of enquiries being kept and the ability to identify the visitors who had previously made an enquiry.

5 Increase visitors' secondary spending in the theme park's retailing and catering outlets from £3 to £4, which means being able to measure visitor numbers and the income at these particular profit centres.

6 Encourage the parent company to allocate an extra £2 million for refurbishment and the purchase of a new ride.

Many performance standards are relatively easy to quantify but many are, by definition, qualitative and are very difficult to measure.

The theme park we are considering would need to devise quality systems to achieve these performance standards. If we take the six examples used above, these might be as follows:

1 More regular maintenance checks, increased spending on maintenance and a 'quality circle' for the ride operators to improve the way the ride is operated.

2 Sophisticated surveys to evaluate levels of customer satisfaction and team meetings to see how customer satisfaction might be increased, what customers like about the attraction, and how they feel they are treated. Specific customers should be 'tracked', all the way round the attraction to see how complaints might be reduced. Individual staff may be given specific responsibilities, and financial resources could be given to the staff to help them carry out these duties.

3 Introduce job rotation and empowerment to increase job satisfaction and the use of performance-related pay to reward good workers and ensure that they do not leave. Regular staff development interviews could be introduced between staff and managers so that early indications of dissatisfaction could be detected and tackled. Develop in-house courses and encourage staff to take formal qualifications.

4 Train staff to do telesales work so that, rather than simply replying to enquiries, they sell the attraction to potential visitors on the telephone.

5 Carry out visitor surveys to identify what retail and catering outlets are currently offering, what visitors would buy if they were on offer, and then provide them.

6 Give positive messages about the attraction to the parent company and prepare a good case to show what extra profit could be generated by the investment of £2 million in the theme park.

It is clearly important that all such systems or indicators are monitored to see if they are meeting their objectives and to see how their effectiveness might be improved. This monitoring is made easier if the system stipulates who has responsibility for implementation and what resources they have at their disposal.

However, this hypothetical system has just looked at single issues rather than at an integrated, holistic quality management system for the attraction as a whole. Furthermore, it focused on the achievement of one-off targets, whereas in reality quality management is more about constant improvement over time, where the one-off targets are just rungs on the quality ladder. It is interesting to look at how the general quality management approaches we discussed earlier can be applied to attractions.

Quality control and attractions

Following such an approach would mean attractions having special quality control inspectors whose responsibility it would be to monitor product and service quality, identify problems and tackle them. Such roles are currently virtually unknown at attractions, although in many cases this function does exist but is carried out by operations managers or duty officers, who also have other duties. At small attractions the owner or manager will usually number quality control among his or her many other responsibilities.

Quality assurance and attractions

Quality assurance means preventing problems occurring in the first place by ensuring that staff perform their duties properly at all times. It places the responsibility for action on the staff involved in the delivery of the product rather than on managers. This is particularly a problem for attractions where many workers are casual staff who may have received little training and might have little commitment to the job. Attraction managers therefore need to devise human resource management systems that encourage all staff to operate the principles of quality assurance.

Total quality control and attractions

This means taking a wider view of the service delivery process so that we look at all factors that might affect the product rather than just focusing on the way in which the service is actually delivered. This is a difficult task in the case of attractions where the business environment is complex and ever changing. It could include matters as diverse as staff training, customer expectations, suppliers and marketing intermediaries.

Total quality management and attractions

Total quality management is concerned with achieving constant, continuous improvement in terms of the product, service delivery and the operation of the attraction. It relates quality to the achievement of the organization's objectives, and is based on the idea that quality must permeate the whole attraction and be the responsibility of every member of staff. For attractions to operate TQM there would be a number of prerequisites that might not be easy to achieve, including:

- being able to set their own objectives and develop their own performance standards – this is very difficult for many public sector attractions where objectives and performance standards may be set by politicians, or at attractions owned by major corporations where objectives and targets may be set by the parent company
- convincing all staff to take an interest in quality when, some of them at least, may be poorly paid, work long hours and have few promotion or career prospects
- being able to plan long term to see how quality will improve in the future and having the power to control their own resources to allow them to achieve their quality objectives. For many public sector attractions, in particular, these twin prerequisites are not realistic because of their volatile business environment and their lack of control over their own resources.

Whichever approach is adopted, implementation will mean a mixture of 'hard' elements, such as procedures and manuals, and 'soft' elements, such as the attitudes of managers and staff.

Quality and different audiences

Attractions have a range of audiences, both internal and external, which will all have their own idea of what constitutes quality at an attraction. Some of the many audiences for attractions are outlined below, together with their likely views on what constitutes quality at an attraction:

- attraction managers, for whom quality is likely to be about the smooth operation of the attraction and the minimum number of customer complaints
- attraction staff, who tend to see quality in terms of their terms and conditions of employment, and how few complaints from customers they have to handle
- customers, who tend to view quality at attractions in relation to how easy the site is to use, how safe and secure they feel on site and to what extent they feel that the attraction offers them value for money
- competitors, who would define quality at another attraction as the aspect of it which gives it competitive advantage, and which might be worthy of imitating

- suppliers, who will define attraction quality in terms of those attractions which are easy to work with and who pay their bills on time
- marketing intermediaries such as tourist information centres and coach operators, who will see quality in terms of popularity; they will see attractions as being of a high quality if a lot of their users or customers want to visit the attraction
- regulators such as trading standards and environmental health departments, who view attractions as being quality attractions if they appear to comply with regulations and operate with safety and hygiene as major priorities
- parent companies, for whom quality means meeting financial targets set by the parent company and increasing their market share
- elected councillors, who see quality at local authority owned attractions as being about keeping within budget, being popular with local people and being a valuable education resource for local schools
- investors, for whom quality equates simply with achieving a good rate of return on investment, year after year
- destination marketing agencies, who judge the quality of attractions in terms of the extent to which they help the destination attract more visitors
- the media, who believe that quality means attractions that are novel and offer interesting news stories, are safe and are perceived to represent good value for money
- professional bodies, who see attraction quality in terms of those which are innovative or gain a reputation for good practice in one or more management functions
- academic institutions such as schools and colleges, who define quality in terms of attractions that offer a good education service or are helpful with student enquiries, and placement requests.

It is also important for attraction managers to decide whether or not they are going to try to gain official external recognition of their quality through schemes such as BS 5750/ISO 9002.

The quality–price rapport

Up to now we have looked at quality as if it were an absolute, whereas in reality, it tends to be relative to issues such as price or cost. In other words, quality tends to exist at different levels in the market in relation to the price paid by the customer or the costs incurred by the attraction in providing the product.

For example, in the case of an inexpensive, mass-produced car, quality might mean that it always starts, is reliable and safe, is comfortable and does an impressive number of miles on a gallon/litre of fuel. At the other extreme, for an expensive, exclusive car, quality can mean things like being hand-made or hand-finished, having luxury upholstery, being capable of driving at high speed and having lots of features included in the price that might be extras on other cars.

Quality is therefore a matter of how one attraction performs in relation to others in the market at a similar price. Being seen as of good quality therefore is probably really about being better than average in relation to competitors.

This concept of a quality–price rapport is particularly interesting in the context of attractions offering free entrance or use. The logic would seem to be that free attractions should offer more basic, simple, lower-level quality features than attractions that charge a high price. However, this is clearly not the case, as many free attractions are owned by the public sector and are so heavily subsidized that they can offer the level of quality features one might expect from an expensive car, whereas in reality the car is being given away free! In this case there is no clear relationship between quality and price at all.

Nevertheless, in many cases a price is charged for using the attraction and managers must decide what level and type of quality they can offer in relation to the price customers pay and the cost of offering the attraction product. Getting the balance right is the key to being perceived by customers as being a value-for-money attraction.

The concept of quality over time

Just as quality is not an absolute, likewise, it is not fixed over time. The concept of what constitutes quality changes over time in response to influences such as:

- the expectations of consumers
- advances in management practice
- changes in legislation and regulations
- the actions of new attractions which are seen as innovators.

In the attractions field, the quality debate is still in its early stages but there is a general feeling that standards are rising, largely due to the demands of customers who are increasingly sophisticated and requiring higher standards. Therefore, an attraction that yesterday would have been viewed as of high quality, would today appear to be of medium quality and will be seen tomorrow as of poor quality if it does not take action to develop its quality.

In the future, there will also be further changes in management theories on the subject of quality and in terms of government regulations.

Constraints on quality management at attractions

Attraction managers face a number of constraints when they try to develop quality management systems, including:

- a lack of finance to fund necessary developments of the product or management systems
- a lack of interest or outright opposition on the part of some staff or the employees as a whole

- a corporate culture that is not conducive to quality management
- different views on what quality means between managers, staff and other stakeholders such as parent companies or councillors, investors and regulators
- differences between the level of quality managers would like to offer and the level which customers are willing to pay for.

Many attraction managers may also have little knowledge or experience of quality management, which may make them cautious or may limit the effectiveness of what they try to do.

Finally, it is important to recognize that many of the factors that contribute to a quality experience for visitors at attractions are outside the control of managers. Examples of these include the weather and the mixture of people using the attraction at any one time. These different people may have very different attitudes and standards of behaviour, and their coming together in the same place at the same time may cause problems and conflicts. It is usually not possible, even if it were desirable, for managers to control access to the site in such a way that could prevent such problems.

Government actions and attraction quality: the case of the UK

Governments are increasingly recognizing the importance of attractions and the role they play in the tourism industry. Some governments, therefore, are taking action to improve their quality, through national and regional tourist boards. This government involvement in the UK dates back a little over a decade.

In 1989 the Association of Scottish Visitor Attractions, under the Scottish Tourist Board, developed a quality assurance scheme. Two years later, the English Tourist Board, as it then was, introduced a National Code of Practice for Visitor Attractions. This evolved into the Visitors' Charter which was reproduced earlier in this chapter. This charter is now in the process of being reviewed.

In 1998, the Southern Tourist Board spearheaded development of the bench-marking initiative in Hampshire which was also discussed earlier in this chapter.

The UK government in the late 1990s realized the importance of attractions for the tourism industry in the country. It set up the 'Action for Attractions' initiative, where the English Tourism Council, the government's tourism development agency for England, worked with leading attraction professionals to develop recommendations to help attractions in England specifically, become more successful in the future.

While specifically relating to England, the recommendations could perhaps be seen to be relevant to the UK as a whole because in its tourism strategy for the entire UK, 'Tomorrow's Tourism', the government identified a need to improve the quality and range of visitor attractions in the UK 'as part of its drive to maintain the UKs competitiveness in the world market'.

This initiative resulted in a large number of recommendations, some of which directly related to the quality of attractions, including the following:

1 Industry training organizations should develop advanced customer care training to build on the success of Welcome Family and make it available across the sector.
2 The Department for Education and Employment (DfEE) should be encouraged to help attractions develop their educational potential.
3 Regional tourist boards and sectoral associations should work together to develop guidance and signpost information technology initiatives across all the sectors.
4 There is a need to co-ordinate training and continuous professional development across the whole sector, possibly by bringing the training needs and professional development of all attractions under one national training organization.
5 One regional tourist board should lead a pilot project on management and continuous professional development to include a mentoring initiative and a leadership development programme.
6 All quality assurance schemes should review training and management development and take-up of schemes such as Investors in People (IIP).
7 Full training is needed for the trainers/advisers/assessors.
8 The Southern Tourist Board (STB) should evaluate the Hampshire/Dorset bench-marking scheme for small/medium attractions and review other relevant experience. The STB should liaise with the English Tourism Council, the proposed attractions advisory group and the regional tourist boards, to develop a voluntary national scheme that is relevant to all attractions and affordable, in order to maximize participation.
9 The English Tourism Council will support the development of the Visitor Attractions Quality Assurance Service (VAQAS) being piloted by the East of England Tourist Board, and liaise with the proposed attractions advisory group members to ensure that sectoral organizations are aware of the initiative and that their views and suggestions are taken on board.
10 The English Tourism Council will continue to seek industry-wide support for VAQAS before its national introduction.
11 The English Tourism Council will publish the revised Visitors' Charter on completion of the review.
12 The English Tourism Council will advocate incentives for investment, so that any changes to the tax system encourage reinvestment.
13 The English Tourism Council will encourage government to revise Planning Policy Guidance Note 21 to include updating section 5.4 on large-scale attractions and emphasis on the following:
    (a) improved pre-planning and feasibility for attractions, including more rigorous analyses of visitor forecasts and economic viability
    (b) greater appreciation that attractions should be distinctive and related to their location

(c) the rejuvenation of existing attractions rather than the development of new ones.

14 Backed by policy support from the English Tourism Council, the regional tourism boards should work with local authorities to examine the impact of tourism proposals within and across their boundaries, and encourage better regional co-ordination of attraction development across these sub-regions (English Tourism Council, 2000).

Conclusion

Quality management in general, and its application to attractions in particular, is still a subject in the early stages of development. However, it is currently a highly fashionable subject and the conventional wisdom appears to be that the key to future success for attractions will be about attaining or maintaining a reputation for quality.

In this chapter we have focused a lot on the situation in the UK, although most of the principles discussed are applicable globally. However, it is important to recognize that in a competitive international market like tourism, quality is a global issue. Indeed, in the case of attractions, many of the ideas on quality which are now accepted in the UK originated from other parts of the world, notably the USA.

Finally, it is likely that the concept of quality in relation to attractions will not be determined by the attractions sector or its managers, or even by government. Instead, it is likely to be consumer driven and will evolve in response to changes in consumer attitudes.

Discussion points and essay questions

1 Discuss the factors which you believe determine visitor satisfaction or dissatisfaction at attractions.
2 Critically evaluate the potential application of quality assurance, total quality control, and total quality management at visitor attractions.
3 Discuss the relationship between quality and price in relation to visitor attractions.

Exercise

Read the Young and Ambrose (1999) paper and look at other literature concerning bench-marking. Then develop your own simple pilot bench-marking manual for attraction operators in your area. If these operators will co-operate with you, try to test your manual and improve it as a result of the testing process. Then write a short evaluation report, highlighting what this exercise has taught you about the development and implementation of bench-marking schemes.

Managing change and planning for the future

Introduction

Managing change is a constant theme in the working life of attraction managers because of the volatile business environment in which they live. This and the unpredictability of much of this change means that its management is often almost totally reactive and ad hoc. The world in which an attraction exists changes and the attraction adapts to the change as quickly and as best it can, within the constraints it operates. Such change may be termed 'external enforced change', and its management is generally of a short-term tactical nature.

Conversely, some managers feel the need to take a longer-term view and choose to try to proactively plan for the future development of their attraction. This may include changes in the mission, direction or culture of the attraction and/or its physical form. Such future planning may be termed 'internal voluntary change' and tends to operate at the strategic level.

External enforced change

There are a number of types of change that may take place in the business environment of an attraction that may make its management feel they have to make changes. These are the motivators of changes, and a number of the main ones are outlined below. While they are listed separately, it is important to recognize that in reality change is not so compartmentalized. Many changes are interrelated while attractions may have to cope with more than one type of change at the same time.

Furthermore, one must acknowledge that what matters most in terms of this type of change is not what actually happens in the business environment but rather the manager's perception of what is happening and what may happen in the near future. The reality and the perception may of course be different, in which case the change that is initiated by the manager may be counterproductive.

The motivation for change

The main types of changing circumstances that can cause managers to feel they must make changes to their attractions include:

1 Changes in consumer behaviour, such as the growing interest in green issues, animal welfare and healthy eating, and the desire to learn something new on a visit to an attraction.
2 New legislation and regulations which affect the attraction's operations.
3 A deterioration in the state of the economy which may result in less attraction visits being made and visitors looking for more attractions which are perceived to offer value for money.
4 Demographic change which threatens to reduce the size of the market which the attraction currently targets.
5 Reductions in visitor numbers and/or income.
6 Complaints about the attraction from existing customers.
7 Poor performance by marketing intermediaries or suppliers.
8 The actions of competitors.
9 The opinions of key stakeholders, such as major investors in the case of private attractions, or councillors in relation to local authority museums.

The implications of change

When considering the implications of the change factors outlined above, four things have to be taken into account:

1 The likely scale of the changes in the business environment.
2 The aspects of the attraction that will be most affected by the factors.
3 What aspects of the attraction need to be changed in response to these factors, and how.
4 The cost of these changes and the timescale for their implementation.

This section looks at all four aspects, both in general and in relation to specific examples of particular types of attraction.

Perhaps the best way to illustrate the general points is through a hypothetical example. Table 20.1 uses the example of a medium-sized traditional zoo and looks at some hypothetical factors and their implications in terms of the four elements outlined above.

Table 20.1 The implications of change: the hypothetical example of a zoo

The hypothetical factor	The scale of change	The aspects of the attraction that will be most affected by the factor	The aspects of the attraction that need to be changed to respond to the factor	The costs and timescales of achieving the desired changes
Rising consumer interest in animal welfare and the dislike of seeing animals in a cage	Very large	Many of the on-site attractions which currently consist of animals in cages, although some are already in larger open areas	Remodelling to create attractive open areas for the animals	High cost but needed quickly to maintain visiyor numbers and place in the market
Small minor changes in hygiene laws	Small	All food outlets, including the restaurant, snack bars and ice cream kiosk	Some minor changes to food storage arrangements and a small amount of staff training	Low cost but needs to be done immediately to comply with the new law
Economic recession in the domestic market	Moderate	Visitor numbers and on-site spending levels	Pricing policies and the type of goods on sale in retail and catering outlets	No real cost but immediate action needed or will lose revenue and visitor numbers
Inability of some souvenir suppliers to deliver on time	Small	Retail sales and complaints from customers about lack of availability	Purchasing policies, in other words, look for new suppliers	No cost – could lead to increased income. Action needed as quickly as possible
Customer complaints about car park security	Small	Customer satisfaction and, ultimately, possibly, visitor numbers if the problem is not resolved	Car park security needs to be enhanced through video cameras and extra lighting	Moderate cost and will take several weeks or a month or two to implement
Investors' demand for higher rates of return on investment	Large	All aspects in terms of generating extra income and reducing costs	In the short term, minor changes to the product to attract more visitors, In the longer term, perhaps a complete change of theme/core attraction in light of changes in consumer attitudes outlined above	Low or no cost in the short term but high cost in the longer term

So far we have concentrated on external enforced change, but there is also internal enforced change. For example, attractions may have to respond to changes in their internal environment which they are unable to prevent. These might include a fire at a theme park that destroys many of the rides. In this situation, the attraction will have to either close in the short term or reduce prices. In the longer term, the incident may be used as an opportunity to redevelop the site, including a change in the core product.

Internal voluntary change

There are many reasons why managers may wish to initiate internal voluntary change, including:

- a desire to achieve competitive advantage
- a wish to change the corporate culture
- to respond to changes in the level of resources available
- to diversify the attraction operation
- to appeal to new market segments
- to impress superiors in the management hierarchy
- to obtain kudos in the industry and/or improve her/his reputation with peers.

Even this brief list shows there are probably conscious and subconscious reasons why managers seek to implement change voluntarily.

One motivating factor which is particularly influential, but may not be well recognized, is the desire to be seen to be up to date with changes in management thinking. They may instigate customer care programmes to show that they operate a customer-centred, market-led approach to their business.

In the case of internal voluntary change, the sequence of change is possibly as follows:

- identification of desired outcomes
- consideration of change required to achieve outcomes
- development of plan for activating change
- implementation of change.

What changes at attractions?

The scope for change at attractions is vast and can cover the following elements:

- the nature of the product that is offered, including the tangible aspects and the service delivery
- the price charged for the product and what discounts or concessions are made available
- the way the product is promoted to potential customers
- the methods of distribution which are used in the marketing of the attraction

- human resource policies
- financial management systems
- management information systems
- operational details, such as periods of queuing and opening hours
- the attraction site or the dates, if it is a special event
- the organization's structure
- the organization's mission
- the culture of the organization.

Obstacles to achieving change

Whatever type of change managers attempt to implement, there will be obstacles either in terms of individual resistance on the part of members of staff, organization-wide obstacles or external constraints.

In terms of individuals, resistance to change may result from a number of possible reasons. It could be because proposals to improve labour productivity might reduce take-home pay or increase the amount of work for individual staff. Some staff may resist change because they feel the management is trying to change the culture of the organization in a way that they think is wrong from a moral or ethical standpoint. On the other hand, their opposition to change may simply be because of fear of change or a fear of the unknown. Finally, opposition can sometimes occur because staff have simlpy misunderstood what is being proposed.

Organization-wide opposition can result from a number of causes, including:

- a lack of the necessary resources, such as the availability of money at the right time and having staff with the appropriate skills and experience
- established organization or structures and decision-making systems that may make change difficult to achieve
- physical assets such as buildings and museum exhibits that are difficult to change or adapt
- internal policies and procedures
- the existing corporate culture.

External constraints to change can come in a number of forms:

- legislation and government regulations
- ideas of what is socially acceptable
- the actions of competitors
- existing contracts and/or relationships with suppliers and marketing intermediaries
- the opinions of industry and other stakeholders.

While obstacles to change exist in all organizations, they are perhaps greatest at particular types of attractions. For example, public sector attractions often have characteristics that make change difficult to achieve, such as:

- statutory control on what they are allowed to do
- external control on their finances
- slow decision-making processes involving committees that may meet only infrequently
- bureaucratic cultures
- human resource policies and recruitment systems which may be inappropriate but are difficult, if not impossible, to change.

In the case of large attractions owned by major corporations the freedom of action of individual attraction managers to implement change in the way they would like may be severely limited because of the policies of the parent company. At the other extreme, many small private or voluntary sector attractions find it difficult to implement change because they either lack the necessary resources and/or because they lack the management skills and experience that is required to put their ideas into practice.

It has to be said that change often does not occur simply because managers do not perceive the need for change, do not feel capable of achieving it or may simply not want to disrupt the status quo. Finally, however, it has to be admitted that change can often be unsuccessful, even where it does occur. Change in itself is not always a good thing; it has to be the right change.

Prerequisites for successful change management

In order to succeed with change management there are a number of prerequisites, including:

- clear objectives
- commitment
- accurate scanning of the business environment
- skilful management of staff
- adequate resources
- sensitive management of the change.

Figure 20.1, based on the ideas of Lewin and further developed by the Open University, is a useful model of change that can be applied to attractions in the form of a checklist.

In spite of all the problems there have been many examples of successful large-scale change at attractions, as well as a myriad of small-scale changes which happen every day. For example, Chessington Zoo in the UK was successfully remodelled as the highly successful theme park, Chessington World of Adventures. This strategy was designed to exploit the growing theme park market and perhaps also to diversify the business away from a total reliance on animals at a time when public concern over animal welfare was growing. Other examples of successful change include:

- the way many museums and galleries, which are national institutions, such as the Science Museum in London, and the Natural History

1 *Preparation*
- Be constantly alert to the possible need for change
- Identify the basic opportunity and level of change
- Be clear about desired outcomes, achieving *specific* improvements – establish a view of the desired state
- Analyse the driving and restraining forces and the potential resistance
- Decide who else needs to be involved in planning the change
- Select a change strategy and approach for anticipating resistance
- Anticipate problems likely to be generated by the change
- Select methods for dealing with resistance
- Draw up a realistic timetable and 'measures' for monitoring and evaluating the progress of the change
- Establish resources and support mechanisms required, including training, technology, facilities, consultants

2 *Unfreezing*
- Allow time for loosening up the organization – unless this is impossible
- Select training and communications approaches consistent with change strategy
- Monitor progress and modify approach if necessary

3 *Changing*
- Change as little as necessary to accomplish the desired improvement
- Keep a 'fire fighting' reserve of time and resources to deal with the unpredictable
- Be prepared to modify the change and/or strategy where it seems to be sensible
- Communicate successes

4 *Refreezing*
- Allocate adequate resources for supporting and maintaining the change
- Consider follow-up training and development
- Implement contingency plans, based on experience, as necessary

5 *Evaluation*
- Undertake follow-up reviews
- Obtain feedback from those affected, let them know you are 'listening'
- Communicate outcomes to those concerned
- Reflect on the process of change and discuss with 'change agents' key lessons for next time.

Figure 20.1
A checklist for change
Source: after Lewin and as further developed by the Open University

Museum in Paris, have introduced 'hands-on' exhibits and developed their retailing activities
- the introduction of special events such as performances of Shakespeare's plays in the grounds of National Trust properties
- the opening of Tate galleries away from London, in Liverpool and St Ives.

Planning for the future

Attraction managers are always having to look ahead and plan for the future. In a sector of tourism where the business environment is constantly changing, competition is fierce and the lead-in time for new developments is long, future planning is essential but difficult. Attractions must be constantly evolving if they are to continue to satisfy customers, stay ahead of competitors and achieve their objectives.

Planning for the future means deciding what needs to happen, when it needs to happen, how it will be implemented and who will be responsible for implementation. For most attractions, future planning is about dealing with a mixture of predictable certainties, foreseeable probabilities and possible events and unforeseen eventualities. This means creating future plans that are structured enough to survive the certainties but flexible enough to deal with the probabilities and possible events together with unforeseen problems and opportunities.

The certainties are perhaps best exemplified by the issue of refurbishment. Every attraction, no matter how well built, will need refurbishment at some time. The period before refurbishment is required will depend on a range of factors, including:

- how well-built the attraction was in the first place
- how quickly or slowly the attraction's fabric deteriorates in normal conditions
- the level of maintenance
- visitor numbers and the nature of the visitors.

Refurbishment may, of course, be put off even when it is needed, usually for financial reasons, but this has a cost in that a degraded attraction may attract fewer visitors.

Therefore, in this case the key to successful attraction management is to predict when major refurbishment will be needed and to ensure that adequate provision has been made in the budget and that time has been made available for the work to be carried out.

In a wider sense this is related to the fact that in many ways future planning is about managing the attraction's product life cycle. Although we know from the discussion in Chapter 3 that the product life cycle concept is flawed as a predictive tool, it is nevertheless a valuable way of making managers focus on the fact that attractions change over time and that there are dangers for those that do not think ahead. This is important as one of the probable or possible events we mentioned above is the probability or possibility that in the next few years the attraction may enter the 'decline' stage, which in itself may trigger the need for a relaunch. While predicting when this stage is likely to be reached is difficult, there are classic signs such as reaching a plateau in terms of visitor numbers, relying on repeat visits with relatively few new visitors and so on. An attraction's future planning should therefore include ideas either on how to prevent the onset of the decline stage or what form a relaunch will take. This could be a change of core theme or product, attracting new market segments or simply trying to change the attraction's image, or all three! This all sounds very neat, but in reality it is far more complex given the fact that all attractions have unique life cycles.

Attractions might also wish to develop ideas on how they might respond to other probable or possible events, such as the likely future activity of competitors and foreseeable changes in the law or government policy.

Finally, and perhaps most difficult of all, is the task of planning for sudden, unforeseen circumstances, which may appear to be a contradiction in terms. However, it is important that attractions have some idea of what they might do in the event of things occurring without warning. Such eventualities might include a strike or a fire. In this case, attractions need to develop contingency plans – this topic is discussed in more detail in Chapter 15.

Future planning must also be proactive and attractions need to develop a clear view of where they want to be in the future in terms of the product offered, the markets served and where the product is perceived to be in the marketplace, when viewed from the customer's point of view. Such future planning might also include how the organization itself might develop in the future and whether or not it will set up new attractions or take over existing ones.

Having decided all this, future plans are only ever totally relevant on the day they are written. From that day onwards the plan is becoming outdated and the circumstances and forecasts on which it is based change. Plans, therefore, need to be constantly reviewed and updated. It may also be advisable to subject the plan to sensitivity analysis, in other words, to see how it would be influenced by events such as an economic recession or a particular change in consumer behaviour.

The obstacles to future planning

In many attraction operations there appears to be a belief that, because of its nature, it is impossible to plan far ahead in the attractions field. This is clearly an exaggeration, but there are real problems with future planning in relation to attractions. These can be briefly summarized as follows:

- The lack of good up-to-date market research data that does not help with identifying trends in consumer behaviour.
- Many attractions lack a clear view of their present market let alone their future market.
- The market can be subject to sudden catastrophic changes due to external factors such as war or civil disorder, for example the impact that the terrorist attacks on the USA in September 2001 had on the global tourism market.
- Technological developments can have a dramatic impact on the attraction product which is difficult to forecast in advance. For example, we still do not know what the full impact of virtual reality technologies will be and when it will be felt.
- Plans may be based on the attitudes, skills and experience of staff who may then leave.
- It is hard to predict cash flow in advance, yet future planning requires a reasonable knowledge of what financial resources are likely to be available in the future, for investment in product development, for example.

- Managers may feel they are so busy coping with the everyday management of the attraction that they have no time for future planning.

Conclusion

In this chapter we have looked at two related aspects of attraction management, namely, the management of change in the current period and near future, and the task of planning for the more distant future. We have seen that both tasks are difficult, with many obstacles to overcome, and that both types of management involve proactive and reactive action from managers.

Discussion points and essay questions

1 Discuss the actions which a manager may take when faced with the changes identified in Table 20.1.
2 Discuss the reasons why managers may voluntarily seek to make changes within their attraction.
3 Critically evaluate the application of the ideas of Lewin contained in Figure 20.1 to the attractions sector.

Exercise

Select an attraction with which you are familiar and identify both external enforced changes and internal voluntary changes you believe it is likely to experience over the next ten years.

Part Four

Case Studies

Introduction

The purpose of these case studies is to provide real-world illustrations of some key issues in the attractions sector, including attraction markets in different countries, and aspects of the development and management of individual attractions.

A conscious attempt has been made to offer the reader a range of case studies that are truly international, rather than just representing one country.

It should be noted that these case studies were written between February and July 2001. They are thus a snapshot at one point in time, and should be read with this in mind.

Case 1

Lessons from the Millennium Dome, London

The Millennium Dome in London lasted just 365 days yet it caused more controversy, perhaps, than any other attraction in history.

This huge temporary attraction was designed to:

- stimulate tourism to London
- help regenerate the depressed Greenwich borough
- provide a showcase for UK designs and companies
- reinforce London's image as a dynamic international city.

From the beginning the project was chiefly associated with government, first the Conservative administration and then New Labour.

Hundreds of millions of pounds of National Lottery money were contributed to the project which cost around £700 million when it finally opened. Its financial problems continued throughout its year of operation, 2000, and after it closed it proved very difficult to find new uses for the site.

On the other hand, this new attraction received 6.5 million visitors in 2000, far more than any other UK paid entry attraction and it was second only to Disneyland Paris, in Europe, as a leisure tourism attraction in terms of visitor numbers. Furthermore it achieved a good 88 per cent visitor satisfaction rating (MORI, 2001).

Nevertheless it was largely perceived to be a failure, so what lessons can future attraction developers learn from this experience? The author thinks these include:

- Recognizing the power of the media to make or break an attraction. People were put off visiting the Dome by the adverse media coverage that made it 'un-cool' to visit the attraction.
- Governments should perhaps steer clear of high profile involvement in attraction projects because this can lead to them being 'political footballs'.
- Ensuring that the marketing before the opening creates a desire to visit and a clear brand awareness among potential visitors.
- Location is clearly important and this can lead to a conflict between the desire to stimulate tourism in deprived areas and the fact that tourists generally like to visit places which have a strong positive image and/or are established tourist 'destinations'.
- People visit attractions more for entertainment than for education; they want to be stimulated and excited, but not lectured.
- Planning needs to take account of the need to avoid 'bottlenecks' which lead to excessive queuing as this reduces customer satisfaction levels.
- Trying to encourage visitors to use public transport for the sake of the environment is a good idea but if things are made too difficult for car drivers, in a country where up to 80 per cent of leisure trips are made by car, visitor numbers will suffer.
- An attraction which is a national project should make every effort to attract people from all parts of the country, as the Dome was perceived to have made little real attempt to attract people from Northern England, Scotland and Wales.
- The use of money gathered from a lottery or taxation for supporting leisure projects is a very sensitive issue as many people think it would be better spent on housing, health and education.
- Gaining sponsorship and private sector investment is a specialized and difficult task which should not be underestimated.
- Successful attractions need a 'Wow' feature and/or a 'unique selling proposition' and this needs to be heavily promoted.

Finally, the Millennium Dome experience teaches us the lesson that business plans need to be realistic. The Dome was perceived as a failure because 12 million visitors were predicted but only 6.5 million actually arrived. This is a huge achievement for a new temporary attraction but it is not seen as such when 12 million were predicted. Business plans are often overoptimistic because of the need to raise funding, but this overoptimism creates unrealistic expectations that result in negative press coverage and even lower visitor numbers. This vicious circle has to be broken or many other attractions will be perceived as 'failures' when they may be successful.

Case 2

The Millennium Commission and attraction projects in the UK

The Millennium Commission was set up in 1998 to support projects designed to celebrate the Millennium. Since then it has spent just under £1400 million on grants to some 190 major projects and 350 smaller ones across the country, many of which are visitor attractions of the kind covered by this book.

An outline of the distribution of these grants is given in Exhibit 2.1.

Several projects supported by the Commission have also had problems such as the Earth Centre in South Yorkshire. However, there have also been definite success stories such as The Lowry Centre and the Eden Project.

The work of the Commission has been rather overshadowed by its investment in the Millennium Dome project in London, which received such bad publicity.

Questions have been asked about whether money from the National Lottery should be invested in attraction projects rather than in other 'good causes'.

A major concern is that project funding has been largely concerned with capital cost rather than revenue and it is feared that many projects may prove non-viable in the longer term. This argument is exacerbated by the fact that the Millennium Commission is due to be wound up in 2005.

The projects supported by the Commission have clearly helped stimulate the tourism industry in many areas, for example:

- in Cornwall, where the Eden Project which combines space age design with the concept of sustainability, has predicted that it will need 750 000 visitors in its first year
- in the city of Salford, the Lowry Centre has helped rejuvenate a waterfront area and hopes to attract 770 000 visitors per annum
- the International Centre for Life in Newcastle-upon-Tyne which expected to receive 225 000 visitors each year
- At-Bristol a hands-on science attraction which had welcomed 533 000 visitors by February 2001, and had received the 'Family Attraction of the Year' award in the *Good Britain Guide 2001*.
- Our Dynamic Earth, in Edinburgh, which attracted 512 000 visitors in its first year, including around 60 000 foreign tourists

However, the work of the Commission has also been criticized for supporting projects that did not have enough popular appeal, for stimulating an oversupply of attractions and for creating unfair competition for private and voluntary sector attractions. It will be several years, however, before we can produce an accurate and fair evaluation of the results of Millennium Commission funding.

Region	Total funds awarded (£)	Millennium projects		Average award (£)	Biggest award (£)	Project receiving biggest award
		Projects	Sites			
Scotland	192 949 129	19	486	10 155 217	35 000 000	Glasgow Science Centre
Northern Ireland	78 383 681	17	124	4 610 805	45 000 000	Odyssey
Wales	129 148 952	9	56	14 349 884	46 000 000	Millennium Stadium
North East	65 213 228	9	91	7 245 914	31 450 000	International Centre for Life
North West	93 368 623	19	102	4 914 138	15 650 000	The Lowry Centre
Yorkshire and Humberside	156 638 324	17	396	9 214 019	40 000 000	The Earth Centre
East Midlands	46 619 641	11	22	4 238 149	26 000 000	National Space Science Centre
West Midlands	84 402 638	11	1010	7 672 967	50 000 000	Millennium Point
East of England	59 786 105	18	18	3 321 450	30 069 000	Norfolk and Norwich Millennium Project
South West	108 509 097	8	59	13 563 637	44 300 000	At-Bristol
South East	95 402 229	25	42	3 321 450	38 000 000	Portsmouth Harbour
Greater London	147 930 099	15	50	9 862 007	50 000 000	Tate Modern
Cross-regional	17 753 000	2	2	8 876 500	14 851 000	Huddersfield Narrow Canal
England-wide	20 100 000	2	412	10 050 000	10 100 000	Millennium Greens
England and Scotland	2 500 000	1	100	2 500 000	2 500 000	Rural Churches in Community Service
England and Wales	28 737 000	2	221	14 368 500	22 100 000	Changing Places
Great Britain and UK wide	56 753 053	5	552	11 350 611	43 500 000	Sustrans
Total	1 387 194 799	190	3743	7 301 025		

Sources: Millennium Commission Annual Report and Accounts, 1999–2000; Locum Destination Review (Spring 2001)

Exhibit 2.1 Funding of Millennium Projects by region

Case 3

Relationship marketing: the RAF Museum, Hendon, UK

The RAF Museum at Hendon is the UK's largest museum, covering the history of military aviation in the UK. Apart from its site at Hendon the museum also has two other sites at Cosford in Shropshire and Stafford in Staffordshire. The museum as a whole possesses and displays over 200 aircraft and interprets the history of the Royal Air Force.

Interest in the subject is very strong among a particular market segment, with other segments having a significant but less intense interest. The RAF Museum recognizes the value of repeat customers and 'brand loyalty', and therefore undertakes a range of relationship marketing activities to maintain customer loyalty and maximize repeat visits, including:

1 A newsletter, 'Plane Talk' which was launched in 2000. It keeps readers up to date with developments at the museum. The winter 2000–1 issue for example told readers about:
   (a) new acquisitions at the museum
   (b) the next phase of the museum's development programme which will involve £10 million investment in new displays and buildings
   (c) profiles of aircraft in the museum collection
   (d) details of special events held in the museum
   (e) news of projects concerning the restoration of old aircraft.
2 A programme of annual events, with particular themes, that are designed to encourage people with special aviation interests to visit the museum sites. In 2000, these events included:
   (a) the Large Model Association model aircraft rally at the Cosford site
   (b) a Millennium Festival of Youth in September 2000
   (c) the 'Evacuee Experience' in October 2000, which re-created the experiences of children who were evacuated during the London 'Blitz'

The 2001 programme of events included 'open cockpit' weekends for those who enjoy sitting in real cockpits, a 'family weekend', a veterans day for ex-RAF personnel, and a day when children could dress up in RAF uniforms. The museum also hosts non-aviation events to encourage people to visit who might not otherwise come were it not for the event. The hope is that they will then become regular visitors to the museum. Some of these such events in 2001 included a balloon rally, a falconry display, and car rallies.

3 Cosford hosts a major annual air show which attracts many repeat visitors. Each June, this air show attracts between 40 000 and 50 000 visitors. The show has now been run continuously since 1978.
4 The museum has a volunteer support group, the Aerospace Museum Society, founded in 1977. These volunteers work on the site in a voluntary capacity in a number of roles from acting as guides to helping restore old aircraft. These volunteers clearly have a very close relationship with the museum.
5 The museum shop offers a mail-order service, including an on-line shopping facility. This keeps the museum in touch with many of its visitors and allows it to earn income from people even when they live thousands of miles away from the museum.
6 The museum also promotes itself as a venue for conferences, and corporate hospitality events. Many businesses are now regular users of the museum's facilities for the corporate market.

These examples show that the RAF Museum fully understands the importance of relationship marketing.

Case 4

Industrial tourism: 'The Potteries', UK

For several centuries, 'The Potteries' region in the UK has been famous for the production of ceramics. The city of Stoke-on-Trent tourism office have turned this into a tourism product, the only real major product the area has to offer tourists. The city now sees visitors coming from all over the world for what can be described as 'ceramics tourism'.

The city promotes a range of attractions which link the history of ceramics production in the area with today's ceramics industry.

A 2001 brochure entitled, 'Visit the Potteries for a China Experience', outlined the elements of the industrial tourism product as follows:

- thirty-three factory shops where visitors can buy ceramic products produced by factories today
- four museums on the theme of ceramics production, one of which gives visitors a chance to have a go at making pottery for themselves
- three specialist retailers who sell antique ceramics products
- three visitor centres that are showcases for locally-based world famous local brands, namely Royal Doulton, Spode, and Wedgwood

- nine factories which offer tours of the production area.

Pottery-themed holidays can also be arranged for groups. The ceramics tourism initiative of the city council has been part funded by the European Community Fund, European Regional Development Fund Objective 2 scheme.

The private sector has also invested in facilities to attract ceramics tourists. For example, Wedgwood has recently opened a larger visitor centre, 'The Wedgwood Story'. It is open seven days per week and incorporates a factory tour with an audio guide. Visitors can make their own ceramics products in the centre, and buy Wedgwood products in the centre shop There are also two catering outlets with a total capacity of 260 people. For the visitor the Wedgwood Centre is not free, a charge is made for admission.

Finally, it is interesting to note that Wedgwood also has a range of high street retail outlets, shared with Waterford Crystal, its sister company, which sell their products in major cities, a logical development of the concept of industrial tourism.

· · · · ·

Case 5

Parcs d'attractions in France

In the past, 'parcs d'attractions' in France have had a difficult time with some significant failures. However, today such parks – leisure parks, amusement parks, theme parks, aquariums and eco-musées – have become a well developed, more successful sector than previously. A guide to these in 1999 identified 265 parks and claimed that in 1999 the parks received some 70 million visitors (Guides Laravière, 1999).

The guide's top-ten such parks in France were as follows:

1 Disneyland Paris, with more than 12 million visitors, which has established itself following its

difficult early days after it opened in 1992. It has five on-site attractions, namely Main Street, Frontierland, Adventureland, Fantasyland, and Discoveryland, supported by hotels, shops, and restaurants. Corporate usage for conferences and its golf course are now significant sources of revenue. A second park is due to open at Disneyland Paris in the near future.

2 Parc Asterix, a 20-hectare park on the edge of Paris based on the comic character, Asterix, which now attracts around 2 million visitors although it is only open between April and October. It consists of reconstructed period 'sets' with live interpreters, together with themed

rides, and spectacles. A hotel has now been built on site and there are generally inexpensive restaurants and fast food outlets.

3 Bagatelle, on the coast in North East France, is an amusement park which was opened originally in 1955, and has a site which covers 30 hectares. It attracts around 500 000 visitors a year who are primarily families taking vacations on this coast. As well as rides it contains gardens and a zoo and it also offers shows and spectacles.

4 Ecomusée d'Alsace, an open-air museum in Eastern France, which receives around 400 000 visitors per annum. It features reconstructed traditional buildings and people in costumes bringing scenes from history to life. There are many special events organized on site and the museum also boasts an on-site hotel and restaurant.

5 Futurosope, in Western France, opened in 1987 as a theme park focused on 'images' and based on state-of-the-art media technologies. It now

Park	Day ticket price: adult	Day ticket price: child
Disneyland Paris	220	170
Parc Asterix	170	120
Bagatelle	98	78
L'Ecomusée d'Alsace	78	48
Futuroscope	195	140
Marineland	120	80
La Mer de Sable	87	77
Nigloland	78	68
OK Corral	83	68
Walibi Schtroumpf	120	100

Source: Guides Laravière (1999)

Exhibit 5.1
Entrance prices at ten French parcs d'attractions, 1999 (French Francs)

Region	Number of parcs d'attractions
Alsace – Lorraine	17
Aquitaine	13
Auvergne-Limousin	12
Bourgogne-Franche-Comté	13
Bretagne	24
Centre	16
Ile-de-France	12
Languedoc-Rousillon	19
Midi-Pyrénées	22
Nord	15
Normandie	20
Pays de la Loire	20
Picardie	7
Poitou-Charentes	8
Provence-Alpes – Cote d'Azur	15
Rhone Alpes	19

Source: Guides Laravière (1999)

Exhibit 5.2
The geographical distribution of 255 parcs d'attractions in France

attracts around 3 million visitors per annum and the number is still growing. It also offers a light show spectacular on summer evenings.

6 Marineland, at Antibes on the French Riviera, was opened in 1970, and now attracts around 1 200 00 visitors. It is a park with a water theme in terms of having an aquarium and dolphin shows, as well as a water slide and swimming pool. It also supports marine conservation work. The site also includes a children's farm, a butterfly jungle, and an adventure golf course.

7 La Mer de Sable, a park opened in 1963, just north of Paris. It is a combination of rides, themed areas (such as the Chinese Quarter), and entertainment. Today it attracts more than 400 000 visitors every year.

8 Nigloland, in the Champagne region, south east of Paris, opened in 1987. It is an open-air park with an emphasis on entertainment, and is targeted at younger children, with a wide range of rides. There is now a hotel on the site and numerous catering outlets. The park now attracts around 500 000 people per year.

9 OK Corral which traces its origins back to 1963 but which has been constantly refurbished and modified since. Located near Marseille, as its name suggests, its theme is that of the American Wild West, with a mixture of rides and reconstructions by costumed staff. It now has a site of 15 hectares and attracts around 500 000 visitors each year.

10 Walibi Schtroumpf, near Metz in Eastern France, a park based on the cartoon characters, the Schtroumpfs or Smurfs. It has had difficult times, being in a region which has seen great unemployment, but it now attracts visitors from Belgium, Luxembourg and Germany too. It is now owned by an American consortium, Premier Parks. It combines rides with scenarios and characters from the Schtroumpf cartoons.

The prices of these attractions are shown in Exhibit 5.1.

The guide also contains details of 254 other parcs d'attractions in France. Exhibit 5.2 shows the geographical distribution of these attractions.

The types of parcs d'attractions in the guide include:

Water parks	27
Aquariums	31
Theme parks	61
Wildlife parks	92
Miscellaneous parks	43

(Guides Laravière, 1999).

It is clear, therefore, that parcs d'attractions are now a popular and diverse phenomenon all over France.

· · · · · ·

Case 6

Visitor attractions in Paris

Paris is one of the world's leading tourist destinations with a wide range of visitor attractions. The *Rough Guide to Paris* lists no fewer than 257 different visitor attractions, based on the definitions used in this book.

The main types of attractions found in Paris, are as follows:

1 Museums of different types including:
   (a) art museums such as the Louvre and the Musée d'Orsay
   (b) museums associated with famous people such as Edith Piaf and Victor Hugo
   (c) history museums such as the Musée de L'Histoire de France
   (d) natural history museums like the Museum National d'Histoire Naturelle
   (e) museums about public services such as the Musée de la Poste
   (f) museums about ethnic communities, for example, the Musée Armenien
   (g) museums about neighbourhoods such as the Musée de Montmartre
   (h) technology-themed museums such as La Villette
   (i) decorative art museums such as the Musée des Arts Decentifs
   (j) museums on unusual, esoteric themes such as the Musée de la Erotisme.

2 Famous monuments such as the Tour Eiffel and L'Arc de Triomphe.

3 Theme parks, on the edge of the city, such as Disneyland Paris, Park Asterix, and Bagatelle.

4 Wildlife-based attractions, notably the Sea Life Centre near Disneyland Paris and the Parc Zoologique in the Bois de Vincennes.

5 The famous cabaret clubs with their risqué shows, including Lido, Folies Bergerès, Crazy Horse, and the Moulin Rouge.

6 Sporting attractions, notably, the Stade de France, with its museum and guided tours, and the Stade Roland Garros, together with the Longchamps racecourse.

7 Cemeteries where famous people are buried, namely Père Lachaise.

8 Cultural centres, for instance, the Fondation Cartier, at the Maison de la Culture des Japan.

9 Parks and gardens including the Luxembourg Gardens, the Jardin D'Acclimation and the Bois de Boulogne.

10 Concert venues, notably the Palais Omnisports de Bercy and the Opéra Bastille.

11 Major libraries such as the Biblioteque Nationale de France.

12 Famous department stores such as Galeries Lafayette and Magasins du Printemps.

13 Specialist shops, including the Fauchon food emporium.

14 Flea markets in different locations, notably Puce St-Ouen Porte de Cligancourt.

The city also hosts a wide variety of events and festivals that attract different markets at different times of the year. Here is a selection of events for every month of the year:

January: International Circus Festival
February: Salon d'Agriculture
March: International Antiques, Primitive and Contemporary Art Fair
April: Paris Marathon
May: French Open Tennis Championships
June: Jazz Festival
July: Tour de France, Finish
August: Classical Music Festival
September: International Dance Festival
October: Prix de L'Arc du Triomphe Horse Race
November: Ecological/Environmental Fair
December: New Year's Eve

Attraction prices in Paris are illustrated in Exhibit 6.1, a city which is renowned for being quite an expensive destination.

In addition, Paris also attracts tourists because of its intangible attractions such as its romantic image, its lifestyle and its reputation for good food.

Exhibit 6.1
Entrance prices at a selection of Paris attractions, 1999 (French Francs)

Attraction	Adult ticket
Musée de Louvre	45
Panthéon	32
Tour Eiffel	59
Musée d'Orsay	40
Catacombs	27
Show and Dinner at the Lido	815 [1]
LaVillette (La Géode)	57 [1]
Centre Pompidou	30 [1]
Notre-Dame	32
L'Arc du Triomphe	35

Note: 1 2001 price.
Source: Baillie *et al.* (1999)

Case 7

Parc du Futuroscope, France

In Chapter 2 we looked at the role Futuroscope has played in the regional development of the Poitou-Charentes region in western France. Futuroscope was developed by local government, in partnership with private and public sector organizations, and opened in 1987. It is now visited by around 3 million people per year. It is a high-tech park based on the moving image and the media. Located in a 60-hectare site, on the edge of Poitiers, it has eighteen major attractions, notably:

- a high resolution cinema
- the Gyrotour, a revolving lift
- a 7000 square metre lake which is the 'stage' for an evening
- light and sound show
- a 360° cinema
- a multimedia magic show
- a 600 square metre IMAX screen cinema
- the Astrotour Simulator
- an 800 monitor screen video wall
- the 'Tapis Magique' that allows visitors to 'fly over' scenes with screens between their feet
- interactive computer games
- a children's game area
- the Cinéma Dynamique
- a 1200 square metre temporary exhibition space
- an Omni Max cinema
- a three-dimensional cinema
- a high-tech multimedia experience on the theme of cinema
- a 35-metre high screen Kinémax cinema
- a hemispheric 900 metre screen solido cinema.

The park now has its own station on the TGV fast train line from Paris to Bordeaux. It is also close to the A10 motorway and is only a few kilometres from Poitiers airport.

Futuroscope is open for eleven months of the year; in 2001 it only closed from 2 January to 2 February. However its spectacular show of the 'Lac des Images' generally only takes place daily between April and August and on some weekends throughout the rest of the year.

The pricing structure is quite complex as can be seen from Exhibit 7.1.

The park offers a range of services for its visitors, including:

- free parking
- cashpoint/ATM machines
- a bureau de change
- baby changing areas
- advice for disabled visitors
- left luggage facilities
- Walkman headsets with commentaries in different languages
- photograph developing outlets
- a pet centre to look after animals while their owners visit the park
- a tourist information office for the region as a whole.

The site offers a range of catering outlets, from fast-food kiosks to traditional restaurants, with prices starting at FFr18 for a sandwich. There is also a large gift shop with a range of themed merchandise.

The site is surrounded by eleven hotels of between one-star and four-star standard. In the peak season in 2000, a package of a two-day ticket and one night in a hotel for two adults and a child,

Type of ticket	Adult	Child
One-day ticket, peak season	210	145
Two-day tickets, peak season	350	200
Evening ticket, peak season	100	60
Evening ticket with snack, peak season	140	90
One-day ticket, off-peak season	145	100

Exhibit 7.1
Ticket prices at Futuroscope, 2000–1 (French Francs)

sharing a room would have cost between FFr1320 and FFr1930, depending on the quality of the hotel. Packages are also available including train travel within France. For example, a family of two adults and two children, in March 2001, travelling from Bordeaux would have paid FFr2522 for rail travel, one night's accommodation in a two-star hotel, and a two-day ticket, for all of them.

A major growing market for Futuroscope is the education market, particularly schools. For example, it has now been estimated that around 20 000 UK schoolchildren visit the park each year. A special supplement in the *Guardian* newspaper in spring 2001 noted that students visited the park to study a wide variety of subjects from geography to language, architecture to media studies, and

natural history to science. The park offers a range of specialist facilities for educational groups, including:

- study packs
- a teachers' area
- a resource centre
- interactive discovery classes
- a converted bus that now functions as a classroom
- a web site.

Futuroscope is now a well-established attraction but its main future challenge will be the need to constantly reinvest in new technology given that it is based on state of the art image technologies.

• • • • •

Case 8

The clubs of Ibiza

The rapidly changing nature of the attractions sector is clearly illustrated by the rise of dance club attractions in various Mediterranean destinations. Traditionally, clubs would have been seen as ancillary support services in destinations just like restaurants and bars. However, in places like Ibiza dance clubs are attractions in the true sense of the word; they are the main reason why many people visit the destination.

Exhibit 8.1 gives details of seven leading Ibiza clubs today. It is clear that the club scene in Ibiza is now big business. For example, if Privilege was full one evening, the takings for that evening alone

would amount to up to £40 000 in entrance charges alone!

The first club opened in 1973 at which time Ibiza was an upmarket 'millionaires playground', following its popularity as a hippy colony in the 1960s. From the late 1970s onwards, British music and dance entrepreneurs and fans began to develop the island as a party destination. Spanish entrepreneurs also became involved in the development of club attractions.

The clubs in Ibiza have a number of characteristics as attractions:

Club	Date opened	Capacity	Entrance charge (pesetas)
Amnesia	1987	5000	4000–6500
El Divino	1993	1500	5000
Eden	1980s	5000	4000–7000
Es Paradis	1975	3500	5000–6000
Pacha	1973	3000	4000–7000
Privilege	1978 (rebranded 1995)	10000	5000–9000
Space	1988	3000	2000–8000

Source: Ministry of Sound (2001)

Exhibit 8.1
The leading clubs of Ibiza, 2001

1 While their clientele is international, they are still very heavily influenced by British tastes.

2 Because the nightlife business is highly fashion-conscious the clubs have to be constantly remodelled and relaunched to keep up with changes in the market.

3 Market appeal requires a club to have unique selling proposition or two! This could be a particular disc jockey or type of music, or a physical feature such as the 120 000 kilogram glass roof at Es Paradis or equipment such as the 80 000-watt sound system at Eden.

4 As the season is only around six months long, owners have to achieve a satisfactory rate of return on their investment over a short, intense period.

5 Much of the labour of the club is international rather than local, which limits the economic benefit the club brings to the island.

6 There are different types of relationships between those who own and manage the club and those who provide the entertainment within them. Some of the latter are employees while others are employed by specialist companies who run special gigs or events, at different clubs, while others are simply self-employed freelancers.

7 Some UK-based clubs run events in venues in Ibiza such as Ministry of Sound.

The clubs have clearly put Ibiza on the world tourism map and have given it an advantage over its competitors. However:

• this market is fickle and fashion-conscious, and Ibiza could lose out if other destinations succeed in developing a better reputation as party places

• the behaviour of some clubbers has upset local opinion, particularly in relation to alcohol and drug abuse. The authorities are trying to control the worst excesses of party tourism on the island.

The island has an infrastructure geared heavily to the needs of the clubbing market, including:

• a wide range of bars to suit all tastes including 'chill-out bars'

• restaurants and fast-food joints, with British, Spanish, and international food at low prices (clubbers do not want to 'waste' too much of their holiday budget on food!)

• a range of accommodation including 'bed and breakfasts', apartments, villas and hotels

• 'chill-out' activities, from yoga and tai-chi classes to a health spa

• 'adrenaline' activities for the daring including bungee catapults, watersports, diving, rock climbing or visiting the island's only casino.

The club scene in Ibiza continues a tradition of hedonistic tourism that dates back several millennia. However, perhaps never in history, with the possible exception of the Romans, has so much investment been made in hedonistic attractions, for such a sophisticated market.

· · · · · ·

Case 9

The product life cycle and Legoland, Denmark

Legoland, Denmark is a themed attraction, built on a 10-hectare site, near Billund, an inland town in Denmark. The attraction has its own hotel and restaurants, and even its own airport.

Created in 1968, it could be seen as a brand extension attraction, promoting as it does the Lego brand of children's building bricks. The focus of the attraction is a miniature village made solely from Lego bricks, 45 million of them. Lego was started in 1934 and is still a family-owned business, while Legoland parks are also found in the UK and the USA.

Legoland opens daily between early April and late October, and entrance prices in 1999 were 130 Danish Kroner for adults and 120 for children. However, when the rides finish operating in the evening, visitors can look at the miniature village, free of charge.

The park has now received more than 30 million visitors since it first opened, with more than half of these visitors coming from outside Denmark. The international market is helped by the fact that Billund airport has direct flights from several European countries.

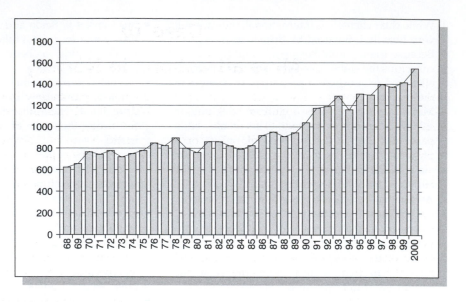

Exhibit 9.1
Legoland visitor
numbers, 1968–2000

Exhibit 9.1 models the evolution of visitor numbers at Legoland between 1968 and 2000. What does this tell us about the application of the product life cycle concept to attractions, a subject dealt with in Chapter 3 of this book?

It is clear that the life cycle curve is not as smooth and clear as product life cycle theory suggests. Some years the market rises, others it falls only to rise again the next year. There was no rapid 'growth' phase nor a clear maturity phase of stable demand. Visitor numbers have grown steadily since 1990 – with the exception of 1994 – after a fairly stagnant period from 1970 to 1990. Is this the result of a relaunch of the attraction or just a reflection of the growth of attraction visiting by Danish tourists, or an increase in international tourism to Denmark?

The fact is we do not know and this is not surprising given that so many factors can affect attraction visiting, many of which are outside the control of the attraction. These include:

- weather – open-air attractions like Legoland will suffer reduced visitor numbers if the summer is cool and rainy
- currency exchange rates – these affect foreign visitor numbers positively or negatively

- state of the Danish economy – this affects domestic demand for attraction-visiting in general
- competition – the opening of new competitive attractions will also affect visitor numbers.

At the same time, Legoland, Denmark will also be affected by:

- the popularity of the Lego brand worldwide
- the opening of Legoland in the UK which may become a 'substitute' for visitors to Legoland, Denmark, by British people.

Of course, Legoland, Denmark, can influence its own visitor numbers through:

- new product development
- innovative marketing, from better promotion to relationship marketing to tactical pricing.

However, as we have seen, attraction life cycles are often:

- uneven and disjointed in contrast with the theory of smooth curves
- affected by factors beyond the control of the attraction.

Case 10

Mine attractions in Norway

Norway has relatively low levels of inbound tourism, partly due to the high cost of living for foreigners. Tourism here tends to focus on particular areas such as Oslo, the fjords of western Norway and, to a lesser but growing extent, the Tromsø area.

However, other regions of the country have their attractions too, some of them based on the history of the country. One such type of attraction is the mine attractions, which we will discuss here.

Perhaps the largest such group of attractions are found around Kongsgruvene, a silver-mining district, in the Telemark region. Three different mines tours are available, including:

- a tour that includes a 2.3 kilometre walk through the tunnels of the mine, where visitors are shown the equipment used by pioneers. The mines are open only from late May to September and the tour cost 55 Norwegian Kroner in 1999
- the Christian VII mine tour offers a two-hour underground tour or an above ground tour of the mine installations and a chance to walk along the route to work taken by the miners
- in the King Frederick's mine you can abseil into the mine and then look around.

At Sakkerhusene visitors can explore the administrative buildings and workers' houses.

The Røros area of Norway is an excellent example of an old town built – literally – on mining, in this case, copper. In 1984 it was added to UNESCO's list of World Heritage sites based on its copper mining heritage. The smelting district of the town has been preserved, as have the homes of the miners. There is a museum based on the old smelting house. Just outside this old-style 'company town' is the Olausgruva Mine. Here visitors walk through part of the original seventeenth-century mine before entering the main mine which did not close until the 1970s. The mine tour cost 40 Norwegian Kroner in 1999 and most tours take place during the summer.

In the North of Norway, near Narvik, are the Giken mines – copper mines which because of the severe climate and short tourist season are only open between 20 June and 18 August. The mining history of the area is told in a local museum.

The arctic island of Svalbard is an extreme environment with a severe climate and an interesting history. Coal was discovered in the seventeenth century but mining did not really commence until the early twentieth century. The mines have been shared by miners of different nationalities, notably Norwegians and Russians.

Mines have been closing in recent years and relatively few now remain open, so soon this form of tourism may be more about industrial heritage than visiting working mines.

Several mine tours are offered in Svalbard including a visit to Mine No. 3 which cost 550 Norwegian Kroner in 1999. Tours are also available to the settlement of Barentsburg, a Russian mining village with its Pomor Museum which explains the story of coal mining by Russians in Svalbard. There is also a mining museum in Ny Ålesund, where the last mine closed in 1962 following a major explosion.

Given the low volume and high seasonality of most Norwegian tourism, visitor numbers at all these mine attractions are often low, a few thousand people per annum. Apart from Røros and Svalbard, the market for most of the other mines is apparently domestic, given that the mines are in areas not well established as destinations for foreign tourists.

Nevertheless, in all the cases discussed here, local authorities have sought to use mine attractions to help stimulate local tourism and the broader economy.

Case 11

Bay Street complex, Malta

Malta attracts well over a million foreign visitors each year but it is currently looking at ways of improving its tourism product, not least through the development of new attractions.

One such project, the Bay Street complex, opened in 2001, a £17.3 million mixed use development in the St George's Bay area of the island, created by a consortium led by Bromille Ltd.

According to an article by Tibbytt of Locum Destination Consultancy, the development is designed to appeal to three market segments:

- the young, mobile domestic market
- tourists staying in four- and five-star hotels in neighbouring Paceville
- all international tourists on the island.

The complex brings together several elements, notably:

- a family entertainment centre
- a hands-on science centre
- restaurants and bars
- retail outlets
- language school.

The architecture is modern in style and the project took just 2.5 years from the beginning of construction to the official opening. The attraction covers 19 000 square metres and its total cost of a little over £17 million was divided up approximately as follows:

site cost	29 per cent
construction	24 per cent
engineering and mechanical work	24 per cent
fitting out and shells for the units	14 per cent
contingencies	9 per cent.

Occupiers are responsible for fitting out their own units and these occupiers are planned to include Marks and Spencer, Naf-Naf and Hard Rock Café, as well as a craft market and a hotel.

The architecture, it is claimed, draws it inspiration from the fortresses of Valletta, and makes great use of natural light.

It is very much a lifestyle-based attraction and it has been consciously designed to attract the local population – where social and economic change has potentially created demand for such an attraction – as well as tourists.

· · · · ·

Case 12

The impact of political change on the attractions sector in Russia

Russia is an excellent example of how political change can affect the attractions sector in a country. It has to be said, as we will see, that the impact in Russia has been rather negative, but let us begin by looking at the positive dimension. The end of communism in Russia allowed new types of attractions to emerge, although many of these were not particularly designed for foreign tourists. These include the new US$360 million cathedral, the Church of Christ the Saviour in Moscow, alternative art galleries, and new retail outlets and restaurants.

In theory, as it is now easier for foreigners to enter the country, inbound tourism should be growing

and providing new visitors for Russian attractions. However, the Russian attractions sector has suffered heavily in recent years in a number of ways, including:

- Political and economic instability, and the perception of rising crime, has actually reduced inbound tourism from the West to Russia.
- The difficult economic situation has led to underinvestment in museums and theatres, which has reduced the quality of the product.
- Many key figures in the arts have left to pursue careers in the West to the detriment of, for

example, the ballet and opera companies of St Petersburg and Moscow.

- The break-up of the Soviet Union has made it more difficult to put together itineraries which link cultural attractions in Russia with those in former Soviet republics such as Uzbekistan, Armenia and Georgia.
- Privatization and economic instability have created major infrastructure problems such as domestic air transport problems and the fragmentation of the Intourist organization. This, too, has constrained the growth of foreign tourists to Russia, particularly in cities in Siberia such as Irkutsk.
- The war in Chechnya has made people wary of visiting resorts such as Sochi.
- The poverty of much of the Russian population has meant that no real large-scale domestic attraction market has yet developed.
- The economic situation and the reduction of subsidies has meant that prices have risen at Russian attractions. For example, in 2000 a tour

of the whole Kremlin complex in Moscow was US$10.

- The new political climate has meant that many former attractions, that were unique, have been closed, or are no longer promoted. For example the former Park of Soviet Economic Achievements has become a place where foreign consumer goods are promoted and sold. Even the future of Lenin's Mausoleum is in doubt!

To date, therefore, it seems that the political and economic change that has taken place since the late 1980s in Russia has had a negative affect on the attractions sector in Russia. As things settle down and the economy recovers, Russia may yet see a growth in its attractions sector. However, given social and cultural change in the country, it is unlikely that this will mean more theatres, museums and classical art museums. It is more likely to involve theme parks, leisure shopping complexes and entertainment centres. Russia has changed for ever, and so has its attraction sector!

· · · · · ·

Case 13

The management of archaeological sites in Greece

Greece has, perhaps, the richest collection of archaeological sites in the world. The management of these sites is perhaps the greatest problem because the number of sites puts a great strain on government resources. Furthermore, the volume of great archaeological sites may also have led to those sites and their value, being rather underrated by the Greeks. However, in recent years the Greek government, together with the European Commission and UNESCO have been trying hard to improve the way in which sites in Greece are both conserved and interpreted for visitors.

Some of the key issues facing archaeological site managers in Greece are as follows:

1 Finding enough money and expert staff to ensure that sites are systematically excavated and then protected.
2 Deciding whether artefacts should be displayed on site or removed to major archaeological museums. In recent years excellent new museums have opened or been remodelled across Greece, from Athens to Mytillene, Heraklion to Thessaloniki. However, it might be

argued that finds should be seen by visitors *in situ* to help them understand the context of such finds and therefore better appreciate their history and significance.
3 Many sites still have little or no on-site interpretation and what there is may be old-fashioned, such as wordy guidebooks or display panels. Little use has yet been made of interactive computer technologies or live interpretation, by actors, at Greek archaeological sites. Clearly, these things could threaten the sense of place at sites but it could attract more visitors. For foreigners, many of whom have little knowledge of ancient Greek history it could also help them better to understand the sites.
4 At most sites visitor services are very limited and of mediocre quality, from toilets to souvenir shops.
5 Many sites appear to be rather under-priced for their inherent quality and rarity value. This reduces the income that could be generated which could then be reinvested in conservation and interpretation.

6 Some guides that double as guardians of the site appear to be undertrained and are unable to do justice to some wonderful sites.

Furthermore, often, even the major Greek sites are not user-friendly to tourists in terms of opening hours. For example, the Acropolis does not open in the evening. It sometimes closes in mid-afternoon. Longer opening hours might help to spread out the visitors more and reduce overcrowding. Evening opening would also give visitors an unforgettable experience.

It is also closed on seven public holidays a year, a lot for a site of world significance. At the same time, the Agora in Athens is only open for six days of the week, as is the Kerameikós and the Tower of Winds.

At the great site of Delphi, the closing time at the weekend is 3 p.m., and there is no shop or café.

One very positive development in recent years has been the growing use of sites for live performances of Greek plays and operas. For example, a festival of ancient dramas takes place every summer at the superbly preserved ancient theatre at Epidaurus, and at the theatre at Dodoni Epirus.

On the one hand it could be argued that Greece represents a refreshingly non-commercialized approach to heritage at its archaeological sites. On the other hand, it could be suggested that Greece, whose tourism market faces growing competition from Mediterranean and Asian destinations, is missing an opportunity to further develop and widen its cultural tourism market. The pressure for change in the way sites are managed could increase as heritage interpretation improves in other parts of the world, and as new places seek to establish themselves as competitive cultural tourism destinations.

· · · · ·

Case 14

Major museums in New York

New York is the home of a plethora of museums of all kinds which attract many visitors to the city, and provide entertainment and education for most tourists to the city at some time during their visit.

The most important groups of museums are based on art, much of it foreign to the USA, including:

1 The Metropolitan Museum of Art, one of the top such museums in the world with more than 2 million works of art featuring everything from European painting to ancient Greek and Roman art, American art to Asian art. It has shops and restaurants and is ostensibly free although a donation of US$10 is requested.
2 MoMA or the Museum of Modern Art is very popular although it is currently undergoing an extensive refurbishment. It features the work of famous artists and architects such as Chagall, Matisse, Magritte, Hopper, Bacon, Pollack, Warhol and Le Corbusier, and charges US$9.50 for admission.
3 The Guggenheim Museum occupies a building designed by Lloyd-Wright and opened in 1959. It contains a variety of works but it is particularly strong on the French Impressionists.

4 The Frick Collection, with an entrance fee of US$7, features an eclectic collection from Gainsborough to El Greco, Fragonard to Rembrandt.
5 The Whitney Museum of American Art is the home of some of the best examples of American painting. Located in a rather undistinguished modern building, it costs US$3.50 to visit.
6 The Cloisters houses private medieval sculpture and archaeological work collections most of it from France and Spain, together with tapestries and tombs. Ostensibly free, a US$10 donation is requested.

Typically for the USA, most of these art museums are based on the private collections of rich benefactors rather than on state-owned collections.

The *Rough Guide to New York* (2000) lists another twenty-five 'art' museums in the city, including the Museum of TV and Radio.

New York also has one of the world's leading natural history museums, the American Museum of Natural History. Again, officially it is free but a donation of US$8 is forcefully requested by the management. This museum dates back to 1869 but it has been refurbished recently and now has more than 30 million exhibits on display. It also incorporates a planetarium and an education centre.

Given the history of New York it is not surprising to find that it has a number of museums dedicated to the lives of different ethnic groups in the city. These groups include Hispanic people, Jewish people, Kurds, the Chinese and Ukranians. There are also museums devoted to the history of Black people in the USA, as well as the National Museum of the American Indian.

A very interesting museum, the Lower East Side Tenement Museum, uses one building to show how different ethnic immigrant groups lived in this neighbourhood from the 1860s onwards. It is also a centre of research and offers tours of the area too. It also publishes a guide to the area which offers self-guided walks looking at the history of groups such as the Irish, Germans, Jews and the Chinese.

Immigration to the country is also at the heart of one of the city's other great museums, the Ellis Island Museum of Immigration. This museum is based in the old immigrant processing station which opened in 1892. As well as exhibitions, dramatic re-enactments, based on the testimony of real immigrants, help bring the immigrants' stories to life for visitors. Poignant personal persecutions of immigrants provide moving evidence of the nature of immigration to the USA. The museum costs US$7 for adults and US$3 for children.

The history of the city is also remembered in the South Street Seaport Center and Museum, which tells the story of the seafaring history of the city. It is situated next to the famous Fulton Fish Market. This museum is a good example of the use of attractions to regenerate urban areas as much of this area was formerly derelict before the museum opened. Now it is an area of shops, restaurants, bars and old ships.

The more recent history of the city and country is told in the Intrepid Sea-Air-Space Museum which is based in an old aircraft carrier berthed on Pier 86. It contains aircraft and space exhibits and is quite interactive. The entrance fee was US$10 in 2000.

Other museums focus on subjects that are peculiar to the city including the New York police force, the subway and even the history of skyscrapers. There is even a museum specially designed for children in Manhattan, the Children's Museum of Manhattan.

The museums of New York have a number of interesting characteristics, notably:

- a large proportion of them, nearly 50 per cent, are based on the arts including painting, sculpture, photography, architecture, and the media
- many of the larger museums are ostensibly free but expect a particular size of donation to be made
- a high percentage of the museums, approximately 80 per cent are in Manhattan rather than the outer boroughs of the city, namely Brooklyn, the Bronx, Queens and Staten Island.

For most visitors to the city, however, the museums are probably a secondary reason for visiting. The primary reasons probably include the busy atmosphere, Broadway shows, the shops, eating, nightlife, baseball, and monuments like the Statue of Liberty and the Empire State Building.

· · · · ·

Case 15

Leading theme parks in the USA

The USA is commonly accepted to be the pioneer and the market leader in the theme park sector. Of the world's twenty most visited theme parks, no fewer than twelve are in the USA. In 1998, its theme parks received some 300 million visits and US $8.7 billion revenue (Amusement Business, 1999).

A selection of the leading theme parks in the USA include the following:

1 Walt Disney World Resort, Orlando, which incorporates:
  (a) Magic Kingdom, a fantasy land, strongly related to the animation films by Disney
  (b) Epcot, with its focus on high-technology rides
  (c) Disney's Animal Kingdom, which involves real animals and Disney animal characters
  (d) Disney – MGM studios, a cinema-based theme park.

It also offers a huge range of shops, entertainment attractions and restaurants, together with three water parks, a sports complex, an international theme park complex, Disney Quest, and the Cirque de Soleil circus. The park is also supported by a range of on-site themed hotels.

2 Universal Orlando, is actually three theme parks, namely Universal Studios, a marine theme park and Island Adventure which incorporates five 'lands' based on high-technology rides. It also has its own shops, restaurants and hotels.

3 Sea World Adventure Park, Orlando, a water themed attraction that combines high-technology rides, with the chance to see great sea mammals and fish such as whales, dolphins and stingrays.

4 Busch Gardens Tampa Bay features state of the art 'white knuckle rides' and a 29-acre 'safari park' which re-creates conditions in Africa so that visitors can see giraffes and elephants, for example, roaming 'free'.

5 Discovery Cove, Orlando, a park which allows visitors to:
   (a) swim with dolphins and other marine creatures and touch them
   (b) see exotic birds in a free-fly aviary
   (c) bathe in a reconstructed 'tropical cove'.

6 Legoland California, a hands-on park, aimed at younger children featuring exhibits made from Lego bricks, and themed rides.

7 Disney's Californian Adventure, Anaheim, a new park which is also the subject of another case study in this book. This attraction covers 55 acres and has as its theme all aspects of the State of California. It also incorporates a reconstruction of 'Hollywood' in its 'golden age' and Paradise Pier, a reconstructed seaside 'boardwalk'.

8 Knotts Berry Farm, California, which combines rides with shows.

9 Six Flags Magic Mountain, California which explains California's history and its present, through rides and shows.

It is clear that the theme park industry in the USA has a number of characteristics:

- the overwhelming majority of major parks are in states with a good all-year round climate such as California and Florida
- most of the parks are owned by a few major attraction corporations such as Disney and Universal
- several leading parks combine themes rather than having a single theme
- some of the parks are non-American concepts such as Legoland California.

Attraction prices in the USA tend to be high, particularly in relation to European parks as can be seen from Exhibit 15.1.

Park	Location	Adult	Child
Walt Disney World Resort	Florida, USA	186[1]	150[1]
Disney California Adventure	California, USA	78[2]	61[2]
Universal Orlando	Florida, USA	63[3]	52[3]
Sea World Adventure Park	Florida, USA	33[4]	27[4]
Busch Gardens	Florida, USA	32[4]	26[4]
Discovery Cove	Florida, USA	147[5]	N/A Over 6s adult price
Legoland California	California, USA	25[4]	20[4]
Six Flags Magic Mountain	California, USA	24[4]	17[4]
Wet 'n' Wild	Florida, USA	20	16
Disneyland Paris	France	39[4]	26[4]
Universal Studios Port Aventura	Spain	28[3]	21[3]

Notes: 1 Five-day Hopper Plus ticket
2 Three-day pass
3 Two-day pass
4 One-day pass
5 Includes swim with dolphins

Exhibit 15.1
Prices for day passes or shortest duration tickets available for adults and children in high season 2001 at selected US and European theme parks (£)

Many of the attractions in California and Florida also offer joint ticket package deals including several attractions, as can be seen from the following examples:

- 'Orlando Flexi Ticket' which gave admission to four parks in 2001 for £113 [adults] or £90 [children]
- 'Adventure Passport' covering Busch Gardens, Tampa Bay and Sea World, Orlando, with a combined cost of £60 [adults] or £49 [children] for visits anytime within a twenty-one day period.

It is interesting that in the USA, children often pay between 77 per cent and 85 per cent of the adult price, although very young children often enjoy free admission. Given that most theme park visitors are families this can make attraction-visiting in the USA particularly expensive. This expenditure is further increased by the great emphasis on merchandising and food and drink sales at US theme parks. These two factors help explain the impressive profitability of theme parks in the USA.

Case 16

Disney California Adventure, USA

Disney's latest attraction in the USA, the Californian Adventure, opened in Anaheim in February 2001, at an estimated cost of $1.4 billion. This is part of an ambitious phase of new development by Disney with new parks opening in Tokyo, Paris, and Hong Kong over the next few years.

The new American park is based on California as a theme and is their second park in Anaheim, alongside Disneyland.

Although the theme park business is healthy in the USA at the moment, there have been commentators who have questioned the prospects for the new park based on the following grounds:

- the USA at the time of opening, appeared to be entering an economic downturn which could affect the overall volume of theme park visitors in the USA
- the US$43 entrance charge which is the same as Disneyland, even though there are far fewer

on-site attractions at California Adventure than at Disneyland

- rising fuel pries in the USA which may discourage tourists from driving to Anaheim
- the company has had several unfortunate incidents in Anaheim including accidents at Disneyland and even an evacuation at a special preview for the California Adventure park.

Industry analysts on the other hand, predict that the new park will, nevertheless, be successful for the company. It will extend the stay, and increase the expenditure of visitors to Anaheim, and will bring more income to Disney because of its two parks, as has happened with the company's four parks in Orlando.

The park has a daily capacity of around 30 000 and there are fears that if the park really takes off it could be overcrowded almost every day.

However, the management of the park is confident it will be successful and will give the visitor a high-quality experience.

Case 17

Special interest attractions in South Africa

South Africa is the wealthiest country in Africa and has a wide range of spectacular natural attractions. One would, therefore, expect it to have a highly developed attractions sector to serve the need of both domestic and foreign tourists. However, this is not the case, because:

- the wealth is unevenly distributed within the country and many people lack the disposable income to indulge in leisure tourism
- the Apartheid era isolated the country from many international markets in the rest of South Africa and beyond.

However, both problems are now being reduced, the latter faster than the former.

Rather than developing general museums and theme parks as major attractions, South Africa, has instead, focused on attracting domestic and foreign tourists by developing special interest attractions, as we will now see:

1 Wineries: South African wine has become well established around the world and many tourists want to visit the wineries. In 2000–1, guidebooks to the country identified nine major wineries which are open to the public, of which the greater concentration is the Stellen busch region. Generally, the wineries offer tours, tastings and a chance for visitors to purchase the wine directly from producers.

2 Aquariums: there are four major aquariums in South Africa in Cape Town, Durban, Kynsna, and Pretoria. The Two Oceans Aquarium is based on the waterfront in Cape Town and has sharks as its main attraction. Sea World in Durban has several dolphin shows as its highlights. The Kynsna aquarium is a small one but it displays the unique Kynsna seahorse. The Pretoria aquarium, more traditionally, is part of a zoo complex.

3 Battlefields: Zululand has five battlefield sites which are used to attract certain market segment to the region. These battles were part of the Zulu and Boer wars and are of interest particularly to South Africans themselves. Most of these sites have visitor centres with multimedia displays and artefacts.

4 Spas: there are three major spa centres in South Africa, at Aventura, Montague and Cilnsdol. Sometimes the spas have been incorporated into luxury resort hotels, such as the Avalon Springs Resort at Montague.

5 Farms: the 'Let's Go' Guide to South Africa lists ten farms which open their gates to visitors and are major attractions. The products of these farms range from cherries to coffee. However, while some of these are purely working farms, others mix farming with offering, for example, accommodation or horse-riding.

6 Game reserves: in addition to national parks, there are smaller game reserves which are managed as visitor attractions. Near Port Elizabeth, for example, there is the Addo Elephant Park, with accommodation and a restaurant, and the Scholia Private Game Reserve which closes at 8.00 p.m. each evening but which also offers night safaris.

7 Specialist museums: the country has a range of museums based on specialist themes such as astronomy, the Boer war, the Siege of Ladysmith and African music.

8 Diamond mines: visitors can visit a working diamond mine such as the Premier Mine near Pretoria.

The success of its tourism industry in recent years seems to suggest that specialist attractions have helped put South Africa on the international tourism map.

. . . . . .

Case 18

The international casino market in New Zealand

As Pearce (1999) noted, 'the promotion of tourism has been one of the explicit rationales for the introduction of casinos in New Zealand'. With this in mind, several cities have opened casinos in recent years.

However, Pearce has shown that, often, casinos have overestimated the potential volume of international visitors. This point is illustrated in Exhibit 18.1.

The research reported by Pearce also indicated that visitors from Taiwan, Singapore and Hong Kong were far more likely to visit casinos during their stay than were visitors from Australia and the UK. Furthermore, casino visitors were more likely to be part of tour groups than non-casino visitors.

The international casino visitors were more likely than other visitors to undertake the following activities during their visit to New Zealand:

- shopping
- museum visiting
- garden visiting
- attending a Maori cultural performance
- visiting a zoo
- jetboarding

Casino	Projected percentage of international visitors	Actual percentage of international visitors
Christchurch	30.0	24.0
Auckland	13.7	10.0

Source: Pearce (1999)

Exhibit 18.1
Projected and actual international visitor numbers at two casinos, 1997

- experiencing a live concert or theatre performance
- taking a scenic boat cruise.

The same research indicated that foreign casino visitors stayed an average of twenty days in New Zealand, and spent an average of NZ$2684 per trip, or NZ$134 per day.

Nevertheless, data published by the National International Visitor Survey in the late 1990s showed that:

- only a fifth of all international visitors actually visited a casino while in New Zealand
- international visitors who do visit a casino made 1.4 casino visits during their stay.

• • • • •

Case 19

Visitor attractions in Brazil

Brazil is a country where tourism is largely based on beaches, festivals and natural attractions such as the Pantanal wetland region. However, it does have a number of interesting attractions of the kind this book is discussing, which we will now briefly consider:

1 Rio de Janeiro has many attractions, in addition to the Carnivale, including:
  (a) Musee Naval e Oceanográfico, a maritime and oceanographic museum
  (b) several cultural centres, several of which are sponsored by banks
  (c) the monastery of Igreja e Mosteiro de Saõ Bento
  (d) the English cemetery at Gamboa
  (e) Museum Histórico Nacional
  (f) the tram museum at Santa Teresa
  (g) the largest collection of primitive art, the Musee Internacional de Arte Naif
  (h) the National Museum and Zoological Museum, both in the Quinta da Boa Viste neighbourhood
  (i) the 200 000 seater Maraconá football stadium
  (j) the Musee do Índio about the country's indigenous Indian population

  (k) the racecourse at Gávea
  (l) samba schools where visitors can learn this Brazilian dance
  (m) the nuclear power station visitor centre at Angra.
2 Minas Gerais and Espírito Santo:
  (a) the Centro de Artesanato Mineiro, a retail outlet for locally produced crafts in Belo Horizonte
  (b) a cultural centre, the Centro de Culture Belo Horizonte
  (c) the historical museum, Abílio Barreto, with its gallery of old photographs
  (d) the Museo do Ouro, looking at the colonial history and gold mining history of Satará, near Belo Horizonte
  (e) the gold mine site at Passagem near Belo Horizonte
  (f) the Basilico do Senhor Bon Jesus de Matosinhos, a pilgrimage site at Congantas
  (g) the Museo do Diamante museum tracing the history of the diamond industry in Diamontina
  (h) Agroturismo attractions in the Venda Nova and Pedro Azul where various farms open to allow visitors to see how they operate and to buy their products.

3 The North-East:
   (a) the Museo Afro-Brasiliero in Salvador which celebrates the Black contribution to Brazilian culture
   (b) the Turtle reserve at Prai do Forte
   (c) the museum of religious art at Marechal Deodoro
   (d) the major anthropological and ethnographic Museo do Humem du Nordeste in Recife
   (e) a pottery museum dedicated to the work of artist Mestre Vitalino, in Caruaru
   (f) the Museo do Algodão in Campina Grande which tells the story of cotton plantations in the area.

4 Amazonia:
   (a) the traditional Ver O Peso market in Belem
   (b) the botanical garden and zoological park of Emilio Gaeldi in Belem
   (c) the dam and hydro-electric plant at Tucvrui
   (d) the Centre for the Preservation of Indian Art near Santarem
   (e) the Teatro Amazon or opera house in Manaus
   (f) monuments and museums dedicated to the pioneers of developing Amazonia such as the monument to the pioneers of Roramia in the city of the same name
   (g) the railway museum at Porto Velho
   (h) the fort of Principe da Beira, an eighteenth-century military base at Guajará-Mirim

5 Brasilia:
   (a) the huge cathedral, opened in 1960, the Catedral Metropolitana Nossa Senhara Apar ecida
   (b) the Planetarium
   (c) a museum dedicated to the gem industry, the Museo Nacional des Gems
   (d) the museum of Brazilian art
   (e) the mixed retail and entertainment complex of the Centro Comercial Gilberto Salamão
   (f) an amusement park, at nearby Goiánia

6 Mato Grosso:
   (a) the cave, Gruta do Lago Azul, Near Bonito
   (b) the ecological visitor centre, Fazenda da Barra Projeto Vivo, near Benito
   (c) the history and natural history museum of Pantanal in Corumbá
   (d) the Casa do Artesão, in Corumbá, a retail outlet for local crafts.

7 São Paulo:
   (a) a museum of Japanese immigration in the city centre
   (b) the new concert hall in the old railway station, the Estacão Júlio Prestes
   (c) Museum de Arte de São Paulo, one of the few Brazilian museums which have a truly international reputation
   (d) the Caso de Bandeirante, a preserved homestead of the early settlers in the city
   (e) the railway museum at Paranapiacaba
   (f) the Fazenda do Pinhol, a well-preserved rural estate, which was involved in coffee production

8 The South:
   (a) the railway museum in Curitiba
   (b) a museum celebrating Polish immigration in Curitiba; there is a similar museum at Araucária
   (c) an ecological reserve on Ilha do Met
   (d) Museum de Milénio and the Casa do Artesanato in Prudentópolis, which celebrates the history and the crafts of the Ukranian settlers respectively
   (e) a visitor centre for the Itaipu hydro-electricity dam
   (f) the Ecomuseu at Santa Catarina with handcraft exhibitions and artefacts of the Azorean settlers
   (g) the Serra do Tabuleiro, half nature reserve, half zoo, which displays the local fauna
   (h) a coal mine which is open to the public at Criciúma
   (i) a small wine museum in Videira
   (j) mission towns and churches, with sound and light shows like San Ignaccio.

This selection shows that Brazil has a variety of attractions but that most of them are based on its colonial history, immigrant groups, industries, arts and crafts, and natural history. The fact that Brazil is not yet a well-developed tourist destination, and the emphasis on beach attractions means that many of the attractions are relatively little visited and are not of high quality.

Finally, controversial, if understandable and well meaning, efforts are now being made to make tourists aware of the realities of life for many Brazilians by offering them tours of the 'favelas or shanty towns' in Brazilian cities. This clearly raises major ethical issues about what should or should not be seen as a legitimate attraction.

Case 20

Sporting attractions

Sport – for participants and spectators – has grown dramatically in recent years. Some sports teams such as the New York Mets and Manchester United are truly global brands, while many other sporting events such as the Olympics, are global media events.

Sports attractions, as we saw in Chapter 3, are becoming an ever more important part of the attractions market. Exhibit 20.1 illustrates the different types of sporting attractions.

The variety of sporting attractions can be appreciated from the following examples:

1 The Stade de France, Paris, where the 1999 World Cup took place. Ninety-minute behind-the-scene tours are offered at a cost of FFr90 for adults, as well as shorter FFr38 tours. There is also a memorabilia shop and two restaurants available to visitors on weekdays. The international appeal of this attraction is shown by the fact that its promotional leaflet is in six languages, including Japanese.
2 The Wimbledon Lawn Tennis Museum, which opened in 1977 to celebrate one hundred years of the Men's Championship, Queen Elizabeth II Silver Jubilee, and the victory in the Ladies Final of the Briton, Virginia Wade. The museum was extended in 1989 but 'it is no longer cutting edge in its approach to interactions on display' (Jones, 2001). According to Jones, visitor numbers in recent years have declined from a peak of 70 000 to around 50 000 in 2001, partly due to increased admission charges. A new behind-the-scenes tour was introduced in 2000 but this is not part of the normal museum visit.
3 The Keith Prowse organization which offers tickets to baseball, ice-hockey and American football games all over the USA.
4 The Rugby Sevens in Hong Kong, every September, during which it is difficult to find a hotel bed due to the international visitors.
5 Spectating at major, famous horse races, from the Dubai Classic to the Prix de L'Arc de Triomphe in Paris and the Kentucky Derby in the USA.
6 Diving sites such as Manado in Indonesia, the Similan and Susin Islands in Thailand and the Great Barrier Reef in Australia.

Human-made sporting attractions and events are often designed to achieve brand extension for both events and teams.

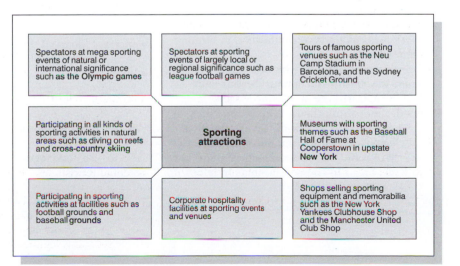

Exhibit 20.1
The different types of sporting attractions

Case 21

Food and drink attractions

Food and drink has been used to attract visitors to countries like France for many years. However, in recent years, food- and drink-based tourism has grown dramatically, although it takes many different forms in different places, including the following:

1 Food- and drink-themed events and festivals from the annual food festival in Hong Kong to the Oyster Festival which takes place every September in Galway, Ireland.
2 Food and drink markets such as the spice market in Istanbul, the Saturday market in Arles, France, or the numerous 'farmers markets' now found in the UK, France and the USA.
3 Famous restaurants which serve classic cuisine and are internationally renowned for their quality, for example, the Restaurant Bocuse in Lyon.
4 Traditional national types of eating establishments such as the tavernas of Greece, and the churrascarios of Brazil.
5 Specialist food retailers, ranging from up-market traditional establishments such as Fauchan in Paris to the delis of New York.
6 Food producers who offer visits to their premises, and opportunities to taste the product. An excellent example of this phenomenon is the Société Roquefort cheese plant in the Midi-Pyrenées region of France, near Millau.
7 Food producers who develop attractions to promote their brand, such as the Cadbury World, chocolate-themed attraction in Birmingham, UK.
8 Drinks manufacturers who offer tours of their premises, including famous brands such as Guinness, Carlsberg and Remy-Martin.
9 Food- and drink-themed museums such as George Duboeufs 'Hamear du Vin' attraction in the Beaujolais region of France, and ecomusées in France based on products ranging from cider to wine, bread to cheese, chestnuts to honey.

10 Restaurants in unusual locations such as the floating restaurants of Aberdeen harbour, Hong Kong.
11 Opportunities for tourists to visit working farms to see food production at first hand, and perhaps even to help feed animals or pick fruit, for example.
12 Places where visitors can see the 'harvesting' of various products such as the spring collection of Maple Syrup in New England, USA.
13 The Ferme-Auberges of France where guests are invited to enjoy traditional regional cuisine based on local produce, at farms.
14 Hotels which offer food- and drink-themed breaks where visitors can learn to cook particular dishes and/or appreciate good wines.

In addition, some areas have developed food and drink routes, and trails linking together various food- and drink-themed attractions in the area. Some focus on a single product such as wine or cheese, while others link all kinds of products from the same area. In Europe, the European Commission has provided funding through its LEADER programme for food and drink trail projects, to help stimulate local tourism.

Recent food crises such as BSE and the controversy over genetically modified foods has focused public interest increasingly on the quality of food and drink we consume. This will:

- increase demand for existing food and drink attractions
- stimulate the growth of attractions based on organically produced food and drink.

With the growing global interest in food and drink, it seems likely that more and more destinations will seek to use food and drink as an attraction for potential tourists.

Case 22

The evolution of wildlife attractions

People have always been attracted by the chance to see wildlife but the nature of wildlife attractions, as we will see, has changed over time.

Until the middle of the twentieth century, the only real forms of wildlife attractions were:

- traditional zoos in which animals were kept in cages, for the entertainment, as well as the education, of city dwellers
- hunting trips, ranging from fishing in the wilderness in the USA, to big game hunting in East Africa
- safaris, largely in Eastern Africa, and affordable by only a tiny minority of people
- circuses where animals were often the main attraction.

Since then, there has been a virtual revolution, let alone evolution, in the nature of wildlife attractions. First, the four types of attractions already mentioned have changed as follows :

1 Public opinion has become less favourable about seeing animals in cages. As a result some zoos have closed, others have been remodelled to give the creatures more space and a more appropriate habitat, and the focus has moved on to conservation.
2 Hunting has been banned in many countries and nature reserves have been created. However, it still continues, often illicitly, in many countries.
3 Safaris have fallen in price and become a more mass-market form of tourism, particularly in Africa.
4 Many circuses are now animal-free as a result of public and governmental opinion.

At the same time, new forms of wildlife attractions have arisen, including:

- aquariums which have often been used in urban regeneration schemes in the USA and Europe. The UK even has a 'chain' of such attractions, the Sea Life Centres. Perhaps people are less concerned about the welfare and rights of fish than they are of animals
- attractions where dolphins and seals perform for visitors such as Sea World in the USA
- scuba-diving on reefs to see the rich marine life for whom the reef is their habitat
- boat trips where tourists are taken to see whales in the wild in the sea
- farm attractions where visitors, particularly children, see farm animals and learn about them as part of a broader agenda of learning more about farming and rural life. Baby animals such as lambs are often a good way of making attractions appeal to young children
- city farms where urban children are introduced to farm animals which they may never otherwise see
- attractions based on particular types of wildlife such as snakes and reptiles, birds, flora or butterflies
- nature reserves where visitors can observe wildlife in its natural habitat
- animal sanctuaries and hospitals where threatened or injured animals are taken for care. Visitor donations in turn help fund this work
- novel forms of attractions such as the 'night safari' in Singapore.

There is no doubt that:

- wildlife will continue to be a great attraction for tourists
- the nature of wildlife attractions will evolve and develop in new ways.

In the next few years we may see the rise of virtual reality wildlife attractions that will help teach people about wildlife without the need to keep animals in captivity.

How long will it be before we have complexes where people come to watch other people living in unusual and artificial circumstances such as stranded on a 'desert island' or re-creating a period from the past, for instance? It would just be another form of 'wildlife tourism'!

Part Five

The Future of Visitor Attractions

Introduction

In the first edition of this book, in 1995, the author endeavoured to forecast how the attractions sector might change in the future. No timescale was applied to these predictions. In the intervening six years, interestingly, some of the forecast changes have started to come true. However, more of them have yet to be fully seen although it now looks even more likely that they will happen. In this section we will first, therefore, revisit some of the predictions made in the first edition in 1995. However, in many cases the original wording will suffice as the changes have yet to fully become reality.

The nature of visitor attractions and their markets will continue to change in the future as they have in the past. However, there is reason to believe that the pace of change may even increase in the future as a result of a number of powerful factors which are discussed below.

We will use the framework of the business environment – namely the macroenvironment and microenvironment – to examine these factors, before briefly going on to look at some other forces that will influence the attractions of the future. Clearly, the factors outlined below will affect attractions over different timescales; some are already having an impact on the attraction business, while the effects of others will not be experienced for a number of years yet. It must be stressed that this section is, of necessity, selective, speculative and subjective.

The macroenvironment

We will start by looking at the macroenvironment using the PEST analysis framework.

Political factors

The following political issues will affect the attraction product and market over the coming years.

Political change in Eastern Europe ● ● ●

The political changes in Eastern Europe and their social and economic ramifications have had less influence on the attractions market than was envisaged in 1995. Eastern European citizens, whose freedom to travel was restricted in the past, now have a great desire to travel to Western Europe and the USA to visit the icons of Western tourism. This should have swelled visitor numbers at major natural and human-made attractions. Given that many such sites (monuments and famous museum collections, for example) are already experiencing problems because of overuse, this is potentially a serious problem. These Eastern European visitors will also want to visit special events in the West, such as rock concerts, the Olympics and traditional events like the Trooping of the Colour. This wish on the part of Eastern Europeans will only be translated slowly into active demand, for only a few currently have enough money for such trips, but many others will follow in due course. Given that the countries of Eastern Europe including 'European' Russia have a population well in excess of 200 million people, the potential of this newly developing market should not be underestimated.

The second way in which political change in Eastern Europe was predicted to affect the attraction market was through the growth of competition. More and more people from the West it was thought would take advantage of the new political climate in the East to visit existing attractions in Eastern Europe, whether they are natural attractions or museums and galleries or music festivals, for example. Eastern Europe currently offers natural attractions which are often underdeveloped by Western standards, but years of state subsidy of the arts and culture have led to high standards in the performing arts and superb collections in museums and galleries that few Westerners have yet seen. This prediction has yet to come to fruition because of political and economic instability in parts of Eastern Europe.

In addition, as the tourism industry of Eastern European countries developed, it was thought new attractions would be introduced that would further increase competition for the existing attractions of Western Europe and the USA. For some Western attraction operators there were thought to be opportunities to develop these new attractions in Eastern Europe, particularly in terms of the types of attractions where people in the East have little or no expertise, such as theme parks. Political and economic instability has also limited this development.

The growing role of the European Union ● ● ●

For attractions in Western Europe, the EU will continue to be a major influence in the future in two main ways. First, it will become increasingly involved in the regulation of the tourism industry and in developing general regulations that will impinge on the operation of attractions. Such regulations will cover matters such as health and safety, working hours, consumer protection and employment law. Second, the EU will initiate campaigns to promote Europe as a whole as a tourist destination and will encourage cross-border co-operation in destination marketing between member countries, particularly in the field of cultural tourism. Both these moves could help boost the attendance figures for foreign visitors at European attractions, particularly at those attractions such as heritage sites and arts festivals that could be described as cultural tourism attractions.

As more and more countries join the EU, the influences noted in the last paragraph will apply to more and more countries. Most importantly, these new countries will principally be in the Mediterranean (Cyprus, Malta and probably Turkey) and Eastern Europe (Poland, Hungary and the Czech Republic, for example). These developments will change the geography of the European attractions business significantly in terms of both supply and demand.

Legislation

As the tourism industry becomes more mature and is given increased recognition by governments around the world, it may become the subject of increased legislation. This may cover issues such as the rights of consumers, health and safety, quality standards, and conservation and environmental protection. Legislation of this kind would clearly have an impact on the management of visitor attractions. Perhaps that is why the tourism industry in general, and the attractions sector specifically, is keen to project the idea that it is regulating itself, thus preventing the need for legislation.

Deregulation and privatization

In many developed countries, particularly in Europe – both West and East – there is a trend towards deregulation and privatization. As far as the attractions sector is concerned this may mean that in future some attractions and events that were formerly owned by the public sector will be transferred to the private or voluntary sectors. At the same time, those attractions that do stay within the public sector may be forced to operate in a much more commercial and entrepreneurial manner.

Civil unrest and war

There currently appears to be a growth in civil unrest and war around the world which is bound to have a negative effect on the attraction market. There are three main aspects to this problem:

1 Manifestations of social dissatisfaction such as strikes and demonstrations.
2 Terrorist activities, where tourists may either be innocent victims or deliberate targets of terrorists intent on disrupting the economy of an

area or country. As far as tourism attractions are concerned the current rise of fascism in Western Europe could become an important form of terrorism, as could the rise of Islamic fundamentalism in countries like Egypt or Turkey.

3 Wars, either between nations or civil wars within nations. This latter form of strife seems to be on the increase, for example in the former countries of Eastern Europe, due to the growth of nationalism.

All these phenomena reduce people's desire to visit attractions in a particular location or may totally destroy the market altogether. Likewise they may make it impossible for tourists to gain access to attractions, even if they wanted to visit them. Conversely, if the hopes of peace in countries like South Africa and in areas like Palestine and Northern Ireland are realized, tourism could indeed develop rapidly.

Economic factors

Economic factors are a vital element in the business environment of attractions because of their effects on both consumer demand and investment in new product development. These factors tend to be of two main types:

1 Those which are created or heavily influenced by the actions of politicians.
2 Those which might be described as 'market forces' which are usually commercially rather than politically inspired.

We will begin by looking at a number of economic issues that are largely political in origin, and then move on to those of the second type.

Currency exchange rates • • •

Currency exchange rates are crucial to international tourist flows. For example, if the dollar is strong more Americans visit Europe and if the pound is strong against the dollar more Britons visit the USA. This is crucial for attractions such as the cultural and heritage attractions of Europe and the theme parks of Florida.

While currencies have generally fluctuated in relation to market forces, the introduction of the 'Euro' in Europe may reduce the impact of these factors, but of course a number of European countries will not be in this 'Euro-zone'.

Wealth distribution • • •

Governments will influence the attraction market in the future through their policies on the distribution of wealth. Depending on the philosophy of particular governments, this will involve:

- taxation policies, both in terms of direct and indirect taxes
- the amount of paid holiday that is accorded by statutory regulations

- relative increases or reductions in the real value of pensions and social security benefits. The growing number of elderly people in developed countries will put severe pressure on the ability of governments to increase state pensions. This may result in a growing role for private pension schemes.

Interest rates

Interest rates affect disposable income which then has an impact on the size and value of the attraction market. They also have an effect on the attraction product in that if rates are high it is harder for attraction operators to fund product development in the form of new buildings and structures, for example.

The state of the economies

At the time of writing most of the developed world is beginning to recover from economic recession. It is likely that in the next few years this recession will give way to a more buoyant economic situation which should stimulate growth in the number of visits to attractions.

Newly industrialized and industrializing countries

Many countries that would formerly have been described as less industrialized or developing or Third World countries are now much more economically developed than they were a few years ago. Such countries are seeing rises in the material wealth of their populations which will increasingly be translated into a desire to travel abroad on holiday. Thus these people will become important new players in the international attraction market. Such countries include China and Brazil. Already we have seen a rapid growth in recent years in South Korea with the country becoming a major player in the attractions market as predicted in the first edition.

As these countries become more economically developed and are able to attend to their immediate priorities such as education, health and housing, they may ultimately be able to become more actively involved in developing attractions within their own country, with the aim of stimulating both domestic and international tourism.

Industrial concentration

In line with trends in other industries, and recent trends in the attractions business, we will continue to see a growth in concentration of ownership in the attractions business in relation to major attractions. A smaller number of corporations will develop and manage the truly mega attractions.

There is as yet no sign of the virtual integration envisaged in the first edition of this book, in that no tour operator or hotel chains have sought to enter the attractions market.

Globalization • • •

In the past five years we have seen the beginning of a truly globalized attractions sector in terms of the mega-attractions, through the activities of Universal and Six Flags, for example, in addition to Disney with its planned new park in Hong Kong. More and more countries may increasingly find their favourite theme park is owned by a foreign company, usually an American company. In future, the author predicts that Asian corporations will also become a driving force in the global attractions business, focusing on theme parks and leisure shopping outlets.

One aspect of this globalization is that it may lead to increased standardization of the attraction product, as these multinational corporations seek to develop attractions in other countries based on the same model as successful attractions in their own country. Ultimately this globalization of the attraction product could also lead to the rise of a 'global attraction market', namely a group of people who may in part decide what countries to visit on the basis of whether or not there is a major attraction there which is managed by a particular corporation.

Certainly, such a globalization of the attraction sector would be in line with that seen in other service sector industries, such as the fast-food business. However, we should perhaps be a little cautious when talking specifically of the attraction business for we have seen how difficult it was for the Disney organization to establish itself in the European market.

We must also keep the issue of globalization in the attractions sector in proportion. Many parts of the attractions sector such as farm attractions, heritage centres and zoos are not becoming globalized. Indeed, it is only really the theme park area where globalization has been evident. However, there are a few signs that the trend may be broadening into other areas, for example:

- The 'Sea Life Centre' brand has now spread from the UK with a centre now open in Paris.
- Famous 'brands' of art museums such as the Guggenheim Foundation are opening new museums around the world.
- Some major museums and galleries are now developing global merchandising businesses.

Sociocultural factors

Consideration of social and cultural factors may be carried out under the following headings.

The demographic 'time bomb' • • •

Throughout most of the developed world the next few years will see an increase in the proportion of the population which is elderly. For many of these people, private pension schemes and improved health services will mean that they have the money and health to be active participants in the tourism market. At the same time younger people will represent a relatively smaller proportion of the market than they have in recent years. Attraction operators will have to recognize this fact in terms of product development and the way they promote attractions. On the other hand, in many developing countries there is still rapid growth in the younger age groups, which also has implications for attraction development in these countries.

The changing family

The family will continue to evolve in a number of ways which have implications for attraction operators, as follows:

- There will be continued growth in the number of single parent families.
- Children will probably continue to become increasingly powerful consumers in their own right and teenage subcultures will continue to grow.
- More and more people, particularly in the 'professional classes', will probably have children when they are between thirty and forty years of age.

The multicultural society

Most developed countries will become increasingly multicultural, and attraction developers must respond to this trend. This means finding attraction products that will be attractive to the different ethnic markets, providing appropriate types of catering, such as halal for example, and operating in a way that is culturally acceptable to people from different ethnic backgrounds. It is important to recognize that there are many different ethnic markets, based on different races, religions and languages, and to treat them separately. At many attractions in Europe, Asia and Australasia, ethnic communities are still heavily underrepresented in the visitor profile. Failure to take action in the future to attract these markets will mean attractions missing out on markets which will become increasingly lucrative.

Disabled visitors

There is a growing belief that better facilities should be provided for disabled tourists and there appears to be growing demand for better leisure opportunities for disabled people. Thus, attractions will have to concentrate on the ways in which they can attract more disabled visitors. Again it is important to remember that disabilities differ. They may be mental or physical, and the physical may include being wheelchair-bound or being hearing-impaired or having problems with sight. The needs of all disabled people are different and they cannot and must not be treated as the same. People often forget how sizeable the disabled visitor market is and therefore it is sensible for attractions to try to attract this market for good commercial reasons as well as because it is socially right to do so. In future, as attitudes change, able-bodied visitors may actually boycott or be less enthusiastic about attractions that are not seen to cater for the disabled.

Concerns over environmental issues • • •

Public interest in environmental issues will evolve in the future and people will expect attractions to keep up to date with these developments. As well as concerns over environmental issues such as pollution, noise and energy conservation, concern with environmental issues may develop to encompass sociocultural and economic impacts. Attractions will come under increasing pressure to prove that they bring social and economic benefits to their area. Ultimately national or international standards may be developed to recognize attractions that are 'environmntally friendly'.

The animal welfare movement • • •

It seems likely that the growth of interest in animal welfare will continue. At one extreme this may mean that attendances at traditional animal attractions such as zoos, circuses and bullfights may fall, while at the other end of the spectrum militant animal welfare activists may begin to target animal attractions for physical attacks. Alternatively these attractions may move their focus away from animals or may improve their product in an attempt to reduce criticism.

The desire for social responsibility in business • • •

There is evidence that some people, at least, are increasingly rewarding companies which operate in a socially responsible way. This is one of the reasons for the success of organizations like the Body Shop. To capitalize on this trend, attraction operators will need to consciously change in a number of ways, including the way they recruit and treat staff, operating in a 'greener' way, sponsoring good causes and taking care that their suppliers also operate in an ethical manner. They may also have to reassure visitors that their catering outlets are offering wholesome food, following the concerns over BSE and 'genetically modified' foods.

Lifestyles and lifestyle marketing • • •

We are now living in the era of lifestyle marketing. Lifestyles are becoming increasingly differentiated as people's levels of sophistication, their aspirations and the myriad of opportunities available to them, allow them to choose their own lifestyle. These lifestyle choices are also increasingly being influenced by the media, and by the intense marketing activity of consumer goods producers. This is being reflected in the fact that marketing now tends to be targeted at people who follow particular lifestyles – healthy, fashion-conscious and so on – rather than just seeing them in terms of their age and sex for example. Attraction marketing needs to reflect this fact, which it often does not do at the moment.

The desire to learn • • •

Tourism surveys are clearly showing that more and more people are looking for opportunities to learn something new on their day trips as well as on their holidays. This trend clearly favours cultural and educational activities, although most attractions can offer opportunities for visitors to learn, whether through special events like craft demonstrations or new attractions such as hands-on science exhibitions. This latter example is particularly important as people increasingly prefer to learn by actively doing something rather than by passively watching others do things.

The computer culture • • •

For more and more people, particularly the young, computers are becoming a major part of their lives. Already, for a large number of people, they are their main leisure activity in terms of playing computer games. When designing new attraction products, operators need to bear this in mind.

The changing concept of heritage • • •

While people will remain interested in the idea of heritage which is represented by castles, stately homes and traditional events, heritage will increasingly have a wider meaning as time passes. Consumer tastes will change as many societies become increasingly multicultural. There will be a growing interest in some 'alternative' types of heritage, as follows:

- The cultural heritage of ethnic communities will become popular.
- The culture of recent decades such as the 1970s or even later will increase.
- Industrial tourism may come to mean service industries that grew up in the past thirty years as well as traditional manufacturing industries.
- Oral history may become a central focus of heritage attractions as it is a more imaginative method of interpretation.
- Forgotten areas of history such as food and drink may become more popular.
- Popular culture such as film, television, music and dance, will come to be seen as an integral part of heritage.

Technological factors

Technological factors in the future will represent both an opportunity and a threat for visitor attractions. Furthermore, some of them will affect the attraction product while others will have an impact on the attraction market.

Virtual reality • • •

Virtual reality is one of the 'buzz' phrases of our time but we are only just starting to appreciate its potential impact on the attraction sector. Those who have thought about this impact see virtual reality as both a potential opportunity and a threat.

Rather than using words or pictures to stimulate images in people's minds, virtual reality technology uses computers to give one the sense of actually 'being there' even if the real 'there' is thousands of miles away or hundreds of years ago. It works directly on the senses. Ultimately, some believe that we will be able to do virtually anything, experience anything. However, currently the technology is at a relatively early stage in its development. Most systems rely on graphics, whereas a true virtual reality system would also appeal to other senses.

Let it be said that virtual reality does not represent a revolution. In many ways it is a natural consequence of the growing sophistication of existing computer games and interactive videos which are now a familiar part of life for many people. There are already indications of how virtual reality could affect the attractions world. A few examples will illustrate this point:

- There are already a number of virtual reality inspired entertainment centres in high streets around the UK such as the Laser Quest complexes. These are attractions in the true sense of the word, based on the interface between computer games, interactive video and virtual reality.
- Flight simulators, which are virtual reality par excellence, are already proving to be popular 'attractions', particularly with corporate clients who often hire them for a day as part of training or corporate hospitality packages.
- There has been a great increase in simulator 'rides' at attractions all over the world.
- Virtual reality has been used extensively in leading museums to bring history to life and to offer imaginative interpretation.

It is clear that there are a number of ways in which the growth of virtual reality represents an *opportunity* for attractions, a few of which are outlined below:

- It could help develop a whole new range of attractions that do not currently exist. What is more, as these attractions would not be based on any physical resource they could be developed anywhere. Thus they could be useful tools for urban regeneration or rural development as they could be located in areas that currently have little or nothing to attract tourists, and where there is a need for economic and social development.
- To install some virtual reality technology might help attractions that have traditionally found it difficult to attract younger visitors.
- For attractions whose main objective is education, virtual reality represents opportunities in that this technology will allow subjects to

'come to life' for students. Likewise it will bring new meaning at heritage centres to the concept of living history.

Furthermore, virtual reality will also be of help in the process of developing new attractions. It will allow attraction planners and designers to create realistic three-dimensional pictures of the proposed attraction and will let them see a visitor's eye view of the potential attraction. This should help them ensure that the attraction is aesthetically pleasing and that it works well from an operational point of view, with fewer queues for example.

Many commentators believe that virtual reality could allow tourism to become a much 'greener' activity. The thinking behind this view is that if one can provide virtual reality experiences in people's own homes or their local high street, it may reduce their desire to travel further afield for leisure experiences. This would then reduce tourism demand, particularly in relation to day trips, which would reduce problems such as the pollution caused by the cars taking people to their leisure experiences.

Furthermore, virtual reality could also help reduce pressure on fragile 'honeypot' attractions if a virtual reality copy could be made available near to the original, on the lines of the Cluny Abbey reconstruction developed by IBM in the 1990s.

However, this does seem a rather naive view that appears to ignore important issues, including:

- that for many people leisure experiences are a social event where interaction with other people is part of the experience
- the status that society attaches to visiting certain sites or indulging in certain activities. It is unlikely that the same such status might be attributed to virtual reality experiences. However, there is no reason why virtual reality should not offer status in its own right, particularly to specific audiences
- the current market for virtual reality is generally rather male orientated and at the younger end of the age range. Therefore, to have the 'greening' effect, virtual reality would have to develop in ways that would widen its market appeal.

Nevertheless, there may well be some scope for using virtual reality to make the attraction sector and its market a little greener. However, the industry may see this as a threat, just one of the threats which some believe virtual reality represents for the attractions business.

The threat is seen to have two main elements:

1 If it is possible to access virtual reality experiences in your local high street or your own home and this does reduce people's desire to travel for a leisure experience, then this clearly represents a threat to established attractions. It could lead to reduced visitor numbers at conventional attractions. That is why many attractions feel they must try to neutralize this threat by incorporating virtual reality into the product they themselves offer.

2 Virtual reality is expensive and there is a feeling that only the larger attractions, owned by organizations with substantial financial resources, will be able to afford to make use of these technologies. The danger, therefore, is that the other attractions that are unable to afford virtual reality will lose visitors to the larger attractions.

There are, of course, wider issues at stake than just the impact of virtual reality on attractions. There is a whole range of social and moral concerns, including:

- the fear that people will become obsessed with virtual reality, in a way that some are already obsessed by computer games, to the extent that they withdraw from social activities and find it easier to relate to machines than to other human beings
- that some virtual reality products, such as the ones based on war games, may further de-sensitize people to violence which could have consequences on behaviour in the longer term
- that some types of virtual reality will be morally highly questionable. For example, 'virtual pornography' is already starting to make its appearance.

Some of the social problems of virtual reality might be lessened if it could be changed from being largely a solitary activity enjoyed by younger males generally to being a communal activity that appealed to a wide cross-section of society.

The future of virtual reality at attractions is clearly linked to the future of virtual reality in general. Some of the most interesting future developments over the next few years include the following:

- Technological developments will improve the quality of sound and graphics and may reduce the need for the relatively clumsy goggles, helmets and suits.
- Virtual reality systems may be developed that will allow a real person, in a virtual reality world, actually to touch things in the virtual reality world and even be touched by them.

There is clearly much potential for virtual reality to be linked to other technological developments such as robotics, and meet the desire of customers for fantasy experiences to create whole new fantasy-world attractions. Perhaps the type of tourism portrayed in the film *Westworld* is not that far away after all!

But we must not get carried away. Virtual reality is not going to sweep through the leisure industry at great speed, making all other forms of activity obsolete. Its impact will be slower, partly because its appeal currently is greater among young males than any other market segment, although this will probably change as the range of available virtual reality experiences grows. Nevertheless, it will undoubtedly change both the attraction product and the market in the years to come. The way in which managers of conventional attractions respond to virtual reality will largely determine whether, overall, it is ultimately an opportunity or a threat.

Home-based entertainment systems ● ● ●

In the future the home will increasingly become an entertainment centre in its own right so that some people may not even leave home in search of leisure experiences. Improvements to hi-fi systems and the growth of computer games and interactive video and television, together with the increase in home ownership and the popularity of gardening and DIY, mean the home will probably become an increasingly important focus for people's leisure activities. Examples of this are the rise of CD-ROMs, DVD and Play Station 2 in recent years. Therefore, attractions may need to exploit technological developments to take the attraction to people's homes rather than expecting them always to visit the attraction.

Smart cards ● ● ●

These cards, which will increasingly allow customers to carry out a wide range of transactions, could be very important for attractions. They may ultimately reduce the need for entrance kiosks and the resulting queues as people would simply use their card to gain admission and pay. These cards could also be used to help potential visitors pre-book simply and without the need to tie up staff on the telephones or exchange correspondence and generate paperwork. However, we are still some way from such a situation at many attractions.

Artificial environments ● ● ●

In the years to come it will be possible to create artificial environments above and below ground and underwater. These will be exciting attractions and will offer a fantasy-style experience for visitors. There are already plans for 'underwater resorts' in Asia and the Mediterranean.

New technology and attraction marketing ● ● ●

New technologies are, slowly, changing the way we market attractions, most notably as follows:

- The growing sophistication of computer databases is facilitating the growth of direct marketing, reducing the need for intermediaries.
- The Internet is breaking down the barriers between promotion and destination by allowing attractions to offer information and take bookings through the same medium at the same time.

This trend will develop rapidly in the future as the Internet becomes more and more important in the lives of consumers. Attractions that do not jump on board this particular bandwagon will find themselves at a distinct disadvantage in the increasingly competitive marketplace.

To sum up then, it can be seen that in terms of the political, economic, social and technological factors, the situation is that in most cases the future will mean the continuing development of trends that are already under way.

The microenvironment

In contrast to the macroenvironment, organizations have a reasonable degree of control or influence over the five key elements in the microenvironment.

The organization

In the future, attractions will be affected by changes in management philosophies in relation to how organizations are managed. These may include:

- a growing concentration on quality as attractions seek to operate quality management systems such as total quality management and bench-marking and gain official recognition for the quality of their operations through ISO 9002, or its possible future successors
- a move towards the flattening of corporate hierarchies and the 'empowerment' of staff, so that they are allowed to show more initiative and take increased responsibility
- placing more emphasis on the recruitment of the right people and on the use of appraisal, staff development and performance-related pay schemes to ensure that they are properly motivated and rewarded
- the increased use of integrated, computerized management information systems to provide managers with sound data on which to base their decisions
- a growth in the professionalism of attraction managers through training and education courses. Larger attractions may recruit managers from other sectors of industry who are first and foremost managers, rather than attraction specialists
- a greater emphasis on marketing, which may well become the central focus of attraction operators, with an increased share of the overall attraction budget, as the concept of being market led becomes accepted by more and more organizations
- a growing desire on the part of organizations to be seen as ethical and socially responsible by people outside the organization.

Suppliers

In line with what is happening in some other industries, attractions may develop stronger links with their suppliers, for a number of reasons. First, the legal concept of product liability means that the attraction may in future be increasingly legally liable for problems that arise at the attraction because of faulty goods and services provided by its suppliers. They will therefore take more of an interest in the activities of their suppliers to protect themselves from possible legal action. Second, the quality of goods and services provided for the attraction by its suppliers have a direct impact on the quality of the attraction product. Attraction operators will therefore want to have more control over their suppliers to ensure that the quality of the product is maintained, because this is essential for long-term success. Both these factors will lead to attractions taking a growing interest in their suppliers in terms of their quality standards, business ethics and management systems.

The problem is that whereas many of the other organizations that have developed close links with their suppliers have relatively few of them, the variety of suppliers used by attractions is enormous and many of them are small one-person businesses. They include souvenir producers, catering suppliers, tradespeople, equipment suppliers, training organizations, maintenance contractors and uniform suppliers, to name but a few. It is therefore very difficult to develop close attraction–supplier relationships.

Marketing intermediaries

As the people who are the interface between attractions and their customers, the role of marketing intermediaries will became increasingly important in the competitive attraction marketplace of the future. Attractions will take more interest in their marketing intermediaries in the years to come to ensure that potential customers are made aware of, and given the right message about, the attraction to maximize the possibilities of them becoming actual visitors.

Again, however, the possible marketing intermediaries are large in number and diverse in nature, which makes it very difficult to develop closer links with them. They can range from libraries and tourist information centres which merely display literature, to journals and newspapers which may produce editorial features on the attraction, to tour and coach operators which may use the attraction to try to encourage people to buy their holidays or coach trips. In the future, the recognition that, perhaps, an attraction's most important marketing intermediaries are its customers through their word-of-mouth recommendations, will be translated into schemes to ensure that this phenomenon becomes a part of the attraction's marketing strategy.

The customers

The growth in the idea of customer-centred marketing will continue and this will mean even more attention being paid to customers, by attractions. This will take a number of forms:

- making those who have never been to the attraction aware of what it has to offer
- impressing first-time users so that they recommend the attraction to friends and relatives, and become regular visitors

- introducing initiatives to develop relationship marketing and particularly 'brand loyalty' among existing customers along the lines of the 'frequent flyer' programmes that airlines are increasingly using to achieve the same aim
- trying to woo back ex-visitors by offering new on-site permanent attractions and special events to give them a reason to visit again.

All these ideas imply an increased role for marketing research, which has often been the 'Cinderella' area of attraction management in the past. There will be a growing recognition that, in addition to factual information about visitors – age, place of residence and so on – there is a need for qualitative research focusing on the opinions and attitudes of visitors. It is important to know how customers think and what makes them visit or not visit attractions.

Attractions will need to become much more sophisticated in the way they segment their market to reflect the complexities of modern society. Customers will have to be looked at in terms of their lifestyle as a whole rather than just their behaviour in relation to attractions.

Competitors

As the attraction market becomes increasingly competitive, attractions will need to devote more effort to analysing their competitors and seeing how they can achieve competitive advantage over them. Competition for attractions exists at a number of levels:

- attractions of a similar type, such as other theme parks or heritage attractions
- attractions which are aimed at the same or similar target market(s) in the same geographical area
- other activities which are popular with the attraction's target market(s). These will not be visitor attractions as such but, instead, will be activities such as eating out, home entertaining, gardening or DIY.

Attractions will need to recognize these different types of competition and will need to look at how they can improve their position in relation to these competitors. In the future the ways in which attractions gain competitive advantage may well change. In the past, price and providing a wide range of attractions on site to appeal to a number of markets was seen as being a good way of ensuring the attraction remained competitive. Two of the ways of achieving competitive advantage that may prove popular in the years to come are:

- focusing on particular market segments rather than trying to appeal to everyone
- selling the attraction on the basis of its concern with social issues such as the environment and animal welfare, and on the basis of its corporate culture.

Furthermore, in the past, and even the present, many public sector attractions have not perceived that they have any competition. In the future, however, as they are privatized or are forced by financial constraints to operate in a more commercial manner, they will have to recognize that they do have competitors and look at how they will compete with them.

The impact of changes in other sectors of the tourism industry

The tourism industry as a whole is changing at a rapid pace and will continue to do so in the future. Some of these changes will have an impact on attractions. Perhaps this can best be illustrated by looking at tourism, sector by sector.

Accommodation sector

Some accommodation establishments have always been seen as attractions as well, such as luxury hotels and holiday centres with related leisure activities on the same site. However, in the future, we may see the development of types of accommodation which are designed to be first and foremost attractions rather than merely places to sleep. For example, we will see the rise of themed hotels and resort complexes (perhaps based on television or historical themes). This may lead to 'fantasy hotels' where people enter an environment where they can live out their fantasies. It could be argued that this trend is already under way to some extent. Some Las Vegas hotels are early examples of this idea, as is The Lost City, at Sun City in Bophuthatswana, South Africa.

Alternatively, the desire of increasingly sophisticated tourists to stay in accommodation that is different to the norm will lead to more and more attractions starting to offer overnight accommodation. Industrial heritage attractions may convert old industrial buildings into self-catering accommodation, while more and more historic houses will offer some sort of service and accommodation. Already, theme parks have added accommodation units on their site, on the model of that provided by Disney in its theme parks. The development of such accommodation will also allow attractions to obtain more conference and exhibition business.

Thus, in the future attractions and established traditional accommodation operators may find themselves increasingly in competition with each other.

Transport sector

Some modes of transport have for many years been regarded as attractions, for example Concorde and the Orient Express. Cruise ships are also developing dramatically to become more like sophisticated floating attractions. On the other hand, attractions know that visitors enjoy unusual types of on-site transport to take them from place to place so they, too, will be trying to use new technology to create unique on-site transport systems.

Destination sector

We now have some mega-attractions that are almost destinations in their own right, on the model of places like Disneyland Paris and Center Parcs. They provide all the attractions, services and entertainment that visitors require, and are therefore largely self-sufficient. Depending on one's philosophy these may either be anathema to the concept of sustainable tourism or may be an opportunity to allow tourists to enjoy themselves without 'polluting' the culture of the host country through the interactions that take place between visitors and hosts. Mega-attraction destinations have therefore become a useful tool in the development of sustainable tourism.

Conversely, many destinations that grew up in years past on the back of successful attractions may find themselves in jeopardy if these core attractions lose their appeal. Perhaps, we have already seen this phenomenon in the case of seaside resorts in Britain and other countries with cool climates, as the interest in sea-bathing, beach activities and seaside pier and theatre entertainment has declined. One day, changes in consumer tastes may also lead to problems for the destinations that have grown up based on attractions such as theme parks (Orlando in Florida, for example). If this happens the destination marketing agencies will need effectively to relaunch the destination or it may go into terminal decline.

Finally, in future, destinations that are trying to reverse decline, diversify their product portfolio or enter the tourism market, will increasingly make use of a particular type of attraction, namely the special event. People who are interested in the theme of the event will visit the place where it is held, even though they may not otherwise have thought of visiting the destination. Such events can therefore be a cost-effective way of attracting new visitors to a destination. Therefore we should expect to see a growing number of new, themed special events in the years to come.

Tour operation sector

For tour operators, attractions are still at the heart of their package holiday product in two ways:

- The presence of attractions encourages tourists to buy packages to particular destinations.
- Organized excursions to attractions provide a useful stream of extra income for tour operators.

Both these factors will continue to be the case while tour operators will explore new attractions in previously little visited destinations to see if they can make them the basis of new package holiday products. This has already been seen in the case of shopping and desert breaks to Dubai, for example.

Travel agency sector

Travel agencies have traditionally had relatively little to do with attractions, except by providing a place where people could book for special events like concerts, or book a package holiday to a major attraction like Disneyland Paris. In the future, however, more attractions may operate a pre-booking system, to prevent overcrowding at peak times, and agencies could use their sophisticated reservation systems to operate this service on behalf of attractions where the entrance charge would generate a sizeable commission for the agent.

Perhaps it is more likely though that the rise of home-based interactive systems and smart cards will allow people to book directly with the attraction, from home, without the need to involve a travel agency.

Support services and infrastructure

This disparate sector has a number of links with the world of attractions that will develop over the coming years:

- More and more attractions will develop catering outlets to maximize on-site expenditure, while off-site catering outlets such as restaurants and fast food chains will seek to become attractions by adding other features to their basic product, such as children's play areas and entertainment.
- Entertainment providers such as nightclubs and theatres will provide an increasingly sophisticated product to attract customers, drawing on some of the technologies and on-site attractions used by visitor attractions.
- Shops will become an even more important source of revenue at attractions, while leisure shopping complexes and individual leisure shopping units will become increasingly important attractions. Themed leisure shops aimed at niche markets will become even more important in the attraction market.
- The operators of tourism infrastructure will seek to earn more revenue by trying to sell themselves as attractions in their own right. For example, airports and the Channel Tunnel may be marketed as industrial tourism attractions.

Tourism education sector

As the size and importance of visitor attractions is increasingly recognized, the world of education and training will respond by developing more courses aimed at improving the quality of attraction managers and staff. These could be formal courses at postgraduate, undergraduate and diploma levels, as well as ongoing courses for staff already in post. Some courses may be organized on the distance-learning model, again for people who are already in employment.

Such education and training must be directly relevant to the everyday working life of managers and needs to be delivered in a flexible way that takes account of the pressures they work under and the times of the year when they are exceptionally busy.

Without such education and training there is a danger that the attractions sector, in particular, and perhaps tourism generally, will never become a truly mature industry that is taken seriously by society in general and key decision-makers in government and finance specifically.

It is also clear that there is a need for considerably more research to be carried out so that we can better understand the nature of attractions, how they are developed and, perhaps most significantly, why people visit them. Some of the key areas for further research include:

- the reasons why people choose to visit particular attractions at particular times
- visitor, and potential visitor, images and perceptions of specific attractions and the product they offer
- the effectiveness of different methods of promotion such as leaflets, advertisements and sales promotions
- the importance of price and the concept of value for money in the consumer's decision-making process
- the role of design and the physical environment of the attraction in determining its success or failure
- improving the way in which we forecast the future size and nature of the attraction market as a whole, and the potential visitor numbers of a specific proposed attraction
- developing better practice in human resource management at attractions, particularly in terms of motivation, reward systems and job satisfaction
- looking at what quality means in the attraction sector and how it can best be delivered
- devising cost-effective ways in which individual attractions can carry out market research that will, in turn, help them make their marketing more effective.

The challenges facing the attraction management of tourism

Throughout the world, therefore, it is clear that the attractions sector will change dramatically over the coming years. This will create great challenge for attraction managers from Barcelona to Bogota, Bombay to Bangkok, Beirut to Baltimore. In the figure below the author highlights some of these challenges.

Conclusion

The factors discussed in this final section of the book will combine in the future to bring about changes in the attraction product, the market and the way that attractions are marketed. The precise nature of these changes will vary in a number of ways:

1 Variation over time: some factors will have an impact in the next year or two, while others will take longer to come to fruition. Furthermore,

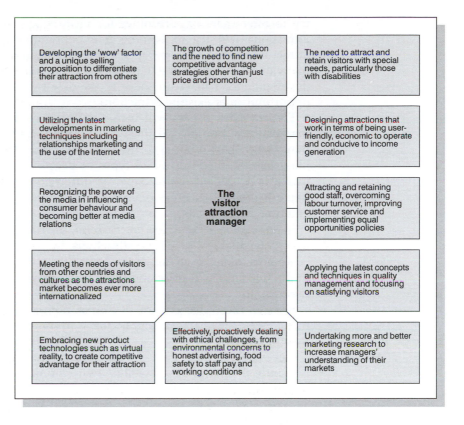

Figure Part 5.1
Challenges facing the visitor attraction manager

some factors may come and go quickly while others will be more permanent.

2 Variation between different types of attractions: theme parks, for example, will face different challenges from those that influence museums, although they may both be affected by some common factors.

3 Variation between different attraction operators: operators will respond to the factors in different ways based on their own unique blend of history, culture and resources.

4 Variation between attractions in different areas: the impact of some of these factors will vary from one geographical area to another, within a particular country.

The situation will undoubtedly also be different in different countries. It is therefore impossible to generalize about the future of attractions, but having said that, there are some basic principles with which commentators would probably find it hard to disagree.

In terms of the *attraction product*, it will undoubtedly become more sophisticated and technology based, although if this trend goes too far there may be a backlash that will bring low-technology attractions back into fashion. The distinctions between different types of attractions will become more blurred. In addition, entertainment-based attractions will try to offer more opportunities for visitors to learn while educational attractions will try to become more entertaining. Ownership of the attraction product will probably become concentrated in fewer hands and many of them will belong to overseas corporations. Finally, technological developments will create new types of attractions and provide new opportunities at existing attractions.

The *attraction market* will increasingly be made up of distinct niche markets based on shared lifestyles, opinions and attitudes. Attractions may target their product to these niches rather than trying to attract a mass market, made up of all types of people. The market will become increasingly global with people of different nationalities displaying a liking for particular types of attractions and people from more countries entering the international attraction marketplace.

In terms of *how attractions are marketed*, the future will see the increased use of technology to allow attractions to communicate directly with customers in their own homes. Furthermore, attractions may be marketed in the future less on price and more on quality and the ethical values of the operator.

Some of these changes are, of course, not unique to attractions, but in many cases, they have already occurred in some industries and are under way in others.

Nevertheless they look set to change the attractions market significantly. For example, a well-known commentator on the attractions business, Stevens, predicted that:

> The next ten years will see remarkable changes in the geography and nature of the visitor attraction industry. The changes currently being experienced in consumer demand will lead to a considerable number of casualties among traditional attractions. Many will become increasingly irrelevant to the interests of the market.
>
> The future is likely to remain relatively positive for those signature attractions that are regarded as 'must see places' on most tourist itineraries. Equally, those attractions that continue to innovate with their product and become market, or customer, focused are more likely to survive. This will necessitate a real commitment to quality as well as becoming price competitive and developing multiple sources of revenue.
>
> In the meantime, the next ten years will see the emergence of the next generation of destination attractions. Many of these will use the Disney model as the prototype for the new genre of attractions. These will provide all-weather, inclusive resort products but operating on a smaller scale than Disney and sited in unusual locations. Others will be founded upon new types of destinations in urban centres.
>
> The emerging economies will soon create resident markets with disposable income and aspirational demands for entertainment and enjoyment in unusual settings. These countries will also offer attractive land and property deals to investors. As a

result, there is likely to be a burst of interest in the potential to create these new destination attractions in these countries. (Stevens, 2000)

The author agrees with these points, but feels we must be realistic about the likely scale and speed of this change. It is likely to affect the mega-attractions first and more fundamentally, although the ripples will be increasingly felt by smaller attractions. Furthermore, change is not likely to occur overnight and be revolutionary but, rather, will be evolutionary, albeit at a rather rapid rate compared to the past.

Some attractions will successfully anticipate the changes, while others will react when they occur. Others will not react and for those attractions the future may be very uncertain or even non-existent!

While everything in the attraction sector is constantly changing, one fact appears to remain true always: attractions are still the core of the whole tourism industry. They are the reason why people make tourist trips, whether the trip is a two-week holiday to see the pyramids and cultural treasures of Egypt or a day trip to a theme park a few miles from home. Without attractions there would be no tourism industry. That is why it is vital for the future of tourism as a whole that we understand how attractions should be developed and managed, and that we seek to put this understanding into practice.

Postscript

At the time of writing (October 2001) the world is still reeling from the effects of the tragic events which took place in New York and Washington on September 11 2001.

Nobody, today, can predict what the long-term impact of these events, and the resulting 'war' may have on the attractions sector, worldwide. Indeed, it could be argued that in the light of these appalling events, the future of the attractions sector is a matter of little importance.

However, we must remember that attractions provide a livelihood for literally millions of people around the world. Therefore we have to do all we can to ensure the continued success of the attractions sector.

Whatever happens, there is no doubt that the horrific events of September 11 2001 will have an impact on the attractions business for years to come.

Bibliography

Adler, J. (1989). Origins of sightseeing. *Annals of Tourism Research*, **16**, 7–29.

Allanson, J. (1993). Land of the rising sun. *Leisure Management*, July.

Ashford, D. M. (1997). Space tourism: how soon will it happen. Proceedings from the IEEE Aerospace Conference, Snowmass, Colorado, 1–8 February.

Ashworth, G. J. and Goodall, B. (1990). *Marketing Tourism Places*. Routledge.

Baillie, K. *et al.* (1999). *Paris: The Rough Guide*. Rough Guides.

Baker, M. J. (1985). *Marketing Strategy and Management*. Macmillan.

Baum, T. (ed.) (1993). *Human Resources in International Tourism*. Butterworth-Heinemann.

Belbin, R. M. (1981). *Management Teams: Why They Succeed or Fail*. Butterworth-Heinemann.

Benckendorff, P. J. (1999). The pricing of leisure attractions: a preliminary study of Queensland establishments. Unpublished report, Tourism Programme, School of Business, James Cook University.

Bentley, J. L. (1989). *Center Parcs*. Pavic.

Beoiley, S. and Denman, R. (1988). *Industrial Heritage Attractions in North West England*. North West Tourist Board.

Berenger, M. P. (1992). L'Evenement comme argument. Unpublished project, CEFSI, Nice.

Bodlender, J., Jefferson, A., Jenkins, C. and Lickorish, L. (1991). *Developing Tourist Attractions: Policies and Perspectives*. Longman.

Boniface, P. (1995). *Managing Quality Cultural Tourism*. Routledge.

Booms, B. H. and Bitner, M. J. (1981). Marketing strategies and organisation structures for services firms. In *Marketing in Services* (J. H. Donnelly and W. R. George, eds), pp. 47–51, American Marketing Association.

Brent-Ritchie, J. R. and Goeldner, C. R. (1994). *Travel, Tourism and Hospitality Research: A Handbook* for *Managers and Researchers*. Wiley.

British Tourist Authority/English Tourism Council (1999). *Sightseeing in the UK*. British Tourist Authority/English Tourism Council.

British Tourist Authority/English Tourism Council (2000). *Sightseeing in the UK*. British Tourist Authority/English Tourism Council.

Brown, J. (1992). The impact of the recession on attendances at major visitor attractions. *Insights*, September, A55–A65.

Brundtland Commission (1987). *Our Common Future*. Oxford University Press.

Buckley, P. J. and Witt, S. F. (1989). Tourism in difficult areas II. *Tourism Management*, June, 138–152.

Cathedral Tourism Advisory Group (1979). *English Cathedrals and Tourism*. English Tourist Board.

Chartered Institute of Marketing (1984). *Definition of Marketing*. Chartered Institute of Marketing.

Cheong, R. (1995). The virtual threat to travel and tourism. *Tourism Management*.

Collins, P., Fukuoka, T. and Nishimura, T. (1994). Zero-gravity sports centres. *Engineering Construction and Operations in Space 4*. ASCE 1, 504–513.

Collins, P., Kuwahara, S., Nishimura, T. and Fukuoka, T. (1997). Design and construction of zero-gravity gymnasium. *Journal of Aerospace Engineering*, **10**, 94–98.

Cooper, C. P. (ed.) (annual). *Progress in Tourism, Recreation and Hospitality Management*. Belhaven.

Cooper, C. P., Fletcher, J., Gilbert, D. and Wanhill, S. (1998) *Tourism: Principles and Practice*. Pitman.

Corke, J. (1988). *Tourism Law*. Elm.

Cowell, D. (1984). *The Marketing of Services*. Butterworth-Heinemann.

Cox, L. J. and Fox, K. (1991). Interactive science and technology attractions. *Insights: Tourism Marketing Intelligence Services*, **8**, A189–A194.

Crossley, J. F. and Jamieson, L. M. (1989). *Introduction to Commercial and Entrepreneurial Recreation*. Sagamore.

Davidson, R. (1994). Themed attractions in Europe. *Insights*, May, A159–A166.

Davidson, R. (1997). *Tourism in Europe*. 2nd edn. Pitman.

Denver Convention and Visitor Bureau (1991). *Annual Report*. Denver Visitor and Convention Bureau.

Department of the Environment/PA Cambridge Economic Consultants (1990a). *An Evaluation of Garden Festivals*. HMSO.

Department of the Environment/PA Cambridge Economic Consultants (1990b). *Tourism and the Inner City.* HMSO.

Dodds, M. (1992). Vive la tradition. *Leisure Management*, November.

Doswell, R. and Gamble, P. R. (1979). *Marketing and Planning Hotels and Tourism Projects.* Hutchinson.

Dreyfus-Signoles, C. (1992). *Structures et organisations du tourisme en France.* Breal.

Drucker, P. F. (1954). *The Practice of Management.* Harper and Row.

Drucker, P. F. (1973). *Management: Tasks, Responsibilities, Practices.* Harper and Row.

English Tourism Council (2000). *English Heritage Monitor.* English Tourism Council.

English Tourist Board (1991). *Tourism and the Environment: Maintaining the Balance.* English Tourist Board.

English Tourist Board (1993a). *Investment in Tourism* (July to December 1992). English Tourist Board.

English Tourist Board and James Nisbet and Partners (1992). *Building a Tourism Business: A Development Guide.* English Tourist Board.

English Tourist Board and Jones Lang Wootton (1989). *Retail, Leisure and Tourism.* English Tourist Board.

Evans, M. (2001). Gardens tourism: is the market really blooming? *Insights*, May, A153–A159.

Faulkner, B., Moscardo, G. and Laws, E. (2001). *Tourism in the 21st Century: Lessons from Experience.* Continuum.

Feifer, M. (1985). *Going Places: The Ways of the Tourist from Imperial Rome to the Present Day.* Macmillan.

Fodness, D. D. and Milner, L. M. (2000). A perceptual mapping approach to theme park visitor segmentation. In *Tourism Management: Towards the New Millennium* (C. Ryan and S. Page, eds), Pergamon.

Foster, D. (1986). *Travel and Tourism Management.* Macmillan.

Frew, E. A. and Shaw, R. N. (1999). The relationship between personalities, gender, and tourist behaviour. *Tourism Management*, **20**, 193–202.

Getz, D. (1991) *Festivals, Special Events and Tourism.* Van Nostrand Reinhold.

Getz, D. (1993). Tourist shopping villages: development and planning strategies. *Tourism Management*, February, 15–26.

Glaser, J. R. (1986). US museums in context. In *The American Museum Experience: In Search of Excellence* (Scottish Museums Council, ed.), HMSO.

Gold, J. R. and Ward, S. V. (eds) (1994). *Place Promotion: The Use of Publicity and Marketing to Sell Towns and Regions.* Wiley.

Gratton, C. (1992). Is there life after Euro-Disney? *Leisure Management*, April, 24–27.

Greenwood, J. (1993). Business interest grows in tourism governance. *Tourism Management*, October, 335–345.

Grönroos, C. L. (1990). Marketing redefined. *Management Decision*, **28**(8).

Guides Laravière (1999). *Le Guide Officiel des Parcs d'Attractions.* Guides Laravière.

Gunn, C. (1985). Getting ready for megatrends in travel attractions. *Tourism Management*, June, 138–41.

Gunn, C. (1988). *Tourism Planning*. Taylor Francis.

Gunn, C. (1994). *Tourism Planning*. 3rd edn. Taylor Francis.

Gunn, C. (1997). *Tourism Planning*. 4th edn. Taylor Francis.

Halewood, C. and Hannam, K. (2001). Viking heritage tourism: authenticity and commodification. *Annals of Tourism Research*, **28**(3), 565–580.

Hall, C. M. (1992). *Hallmark Tourist Events: Impacts, Management and Planning*. Belhaven.

Harmsworth, S. (1993). The present status of the spa/health farm industry in the UK. *Insights*, March, B49–B60.

Harris, N. D. (1989). *Service Operations Management*. Cassell.

Henley Centre (1989). Leisure futures. *Time Use Survey*, Spring.

Hewison, R. (1987). *The Heritage Industry: Britain in a Climate of Decline*. Methuen.

Hickman, L. E. and Hawkins, D. E. (1989). *Tourism in Contemporary Society*. Prentice Hall.

Holloway, J. C. and Robinson, C. (1995). *Marketing for Tourism*. 3rd edn. Pitman.

Home, D. (1984). *The Great Museum*. Pluto.

Inskeep, E. (1991). *Tourism Planning*. Van Nostrand Reinhold.

Jacobson, J. K. S. (1997). The making of an attraction. *Annals of Tourism Research*, **24**, 341–356.

Jakle, J. A. (1985). *The Tourist: Travel in Twentieth Century North America*. University of Nebraska Press.

Jansen-Verbeke, M. (1991a). Leisure and shopping: a magic concept for the tourism industry. *Tourism Management*, March, 9–14.

Jansen-Verbeke, M. (1991b). Leisure and shopping: tourism product mix. In *Marketing Tourism Places* (G. Ashworth and B. Goodall, eds) pp. 129–137, Routledge.

Januarius, M. (1992). *Leisure Management*.

Jefferson, A. and Lickorish, L. (1988). *Marketing Tourism*. Longman.

Johnson, D. E. and Collins, B. J. (2001). Center Parcs UK: leisure development which achieves bio-diversity gains. *Managing Leisure*, **6**, 63–73.

Johnson, G. and Scholes, K. (1993). *Exploring Corporate Strategy*. 3rd edn. Prentice Hall.

Johnson, P. and Thomas, B. (1990). *Report on a Group of Visitors to Beamish Museum*. Tourism Working Paper No. 9. Department of Economics, University of Durham.

Johnson, P. and Thomas, B. (1991). The comparative analysis of tourist attractions. In *Progress in Tourism, Recreation and Hospitality Management* (C. P. Cooper, ed.) pp. 114–129, Belhaven.

Johnson, P. and Thomas, B. (1992a). *Tourism, Museums and the Local Economy*. Edward Elgar.

Johnson, P. and Thomas, B. (eds) (1992b). *Choice and Demand in Tourism*. Mansell.

Jones, A. (2001). Brand extension in tourist attractions: success factors. *Insights*, May, D35–D39.

Joppe, M., Martin, D. W. and Waalen, J. (2001). Toronto's image as a destination: a comparative importance – satisfaction analysis by origin of visitor. *Journal of Travel Research*, February, 252–260.

Judd, D. R. (1995). Promoting tourism in US cities. *Tourism Management*, **11**, 175–187.

Kau, A. (2000). Evaluating the attractiveness of a new theme park: a cross cultural composition. In *Tourism Management: Towards the New Millennium* (C. Ryan and S. Page, eds) Pergamon.

Keynote Publications (1992). *Tourist Attractions*. Keynote Publications.

Kinnaird, V. and Hall, D. (eds) (1994). *Tourism: A Gender Analysis*. Wiley.

Kotler, P. (1994a) *Principles of Marketing*. 6th edn. Prentice Hall (1st edn, 1980).

Kotler, P. (1994b). *Marketing Management: Analysis, Planning, Implementation and Control*. 8th edn. Prentice Hall.

Krippendorf, J. (1987). *The Holiday Makers*. Heinemann.

Lanquar, R. (1992). *L'Empire Disney*. Presses Universitaires de France.

Law, C. M. (1993). *Urban Tourism: Attracting Visitors to Large Cities*. Mansell.

Laws, E. (1991). *Tourism Marketing: Service and Quality Management Perspectives*. Thomnes.

Laws, E., Faulkner, B. and Moscardo, G. (eds) (1998). *Embracing and Managing Change*. Routledge.

Lawson, F. and Baud-Bovey, M. (1977) *Tourism and Recreational Development*. Architectural Press.

Leiper, N. (1997). Big success, big mistake, at big banana: marketing strategies in road-side attractions and theme parks. *Journal of Travel and Tourism Marketing*, **6**, 103–121.

Leisure Consultants (1990a). *What's the Attraction?* Vol. 1: *A Guide for Operators*. Leisure Consultants.

Leisure Consultants (1990b). *What's the Attraction?* Vol. 2: *Market Research and Forecasts*. Leisure Consultants.

Leisure Consultants (1994). *Leisure Forecasts 1994–1998: Leisure Away From Home*. Leisure Consultants.

Levitt, T. (1960). Marketing myopia. *Harvard Business Review*, July–August, 45–6.

Lew, A. (1994). A framework of tourist attraction research. In *Travel, Tourism and Hospitality Research* (J. Brent Ritchie and C. Goeldner, eds) pp. 291–304, 2nd edn, Wiley.

Lew, A. A. (1987). A framework of tourist attraction research. *Annals of Tourism Research*, **14**(4), 553–575.

Lewin, K. (1947). Feedback problems of social diagnosis and action. Part II–B4. Frontiers in group dynamics. *Human Relations*, **1**, 147–153.

Lewin, K. (1951). *Field Theory in Social Science*. Harper and Brothers.

Lewis, R. C. and Chambers, R. G. (1989). *Market Leadership in Hospitality*. Van Nostrand Reinhold.

Lord, G. D. and Lord, B. (eds) (1991). *The Manual of Museum Planning*. Museum Enterprises Ltd and HMSO.

Lumley, R. (ed.) (1988). *The Museum Time Machine: Putting Culture on Display*. Routledge.

Lundberg, D. E. (1989). *The Tourist Business*. 5th edn. Van Nostrand Reinhold.

MacCannell, D. (1990). *The Tourist*. 2nd edn. Schocken.

Martin, B. and Mason, S. (1993). The future for attractions: meeting the needs of new consumers. *Tourism Management*, February, 34–40.

Martin, B. and Mason, S. (1993). The future for attractions : meeting the needs of the new customers. *Tourism Management*, **14**, 34–40.

Mathieson, A. and Wall, G. (1982). *Tourism: Economic, Physical and Social Impacts*. Longman.

McClung, G. W. (2000). Theme park selection: factors influencing attendance. In *Tourism Management: Towards the New Millennium* (C. Ryan and S. Page, eds), Pergamon.

McKeever, E. (1992). Potential for growth. *Leisure Management*, November.

Middleton, V. T. C. (1990). *New Visions for Independent Museums in the UK*. Association of Independent Museums.

Middleton, V. T. C. (1994). *Marketing in Travel and Tourism*. 2nd edn. Butterworth-Heinemann (1st edn, 1988).

Mill, R. C. and Morrison, A. M. (1992). *The Tourism System*. 2nd edn. Prentice Hall.

Mills, P. (ed.) (1992). *Quality in the Leisure Industry*. Longman.

Ministry of Sound (2001). Misguided Ibiza.

Mintzberg, H. (1973). *The Nature of Management Work*. Harper and Row.

MORI (2001). Research reported in *Locum Destination Review*, Spring 2001.

Moscardo, G. (1999). *Making Visitors Mindfull*. Sagamore Press.

Moutinho, L. (1998). Amusement park visitor behaviour: Scottish attitudes. *Tourism Management*, **9**. pp. 291–299.

Murphy, P. E. (1985). *Tourism: A Community Approach*. Methuen.

Myerscough, J. (1988). *The Economic Importance of the Arts in Britain*. Policy Studies Institute.

National Audit Office (1992). *Protecting and Managing English Heritage Property*. HMSO.

National Economic Development Office (1989). *Recruitment Challenges: Case Studies in Tackling the Labour Squeeze in Tourism and Leisure*. HMSO.

Neaves, P. (1993). Adding value. *Leisure Management*, January, 55–56.

Nilson, R. and Edgington, C. (1982). Risk management: a tool for parks and recreation administrators. *Parks and Recreation*, August, 34–37.

Nolan, M. and Nolan, S. (1992). Religious sites as tourist attractions in Europe. *Annals of Tourism Research*, **19**(1),68–78.

Office of Population, Censuses, and Surveys (1991). *Leisure Day Visits in Great Britain, 1988–1989*. HMSO.

Paynter, I. (1991). Farm attractions. *Insights*, September, B17–B22.

Pearce, D. (1989) *Tourist Development*. Longman.

Pearce, D. and Butler, R. W. (1992). *Tourism Research: Critiques and Challenges*. Routledge.

Pearce, D., Benchendorff, P. J. and Johnstone, S. (2000). Tourist attractions: evolution, analysis and prospects. In *Tourism in the 21st Century: Lessons from Experience* (B. Faulkner et al., eds), Continuum.

Pearce, P. L. (1991). Analysing tourist attractions. *Journal of Tourism Studies*, **2**, 46–55.

Pearce, P. L. (1998). Marketing and management trends in tourist attractions. *Asia Pacific-Journal of Tourism Research*, 3, 1–8.

Peters, T. (1989). *Thriving on Chaos*. Pan.

Poon, A. (1993). *Tourism, Technology and Competitive Strategies*. CAB International.

Porter, M. E. (1985). *Competitive Advantage: Creating and Sustaining Superior Performance*. Free Press.

Prentice, R. (1993). *Tourism and Heritage Attractions*. Routledge.

Product Development Department, English Tourist Board (1992). Theme parks. *Insights*, January, B47–B54.

Projection 2000 (1990). *Theme Parks*. Projection 2000.

Renaghan, L. M. (1981). A new marketing mix for the hospitality industry. *Cornell Hotel and Restaurant Administration Quarterly*, April, 31–35.

Richards, G. (ed.) (1996). *Cultural Tourism in Europe*. CAB International.

Richards, G. and Richards, B. (1991). International Themes. *Leisure Management*, October, 46–48.

Richards, W. (1992). *How to Market Tourist Attractions, Festivals and Special Events*. Longman.

Rinschede, G. (1992). Forms of religious tourism. *Annals of Tourism Research*, 19, 51–67.

Robinson, K. (1994). Future for tourist attractions. *Insights: Tourism Marketing Intelligence Service*, **5**, D29–D40.

Robinson, M. and Hind, D. (1992). Quality north open to view: a case study in developing industry tourism. Paper presented at Tourism in Europe: The 1992 Conference, Durham Castle, Durham.

Rogers, H. A. and Slinn, L. A. (1993) *Tourism: Management of Facilities*. Longman.

Rural Development Commission/PA Cambridge Economic Consultants (1991). *The Economic Impact of Holiday Villages*. Rural Research Series Number 11, PA Cambridge Economic Consultants.

Ryan, C. (1991). *Recreational Tourism: A Social Science Perspective*. Routledge.

Ryan, C. (1995). *Researching Tourist Satisfaction: Issues, Concepts and Problems*. Routledge.

Ryan, C. and Page, S. (eds) (2000) *Tourism Management: Towards the New Millennium*. Pergamon.

Sasser, W. E., Olsen, P. R. and Wyckoff, D. D. (1978). *Management of Service Operations: Texts, Costs and Readings*. Allyn and Bacon.

Scottish Tourist Board (1991). *Visitor Attractions: A Development Guide*. Scottish Tourist Board.

Screven, C. G. (ed.) (1999). *Visitor Studies Bibliography*. 4th edn. Screven and Associates.

Shackley, M. (ed.) (1998). *Visitor Management: Case Studies from World Heritage Sites*. Butterworth-Heinemann.

Shepstone, T. and Curtis, S. (1992). Domestic emphasis. *Leisure Management*, November.

Smith, S. L. J. (1989). *Tourism Analysis*. Longman.

Speakman, L. and Bramwell, B. (1992). *Sheffield Works: An Evaluation of a Factory Tourism Scheme*. Centre for Tourism Occasional Paper Number 1, Sheffield City Polytechnic.

Stevens, T. R. (1991). Visitor attractions: their management and contribution to tourism. In *Progress in Tourism, Recreation and Hospitality Management* (C. P. Cooper, ed.) pp. 105–113, Belhaven.

Stevens, T. R. (2000). The future of visitor attractions, *Travel and Tourism Analyst*, **1**, 61–85.

Swarbrooke, J. S. (1993). The future of heritage attractions. *Insights*, January, D15–D20.

Theobald, W. (ed.) (1994). *Global Tourism: The Next Decade*. Butterworth-Heinemann.

Torkildsen, G. (1993). *Torkildsen's Guide to Leisure Management*. Longman.

Tourism Canada (1986). *The US Travel Market Study*. Tourism Canada.

Tourism Concern (1992). *Beyond the Green Horizon*. World Wildlife Fund.

Tourism Planning and Research Associates (1993). *The European Tourist: A Market Profile*. Tourism Planning and Research Associates.

Tourism Research and Marketing (1990). *UK Theme Parks: A Market Report*. Tourism Research and Marketing.

Travel and Tourism Intelligence. City Reports: No. 3 (1997); No. 1 (1999); No. 2 (1999); No. 3 (1999); No. 4 (1999); No. 1 (2000); No. 2 (2000); No. 3 (2000).

Tuckman, B. W. (1965). Development sequence in small groups. *Psychological Bulletin*, **63**.

Turley, S. K. (1999). Exploring the future of the traditional UK Zoo. *Journal of Vacation Marketing*, **5**(4), 340–355.

Urry, J. (1990). *The Tourist Gaze: Leisure and Travel in Contemporary Societies*. Sage.

Uzzell, D. (ed.) (1989). *Heritage Interpretation*. Vol. 2. Belhaven.

Van Harssel, J. (ed.) (1994). *Tourism: An Exploration*. 3rd edn. Prentice Hall.

Van Linge, J. H. (1992). How to out-zoo the zoo. *Tourism Management*, March, 115–177.

Vergo, P. (ed.) (1989). *The New Museology*. Reaktion.

Vittersø, J., Vorkinn, M., Vistad, O. I. and Vaagland, J. (2000). Tourist experiences at attractions. *Annals of Tourism Reserch*, **27**(2), 432–448.

Walsh-Heron, J. and Stevens, T. (1990). *The Management of Visitor Attractions and Events*. Prentice Hall.

Wanhill, S. (2000). Mines: a tourist attraction. Coal mining in industrial South Wales. *Journal of Travel Research*, **39**, August, 60–69.

Witt, S. F. (1988). Mega-events and mega-attractions. *Tourism Management*, March, 76–77.

Witt, S. F. and Moutinho, L. (eds) (1989). *Tourism Marketing and Management Handbook*. Prentice Hall.

Witt, S. F. and Witt, C. (1991). *Modelling and Forecasting Demand in Tourism*. Academic Press.

Witt, S. F., Brooke, M. Z. and Buckley, P. (1991). *The Management of International Tourism*. Unwin Hyman.

Wong, K. F. and Cheung, P. W. Y. (1999). Strategic theming in theme park marketing. *Journal of Vacation Marketing*, **5**(4), 319–332.

Wood, H. (1991a). Case study: Thorpe Park. In *Case Studies in Tourism Management* (G. Richards, ed.), University of North London.

Wood, H. (1991b). Case study: the Tower of London. In *Case Studies in Tourism Management* (G. Richards, ed.), University of North London.

Wood, H. (1991c). Case study: Victoria and Albert Museum. In *Case Studies in Tourism Management* (G. Richards, ed.), University of North London.

Wooder, S. (1992). Industrial tourism. *Insights*, March, B63–B69.

World Tourism Organization (1993) *Sustainable Tourism Development: Guide for Local Planners*. World Tourism Organization.

Yale, P. (1997). *Tourism Attractions and Heritage Tourism*. 2nd edn. Elm.

Young, S. and Ambrose, T. (1999). Benchmarking visitor attractions. Hampshire pilot project. *Insights*, November, A71 – A80.

Index